MPI—The Complete Reference

Volume 1, The MPI Core

Scientific and Engineering Computation

Janusz S. Kowalik, editor

The High Performance Fortran Handbook
by Charles H. Koelbel, David B. Loveman, Robert S. Schreiber, Guy L. Steele Jr. and Mary E. Zosel, 1993

Using MPI: Portable Parallel Programming with the Message-Passing Interface
by William Gropp, Ewing Lusk, and Anthony Skjellum, 1994

PVM: Parallel Virtual Machine—A User's Guide and Tutorial for Network Parallel Computing
by Al Geist, Adam Beguelin, Jack Dongarra, Weicheng Jiang, Bob Manchek, and Vaidy Sunderam, 1994

Enabling Technologies for Petaflops Computing
by Thomas Sterling, Paul Messina, and Paul H. Smith, 1996

An Introduction to High-Performance Scientific Computing
by Lloyd D. Fosdick, Elizabeth R. Jessup, Carolyn J. C. Schauble, and Gitta Domik, 1997

Practical Parallel Programming
by Gregory V. Wilson, 1997

Using PLAPACK
by Robert A. van de Geijn, 1997

Fortran 95 Handbook
by Jeanne C. Adams, Walter S. Brainerd, Jeanne T. Martin, Brian T. Smith, and Jerrold J. Wagener, 1997

MPI—The Complete Reference: Volume 1, The MPI Core, second edition
by Marc Snir, Steve Otto, Steven Huss-Lederman, David Walker, and Jack Dongarra, 1998

MPI—The Complete Reference: Volume 2, The MPI-2 Extensions
by William Gropp, Steven Huss-Lederman, Andrew Lumsdaine, Ewing Lusk, Bill Nitzberg, William Saphir, and Marc Snir, 1998

MPI—The Complete Reference

Volume 1, The MPI Core
second edition

Marc Snir
Steve Otto
Steven Huss-Lederman
David Walker
Jack Dongarra

The MIT Press
Cambridge, Massachusetts
London, England

Parts of this book come from "MPI: A Message-Passing Interface Standard" and "MPI-2: Extensions to the Message-Passing Interface" by the Message Passing Interface Forum, © the University of Tennessee. These sections were reprinted by permission of the University of Tennessee.

This book was set in LATEX by the authors and was printed and bound in the United States of America.

Library of Congress Cataloging-in-Publication Data

MPI—the complete reference/Marc Snir . . . [et. al.]. William Gropp . . . [et al.].
    p.   cm.—(Scientific and engineering computation)
  Includes bibliographical references (p.) and index.
  Contents: Vol. 1. The MPI core—Vol. 2. The MPI-2 extensions.
  ISBN 0-262-69215-5 (v. 1: pbk. : alk. paper).—ISBN 0-262-57123-4 (v. 2: pbk. : alk. paper). —ISBN 0-262-69216-3 (2-vol. set)
  1. Parallel programming (Electronic computers) 2. Subroutines (Computer programs) I. Snir, Marc. II. Gropp, William. III. Series.
QA76.642.M65   1998
004'.35—dc21   98-25604
                                                                                                        CIP

1 0 9 8 7 6 5

Contents

Series Foreword

The world of modern computing potentially offers many helpful methods and tools to scientists and engineers, but the fast pace of change in computer hardware, software, and algorithms often makes practical use of the newest computing technology difficult. The Scientific and Engineering Computation series focuses on rapid advances in computing technologies, with the aim of facilitating transfer of these technologies to applications in science and engineering. It will include books on theories, methods, and original applications in such areas as parallelism, large-scale simulations, time-critical computing, computer-aided design and engineering, use of computers in manufacturing, visualization of scientific data, and human-machine interface technology.

The series is intended to help scientists and engineers understand the current world of advanced computation and to anticipate future developments that will affect their computing environments and open up new capabilities and modes of computation.

This book is about the Message Passing Interface (MPI), a widely used message passing library standard. It covers the MPI functions included in MPI Version 1. Together with *MPI—The Complete Reference: Volume 2, The MPI-2 Extensions* by William Gropp, Steven Huss-Lederman, Andrew Lumsdaine, Ewing Lusk, Bill Nitzberg, William Saphir, and Marc Snir (also in this series), it provides an annotated reference manual for all of MPI. The reader can consult a third book in the series, *Using MPI: Portable Parallel Programming with the Message Passing Interface*, by William Gropp, Ewing Lusk, and Anthony Skjellum, for a tutorial introduction to MPI.

Janusz S. Kowalik

Preface

The Message Passing Interface Standard

MPI, the Message Passing Interface, is a standardized and portable message-passing system designed by a group of researchers from academia and industry to function on a wide variety of parallel computers. The standard defines the syntax and semantics of a core of library routines useful to a wide range of users writing portable message-passing programs in Fortran, C, or C++. Version 1 of this standard (hereafter called MPI-1 [16]) was released in summer 1994. Since its release, the MPI specification has become the leading standard for message-passing libraries for parallel computers. More than a dozen implementations exist, on a wide variety of platforms. Every vendor of high-performance parallel computers offers an MPI implementation as part of the standard system software, and there are a number of freely available implementations for heterogeneous networks of workstations and symmetric multiprocessors, for both Unix and Windows NT. An important reason for the rapid adoption of MPI was the representation on the MPI Forum, which designed MPI, by all segments of the parallel computing community: vendors, library writers, and application scientists.

The MPI-1 standardization effort involved over 80 people from 40 organizations, mainly from the United States and Europe. Most of the major vendors of concurrent computers at the time were involved in MPI, along with researchers from universities, government laboratories, and industry. The standardization process began with the Workshop on Standards for Message Passing in a Distributed Memory Environment, sponsored by the Center for Research on Parallel Computing, held April 29–30, 1992, in Williamsburg, Virginia [35]. A preliminary draft proposal was put forward by Dongarra, Hempel, Hey, and Walker in November 1992, and a revised version was completed in February 1993 [11].

In November 1992, a meeting of the MPI working group was held in Minneapolis, at which it was decided to place the standardization process on a more formal footing. The MPI working group met every 6 weeks throughout the first 9 months of 1993. The draft MPI standard was presented at the Supercomputing '93 conference in November 1993. After a period of public comments, which resulted in some changes in MPI, version 1.0 of MPI was released in May 1994.

These meetings and the e-mail discussion together constituted the MPI Forum, membership of which has been open to all members of the high performance computing community.

Version 1 of MPI deliberately omitted a number of topics important to parallel computing, since the Forum wished to complete its work in a limited time. Beginning in the spring of 1995, the Forum reconvened in order to address these issues and others that had arisen as experience was gained with the implementation and use of MPI-1. The "new" MPI Forum was comprised of both veterans of MPI-1 and new participants. It followed the same open process as before, encouraging anyone who wished to attend meetings and to participate in the e-mail discussions that took place between meetings.

In July 1997 the MPI Forum completed the definition of MPI-2 [17]. It includes significant extensions to the MPI-1 programming model, a number of improvements to the MPI-1 standard, and clarifications to parts of the MPI specification that had been subject to misinterpretation.

About This Book

This book serves as an annotated reference manual for MPI-1, and presents a complete specification of this part of the standard. We repeat the material already published in the MPI-1 specification document [15], though an attempt to clarify has been made. The annotations mainly take the form of explaining why certain design choices were made, how users are meant to use the interface, and how MPI implementors should construct a version of MPI. Many detailed, illustrative programming examples are also given, with an eye toward illuminating the more advanced or subtle features of MPI.

The complete interface is presented in this book, and we are not hesitant to explain even the most esoteric features or consequences of the standard. As such, this volume does not work as a gentle introduction to MPI, nor as a tutorial. For such purposes, we recommend the companion volume in this series by William Gropp, Ewing Lusk, and Anthony Skjellum, *Using MPI: Portable Parallel Programming with the Message-Passing Interface*. The parallel application developer will want to have copies of both books handy.

For a first reading, and as a good introduction to MPI, the reader should first read: Chapter 1, through Section 1.7; the material on point to point communications covered in Sections 2.1 through 2.5 and Section 2.8; the simpler forms of collective communications explained in Sections 4.1 through 4.8; and the basic introduction to communicators given in Sections 5.1 through 5.2. This will give a fair understanding of MPI, and will allow the construction of parallel applications of moderate complexity.

About the Second Edition

The second, revised edition of this book reflects the additions, corrections, and clarifications to MPI-1 done in MPI-2. In certain cases MPI-2 introduced new functions, to replace "deprecated" MPI-1 functions which where awkward to use or lacked desired features. The deprecated functions are still part of the standard, but use of the new functions is recommended. In such cases, this book presents the new functions, and lists the old deprecated functions only for reference. MPI-2 added a C++ binding for the MPI library, and we present here the C++ binding for the functions described in this book. In addition, this edition corrects errors that readers found in the first edition. We are grateful for their help.

Neither *MPI—The Complete Reference: Volume 2, The MPI-2 Extensions* nor this book are official versions of the MPI standard; the standard is available from http://www.mpi-forum.org. In the case of any difference between these books and the standard, the standard takes precedence.

MIT Press is maintaining a Web page for this book, by which one can gain access to errata and corrections, should they be necessary. The URL for this page is http://mitpress.mit.edu/book-home.tcl?isbn=0262629155.

Acknowledgments

This book is based on the hard work of many people in the MPI Forum. The authors gratefully recognize the members of the Forum, especially the contributions made by members who served in positions of responsibility during the development of MPI-1: Lyndon Clarke, James Cownie, Al Geist, William Gropp, Rolf Hempel, Robert Knighten, Richard Littlefield, Ewing Lusk, Paul Pierce, and Anthony Skjellum. The second edition of this book incorporates the work involved in MPI-2. The second volume of this book contains acknowledgements for the work of people in the MPI-2 process. However, several people were of special importance in the material included in this volume. The authors are indebted to those who are volume 2 authors and helped with details of the first volume: William Gropp, Andrew Lumsdaine, Ewing Lusk, Bill Nitzberg, and William Saphir. In addition, several people served in positions of responsibility in developing MPI-2 who have yet to be mentioned: Anthony Skjelum and Jeff Squyres. Other contributors to MPI-1 were: Ed Anderson, Robert Babb, Joe Baron, Eric Barszcz, Scott Berryman, Rob Bjornson, Nathan Doss, Anne Elster, Jim Feeney, Vince Fernando, Sam Fineberg, Jon Flower, Daniel Frye, Ian Glendinning, Adam Greenberg, Robert Harrison,

Leslie Hart, Tom Haupt, Don Heller, Tom Henderson, Anthony Hey, Alex Ho, C.T. Howard Ho, Gary Howell, John Kapenga, James Kohl, Susan Krauss, Bob Leary, Arthur Maccabe, Peter Madams, Alan Mainwaring, Oliver McBryan, Phil McKinley, Charles Mosher, Dan Nessett, Peter Pacheco, Howard Palmer, Sanjay Ranka, Peter Rigsbee, Arch Robison, Erich Schikuta, Mark Sears, Ambuj Singh, Alan Sussman, Robert Tomlinson, Robert G. Voigt, Dennis Weeks, Stephen Wheat, and Steven Zenith. We especially thank William Gropp and Ewing Lusk for help in formatting this volume.

Support for MPI meetings came in part from ARPA and NSF under grant ASC-9310330, NSF Science and Technology Center Cooperative agreement No. CCR-8809615, and the Commission of the European Community through Esprit Project P6643. The University of Tennessee also made financial contributions to the MPI Forum.

MPI—The Complete Reference

Volume 1, The MPI Core

1 Introduction

In this chapter we summarize the goals and scope of MPI. We also describe notations used in this book and some MPI conventions and design characteristics that make the rest of the book easier to understand. We also discuss the meaning of MPI-1 deprecated functions. We address language binding issues here that are common to all chapters. We conclude with comments on implementation and runtime issues. Most of the material in this chapter is repeated in terms and definitions contained in the companion book *MPI—The Complete Reference: Volume 2, The* MPI-2 *Extensions.* It is included in both volumes for completeness.

1.1 Message Passing and Standardization

Message passing is a programming paradigm used widely on parallel computers, especially Scalable Parallel Computers (SPCs) with distributed memory, and on Networks of Workstations (NOWs). Although there are many variations, the basic concept of processes communicating through messages has been well understood for some time.

When the MPI Forum started its activity in 1992, proprietary message passing libraries were available on several SPC systems, and were used to develop significant parallel applications. Code portability was hampered by the differences between these libraries. Several public-domain systems had demonstrated that a message-passing system could be efficiently and portably implemented. It was thus an appropriate time to define both the syntax and semantics of a standard core of library routines that would be useful to a wide range of users and efficiently implementable on a wide range of computers. This effort has been undertaken from 1992 to 1994 by the Message Passing Interface (MPI) Forum, a group of more than 80 people from 40 organizations, representing vendors of parallel systems, industrial users, industrial and national research laboratories, and universities.

The designers of MPI sought to make use of the most attractive features of a number of existing message-passing systems, rather than selecting one of them and adopting it as the standard. Thus, MPI has been strongly influenced by work at the IBM T. J. Watson Research Center [1, 2], Intel's NX/2 [29], Express [28], nCUBE's Vertex [27], p4 [5, 6], and PARMACS [3, 7]. Other important contributions have come from Zipcode [30, 31], Chimp [13, 14], PVM [19, 33], Chameleon [21], and PICL [20]. The MPI Forum identified some critical shortcomings of existing message-passing systems, in areas such as complex data layouts or support for modularity and safe communication. This led to the introduction of new features in MPI.

Version 1 of the MPI standard defines the user interface and functionality for a wide range of message-passing capabilities. Since its completion in May of 1994, MPI has become widely accepted and used. It is now a standard offering on all parallel computers. A number of implementations are freely available available for heterogeneous networks of workstations, as well as for single parallel machines. A large amount of scientific and engineering software has been developed using MPI, including many freely available libraries. Because of this, MPI has achieved one of its goals — adding credibility to parallel computing. Third-party vendors, researchers, and others now have a reliable and portable way to express message-passing parallel programs.

The major goal of MPI, as with most standards, is a degree of portability across different machines. The expectation is for a degree of portability comparable to that given by programming languages such as Fortran. This means that the same message-passing source code can be executed on a variety of machines as long as the MPI library is available, while some tuning might be needed to take best advantage of the features of each system. Though message passing is often thought of in the context of distributed-memory parallel computers, the same code can run well on a shared-memory parallel computer. It can run on a network of workstations, or, indeed, as a set of processes running on a single workstation. Knowing that efficient MPI implementations exist across a wide variety of computers gives a high degree of flexibility in code development, debugging, and in choosing a platform for production runs.

Another type of compatibility offered by MPI is the ability to run transparently on heterogeneous systems, that is, collections of processors with distinct architectures. It is possible for an MPI implementation to span such a heterogeneous collection yet provide a virtual computing model that hides many architectural differences. The user need not worry whether the code is sending messages between processors of like or unlike architecture. The MPI implementation will automatically do any necessary data conversion and utilize the correct communication protocol. However, MPI does not prohibit implementations that are targeted to a single, homogeneous system, and does not mandate that distinct implementations be interoperable. Users that wish to run on an heterogeneous system must use an MPI system designed to support heterogeneity.

Portability is central but the standard will not gain wide usage if this was achieved at the expense of performance. For example, Fortran is commonly used over assembly languages because compilers are almost always available that yield acceptable performance compared to the non-portable alternative of assembly languages. A crucial point is that MPI was carefully designed so as to allow efficient implementations. The design choices seem to have been made correctly, since MPI implementations over a wide range of platforms have achieved high performance, and have largely replaced vendor-specific systems.

An important design goal of MPI was to allow efficient implementations across machines of differing characteristics. For example, MPI carefully avoids specifying how operations will take place. It only specifies what an operation does logically. As a result, MPI can be easily implemented on systems that buffer messages at the sender, receiver, or do no buffering at all. Implementations can take advantage of specific features of the communication subsystem of various machines. On machines with intelligent communication coprocessors, much of the message passing protocol can be offloaded to this coprocessor. On other systems, most of the communication code is executed by the main processor. Another example is the use of opaque objects in MPI. By hiding the details of how MPI-specific objects are represented, each implementation is free to do whatever is best under the circumstances.

Another design choice leading to efficiency is the avoidance of unnecessary work. MPI was carefully designed so as to avoid a requirement for large amounts of extra information with each message, or the need for complex encoding or decoding of message headers. MPI also avoids extra computation or tests in critical routines since this can degrade performance. Another way of minimizing work is to encourage the reuse of previous computations. MPI provides this capability through constructs such as persistent communication requests and caching of attributes on communicators. The design of MPI avoids the need for extra copying and buffering of data: in many cases, data can be moved from the user memory directly to the wire, and be received directly from the wire to the receiver memory.

MPI was designed to encourage overlap of communication and computation, so as to take advantage of intelligent communication agents, and to hide communication latencies. This is achieved by the use of nonblocking communication calls, which separate the initiation of a communication from its completion.

Scalability is an important goal of parallel processing. MPI allows or supports scalability through several of its design features. For example, an application can create subgroups of processes that, in turn, allows collective communication operations to limit their scope to the processes involved. Another technique used is to provide functionality that does not require local computation that scales as the number of processes. For example, a two-dimensional Cartesian topology can be subdivided into its one-dimensional rows or columns without explicitly enumerating the processes.

Finally, MPI, as with all good standards, is valuable in that it defines a known, minimum behavior of message-passing implementations. This relieves the programmer from having to worry about certain problems that can arise. One example is that MPI guarantees that the underlying transmission of messages is reliable. The user need not check if a message is received correctly.

1.2   Who Should Use This Standard?

The MPI standard is intended for use by all those who want to write portable message-passing programs in Fortran, C, and C++. This includes individual application programmers, developers of software designed to run on parallel machines, and creators of environments and tools. In order to be attractive to this wide audience, the standard has provided a simple, easy-to-use interface for the basic user while not semantically precluding the high-performance message-passing operations available on advanced machines.

1.3   What Platforms Are Targets for Implementation?

The attractiveness of the message-passing paradigm at least partially stems from its wide portability. Programs expressed this way may run on distributed-memory multicomputers, shared-memory multiprocessors, networks of workstations, and combinations of all of these. The paradigm will not be made obsolete by architectures combining the shared- and distributed-memory views, or by increases in network speeds. MPI is implemented on a great variety of machines, including those "machines" consisting of collections of other machines, parallel or not, connected by a communication network.

The interface is suitable for use by fully general Multiple Instruction, Multiple Data (MIMD) programs, or Multiple Program, Multiple Data (MPMD) programs, where each process follows a distinct execution path through the same code, or even executes a different code. It is also suitable for those written in the more restricted style of Single Program, Multiple Data (SPMD), where all processes follow the same execution path through the same program. Although support for threads is not required, the interface has been designed so as not to prejudice their use.

Many proprietary, native implementations of MPI, and public domain, portable implementation of MPI are now available. See Section 9.4 for more information about MPI implementations.

1.4   What Is Included in MPI?

Version 1 of the MPI standard includes:

- Point-to-point communication (Chapter 2 and Chapter 3)
- Collective operations (Chapter 4)
- Process groups (Chapter 5)
- Communication domains (Chapter 5)
- Process topologies (Chapter 6)
- Environmental Management and inquiry (Chapter 7)
- Profiling interface (Chapter 8)
- Bindings for Fortran and C

To these MPI-2 added:

- Dynamic process management
- Input/Output
- One-sided operations
- Bindings for C++

MPI-2 also specifies the interaction of MPI with threads and provides extension mechanisms and various facilities for tool developers. Also, "Fortran" has come to mean Fortran 90 rather than Fortran 77.

Most of these MPI-2 extensions are described in the companion book *MPI— The Complete Reference: Volume 2, The MPI-2 Extensions* by William Gropp, Steven Huss-Lederman, Andrew Lumsdaine, Ewing Lusk, Bill Nitzberg, William Saphir, and Marc Snir also published in this series. This book will be henceforward referred to as Book II. References to Book II are indicated by a section number of page number prefaced with a Roman numeral two. For example, Chapter 2 of *MPI—The Complete Reference: Volume 2, The MPI-2 Extensions* is written as Chapter II-2.

Part of the MPI-2 material which closely relates to MPI-1 functions has been included in this book.

As large as MPI may seem, there still are many features that were considered and not included in MPI. This happened for a number of reasons: the feeling that not enough experience was available on some of these topics; the limited applicability of some of the features; and the concern that additional features would burden implementations without adding much value to users. Features that are not included can always be offered as extensions by specific implementations.

1.5   Version of MPI

The original MPI standard was created by the Message Passing Interface Forum (MPIF). The public release of version 1.0 of MPI was made in May 1994. The MPI Forum began meeting again in March 1995. One of the first tasks undertaken was to make clarifications and corrections to the MPI standard. The changes from version 1.0 to version 1.1 of the MPI standard were limited to "corrections" that were deemed urgent and necessary. This work was completed in June 1995 when version 1.1 of the standard was released [16]. In July 1997 the Forum completed version 2.0 of MPI. This book reflects version 2.0 of the MPI standard [17].

The official documents of the Forum, including the the standard, are available from the MPI Forum Web page at `http://www.mpi-forum.org`. Both Postscript and HTML versions are available. Neither *MPI—The Complete Reference: Volume 2, The MPI Extensions* nor this book are official versions of the MPI standard; in the case of any difference between these books and the standards, the standards take precedence.

1.6   MPI Conventions and Design Choices

In this section we explain notation used throughout the book to help the reader navigate the various parts of the MPI standard.

1.6.1   Document Notation

As in the standard itself, we set off with specific notation certain classes of remarks that are not part of the description of the MPI standard.

Rationale.   The rationale for the design choices made in the interface specification is set off in this format. Some readers may wish to skip these sections, while readers interested in interface design may want to read them carefully. ☐

Advice to users.   Material aimed at users and that illustrates usage is set off in this format. Some readers may wish to skip these sections, while readers interested in programming in MPI may want to read them carefully. ☐

Advice to implementors.   Material that is primarily commentary to implementors is set off in this format. Some readers may wish to skip these sections, while readers interested in MPI implementations may want to read them carefully. ☐

1.6.2   Naming Conventions

MPI-1 loosely followed an object oriented design. Most MPI routines are acting on MPI objects. In C++, these objects are instances of C++ classes, and the MPI routines are methods of these classes, or member functions of these classes. MPI-1 generally used naming conventions that reflect this design. In many cases, MPI-1 names for C functions are of the form Class_action_subset and in Fortran of the form CLASS_ACTION_SUBSET, but this rule is not uniformly applied. In MPI-2, an attempt has been made to standardize names of new functions according to the following rules. In addition, the C++ bindings for MPI-1 functions also follow these rules (see Section 1.9.4). C and Fortran names for MPI-1 functions have not been changed.

• In C, names of routines associated with a particular type of MPI object should be of the form Class_action_subset or, if no subset exists, of the form Class_action. In Fortran, all routines associated with a particular type of MPI object should be of the form CLASS_ACTION_SUBSET or, if no subset exists, of the form CLASS_ACTION. In C++, all entities are defined within the **MPI** namespace and a routine associated with a particular type of MPI object is a method on **Class**. Thus, the entire C++ function name is **MPI::Class::Action_subset**. If the routine is associated with a certain class, but does not make sense as an object method, it is a static member function of the class.

• If the routine is not associated with a class, the name should be of the form Action_subset in C, ACTION_SUBSET in Fortran, and in C++ should be scoped in the **MPI** namespace, **MPI::Action_subset**.

• The names of certain actions have been standardized. In particular, **Create** creates a new object, **Get** retrieves information about an object, **Set** sets this information, **Delete** deletes information, and **Is** asks whether or not an object has a certain property.

These rules are strictly followed by the C++ binding, but are sometimes violated by the C and Fortran bindings, especially in MPI-1. The most common exceptions are the omission of the **Class** name from the routine and the omission of the **Action** where one can be inferred. In such cases, the language neutral name is the same as for C and Fortran, but differs from the C++ name. An example of this is the language neutral name of MPI_FINALIZED, with C name MPI_Finalized and Fortran name MPI_FINALIZED, but a C++ name of MPI::Is_finalized.

Rationale.   The naming conventions are often violated so as to have shorter names for common operations. Thus, MPI_SEND, rather than MPI_COMM_SEND, as would be required by a strict application of the naming conventions. Also, the MPI-1 Forum did not follow an explicit set of rules so that violations are more frequent in MPI-1 than in MPI-2. ▯

MPI identifiers are limited to 30 characters (31 with the profiling interface). This is done to avoid exceeding the limit on some compilation systems.

1.6.3   Procedure Specification

MPI procedures are specified using a language-independent notation. The arguments of procedure calls are marked as IN, OUT or INOUT. The meanings of these are:

- if the call may use the input value but does not update an argument, it is marked IN,
- if the call may update an argument but does not use its input value, it is marked OUT, and
- if the call may both use and update an argument, it is marked INOUT.

There is one special case—if an argument is a handle to an opaque object (these terms are defined in Section 1.8.1), and the object is updated by the procedure call, then the argument is marked OUT. It is marked this way even though the handle itself is not modified—we use the OUT attribute to denote that what the handle *references* is updated. Thus, in C++, IN arguments are either references or pointers to `const` objects. Similarly, a send buffer is marked as an IN argument and a receive buffer is marked as an OUT argument.

Rationale.   The definition of MPI tries to avoid, to the largest extent possible, the use of INOUT arguments, because such use is error-prone, especially for scalar arguments. ▯

MPI's use of IN, OUT and INOUT does not always translate into the corresponding language concept in bindings (e.g., `INTENT` in Fortran 90 bindings or `const` in C++ bindings). For example, receive calls return information about the received message in an OUT `status` argument. However, a special constant value (MPI_STATUS_IGNORE) can be passed in the `status` argument, to indicate that no status need be computed and returned by the receive call.

In several cases an argument is used as IN by some processes and OUT by other processes. Such an argument is, syntactically, an INOUT argument and is marked as such, although semantically it is not used in one call both for input and for output on a single process.

Another frequent situation arises when an argument value is needed only by a subset of the processes. When an argument is not significant at a process, then an arbitrary value can be passed as an argument.

Unless specified otherwise, an argument of type OUT or type INOUT cannot be aliased with any other argument passed to an MPI procedure. Two arguments are aliased if they refer to the same or overlapping storage locations. An example of argument aliasing in C appears below. If we define a C procedure like this,

```c
void copyIntBuffer( int *pin, int *pout, int len )
{
    int i;
    for (i=0; i<len; ++i) *pout++ = *pin++;
}
```

then a call to it in the following code fragment has aliased arguments.

```c
int a[10];
copyIntBuffer( a, a+3, 7 );
```

Although the C language allows this, such usage of MPI procedures is forbidden unless otherwise specified. Note that Fortran prohibits aliasing of arguments.

All MPI functions are first specified in the language-independent notation. Immediately below this, the ISO C version of the function is shown, followed by a version of the same function in Fortran and then in C++. Fortran in this book refers to Fortran 90; see Section 1.9.

1.7   Semantic Terms

When discussing MPI procedures the following semantic terms are used.

blocking: A procedure is blocking if return from the procedure indicates the user is allowed to reuse resources specified in the call.

nonblocking: A procedure is nonblocking if the procedure may return before the operation affected by the procedure call completes, and before the user is allowed to reuse resources (such as buffers) specified in the call. A call to a nonblocking procedure **starts** an operation. The call **completes** when the procedure returns, but the operation started may not be completed yet, if the call is nonblocking. The operation **completes** when all changes in the calling process state effected by the call have taken place, and the user is allowed to reuse all resources specified in the call. Thus, a send operation completes when data have been copied out of the sender memory, and the send buffer can be reused. This completion is an asynchronous event that may occur after the send call returned, while the sending process executes unrelated code. It may also occur before the communication initiated by the send operation completes (the data may not have been received yet).

Typically, a **request** object is associated with an operation when the operation is started by a nonblocking procedure. The user can use this object to test or wait for the completion of the operation. When the test succeeds or the wait completes, then the request is **completed** and the operation completion becomes visible to the calling process. Note that the word "complete" is used with respect to operations, requests, and communications, and refers to a possibly distinct event in each case.

local: A procedure is local if completion of the procedure does not depend on the execution of MPI calls by other processes.

non-local: A procedure is non-local if completion of the procedure may require the execution of some MPI procedure on another process.

collective: A procedure is collective if all processes in a process group need to invoke the procedure. A collective call may or may not be **synchronizing**. If it is, then the completion of the call on any process in the group will require that all other processes in the group start their matching call. Collective calls over the same communicator must be executed in the same order by all members of the process group.

predefined: A predefined datatype is a datatype with a predefined (constant) name (such as MPI_INT, MPI_FLOAT_INT, or MPI_UB) or a datatype constructed with MPI_TYPE_CREATE_F90_INTEGER, MPI_TYPE_CREATE_F90_REAL, or MPI_TYPE_CREATE_F90_COMPLEX. The former are **named** whereas the latter are **un-named**.

derived: A derived datatype is any datatype that is not predefined.

portable: A datatype is portable if it is a predefined datatype or is derived from a portable datatype using only the type constructors MPI_TYPE_CONTIGUOUS, MPI_TYPE_VECTOR, MPI_TYPE_INDEXED, MPI_TYPE_INDEXED_BLOCK, MPI_TYPE_CREATE_SUBARRAY, MPI_TYPE_DUP, and MPI_TYPE_CREATE_DARRAY. Such a datatype is portable because all displacements in the datatype are in terms of extents of one predefined datatype. Therefore, if such a datatype fits a data layout in one memory, it will fit the corresponding data layout in another memory if the same declarations were used, even if the two systems have different architectures. On the other hand, if a datatype was constructed using MPI_TYPE_CREATE_HINDEXED, MPI_TYPE_CREATE_HVECTOR or MPI_TYPE_CREATE_STRUCT, then the datatype contains explicit byte displacements (e.g., providing padding to meet alignment restrictions). These displacements are unlikely to be chosen correctly if they fit data layout on one memory, but are used for data layouts on another process running on a processor with a different architecture.

equivalent: Two datatypes are equivalent if they appear to have been created with the same sequence of calls (and arguments) and thus have the same typemap. Two equivalent datatypes do not necessarily have the same cached attributes or the same names.

1.8 Function Argument Data Types

Here we discuss the host language datatypes used in calling MPI functions.

1.8.1 Opaque Objects

MPI manages **system memory** that is used for buffering messages and for storing internal representations of various MPI objects such as groups, communicators, datatypes, etc. This memory is not directly accessible to the user, and objects stored there are **opaque**: their size and structure are not visible to the user. Opaque objects are accessed via **handles** that exist in user space. MPI procedures that operate on opaque objects are passed handle arguments to access these objects. In addition to their use by MPI calls for object access, handles can participate in assignments and comparisons.

In Fortran, all handles have type INTEGER. In C and C++, a different handle type is defined for each category of objects. In addition, handles themselves are distinct objects in C++. The C and C++ types must support the use of the assignment and equality operators.

Advice to implementors. In Fortran, the handle can be an index into a table of opaque objects in a system table; in C it can be such an index or a pointer to the object. C++ handles can simply "wrap up" a table index or pointer. ☐

Opaque objects are allocated and deallocated by calls that are specific to each object type. These are listed in the sections where the objects are described. The calls accept a handle argument of matching type. In an allocate call this is an OUT argument that returns a valid reference to the object. In a call to deallocate, this is an INOUT argument that returns with an "invalid handle" value. MPI provides an "invalid handle" constant for each object type. Comparisons to this constant are used to test for validity of the handle.

A call to a deallocate routine invalidates the handle and marks the object for deallocation. The object is not accessible to the user after the call. However, MPI need not deallocate the object immediately. Any operation pending (at the time of the deallocate) that involves this object will complete normally; the object will be deallocated afterwards.

An opaque object and its handle are significant only at the process where the object was created and cannot be transferred to another process.

MPI provides certain predefined opaque objects and predefined, static handles to these objects. The user must not free such objects. In C++, this is enforced by declaring the handles to these predefined objects to be static const.

Rationale. This design hides the internal representation used for MPI data structures, thus allowing similar calls in C, C++, and Fortran. It also avoids conflicts with the typing rules in these languages, and easily allows future extensions of functionality. The mechanism for opaque objects used here loosely follows the POSIX Fortran binding standard [22].

The explicit separation of handles in user space and objects in system space allows space-reclaiming and deallocation calls to be made at appropriate points in the user program. If the opaque objects were in user space, one would have to be very careful not to go out of scope before any pending operation requiring that object completed. The specified design allows an object to be marked for deallocation, the user program can then go out of scope, and the object itself still persists until any pending operations are complete.

The requirement that handles support assignment/comparison is made since such operations are common. This restricts the domain of possible implementations. The alternative would have been to allow handles to have been an arbitrary, opaque type. This would force the introduction of routines to do assignment and comparison, adding complexity, and was therefore ruled out. ▯

Advice to users. A user may accidently create a dangling reference by assigning to a handle the value of another handle, and then deallocating the object associated with these handles. Conversely, if a handle variable is deallocated before the associated object is freed, then the object becomes inaccessible (this may occur, for example, if the handle is a local variable within a subroutine, and the subroutine is exited before the associated object is deallocated). It is the user's responsibility to avoid adding or deleting references to opaque objects, except as a result of MPI calls that allocate or deallocate such objects. □

Advice to implementors. The intended semantics of opaque objects is that opaque objects are separate from one another; each call to allocate such an object copies all the information required for the object. Implementations may avoid excessive copying by substituting referencing for copying. For example, a derived datatype may contain references to its components, rather then copies of its components; a call to MPI_COMM_GROUP may return a reference to the group associated with the communicator, rather than a copy of this group. In such cases, the implementation must maintain reference counts, and allocate and deallocate objects in such a way that the visible effect is as if the objects were copied. □

1.8.2 Array Arguments

An MPI call may need an argument that is an array of opaque objects. Such an array is accessed via an array of handles. The array-of-handles is a regular array with entries that are handles to objects of the same type in consecutive locations in the array. Whenever such an array is used, an additional len argument is required to indicate the number of valid entries (unless this number can be derived otherwise). The valid entries are at the beginning of the array; len indicates how many of them there are, and need not be the size of the entire array. The same approach is followed for other array arguments. In some cases NULL handles are considered valid entries.

1.8.3 State

MPI procedures use at various places arguments with *state* types. The values of such a data type are all identified by names, and no operation is defined on them. For example, the MPI_TYPE_CREATE_SUBARRAY routine has a state argument order with values MPI_ORDER_C and MPI_ORDER_FORTRAN.

1.8.4 Named Constants

MPI procedures sometimes assign a special meaning to a special value of a basic type argument; for example, tag is an integer-valued argument of point-to-point communication operations, with a special wild-card value, MPI_ANY_TAG. Such arguments will have a range of regular values that is a proper subrange of the range of values of the corresponding basic type; special values (such as MPI_ANY_TAG) will be outside the regular range. The range of regular values for an argument such as tag can be queried using the MPI environmental inquiry functions. The range of other values, such as source, depends on values given by other MPI routines (in the case of source it is the communicator size).

MPI also provides predefined named constant handles, such as MPI_COMM-WORLD.

All named constants, with the exceptions noted for Fortran, can be used in initialization expressions or assignments.[1] These constants do not change values during execution. Opaque objects accessed by constant handles are defined and do not change value between MPI initialization (MPI_INIT) and MPI completion (MPI_FINALIZE).

1.8.5   Choice

MPI functions sometimes use arguments with a *choice* (or union) data type. Distinct calls to the same routine may pass by reference actual arguments of different types. The mechanism for providing such arguments will differ from language to language. For Fortran, the book uses <type> to represent a choice variable; for C and C++, we use void *.

1.8.6   Addresses

Some MPI procedures use *address* arguments that represent an absolute address in the calling program. The datatype of such an argument is MPI_Aint in C, MPI::Aint in C++ and INTEGER (KIND=MPI_OFFSET_KIND) in Fortran.

1.8.7   File Offsets

For I/O (defined in MPI-2) there is a need to give the size, displacement, and offset into a file. These quantities can easily be larger than 32 bits which can be the default size of a Fortran integer. To overcome this, these quantities are declared to be INTEGER (KIND=MPI_OFFSET_KIND) in Fortran. In C one uses MPI_Offset whereas in C++ one uses MPI::Offset.

1.9   Language Binding

This section defines the rules for MPI language binding in general and for Fortran, ISO C, and C++, in particular. (Note that ANSI C has been replaced by ISO

---

[1] They still are not quite the same as language constants. For example, they cannot be used as case labels in a C switch statement.

C.) Defined here are various object representations, as well as the naming conventions used for expressing this standard. The actual calling sequences are defined elsewhere.

Since the word PARAMETER is a keyword in the Fortran language, we use the word "argument" to denote the arguments to a subroutine. These are normally referred to as parameters in C and C++, however, we expect that C and C++ programmers will understand the word "argument" (which has no specific meaning in C/C++), thus allowing us to avoid unnecessary confusion for Fortran programmers.

1.9.1 Deprecated Names and Functions

A number of chapters refer to deprecated or replaced MPI-1 constructs. These are constructs that continue to be part of the MPI standard, but that users are recommended to discontinue using, since MPI-2 provides better solutions. For example, the Fortran binding for MPI-1 functions that have address arguments uses INTEGER. This is not consistent with the C binding, and causes problems on machines with 32-bit INTEGERs and 64-bit addresses. In MPI-2, these functions have new names, and new bindings for the address arguments. The use of the old functions is deprecated. For consistency, here and in a few other cases, new C functions are also provided, even though the new functions are equivalent to the old functions. The old names are deprecated. Another example is provided by the MPI-1 predefined datatypes MPI_UB and MPI_LB. They are deprecated, since their use is awkward and error-prone, while the MPI-2 function MPI_TYPE_CREATE_RESIZED provides a more convenient mechanism for achieving the same purpose.

Table 1.1 provides a list of all of the deprecated constructs.

1.9.2 Fortran Binding Issues

MPI-1 provided bindings for Fortran 77. MPI-2 retains these bindings but they are now interpreted in the context of the Fortran 90 standard. MPI can still be used with most Fortran 77 compilers, as noted below. When the term Fortran is used it means Fortran 90.

All MPI names have an MPI_ prefix, and all characters are capitals. Programs must not declare variables, parameters, or functions with names beginning with the prefix MPI_. To avoid conflicting with the profiling interface, programs should also avoid functions with the prefix PMPI_. This is mandated to avoid possible name collisions. Since Fortran is case insensitive, linkers may use either lowercase or uppercase when resolving Fortran names. Users of case-sensitive languages should avoid the "mpi_" and "pmpi_" prefixes.

Table 1.1
Deprecated functions, constants, and typedefs in MPI.

Deprecated	MPI-2 Replacement
MPI_ADDRESS	MPI_GET_ADDRESS
MPI_TYPE_HINDEXED	MPI_TYPE_CREATE_HINDEXED
MPI_TYPE_HVECTOR	MPI_TYPE_CREATE_HVECTOR
MPI_TYPE_STRUCT	MPI_TYPE_CREATE_STRUCT
MPI_TYPE_EXTENT	MPI_TYPE_GET_EXTENT
MPI_TYPE_UB	MPI_TYPE_GET_EXTENT
MPI_TYPE_LB	MPI_TYPE_GET_EXTENT
MPI_LB	MPI_TYPE_CREATE_RESIZED
MPI_UB	MPI_TYPE_CREATE_RESIZED
MPI_ERRHANDLER_CREATE	MPI_COMM_CREATE_ERRHANDLER
MPI_ERRHANDLER_GET	MPI_COMM_GET_ERRHANDLER
MPI_ERRHANDLER_SET	MPI_COMM_SET_ERRHANDLER
MPI_Handler_function	MPI_Comm_errhandler_fn
MPI_KEYVAL_CREATE	MPI_COMM_CREATE_KEYVAL
MPI_KEYVAL_FREE	MPI_COMM_FREE_KEYVAL
MPI_DUP_FN	MPI_COMM_DUP_FN
MPI_NULL_COPY_FN	MPI_COMM_NULL_COPY_FN
MPI_NULL_DELETE_FN	MPI_COMM_NULL_DELETE_FN
MPI_Copy_function	MPI_Comm_copy_attr_function
COPY_FUNCTION	COMM_COPY_ATTR_FN
MPI_Delete_function	MPI_Comm_delete_attr_function
DELETE_FUNCTION	COMM_DELETE_ATTR_FN
MPI_ATTR_DELETE	MPI_COMM_DELETE_ATTR
MPI_ATTR_GET	MPI_COMM_GET_ATTR
MPI_ATTR_PUT	MPI_COMM_SET_ATTR

All MPI Fortran subroutines have a return code in the last argument. A few MPI operations that are functions do not have the return code argument. The return code value for successful completion is MPI_SUCCESS. Other error codes are implementation-dependent. Error codes are discussed in Section 7.5. The following **reference constants** cannot be used in initialization expressions or assignments in Fortran:

```
MPI_BOTTOM
MPI_STATUS_IGNORE
MPI_STATUSES_IGNORE
MPI_ERRCODES_IGNORE
MPI_IN_PLACE
MPI_ARGV_NULL
MPI_ARGVS_NULL
```

Advice to implementors.   In Fortran the implementation of these special constants may require the use of language constructs that are outside the Fortran standard. Using special values for the constants (e.g., by defining them through `parameter` statements) is not possible because an implementation cannot distinguish these values from legal data. Typically, these constants are implemented as predefined static variables (e.g., a variable in an MPI-declared `COMMON` block), relying on the fact that the target compiler passes data by address. Inside the subroutine, this address can be extracted by some mechanism outside the Fortran standard (e.g., by Fortran extensions or by implementing the function in C). □

Constants representing the maximum length of a string are one smaller in Fortran than in C and C++ as discussed in Section II-2.2.8.

Handles are represented in Fortran as `INTEGER`s. Binary-valued variables are of type `LOGICAL`.

Array arguments are indexed from one. Address arguments are `INTEGER`s of kind `MPI_ADDRESS_KIND`. File displacements are `INTEGER`s of kind `MPI_OFFSET_KIND`.

The MPI Fortran binding is inconsistent with the Fortran 90 standard in several respects. These inconsistencies, such as those related to register optimization problems, have implications for user codes that are discussed in detail in Section II-8.2.2. The binding is also inconsistent with Fortran 77.

- An MPI subroutine with a choice argument may be called with different argument types.
- An MPI subroutine with an assumed-size dummy argument may be passed an actual scalar argument.
- Many MPI routines assume that actual arguments are passed by address and that arguments are not copied on entrance to or exit from the subroutine.
- An MPI implementation may read or modify user data (e.g., communication buffers used by nonblocking communications) concurrently with a user program executing outside MPI calls.

- Several named "constants," such as MPI_BOTTOM, MPI_STATUS_IGNORE, and MPI_ERRCODES_IGNORE, are not ordinary Fortran constants and require a special implementation. See Section 1.8.4 for more information.

Additionally, MPI is inconsistent with Fortran 77 in a number of ways, as noted below.

- MPI identifiers exceed 6 characters.
- MPI identifiers may contain underscores after the first character.
- MPI requires an include file, mpif.h. On systems that do not support include files, the implementation should specify the values of named constants.
- Many routines in MPI-2 have KIND-parameterized integers (e.g., MPI_ADDRESS_KIND and MPI_OFFSET_KIND) that hold address information. On systems that do not support Fortran 90-style parameterized types, INTEGER*8 or INTEGER should be used instead.
- The memory allocation routine MPI_ALLOC_MEM can't be usefully used in Fortran without a language extension that allows the allocated memory to be associated with a Fortran variable.

1.9.3   C Binding Issues

We use the ISO C declaration format. All MPI names have an MPI_ prefix, defined constants are in all capital letters, and defined types and functions have exactly one capital letter immediately following the prefix. Programs must not declare variables or functions with names beginning with the prefix MPI_. To support the profiling interface, programs should not declare functions with names beginning with the prefix PMPI_.

The definition of named constants, function prototypes, and type definitions must be supplied in an include file mpi.h.

Almost all C functions return an error code. The successful return code will be MPI_SUCCESS, but failure return codes are implementation dependent (see Section 7.5).

Type declarations are provided for handles to each category of opaque objects.

Array arguments are indexed from zero.

Logical flags are integers with value 0 meaning "false" and a non-zero value meaning "true."

Choice arguments are pointers of type void *.

Address arguments are of MPI-defined type MPI_Aint. File displacements are of type MPI_Offset. MPI_Aint is defined to be an integer of the size needed to hold any valid address on the target architecture. MPI_Offset is defined to be an integer of the size needed to hold any valid file size on the target architecture.

1.9.4   C++ Binding Issues

The C++ bindings to MPI were added as part of MPI-2. To make the text cohesive, the C++ binding that apply to functions in this book (mostly former MPI-1 functions) are included. Further discussion on the C++ bindings can be found in II-8.1.

There are places in the standard that give rules for C and not for C++. In these cases, the C rule should be applied to the C++ case, as appropriate. In particular, the C++ values of constants given in the text are the ones for C and Fortran. In general, it is easy to determine the C++ constant from the C constant. To help C++ users, the first reference to a constant listed in the index under the C name also has the C++ name in the text. There are also several C++ types that do not exist in C, including MPI::BOOL, MPI::COMPLEX, MPI::DOUBLE_-COMPLEX, and MPI::LONG_DOUBLE_COMPLEX. Several C++ types have names that are not easily derivable from the C name including MPI::F_COMPLEX, MPI::F_-DOUBLE_COMPLEX, MPI::TWOINT, MPI::TWOREAL, MPI::TWODOUBLE_PRECISION, and MPI::TWOINTEGER. There is also the C++ only error handler MPI::ERRORS_-THROW_EXCEPTIONS. Finally, there is no constant comparable to MPI_STATUS_-IGNORE.

We use the ANSI C++ declaration format. All MPI names are declared within the scope of a namespace called `MPI` and therefore are referenced with an `MPI::` prefix. Defined constants are in all capital letters, and class names, defined types, and functions have only their first letter capitalized. Programs must not declare variables or functions in the `MPI` namespace. This is mandated to avoid possible name collisions.

The members of the `MPI` namespace are those classes corresponding to objects implicitly used by MPI. An abbreviated definition of the `MPI` namespace for MPI-1 and its member classes is as follows:

```
namespace MPI {
  class Comm                            {...};
  class Intracomm : public Comm         {...};
  class Graphcomm : public Intracomm    {...};
  class Cartcomm  : public Intracomm    {...};
  class Intercomm : public Comm         {...};
  class Datatype                        {...};
```

```
class Errhandler                        {...};
class Exception                         {...};
class Group                             {...};
class Op                                {...};
class Request                           {...};
class Prequest   : public Request       {...};
class Status                            {...};
};
```

Additionally, the following classes are defined for MPI-2:

```
namespace MPI {
  class File                            {...};
  class Grequest   : public Request     {...};
  class Info                            {...};
  class Win                             {...};
};
```

Note that there are a small number of derived classes and that virtual inheritance is *not* used. To the greatest extent possible, the C++ bindings for MPI functions are member functions of these classes.

The definition of named constants, function prototypes, and type definitions must be supplied in an include file mpi.h.

Advice to implementors.   The file mpi.h may contain both the C and C++ definitions. Usually one can simply use a pre-defined preprocessor symbol (generally __cplusplus, but not required) to see if one is using C++ to protect the C++ definitions. It is possible that a C compiler will require that the source protected this way be legal C code. In this case, all the C++ definitions can be placed in a different include file and the "#include" directive can be used to include the necessary C++ definitions in the mpi.h file. ☐

C++ functions that create objects or return information usually place the object or information in the return value. Since the language neutral prototypes of MPI functions include the C++ return value as an OUT parameter, semantic descriptions of MPI functions refer to the C++ return value by that parameter name (see Section II-8.1.11). The remaining C++ functions return void.

In some circumstances, MPI permits users to indicate that they do not want a return value. For example, the user may indicate that the status is not to be filled in. Unlike C and Fortran where this is achieved through a special input value, in C++ this is done by having two bindings where one has the optional argument and one does not.

C++ functions do not return error codes. If the default error handler has been set to MPI::ERRORS_THROW_EXCEPTIONS, the C++ exception mechanism is used to signal an error by throwing an `MPI::Exception` object.

It should be noted that the default error handler (i.e., MPI::ERRORS_ARE_-FATAL) on a given type has not changed. User error handlers are also permitted. MPI::ERRORS_RETURN simply returns control to the calling function; there is no provision for the user to retrieve the error code.

User callback functions that return integer error codes should not throw exceptions; the returned error will be handled by the MPI implementation by invoking the appropriate error handler.

Advice to users.   C++ programmers that want to handle MPI errors on their own should use the MPI::ERRORS_THROW_EXCEPTIONS error handler, rather than MPI::ERRORS_RETURN, which is used for that purpose in C. Care should be taken using exceptions in mixed language situations. ☐

Opaque object handles must be objects in themselves, and have the assignment and equality operators overridden to perform semantically like their C and Fortran counterparts.

Array arguments are indexed from zero.

Logical flags are of type `bool`.

Choice arguments are pointers of type `void *`.

Address arguments are of MPI-defined integer type MPI::Aint, defined to be an integer of the size needed to hold any valid address on the target architecture. Analogously, MPI::Offset is an integer to hold file offsets.

Most MPI functions are methods of MPI C++ classes. MPI class names are generated from the language neutral MPI types by dropping the `MPI_` prefix and scoping the type within the `MPI` namespace. For example, MPI_DATATYPE becomes `MPI::Datatype`.

The names of MPI-2 functions generally follow the naming rules given. In some circumstances, the new MPI-2 function is related to an MPI-1 function with a name that does not follow the naming conventions. In this circumstance, the language-neutral name is analogous to the MPI-1 name even though this gives an MPI-2 name that violates the naming conventions. The C and Fortran names are the same as the language-neutral name in this case. However, the C++ names for MPI-1 do reflect the naming rules and can differ from the C and Fortran names. Thus, the analogous name in C++ to the MPI-1 name is different from the language-neutral name. This results in the C++ name differing from the language-neutral name. An example of this is the language-neutral name of MPI_FINALIZED and a C++ name of MPI::Is_finalized.

In C++, function `typedefs` are made publicly within appropriate classes. However, these declarations then become somewhat cumbersome, as in the following case. The complete typedef for the generalized request query callback function would look like

```
namespace MPI {
  class Request {
    // ...
  };

  class Grequest : public MPI::Request {
    // ...
    typedef int Query_function(void* extra_state,
                               MPI::Status& status);
  };
};
```

Rather than including this scaffolding when declaring C++ `typedefs`, we use an abbreviated form. In particular, we explicitly indicate the class and namespace scope for the `typedef` of the function. Thus, the example above is shown in the text as follows:

```
typedef int MPI::Grequest::Query_function(void* extra_state,
                                          MPI::Status& status);
```

Besides the member functions which constitute the C++ language bindings for MPI, the C++ language interface has additional functions (as required by the C++ language). In particular, the C++ language interface defines methods for construction, destruction, copying, assignment, comparison, and mixed-language operability for all MPI member classes.

The default constructor and destructor are prototyped as follows:

```
MPI::<CLASS>()
```

```
~MPI::<CLASS>()
```

In terms of construction and destruction, opaque MPI user-level objects behave like handles. Default constructors for all MPI objects except MPI::Status create corresponding MPI::*_NULL handles. That is, when an MPI object is instantiated, comparing it with its corresponding MPI::*_NULL object will return true. The default constructors do not create new MPI opaque objects. Some classes have a member function Create() for this purpose.

The destructor for each MPI user-level object does *not* invoke the corresponding MPI_*_FREE function (if it exists).

The copy constructor and assignment operator are prototyped as follows:

```
MPI::<CLASS>(const MPI::<CLASS>& data)
```

```
MPI::<CLASS>& MPI::<CLASS>::operator=(const MPI::<CLASS>& data)
```

In terms of copying and assignment, opaque MPI user-level objects behave like handles. Copy constructors perform handle-based (shallow) copies. MPI::Status objects are exceptions to this rule. These objects perform deep copies for assignment and copy construction.

The comparison operators are prototyped as follows:

```
bool MPI::<CLASS>::operator==(const MPI::<CLASS>& data) const
```

```
bool MPI::<CLASS>::operator!=(const MPI::<CLASS>& data) const
```

The member function operator==() returns true only when the handles reference the same internal MPI object, false otherwise. operator!=() returns the boolean complement of operator==(). However, since the Status class is not a handle to an underlying MPI object, it does not make sense to compare Status instances. Therefore, the operator==() and operator!=() functions are not defined on the Status class.

Constants are singleton objects and are declared const. Note that not all globally defined MPI objects are constant. For example, MPI::COMM_WORLD and MPI::COMM_SELF are not const.

1.10 Processes

An MPI program consists of autonomous processes, each executing its own code, in an MIMD style. The codes executed by each process need not be identical. The processes communicate via calls to MPI communication primitives. Typically, each process executes in its own address space, although shared-memory implementations of MPI are possible.

MPI specifies the behavior of a parallel program assuming that processes communicate only by using MPI calls. The interaction of MPI calls with other possible means of communication, such as shared memory, I/O, signals or semaphores is not specified. High-quality implementations should strive to make the results of such interactions intuitive to users, and attempt to document restrictions where deemed necessary.

Advice to users.   There is no requirement that MPI processes be the same as POSIX processes. □

Advice to implementors.   Implementations that support such additional interprocess communication mechanisms are expected to document how these interact with MPI. □

The interaction of MPI and threads is defined in Section II-2.1.

1.11   Error Handling

MPI provides the user with reliable message transmission. A message sent is always received correctly, and the user does not need to check for transmission errors, timeouts, or other error conditions. In other words, MPI does not provide mechanisms for dealing with failures in the communication system. If the MPI implementation is built on an unreliable underlying mechanism, then it is the job of the implementor of the MPI subsystem to insulate the user from this unreliability, or to reflect unrecoverable errors as failures. Whenever possible, such failures will be reflected as errors in the relevant communication call. Similarly, MPI itself provides no mechanisms for handling processor failures.

Of course, MPI programs may still be erroneous. A **program error** can occur when an MPI call is made with an incorrect argument (non-existent destination in a send operation, buffer too small in a receive operation, etc.). This type of error would occur in any implementation. In addition, a **resource error** may occur when a program exceeds the amount of available system resources (number of pending messages, system buffers, etc.). The occurrence of this type of error depends on the amount of available resources in the system and the resource allocation mechanism used; this may differ from system to system. A high-quality implementation will provide generous limits on the important resources so as to alleviate the portability problem this represents.

In C and Fortran, almost all MPI calls return a code that indicates successful completion of the operation. Whenever possible, MPI calls return an error code if an error occurred during the call. By default, an error detected during the execution of the MPI library causes the parallel computation to abort, except for file operations. However, MPI provides mechanisms for users to change this default and to handle recoverable errors. The user may specify that no error is fatal, and handle error codes returned by MPI calls by himself or herself. Also, the user may provide his or her own error-handling routines, which will be invoked whenever an MPI call returns abnormally. The MPI error handling facilities are described in 7.5.1. The return values of C++ functions are not error codes. If the default error handler has been set to MPI::ERRORS_THROW_EXCEPTIONS, the C++ exception mechanism is used to signal an error by throwing an `MPI::Exception` object.

Several factors limit the ability of MPI calls to return with meaningful error codes when an error occurs. MPI may not be able to detect some errors; other errors may be too expensive to detect in normal execution mode; finally, some errors may be "catastrophic" and may prevent MPI from returning control to the caller in a consistent state.

Another subtle issue arises because of the nature of asynchronous communications: MPI calls may initiate operations that continue asynchronously after the call returns. Thus, the operation may return with a code indicating successful completion, yet later cause an error exception to be raised. If there is a subsequent call that relates to the same operation (e.g., a call that verifies that an asynchronous operation has completed) then the error argument associated with this call will be used to indicate the nature of the error. In a few cases, the error may occur after all calls that relate to the operation have completed, so that no error value can be used to indicate the nature of the error (e.g., an error on the receiver in a send with the ready mode). Such an error must be treated as fatal, since information cannot be returned for the user to recover from it.

MPI does not specify the state of a computation after an erroneous MPI call has occurred. The desired behavior is that a relevant error code be returned, and the effect of the error be localized to the greatest possible extent. For example, it is highly desirable that an erroneous receive call will not cause any part of the receiver's memory to be overwritten beyond the area specified for receiving the message.

Implementations may go beyond the MPI standard in supporting in a meaningful manner MPI calls that are defined by the standard to be erroneous. For example, MPI specifies strict type-matching rules between matching send and receive operations: it is erroneous to send a floating-point variable and receive an integer. Implementations may go beyond these type matching rules, and provide automatic type conversion in such situations. It will be helpful to generate warnings for such non-conforming behavior.

MPI-2 defines a way for users to create new error codes as defined in Section II-6.5.

1.12   Implementation Issues

There are a number of areas where an MPI implementation may interact with the operating environment and system. While MPI does not mandate that any services (such as signal handling) be provided, it does strongly suggest the behavior to be provided if those services are available. This is an important point in achieving portability across platforms that provide the same set of services.

1.12.1   Independence of Basic Runtime Routines

MPI programs require that library routines that are part of the basic language environment (such as WRITE in Fortran and printf() and malloc() in ISO C) and are executed after MPI_INIT and before MPI_FINALIZE operate independently and that their *completion* is independent of the action of other processes in an MPI program.

Note that this in no way prevents the creation of library routines that provide parallel services whose operation is collective. However, the following program is expected to complete in an ISO C environment regardless of the size of MPI_COMM_-WORLD (assuming that printf() is available at the executing nodes).

```
int rank;
MPI_Init((void *)0, (void *)0);
MPI_Comm_rank(MPI_COMM_WORLD, &rank);
if (rank == 0) printf("Starting program\n");
MPI_Finalize();
```

The corresponding Fortran and C++ programs are also expected to complete.

An example of what is *not* required is any particular ordering of the action of these routines when called by several tasks. For example, MPI makes neither requirements nor recommendations for the output from the following program (again assuming that I/O is available at the executing nodes).

```
MPI_Comm_rank(MPI_COMM_WORLD, &rank);
printf("Output from task rank %d\n", rank);
```

In addition, calls that fail because of resource exhaustion or other error are not considered a violation of the requirements here (however, they are required to complete, just not to complete successfully).

1.12.2 Interaction with Signals

MPI does not specify the interaction of processes with signals and does not require that MPI be signal-safe. The implementation may reserve some signals for its own use. It is required that the implementation document which signals it uses, and it is strongly recommended that it not use `SIGALRM`, `SIGFPE`, or `SIGIO`. Implementations may also prohibit the use of MPI calls from within signal handlers.

In multithreaded environments, users can avoid conflicts between signals and the MPI library by catching signals only on threads that do not execute MPI calls. High quality single-threaded implementations will be signal-safe: an MPI call suspended by a signal will resume and complete normally after the signal is handled.

2 Point-to-Point Communication

In this chapter we present a fundamental capability in message passing systems: the mechanisms for transferring data between two processes. We discuss a number of important ideas that exist throughout MPI including the use of datatypes in all messages. We describe blocking and nonblocking operations along with the communication modes that MPI supports. We present some of the important underlying assumptions in MPI including data conversion and type matching, buffering, and ordering and fairness between messages. Other topics include probing for messages and persistent communication when similar messages are repeatedly sent.

2.1 Introduction and Overview

The basic communication mechanism of MPI is the transmittal of data between a pair of processes, one side sending, the other, receiving. We call this "point to point communication." Almost all the constructs of MPI are built around the point to point operations and so this chapter is fundamental. It is also quite a long chapter for the following reasons: there are many variants to the point to point operations; there is much to say in terms of the semantics of the operations; and related topics, such as probing for messages, are explained here because they are used in conjunction with the point to point operations.

MPI provides a set of send and receive functions that allow the communication of **typed** data with an associated **tag**. Typing of the message contents is necessary for heterogeneous support—the type information is needed so that correct data representation conversions can be performed as data is sent from one architecture to another. The tag allows selectivity of messages at the receiving end: one can receive on a particular tag, or one can use a "wild-card" value for this quantity, allowing reception of messages with any tag. Message selectivity on the source process of the message is also provided.

A fragment of C code appears in Example 2.1 for the example of process 0 sending a message to process 1. The code executes on both process 0 and process 1. Process 0 sends a character string using `MPI_Send()`. The first three parameters of the send call specify the data to be sent: the outgoing data is to be taken from `msg`; it consists of `strlen(msg)+1` entries, each of type `MPI_CHAR`. (The string `"Hello there"` contains `strlen(msg)=11` significant characters. In addition, we are also sending the `'\0'` string terminator character.) The fourth parameter specifies the message destination, which is process 1. The fifth parameter specifies the message tag. Finally, the last parameter is a **communicator** that specifies a **communication domain** for this communication. Among other things, a communicator serves to define a set of processes that can be contacted. Each such process is labeled by a process **rank**. Process ranks are integers and are discovered by inquiry to a communicator (see the call to `MPI_Comm_rank()`). `MPI_COMM_WORLD` is a default communicator provided upon start-up that defines an initial communication domain for all the processes that participate in the computation. Much more will be said about communicators in Chapter 5.

The receiving process specified that the incoming data was to be placed in `msg` and that it had a maximum size of 20 entries, of type `MPI_CHAR`. The variable `status`, set by `MPI_Recv()`, gives information on the source and tag of the message and how many elements were actually received. For example, the receiver can examine this variable to find out the actual length of the character string received. Datatype matching (between sender and receiver) and data conversion on heterogeneous systems are discussed in more detail in Section 2.3.

Example 2.1   C code. Process 0 sends a message to process 1.

```
char msg[20];
int myrank, tag = 99;
MPI_Status status;
...
MPI_Comm_rank(MPI_COMM_WORLD, &myrank);  /* find my rank */
if (myrank == 0) {
  strcpy(msg, "Hello there");
  MPI_Send(msg, strlen(msg)+1, MPI_CHAR, 1, tag, MPI_COMM_WORLD);
} else if (myrank == 1) {
  MPI_Recv(msg, 20, MPI_CHAR, 0, tag, MPI_COMM_WORLD, &status);
}
```

The Fortran version of this code is shown in Example 2.2. The Fortran code is essentially identical to the C code. All MPI calls are procedures, and an additional parameter is used to return the value returned by the corresponding C function. Note that Fortran strings have fixed size and are not null-terminated. The receive operation stores `"Hello there"` in the first 11 positions of `msg`.

Example 2.2   Fortran code. Process 0 sends a message to process 1.

```
CHARACTER*20 msg
```

```
INTEGER myrank, ierr, status(MPI_STATUS_SIZE)
INTEGER :: tag = 99
...
CALL MPI_COMM_RANK(MPI_COMM_WORLD, myrank, ierr)
IF (myrank .EQ. 0) THEN
   msg = "Hello there"
   CALL MPI_SEND(msg, 11, MPI_CHARACTER, 1, &
                 tag, MPI_COMM_WORLD, ierr)
ELSE IF (myrank .EQ. 1) THEN
   CALL MPI_RECV(msg, 20, MPI_CHARACTER, 0, &
                 tag, MPI_COMM_WORLD, status, ierr)
END IF
```

The C++ code appears in Example 2.3. It is very similar to the C code. Almost all MPI calls are methods of suitable MPI classes. In this example, all calls are methods of the communicator class.

Example 2.3   C++ code. Process 0 sends a message to process 1.

```
char msg[20];
const int tag = 99;
MPI::Status status;
...
int myrank = MPI::COMM_WORLD.Get_rank();
if (myrank == 0) {
  strcpy(msg, "Hello there");
  MPI::COMM_WORLD.Send(msg, strlen(msg)+1, MPI::CHAR, 1, tag);
} else if (myrank == 1)
  MPI::COMM_WORLD.Recv(msg, 20, MPI::CHAR, 0, tag, status);
```

These examples employ *blocking* send and receive functions. The send call blocks until the send buffer can be reclaimed (i.e., after the send, process 0 can safely overwrite the contents of msg). Similarly, the receive function blocks until the receive buffer actually contains the contents of the message. MPI also provides *nonblocking* send and receive functions that allow the possible overlap of message transmittal with computation, or the overlap of multiple message transmittals with one another. Non-blocking functions always come in two parts: the posting functions, which begin the requested operation; and the test-for-completion functions, which allow the application program to discover whether the requested operation has completed.

Our chapter begins by explaining blocking functions in detail, in Section 2.2–2.7, while nonblocking functions are covered later, in Sections 2.8–2.12.

We have already said rather a lot about a simple transmittal of data from one process to another, but there is even more. To understand why, we examine two aspects of the communication: the semantics of the communication primitives, and the underlying protocols that implement them. Consider the previous example, on process 0, after the blocking send has completed. The question arises: if the send has completed, does this tell us anything about the receiving process? Can we know that the receive has finished, or even, that it has begun?

Such questions of semantics are related to the nature of the underlying protocol implementing the operations. If one wishes to implement a protocol minimizing the copying and buffering of data, the most natural semantics might be the "rendezvous" version, where completion of the send implies the receive has been initiated (at least). On the other hand, a protocol that attempts to block processes for the minimal amount of time will necessarily end up doing more buffering and copying of data and will have "buffering" semantics.

The trouble is, one choice of semantics is not best for all applications, nor is it best for all architectures. Because the primary goal of MPI is to standardize operations, yet not sacrifice performance, the decision was made to include all the major choices for point to point semantics in the standard.

The above complexities are manifested in MPI by the existence of **modes** for point to point communication. Both blocking and nonblocking communications have modes. The mode allows one to choose the semantics of the send operation and, in effect, to influence the underlying protocol of the transfer of data.

In **standard** mode the completion of the send does not necessarily mean that the matching receive has started, and no assumption should be made in the application program about whether the out-going data is buffered by MPI. In **buffered** mode the user can guarantee that a certain amount of buffering space is available. The catch is that the space must be explicitly provided by the application program. In **synchronous** mode rendezvous semantics between sender and receiver are used. Finally, there is **ready** mode. This allows the user to exploit extra knowledge to simplify the protocol and potentially achieve higher performance. In a ready-mode send, the user asserts that the matching receive already has been posted. Modes are covered in Section 2.13.

2.2 Blocking Send and Receive Operations

This section describes standard-mode, blocking sends and receives.

2.2.1 Blocking Send

MPI_SEND(buf, count, datatype, dest, tag, comm)

IN	buf	initial address of send buffer (choice)
IN	count	number of entries to send (integer)
IN	datatype	datatype of each entry (handle)
IN	dest	rank of destination (integer)
IN	tag	message tag (integer)
IN	comm	communicator (handle)

```
int MPI_Send(void* buf, int count, MPI_Datatype datatype, int dest,
    int tag, MPI_Comm comm)
```

```
MPI_SEND(BUF, COUNT, DATATYPE, DEST, TAG, COMM, IERROR)
    <type> BUF(*)
    INTEGER COUNT, DATATYPE, DEST, TAG, COMM, IERROR
```

```
void MPI::Comm::Send(const void* buf, int count, const
    MPI::Datatype& datatype, int dest, int tag) const
```

MPI_SEND performs a standard-mode, blocking send. The semantics of this function are described in Section 2.4. The arguments to MPI_SEND are described in the following subsections.

MPI_SEND can return the error codes MPI_ERR_BUFFER, MPI_ERR_COUNT, MPI_-ERR_TYPE, MPI_ERR_RANK, MPI_ERR_TAG, or MPI_ERR_COMM to indicate an invalid buf, count, datatype, dest, tag or comm argument, respectively. The same holds for other MPI functions with such arguments. The corresponding C++ error values are MPI::ERR_BUFFER, MPI::ERR_COUNT, MPI::ERR_TYPE, MPI::ERR_RANK, MPI::ERR_TAG, and MPI::ERR_COMM.

2.2.2 Send Buffer and Message Data

The send buffer specified by MPI_SEND consists of count successive entries of the type indicated by datatype, starting with the entry at address buf. Note that we specify the message length in terms of number of *entries*, not number of *bytes*. The former is machine independent and facilitates portable programming. The count may be zero, in which case the data part of the message is empty.

The possible values of the **datatype** argument correspond to the basic datatypes of the host language. Possible values for this argument that correspond to C types are listed below.

MPI datatype	C datatype
MPI_CHAR	signed char
MPI_SIGNED_CHAR	signed char
MPI_UNSIGNED_CHAR	unsigned char
MPI_SHORT	signed short
MPI_UNSIGNED_SHORT	unsigned short
MPI_INT	signed int
MPI_UNSIGNED	unsigned int
MPI_LONG	signed long
MPI_UNSIGNED_LONG	unsigned long
MPI_FLOAT	float
MPI_DOUBLE	double
MPI_LONG_DOUBLE	long double
MPI_WCHAR	wchar_t (MPI-2)
MPI_BYTE	
MPI_PACKED	

Possible values of this argument that correspond to Fortran types are listed below.

MPI datatype	Fortran datatype
MPI_INTEGER	INTEGER
MPI_REAL	REAL
MPI_DOUBLE_PRECISION	DOUBLE PRECISION
MPI_COMPLEX	COMPLEX
MPI_LOGICAL	LOGICAL
MPI_CHARACTER	CHARACTER(1)
MPI_BYTE	
MPI_PACKED	

The possible C++ values of this argument are listed below.

C++ bindings for MPI datatypes	C++ datatypes
MPI::CHAR	signed char
MPI::SIGNED_CHAR	signed char
MPI::UNSIGNED_CHAR	unsigned char

MPI::SHORT	`signed short`
MPI::INT	`signed int`
MPI::LONG	`signed long`
MPI::UNSIGNED_SHORT	`unsigned short`
MPI::UNSIGNED	`unsigned int`
MPI::UNSIGNED_LONG	`unsigned long`
MPI::FLOAT	`float`
MPI::DOUBLE	`double`
MPI::LONG_DOUBLE	`long double`
MPI::WCHAR	`wchar_t`
MPI::BOOL	`bool`
MPI::COMPLEX	`Complex<float>`
MPI::DOUBLE_COMPLEX	`Complex<double>`
MPI::LONG_DOUBLE_COMPLEX	`Complex<long double>`
MPI::BYTE	
MPI::PACKED	
MPI::INTEGER	(Fortran)
MPI::REAL	(Fortran)
MPI::DOUBLE_PRECISION	(Fortran)
MPI::LOGICAL	(Fortran)
MPI::CHARACTER	(Fortran)
MPI::F_COMPLEX	(Fortran)
MPI::F_DOUBLE_COMPLEX	(Fortran)

Normally, C programs will only use datatypes that correspond to C types, and similarly for Fortran or C++. However, constants for Fortran types are defined in C, and vice versa; C++ also has constants for all Fortran types. "Cross-language" types facilitate language interoperability, as explained in Section II-2.2.

Both datatypes MPI_CHAR and MPI_SIGNED_CHAR correspond to the C datatype `signed char`. The first should be used when the corresponding C variable is intended to represent a character, while the second should be used when this variable is intended to represent a (very short) signed integer. In some (rare) cases, their use for communication in a heterogeneous environment can lead to different outcomes – this is explained in Section 2.3.2. MPI-1.1 defined MPI_CHAR to be `signed char`. When MPI-2 added MPI_SIGNED_CHAR it would have made sense to clarify that MPI_CHAR should be `char`. However, this was not done.

The MPI_WCHAR corresponds to the type `wchar_t` defined in `<stddef.h>` to hold Unicode characters.

The datatypes MPI_BYTE and MPI_PACKED do not correspond to a Fortran or C datatype. A value of type MPI_BYTE consists of a byte (8 binary digits). A byte is uninterpreted and is different from a character. Different machines may have different representations for characters, or may use more than one byte to represent characters. On the other hand, a byte has the same binary value on all machines. The use of MPI_PACKED is explained in Section 3.12.

MPI requires support of the datatypes listed above, which match the basic data types of Fortran, C, and C++. MPI also requires that additional MPI datatypes be provided to match any supported, nonstandard data type of a host language. Some examples are: MPI_LONG_LONG (MPI::LONG_LONG, in C++), for C integers declared to be of type long long; MPI_UNSIGNED_LONG_LONG (MPI::UNSIGNED_LONG_LONG, in C++), for C integers declared to be of type unsigned long long; MPI_DOUBLE_-COMPLEX (MPI::DOUBLE_COMPLEX, in C++ and required) for double precision complex in Fortran declared to be of type DOUBLE COMPLEX; MPI_REAL2, MPI_-REAL4 and MPI_REAL8 (MPI::REAL2, MPI::REAL4 and MPI::REAL8, respectively, in C++) for Fortran reals, declared to be of type REAL*2, REAL*4 and REAL*8, respectively; MPI_INTEGER1, MPI_INTEGER2 and MPI_INTEGER4 (MPI::INTEGER1, MPI::INTEGER2 and MPI::INTEGER4, respectively, in C++) for Fortran integers, declared to be of type INTEGER*1, INTEGER*2 and INTEGER*4, respectively. Constants for optional data types of any language should be defined in all three languages. MPI provides a mechanism for users to define datatypes that match Fortran INTEGER, REAL and COMPLEX parameterized types declared using a KIND type parameter. This is explained in Section II-8.2.5. In addition, MPI provides a mechanism for users to define new, derived, datatypes. This is explained in Chapter 3.

2.2.3   Message Envelope

In addition to data, messages carry information that is used to distinguish and selectively receive them. This information consists of a fixed number of fields, which we collectively call the **message envelope**. These fields are

source, **destination**, **tag**, and **communicator**.

The message source is implicitly determined by the identity of the message sender. The other fields are specified by arguments in the send operation.

The comm argument specifies the **communicator** used for the send operation. The communicator is a local object that represents a **communication domain**. A communication domain is a global, distributed structure that allows processes in a **group** to communicate with each other, or to communicate with processes in another group. A communication domain of the first type (communication within a group) is represented by an **intracommunicator**, whereas a communication domain of the second type (communication between groups) is represented by an

intercommunicator. Processes in a group are ordered, and are identified by their integer **rank**. Processes may participate in several communication domains; distinct communication domains may have partially or even completely overlapping groups of processes. Each communication domain supports a disjoint stream of communications. Thus, a process may be able to communicate with another process via two distinct communication domains, using two distinct communicators. The same process may be identified by a different rank in the two domains; and communications in the two domains do not interfere. MPI applications begin with a default communication domain that includes all processes available at job startup; the default communicator MPI_COMM_WORLD (MPI::COMM_WORLD, in C++) represents this communication domain. Communicators are explained further in Chapter 5.

The message destination is specified by the dest argument. The range of valid values for dest is 0,...,n-1, where n is the number of processes in the group. This range includes the rank of the sender: if comm is an intracommunicator, then a process may send a message to itself. If the communicator is an intercommunicator, then destinations are identified by their rank in the remote group.

The integer-valued message tag is specified by the tag argument. This integer can be used by the application to distinguish messages. The range of valid tag values is 0,...,UB, where the value of UB is implementation-dependent. It is found by querying the value of the attribute MPI_TAG_UB (MPI::TAG_UB, in C++), as described in Chapter 7. MPI requires that UB be no less than 32767.

2.2.4 Comments on Send

Advice to users.   Communicators provide an important encapsulation mechanism for libraries and modules. They allow modules to have their own communication space and their own process numbering scheme. Chapter 5 discusses functions for defining new communicators and use of communicators for library design.

Users that are comfortable with the notion of a flat name space for processes and a single communication domain, as offered by most existing communication libraries, need only use the predefined variable MPI_COMM_WORLD as the comm argument. This will allow communication with all the processes available at initialization time. ▯

Advice to implementors.   The message envelope is often encoded by a fixed-length message header. This header carries a communication domain id (sometimes referred to as the **context id**). This id need not be system wide unique; nor does it need to be identical at all processes within a group. It is sufficient that each ordered pair of communicating processes agree to associate a particular id value with each communication domain they use. In addition, the header will usually carry message source and tag; source can be represented as rank within group or as an absolute task id.

The context id can be viewed as an additional tag field. It differs from the regular message tag in that wild card matching is not allowed on this field, and that value setting for this field is controlled by communicator manipulation functions. []

2.2.5   Blocking Receive

MPI_RECV(buf, count, datatype, source, tag, comm, status)

OUT	buf	initial address of receive buffer (choice)
IN	count	max number of entries to receive (integer)
IN	datatype	datatype of each entry (handle)
IN	source	rank of source (integer)
IN	tag	message tag (integer)
IN	comm	communicator (handle)
OUT	status	return status (Status)

```
int MPI_Recv(void* buf, int count, MPI_Datatype datatype, int source,
    int tag, MPI_Comm comm, MPI_Status *status)
```

```
MPI_RECV(BUF, COUNT, DATATYPE, SOURCE, TAG, COMM, STATUS, IERROR)
    <type> BUF(*)
    INTEGER COUNT, DATATYPE, SOURCE, TAG, COMM,
    STATUS(MPI_STATUS_SIZE), IERROR
```

```
void MPI::Comm::Recv(void* buf, int count,
    const MPI::Datatype& datatype, int source, int tag,
    MPI::Status& status) const
```

```
void MPI::Comm::Recv(void* buf, int count,
    const MPI::Datatype& datatype, int source, int tag) const
```

MPI_RECV performs a standard-mode, blocking receive. The semantics of this function are described in Section 2.4. The arguments to MPI_RECV are described in the following subsections.

MPI_RECV can return the error codes MPI_ERR_BUFFER, MPI_ERR_COUNT, MPI_-ERR_TYPE, MPI_ERR_RANK, MPI_ERR_TAG, or MPI_ERR_COMM (MPI::ERR_COMM, in

C++) to indicate an invalid buf, count, datatype, source, tag or comm argument, respectively.

2.2.6   Receive Buffer

The receive buffer consists of storage sufficient to contain count consecutive entries of the type specified by datatype, starting at address buf. The length of the received message must be less than or equal to the length of the receive buffer. An overflow error occurs if all incoming data do not fit, without truncation, into the receive buffer. If a message that is shorter than the receive buffer arrives, then the incoming message is stored in the initial locations of the receive buffer, and the remaining locations are not modified. MPI_RECV may return the error code MPI_ERR_TRUNCATE (MPI::ERR_TRUNCATE, in C++) if a truncation occurs.

2.2.7   Message Selection

The selection of a message by a receive operation is governed by the value of its message envelope. A message can be received if its envelope matches the source, tag and comm values specified by the receive operation. The receiver may specify a wildcard value for source (MPI_ANY_SOURCE, MPI::ANY_SOURCE), and/or a wildcard value for tag (MPI_ANY_TAG, MPI::ANY_TAG), indicating, respectively, that any source and/or tag are acceptable. One cannot specify a wildcard value for comm.

The argument source, if different from MPI_ANY_SOURCE, is specified as a rank within the process group associated with the communicator (remote process group, for intercommunicators). The range of valid values for the source argument is $\{0,...,n-1\} \cup \{MPI\_ANY\_SOURCE\}$, where n is the number of processes in this group. This range includes the receiver's rank: if comm is an intracommunicator, then a process may receive a message from itself. The range of valid values for the tag argument is $\{0,...,UB\} \cup \{MPI\_ANY\_TAG\}$.

2.2.8   Return Status

The receive call does not specify the size of an incoming message, but only an upper bound. The source or tag of a received message may not be known if wildcard values were used in a receive operation. Also, if multiple requests are completed by a single MPI function (see Section 2.9), a distinct error code may be returned for each request. (Usually, the error code is returned as the value of the function in C, and as the value of the IERROR argument in Fortran.)

This information is returned by the status argument of MPI_RECV. The type of status is defined by MPI. Status variables need to be explicitly allocated by the user, that is, they are not system objects.

In C, status is a structure of type MPI_Status that contains three fields named MPI_SOURCE, MPI_TAG, and MPI_ERROR; the structure may contain additional fields. Thus, status.MPI_SOURCE, status.MPI_TAG and status.MPI_ERROR contain the source, tag and error code, respectively, of the received message.

(The error code returned in status by MPI_SEND is not significant. Cases where this field is significant are discussed in Section 2.9.)

In Fortran, status is an array of INTEGERs of length MPI_STATUS_SIZE. The three constants MPI_SOURCE, MPI_TAG and MPI_ERROR are the indices of the entries that store the source, tag, and error fields. Thus status(MPI_SOURCE), status(MPI_TAG) and status(MPI_ERROR) contain, respectively, the source, the tag and the error code of the received message.

In C++, status is an object of type MPI::Status with member functions for accessing the values of the source, tag, and error values, respectively. They are defined as:

```
int MPI::Status::Get_source() const
```

```
int MPI::Status::Get_tag() const
```

```
int MPI::Status::Get_error() const
```

It is possible for users to set the values in the three visible status fields. As a general rule, users should not modify the values contained in a status. Doing so will lead to unpredictable results when MPI interprets these fields. An exception to this statement is status arguments in generalized requests in MPI-2 as discussed in Section II-6.3. In Fortran and C these fields can be set directly by accessing, respectively, the array and struct directly. In C++, this requires accessor functions in the same way that member functions were provided for getting these values. In C++ these functions are:

```
void MPI::Status::Set_source(int source)
```

```
void MPI::Status::Set_tag(int tag)
```

```
void MPI::Status::Set_error(int error)
```

The status argument also returns information on the length of the message received. However, this information is not directly available as a field of the status variable and a call to MPI_GET_COUNT is required to "decode" this information.

MPI_GET_COUNT(status, datatype, count)

IN	status	return status of receive operation (Status)
IN	datatype	datatype of each receive buffer entry (handle)
OUT	count	number of received entries (integer)

```
int MPI_Get_count(MPI_Status *status, MPI_Datatype datatype,
    int *count)
```

```
MPI_GET_COUNT(STATUS, DATATYPE, COUNT, IERROR)
    INTEGER STATUS(MPI_STATUS_SIZE), DATATYPE, COUNT, IERROR
```

```
int Status::Get_count(const MPI::Datatype& datatype) const
```

MPI_GET_COUNT takes as input the status set by MPI_RECV and computes the number of entries received. The number of entries is returned in count. The datatype argument should match the argument provided to the receive call that set status. Section 3.5 explains that MPI_GET_COUNT may return, in certain situations, the value MPI_UNDEFINED (MPI::UNDEFINED, in C++). MPI_UNDEFINED is an MPI named constant that is used to represent an undefined integer value.

The information returned by the status argument is sometimes superfluous. Yet, even when the information is not needed, the user must allocate a status data structure, and the MPI function MPI_Recv must fill up the status structure, incurring a nonnegligible overhead in the process. To avoid the inconvenience and the overhead, users can pass MPI_STATUS_IGNORE as input to the status argument. The MPI_RECV function does not attempt to return any status information when it recognizes this special value. This same optimization for the use of MPI_STATUS_IGNORE as the value for status applies to all MPI functions that return a status. In C++, there is no analogue of MPI_STATUS_IGNORE. Rather, when one does not want a status to be filled, one simply omits the status argument altogether. All MPI functions that take a status argument thus have overloaded bindings in C++ (one with, and one without, the status argument) to realize the MPI_STATUS_IGNORE optimization.

MPI_STATUS_IGNORE is a reference constant (see Section 1.9, page 14). It cannot be used in Fortran, except as a status argument.

Advice to users.   MPI_STATUS_IGNORE is not a special status; for example, it is not, in C, a structure of type MPI_Status. Instead, it is a special value that can be passed as status argument. □

Advice to implementors.   Fortran interfaces that state an intent for arguments of MPI functions should declare status as INOUT, not OUT. ☐

2.2.9   Comments on Receive

Note the asymmetry between send and receive operations. A receive operation may accept messages from an arbitrary sender, but a send operation must specify a unique receiver. This matches a "push" communication mechanism, where data transfer is effected by the sender, rather than a "pull" mechanism, where data transfer is effected by the receiver.

Source equal to destination is allowed, that is, a process can send a message to itself. However, for such a communication to succeed, it is required that the message be buffered by the system between the completion of the send call and the start of the receive call. The amount of buffer space available and the buffer allocation policy are implementation-dependent. Therefore, it is unsafe and non-portable to send self-messages with the standard-mode, blocking send and receive operations described so far, since this may lead to deadlock. More discussions of this appear in Section 2.4.

Advice to users.   A receive operation must specify the type of the entries of the incoming message, and an upper bound on the number of entries. In some cases, a process may expect several messages of different lengths or types. The process will post a receive for each message it expects and use message tags to disambiguate incoming messages.

In other cases, a process may expect only one message, but this message is of unknown type or length. If there are only a few possible kinds of incoming messages, then each such kind can be identified by a different tag value. The function MPI_PROBE described in Section 2.10 can be used to check for incoming messages without actually receiving them. The receiving process can first test the tag value of the incoming message and then receive it with an appropriate receive operation.

In the most general case, it may not be possible to represent each message kind by a different tag value. A two-phase protocol may be used: the sender first sends a message containing a description of the data, then the data itself. The two messages are guaranteed to arrive in the correct order at the destination, as discussed in Section 2.4. An alternative approach is to use the packing and unpacking functions described in Section 3.12. These allow the sender to pack in one message a description of the data, followed by the data itself, thus creating a "self-typed" message. The receiver can first extract the data description and next use it to extract the data itself.

Superficially, tags and communicators fulfill a similar function. Both allow one to partition communications into distinct classes, with sends matching only receives from the same class. Tags offer imperfect protection since wildcard receives circumvent the protection provided by tags, while communicators are allocated and managed using special, safer operations. It is preferable to use communicators to provide protected communication domains across modules or libraries. Tags are used to discriminate between different kinds of messages within one module or library.

MPI offers a variety of mechanisms for matching incoming messages to receive operations. Oftentimes, matching by sender or by tag will be sufficient to match sends and receives correctly. Nevertheless, it is preferable to avoid the use of wildcard receives whenever possible. Narrower matching criteria result in safer code, with fewer opportunities for message mismatch or nondeterministic behavior. Narrower matching criteria may also lead to improved performance. ☐

Rationale.   Why is status information returned via a special **status** variable?

Some libraries return this information via INOUT **count**, **tag** and **source** arguments, thus using them both to specify the selection criteria for incoming messages and to return the actual envelope values of the received message. The use of a separate argument prevents errors associated with INOUT arguments (for example, using the MPI_ANY_TAG constant as the tag argument in a receive). Another potential source of errors, for nonblocking communications, is that status information may be updated after the call that passed in **count**, **tag** and **source**. In "old-style" designs, an error could occur if the receiver accesses or deallocates these variables before the communication completed. Instead, in the MPI design for nonblocking communications, the **status** argument is passed to the call that completes the communication, and is updated by this call.

Other libraries return status by calls that refer implicitly to the "last message received." This is not thread-safe.

Why isn't **count** a field of the **status** variable?

On some systems, it may be faster to receive data without counting the number of entries received. Incoming messages do not carry an entry count. Indeed, when user-defined datatypes are used (see Chapter 3), it may not be possible to compute such a count at the sender. Instead, incoming messages carry a byte count. The translation of a byte count into an entry count may be time consuming, especially for user-defined datatypes, and may not be needed by the receiver. The current design avoids the need for computing an entry count in those situations where the count is not needed.

Note that the current design allows implementations that compute a count during receives and store the count in a field of the status variable. □

Advice to implementors. Even though no specific behavior is mandated by MPI for erroneous programs, the recommended handling of overflow situations is to return, in status, information about the source, tag and size of the incoming message. The receive operation will return an error code. A quality implementation will also ensure that memory that is outside the receive buffer will not be overwritten.

In the case of a message shorter than the receive buffer, MPI is quite strict in that it allows no modification of the other locations in the buffer. A more lenient statement would allow for some optimizations but this is not allowed. The implementation must be ready to end a copy into the receiver memory exactly at the end of the received data, even if it is at a non-word-aligned address. □

2.3   Datatype Matching and Data Conversion

2.3.1   Type Matching Rules

One can think of message transfer as consisting of the following three phases.

1. Data is copied out of the send buffer and a message is assembled.
2. A message is transferred from sender to receiver.
3. Data is copied from the incoming message and disassembled into the receive buffer.

Type matching must be observed at each of these phases. The type of each variable in the send buffer must match the type specified for that entry by the send operation. The type specified by the send operation must match the type specified by the receive operation. Finally, the type of each variable in the receive buffer must match the type specified for that entry by the receive operation. A program that fails to observe these rules is erroneous.

To define type matching precisely, we need to deal with two issues: matching of types of variables of the host language with types specified in communication operations, and matching of types between sender and receiver.

The types between a send and receive match if both operations specify identical type names. That is, MPI_INTEGER matches MPI_INTEGER, MPI_REAL matches MPI_REAL, and so on. On the other hand, MPI_INT does not match MPI_LONG, even on systems where int and long have the same representation. The one exception to this rule is that the type MPI_PACKED can match any other type (Section 3.12).

The type of a variable matches the type specified in the communication operation if the datatype name used by that operation corresponds to the basic type of the host program variable. For example, an entry with type name MPI_INTEGER matches a Fortran variable of type INTEGER. Tables showing this correspondence for Fortran and C appear in Section 2.2.2. There are two exceptions to this rule: an entry with type name MPI_BYTE or MPI_PACKED can be used to match any byte of storage (on a byte-addressable machine), irrespective of the datatype of the variable that contains this byte. The type MPI_BYTE allows one to transfer the binary value of a byte in memory unchanged. The type MPI_PACKED is used to send data that has been explicitly packed with calls to MPI_PACK, or receive data that will be explicitly unpacked with calls to MPI_UNPACK (Section 3.12).

The following examples illustrate type matching.

Example 2.4   Sender and receiver specify matching types.

```
CALL MPI_COMM_RANK(comm, rank, ierr)
IF (rank.EQ.0) THEN
   CALL MPI_SEND(a(1), 10, MPI_REAL, 1, tag, comm, ierr)
ELSE IF (rank.EQ.1) THEN
   CALL MPI_RECV(b(1), 15, MPI_REAL, 0, tag, comm, status, ierr)
END IF
```

This code is correct if both a and b are real arrays of size ≥ 10. (In Fortran, it might be correct to use this code even if a or b have size < 10, e.g., a(1) might be be equivalenced to an array with ten reals.)

Example 2.5   Sender and receiver do not specify matching types.

```
CALL MPI_COMM_RANK(comm, rank, ierr)
IF (rank.EQ.0) THEN
   CALL MPI_SEND(a(1), 10, MPI_REAL, 1, tag, comm, ierr)
ELSE IF (rank.EQ.1) THEN
   CALL MPI_RECV(b(1), 40, MPI_BYTE, 0, tag, comm, status, ierr)
END IF
```

This code is erroneous, since sender and receiver do not provide matching datatype arguments.

Example 2.6   Sender and receiver specify communication of untyped values.

```
CALL MPI_COMM_RANK(comm, rank, ierr)
IF (rank.EQ.0) THEN
   CALL MPI_SEND(a(1), 40, MPI_BYTE, 1, tag, comm, ierr)
ELSE IF (rank.EQ.1) THEN
   CALL MPI_RECV(b(1), 60, MPI_BYTE, 0, tag, comm, status, ierr)
END IF
```

This code is correct, irrespective of the type and size of a and b (unless this results in an out of bound memory access).

Type MPI_CHARACTER   The type MPI_CHARACTER matches one character of a Fortran variable of type CHARACTER, rather then the entire character string stored in the variable. Fortran variables of type CHARACTER or substrings are transferred as if they were arrays of characters. This is illustrated in the example below.

Example 2.7   Transfer of Fortran CHARACTERs.

```
CHARACTER*10 a
CHARACTER*10 b

CALL MPI_COMM_RANK(comm, rank, ierr)
IF (rank.EQ.0) THEN
   CALL MPI_SEND(a, 5, MPI_CHARACTER, 1, tag, comm, ierr)
ELSE IF (rank.EQ.1) THEN
   CALL MPI_RECV(b(6:10),5,MPI_CHARACTER,0,tag,comm,status,ierr)
END IF
```

The last five characters of string b at process 1 are replaced by the first five characters of string a at process 0.

Advice to users.   If a buffer of type MPI_BYTE is passed as an argument to MPI_SEND, then MPI will send the data stored at contiguous locations, starting from the address indicated by the buf argument. This may have unexpected results when the data layout is not as a casual user would expect it to be. For example, some Fortran compilers implement variables of type CHARACTER as a structure that contains the character length and a pointer to the actual string. In such an environment, sending and receiving a Fortran CHARACTER variable using the MPI_BYTE type will not have the anticipated result of transferring the character string. For this reason, the user is advised to use typed communications whenever possible. ☐

Rationale.   Why does MPI force the user to specify datatypes? After all, type information is available in the source program.

MPI is meant to be implemented as a library, with no need for additional preprocessing or compilation. Thus, one cannot assume that a communication call has information on the datatype of variables in the communication buffer. This information must be supplied at calling time, either by calling a different function for each datatype, or by passing the datatype information as an explicit parameter. Datatype information is needed for heterogeneous support and is further discussed in Section 2.3.2. ☐

Advice to implementors.   Some compilers pass Fortran CHARACTER arguments as a structure with a length and a pointer to the actual string. In such an environment, MPI send or receive calls need to dereference the pointer in order to reach the string. Many compilers pass Fortran CHARACTER arguments as two arguments: string and length. In such an environment, MPI send or receive calls should ignore the second (length) argument. ☐

2.3.2   Data Conversion

One of the goals of MPI is to support parallel computations across heterogeneous environments. Communication in a heterogeneous environment may require data conversions. We use the following terminology.

Type conversion changes the datatype of a value, for example, by rounding a REAL to an INTEGER.

Representation conversion changes the binary representation of a value, for example, changing byte ordering, or changing 32-bit floating point to 64-bit floating point.

The type matching rules imply that MPI communications never do type conversion. On the other hand, MPI requires that a representation conversion be performed when a typed value is transferred across environments that use different representations for such a value. MPI does not specify the detailed rules for representation conversion. Such a conversion is expected to preserve integer, logical or character values, and to convert a floating point value to the nearest value that can be represented on the target system.

Overflow and underflow exceptions may occur during floating point conversions. Conversion of integers or characters may also lead to exceptions when a value that can be represented in one system cannot be represented in the other system. An exception occurring during representation conversion results in a failure of the communication. An error occurs either in the send operation, or the receive operation, or both.

If a value sent in a message is untyped (i.e., of type MPI_BYTE), then the binary representation of the byte stored at the receiver is identical to the binary representation of the byte loaded at the sender. This holds true, whether sender and receiver run in the same or in distinct environments. No representation conversion is done.

If a value is sent with type MPI_CHAR, then the value is assumed to represent a character. A representation conversion will occur if this is needed to preserve character encoded. The same holds for values of type MPI::CHAR, MPI_WCHAR, MPI::WCHAR or MPI_CHARACTER. On the other hand, if a value is sent with type MPI_SIGNED_CHAR or MPI_UNSIGNED_CHAR, then the value is assumed to be an integer (signed or unsigned, respectively). Conversions should preserve this integer value. Assume, for example, that system A uses an ASCII encoding for characters, system B uses and EBCDIC encoding, but both use 8 bits in two's complement for signed chars arithmetic. Then no conversion will occur if a value of type MPI_SIGNED_CHAR is sent from A to B; on the other hand, a conversion (from ASCII to EBCDIC) will occur if a value of type MPI_CHAR is sent from A to B.

No representation conversion need occur when an MPI program executes in a homogeneous system, where all processes run in the same environment.

Consider the three examples, 2.4–2.6. The first program is correct, assuming that a and b are REAL arrays of size ≥ 10. If the sender and receiver execute in different environments, then the ten real values that are fetched from the send buffer will be converted to the representation for reals on the receiver site before they are stored in the receive buffer. While the number of real elements fetched from the send buffer equal the number of real elements stored in the receive buffer, the number of bytes stored need not equal the number of bytes loaded. For example, the sender may use a four byte representation and the receiver an eight byte representation for reals.

The second program is erroneous, and its behavior is undefined.

The third program is correct. The exact same sequence of forty bytes that were loaded from the send buffer will be stored in the receive buffer, even if sender and receiver run in a different environment. The message sent has exactly the same length (in bytes) and the same binary representation as the message received. If a and b are of different types, or if they are of the same type but different data representations are used, then the bits stored in the receive buffer may encode values that are different from the values they encoded in the send buffer.

Representation conversion also applies to the envelope of a message. The source, destination and tag are all integers that may need to be converted.

2.3.3   Comments on Data Conversion

Advice to implementors.   The datatype matching rules do not require messages to carry data type information. Both sender and receiver provide complete data type information. In a heterogeneous environment, one can either use a machine independent encoding such as XDR[32], or have the receiver convert from the sender representation to its own, or even have the sender do the conversion.

Additional type information might be added to messages in order to allow the system to detect mismatches between datatype at sender and receiver. This might be particularly useful in a slower but safer debug mode for MPI. ☐

2.4   Semantics of Blocking Point-to-Point

This section describes the main properties of the send and receive calls introduced in Section 2.2. Interested readers can find a more formal treatment of the issues in this section in [10].

2.4.1   Buffering and Safety

The receive described in Section 2.2.5 can be started whether or not a matching send has been posted. That version of receive is **blocking**. It returns only after the receive buffer contains the newly received message. A receive could complete before the matching send has completed (of course, it can complete only after the matching send has started).

The send operation described in Section 2.2.1 can be started whether or not a matching receive has been posted. That version of send is **blocking**. It does not return until the message data and envelope have been safely stored away so that the sender is free to access and overwrite the send buffer. The send call is also potentially **non-local**. The message might be copied directly into the matching receive buffer, or it might be copied into a temporary system buffer. In the first case, the send call will not complete until a matching receive call occurs, and so, if the sending process is single-threaded, then it will be blocked until this time. In the second case, the send call may return ahead of the matching receive call, allowing a single-threaded process to continue with its computation. The MPI implementation may make either of these choices. It might block the sender or it might buffer the data. The choice may depend on the current system state (e.g., whether memory is available to buffer the message).

Message buffering decouples the send and receive operations. A blocking send might complete as soon as the message was buffered, even if no matching receive has been executed by the receiver. On the other hand, message buffering can be expensive, as it entails additional memory-to-memory copying, and it requires the allocation of memory for buffering. The choice of the right amount of buffer space to allocate for communication and of the buffering policy to use is application and implementation-dependent. Therefore, MPI offers the choice of several communication modes that allow one to control the choice of the communication protocol. Modes are described in Section 2.13. The choice of a buffering policy for the standard mode send described in Section 2.2.1 is left to the implementation. In any case, lack of buffer space will not cause a standard send call to fail, but will merely cause it to block. In well-constructed programs, this results in a useful throttle effect. Consider a situation where a producer repeatedly produces new values and sends them to a consumer. Assume that the producer produces new values faster than the consumer can consume them. If standard sends are used, then the producer will be automatically throttled, as its send operations will block when buffer space is unavailable.

In ill-constructed programs, blocking may lead to a **deadlock** situation, where all processes are blocked, and no progress occurs. Such programs may complete when sufficient buffer space is available, but will fail on systems that do less buffering, or when data sets (and message sizes) are increased. Since any system will run out of buffer resources as message sizes are increased, and some implementations may want to provide little buffering, MPI takes the position that **safe** programs do not rely on system buffering, and will complete correctly irrespective of the buffer allocation policy used by MPI. Buffering may change the performance of a safe program, but it doesn't affect the result of the program.

MPI does not enforce a safe programming style. Users are free to take advantage of knowledge of the buffering policy of an implementation in order to relax the safety requirements, though doing so will lessen the portability of the program.

The following examples illustrate safe programming issues.

Example 2.8   An exchange of messages.

```
CALL MPI_COMM_RANK(comm, rank, ierr)
IF (rank.EQ.0) THEN
    CALL MPI_SEND(sendbuf, count, MPI_REAL, 1, tag, comm, ierr)
    CALL MPI_RECV(recvbuf, count, MPI_REAL, 1, tag, comm, status, &
                  ierr)
ELSE IF (rank.EQ.1) THEN
    CALL MPI_RECV(recvbuf, count, MPI_REAL, 0, tag, comm, status, &
                  ierr)
    CALL MPI_SEND(sendbuf, count, MPI_REAL, 0, tag, comm, ierr)
END IF
```

This program succeeds even if no buffer space for data is available. The program is safe and will always complete correctly.

Example 2.9   An attempt to exchange messages.

```
CALL MPI_COMM_RANK(comm, rank, ierr)
IF (rank.EQ.0) THEN
    CALL MPI_RECV(recvbuf, count, MPI_REAL, 1, tag, comm, status, &
                  ierr)
    CALL MPI_SEND(sendbuf, count, MPI_REAL, 1, tag, comm, ierr)
ELSE IF (rank.EQ.1) THEN
    CALL MPI_RECV(recvbuf, count, MPI_REAL, 0, tag, comm, status, &
                  ierr)
    CALL MPI_SEND(sendbuf, count, MPI_REAL, 0, tag, comm, ierr)
END IF
```

The receive operation of the first process must complete before its send, and can complete only if the matching send of the second processor is executed. The receive operation of the second process must complete before its send and can complete only if the matching send of the first process is executed. This program will always deadlock.

Example 2.10   An exchange that relies on buffering.

```
CALL MPI_COMM_RANK(comm, rank, ierr)
IF (rank.EQ.0) THEN
    CALL MPI_SEND(sendbuf, count, MPI_REAL, 1, tag, comm, ierr)
```

```
    CALL MPI_RECV(recvbuf, count, MPI_REAL, 1, tag, comm, status, &
                 ierr)
ELSE IF (rank.EQ.1) THEN
    CALL MPI_SEND(sendbuf, count, MPI_REAL, 0, tag, comm, ierr)
    CALL MPI_RECV(recvbuf, count, MPI_REAL, 0, tag, comm, status, &
                 ierr)
END IF
```

The message sent by each process must be copied somewhere before the send operation returns and the receive operation starts. For the program to complete, it is necessary that at least one of the two messages be buffered. Thus, this program will succeed only if the communication system will buffer at least count words of data. Otherwise, the program will deadlock. The success of this program will depend on the amount of buffer space available in a particular implementation, on the buffer allocation policy used, and on other concurrent communication occurring in the system. This program is unsafe.

Advice to users.   Safety is a very important issue in the design of message passing programs. MPI offers many features that help in writing safe programs, in addition to the techniques that were outlined above. Nonblocking message passing operations, as described in Section 2.8, can be used to avoid the need for buffering outgoing messages. This eliminates deadlocks due to lack of buffer space, and potentially improves performance, by avoiding the overheads of allocating buffers and copying messages into buffers. Use of other communication modes, described in Section 2.13, can also avoid deadlock situations due to lack of buffer space.

Quality MPI implementations attempt to be lenient to the user, by providing buffering for standard blocking sends whenever feasible. Programs that require buffering in order to progress will not typically break, unless they move large amounts of data. The caveat, of course, is that "large" is a relative term.

Safety is further discussed in Section 9.2. □

2.4.2   Order

Messages are *non-overtaking*. Conceptually, one may think of successive messages sent by a process to another process as ordered in a sequence. Receive operations posted by a process are also ordered in a sequence. Each incoming message matches the first matching receive in the sequence. This is illustrated in Figure 2.1. Process zero sends two messages to process one and process two sends three messages to

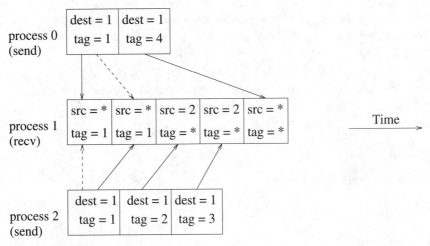

Figure 2.1
Messages are matched in order.

process one. Process one posts five receives. All communications occur in the same communication domain. The first message sent by process zero and the first message sent by process two can be received in either order, since the first two posted receives match either. The second message of process two will be received before the third message, even though the third and fourth receives match either.

Thus, if a sender sends two messages in succession to the same destination, and both match the same receive, then the receive cannot get the second message if the first message is still pending. If a receiver posts two receives in succession, and both match the same message, then the second receive operation cannot be satisfied by this message, if the first receive is still pending.

These requirements further determine matching of sends and of receives. They guarantee that message-passing code is deterministic, if processes are single-threaded and the wildcard MPI_ANY_SOURCE is not used in receives. Some other MPI functions, such as MPI_CANCEL or MPI_WAITANY, are additional sources of nondeterminism.

In a single-threaded process all communication operations are ordered according to program execution order. The situation is different when processes are multithreaded. The semantics of thread execution may not define a relative order between two communication operations executed by two distinct threads. The operations are logically concurrent, even if one physically precedes the other. In this case, no order constraints apply. Two messages sent by concurrent threads can be received in any order. Similarly, if two receive operations that are logically concurrent receive two successively sent messages, then the two messages can match the receives in either order.

It is important to understand what is guaranteed by the ordering property and what is not. Between any pair of communicating processes, messages flow in order. This does not imply a consistent, total order on communication events in the system. Consider the following example.

Example 2.11   Order preservation is not transitive.

```
MPI::Intracomm comm;
int tag, count;
float *buf1, *buf2;
...
int rank = comm.Get_rank();
if (rank == 0) {
  comm.Send(buf1, count, MPI::FLOAT, 2, tag);
  comm.Send(buf2, count, MPI::FLOAT, 1, tag);
} else if (rank == 1) {
  comm.Recv(buf2, count, MPI::FLOAT, 0, tag);
  comm.Send(buf2, count, MPI::FLOAT, 2, tag);
} else if (rank == 2) {
  comm.Send(buf1, count, MPI::FLOAT, MPI::ANY_SOURCE, tag);
  comm.Send(buf2, count, MPI::FLOAT, MPI::ANY_SOURCE, tag);
}
```

Process zero sends a message to process two and next sends a message to process one. Process one receives the message from process zero, then sends a message to process two. Process two receives two messages, with **source = dontcare**. The two incoming messages can be received by process two in any order, even though process one sent its message after it received the second message sent by process zero. The reason is that communication delays can be arbitrary and MPI does not enforce global serialization of communications. Thus, the somewhat paradoxical outcome illustrated in Figure 2.2 can occur. If process zero had sent directly two messages to process two then these two messages would have been received in order. Since it relayed the second message via process one, then the messages may now arrive out of order. In practice, such an occurrence is unlikely.

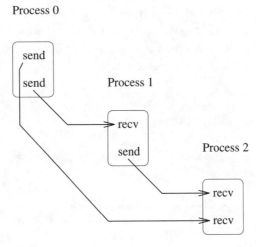

Figure 2.2
Order preserving is not transitive.

2.4.3 Progress

If a pair of matching send and receives have been initiated on two processes, then at least one of these two operations will complete, independently of other actions in the system. The send operation will complete, unless the receive is satisfied by another message. The receive operation will complete, unless the message sent is consumed by another matching receive posted at the same destination process.

Advice to implementors.   This requirement imposes constraints on implementation strategies. Suppose, for example, that a process executes two successive blocking send calls. The message sent by the first call is buffered, and the second call starts. Then, if a receive is posted that matches this second send, the second message should be able to overtake the first one. $\Box$

2.4.4 Fairness

MPI makes no guarantee of *fairness* in the handling of communication. Suppose that a send is posted. Then it is possible that the destination process repeatedly posts a receive that matches this send, yet the message is never received, because it is repeatedly overtaken by other messages, sent from other sources. The scenario requires that the receive used the wildcard MPI_ANY_SOURCE as its source argument.

Similarly, suppose that a receive is posted by a multithreaded process. Then it is possible that messages that match this receive are repeatedly consumed, yet the receive is never satisfied, because it is overtaken by other receives posted at this node by other threads. It is the programmer's responsibility to prevent starvation in such situations.

2.5   Example—Jacobi Iteration

We shall use the following example to illustrate the material introduced so far, and to motivate new functions.

Example 2.12   Jacobi iteration – sequential code

```
REAL A(0:n+1,0:n+1), B(1:n,1:n)
...

! Main Loop
DO WHILE(.NOT.converged(A))
   ! perform 4 point stencil
   DO j=1, n
     DO i=1, n
        B(i,j) =0.25*(A(i-1,j)+A(i+1,j)+A(i,j-1)+A(i,j+1))
     END DO
   END DO

   ! copy result back into array A
   DO j=1,n
     DO i=1,n
        A(i,j) = B(i,j)
     END DO
   END DO
END DO
```

The code fragment describes the main loop of an iterative solver where, at each iteration, the value at a point is replaced by the average of the North, South, East and West neighbors (a four point stencil is used to keep the example simple). Boundary values do not change. We focus on the inner loop, where most of the computation is done, and use Fortran 90 syntax, for clarity.

1D partition   **2D partition**

Figure 2.3
Block partitioning of a matrix.

Since this code has a simple structure, a data-parallel approach can be used to derive an equivalent parallel code. The array is distributed across processes, and each process is assigned the task of updating the entries on the part of the array it owns.

A parallel algorithm is derived from a choice of data distribution. The distribution should be balanced, allocating (roughly) the same number of entries to each processor; and it should minimize communication. Figure 2.3 illustrates two possible distributions: a 1D (block) distribution, where the matrix is partitioned in one dimension, and a 2D (block,block) distribution, where the matrix is partitioned in two dimensions.

Since the communication occurs at block boundaries, communication volume is minimized by the 2D partition which has a better area to perimeter ratio. However, in this partition, each processor communicates with four neighbors, rather than two neighbors in the 1D partition. When the ratio of n/P (P number of processors) is small, communication time will be dominated by the fixed overhead per message, and the first partition will lead to better performance. When the ratio is large, the second partition will result in better performance. In order to keep the example simple, we shall use the first partition; a realistic code would use a "polyalgorithm" that selects one of the two partitions, according to problem size, number of processors, and communication performance parameters.

The value of each point in the array B is computed from the value of the four neighbors in array A. Communications are needed at block boundaries in order to receive values of neighbor points which are owned by another processor. Communications are simplified if an overlap area is allocated at each processor for storing the values to be received from the neighbor processor. Essentially, storage is allocated for each entry both at the producer and at the consumer of that entry. If an entry is produced by one processor and consumed by another, then storage is

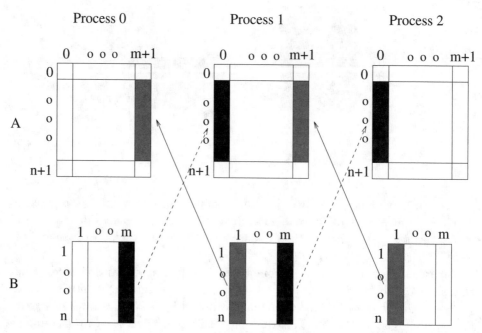

Figure 2.4
1D block partitioning with overlap and communication pattern for jacobi iteration.

allocated for this entry at both processors. With such a scheme there is no need for dynamic allocation of communication buffers, and the location of each variable is fixed. Such a scheme works whenever the data dependencies in the computation are fixed and simple. In our case, they are described by a four point stencil. Therefore, a one-column overlap is needed, for a 1D partition.

We shall partition array A with one column overlap. No such overlap is required for array B. Figure 2.4 shows the extra columns in A and how data is transferred for each iteration.

We shall use an algorithm where all values needed from a neighbor are brought in one message. Coalescing of communications in this manner reduces the number of messages and generally improves performance.

The resulting parallel algorithm is shown below.

Example 2.13   Jacobi iteration—first version of parallel code

```
...
REAL, DIMENSION(:,:), ALLOCATABLE :: A, B
```

```
...
! Compute number of processes and myrank
CALL MPI_COMM_SIZE(comm, p, ierr)
CALL MPI_COMM_RANK(comm, myrank, ierr)

! Compute size of local block
m = n/p
IF (myrank.LT.(n-p*m)) THEN
   m = m+1
END IF

! Allocate local arrays
ALLOCATE (A(0:n+1,0:m+1), B(n,m))
...
! Main loop
DO WHILE (.NOT. converged(A))
   ! Compute
   DO j=1,m
     DO i=1,n
       B(i,j) = 0.25*(A(i-1,j)+A(i+1,j)+A(i,j-1)+A(i,j+1))
     END DO
   END DO
   DO j=1,m
     DO i=1,n
        A(i,j) = B(i,j)
     END DO
   END DO

   ! Communicate
   IF (myrank.GT.0) THEN
      CALL MPI_SEND(B(1,1), n, MPI_REAL, myrank-1, tag, comm, ierr)
   END IF
   IF (myrank.LT.p-1) THEN
      CALL MPI_SEND(B(1,m), n, MPI_REAL, myrank+1, tag, comm, ierr)
   END IF
   IF (myrank.GT.0) THEN
   CALL MPI_RECV(A(1,0), n, MPI_REAL, myrank-1, tag, comm, &
               MPI_STATUS_IGNORE, ierr)
```

```
      END IF
      IF (myrank.LT.p-1) THEN
         CALL MPI_RECV(A(1,m+1), n, MPI_REAL, myrank+1, tag, comm, &
                       MPI_STATUS_IGNORE, ierr)
      END IF
END DO
```

This code has a communication pattern similar to the code in Example 2.10. It is unsafe, since each processor first sends messages to its two neighbors, next receives the messages they have sent.

One way to get a safe version of this code is to alternate the order of sends and receives: odd rank processes will first send, next receive, and even rank processes will first receive, next send. Thus, one achieves the communication pattern of Example 2.8.

The modified main loop is shown below. We shall later see simpler ways of dealing with this problem.

Example 2.14   Main loop of Jacobi iteration—safe version of parallel code

```
...
! Main loop
DO WHILE(.NOT. converged(A))
   ! Compute
   DO j=1,m
      DO i=1,n
         B(i,j) = 0.25*(A(i-1,j)+A(i+1,j)+A(i,j-1)+A(i,j+1))
      END DO
   END DO
   DO j=1,m
      DO i=1,n
         A(i,j) = B(i,j)
      END DO
   END DO

   ! Communicate
   IF (MOD(myrank,2).EQ.1) THEN
      CALL MPI_SEND(B(1,1), n, MPI_REAL, myrank-1, tag, comm, ierr)
      IF (myrank.LT.p-1) THEN
```

```
                CALL MPI_SEND(B(1,m), n, MPI_REAL, myrank+1, tag, comm, &
                        ierr)
        END IF
        CALL MPI_RECV(A(1,0), n, MPI_REAL, myrank-1, tag, comm, &
                    MPI_STATUS_IGNORE, ierr)
        IF (myrank.LT.p-1) THEN
            CALL MPI_RECV(A(1,m+1), n, MPI_REAL, myrank+1, tag,  comm, &
                        status, ierr)
        END IF
    ELSE    ! myrank is even
        IF (myrank.GT.0) THEN
            CALL MPI_RECV(A(1,0), n, MPI_REAL, myrank-1, tag, comm, &
                        MPI_STATUS_IGNORE, ierr)
        END IF
        IF (myrank.LT.p-1) THEN
            CALL MPI_RECV(A(1,m+1), n, MPI_REAL, myrank+1, tag, comm, &
                        MPI_STATUS_IGNORE, ierr)
        END IF
          IF (myrank.GT.0) THEN
            CALL MPI_SEND(B(1,1), n, MPI_REAL, myrank-1, tag, comm, ierr)
        END IF
        IF (myrank.LT.p-1) THEN
            CALL MPI_SEND(B(1,m), n, MPI_REAL, myrank+1, tag, comm, &
                        ierr)
        END IF
    END IF
END DO
```

2.6 Send-Receive

The exchange communication pattern exhibited by the last example is sufficiently frequent to justify special support. The **send-receive** operation combines, in one call, the sending of one message to a destination and the receiving of another message from a source. The source and destination are possibly the same. Send-receive is useful for communications patterns where each node both sends and receives messages. One example is an exchange of data between two processes. Another example is a shift operation across a chain of processes. A safe program that implements such shift will need to use an odd/even ordering of communications, similar to the one used in Example 2.14. When send-receive is used, data flows simultaneously in both directions (logically, at least) and cycles in the communication pattern do not lead to deadlock.

Send-receive can be used in conjunction with the functions described in Chapter 6 to perform shifts on logical topologies. Also, send-receive can be used for implementing remote procedure calls: one blocking send-receive call can be used for sending the input parameters to the remote process and receiving back the output parameters from that process.

There is compatibility between send-receive and normal sends and receives. A message sent by a send-receive can be received by a regular receive or probed by a regular probe, and a send-receive can receive a message sent by a regular send.

MPI_SENDRECV(sendbuf, sendcount, sendtype, dest, sendtag, recvbuf, recvcount,
    recvtype, source, recvtag, comm, status)

IN	sendbuf	initial address of send buffer (choice)
IN	sendcount	number of entries to send (integer)
IN	sendtype	type of entries in send buffer (handle)
IN	dest	rank of destination (integer)
IN	sendtag	send tag (integer)
OUT	recvbuf	initial address of receive buffer (choice)
IN	recvcount	max number of entries to receive (integer)
IN	recvtype	type of entries in receive buffer (handle)
IN	source	rank of source (integer)
IN	recvtag	receive tag (integer)
IN	comm	communicator (handle)
OUT	status	return status (Status)

```
int MPI_Sendrecv(void *sendbuf, int sendcount, MPI_Datatype sendtype,
    int dest, int sendtag, void *recvbuf, int recvcount,
    MPI_Datatype recvtype, int source, int recvtag, MPI_Comm comm,
    MPI_Status *status)
```

```
MPI_SENDRECV(SENDBUF, SENDCOUNT, SENDTYPE, DEST, SENDTAG, RECVBUF,
    RECVCOUNT, RECVTYPE, SOURCE, RECVTAG, COMM, STATUS, IERROR)
    <type> SENDBUF(*), RECVBUF(*)
    INTEGER SENDCOUNT, SENDTYPE, DEST, SENDTAG, RECVCOUNT, RECVTYPE,
    SOURCE, RECVTAG, COMM, STATUS(MPI_STATUS_SIZE), IERROR
```

```
void MPI::Comm::Sendrecv(const void *sendbuf, int sendcount, const
    MPI::Datatype& sendtype, int dest, int sendtag, void *recvbuf,
    int recvcount, const MPI::Datatype& recvtype, int source,
    int recvtag, MPI::Status& status) const
```

```
void MPI::Comm::Sendrecv(const void *sendbuf, int sendcount, const
    MPI::Datatype& sendtype, int dest, int sendtag, void *recvbuf,
    int recvcount, const MPI::Datatype& recvtype, int source,
    int recvtag) const
```

MPI_SENDRECV executes a blocking send and receive operation. Both the send and receive use the same communicator, but have distinct tag arguments. The send buffer and receive buffers must be disjoint, and may have different lengths and datatypes. The next function handles the case where the buffers are not disjoint.

The semantics of a send-receive operation is what would be obtained if the caller forked two concurrent threads, one to execute the send, and one to execute the receive, followed by a join of these two threads.

MPI_SENDRECV_REPLACE(buf, count, datatype, dest, sendtag, source, recvtag, comm, status)

INOUT	buf	initial address of send and receive buffer (choice)
IN	count	number of entries in send and receive buffer (integer)
IN	datatype	type of entries in send and receive buffer (handle)
IN	dest	rank of destination (integer)
IN	sendtag	send message tag (integer)
IN	source	rank of source (integer)
IN	recvtag	receive message tag (integer)
IN	comm	communicator (handle)
OUT	status	status object (Status)

```
int MPI_Sendrecv_replace(void* buf, int count, MPI_Datatype datatype,
    int dest, int sendtag, int source, int recvtag, MPI_Comm comm,
    MPI_Status *status)
```

```
MPI_SENDRECV_REPLACE(BUF, COUNT, DATATYPE, DEST, SENDTAG, SOURCE,
    RECVTAG, COMM, STATUS, IERROR)
    <type> BUF(*)
    INTEGER COUNT, DATATYPE, DEST, SENDTAG, SOURCE, RECVTAG, COMM,
    STATUS(MPI_STATUS_SIZE), IERROR
```

```
void MPI::Comm::Sendrecv_replace(void* buf, int count, const
   MPI::Datatype& datatype, int dest, int sendtag, int source,
   int recvtag, MPI::Status& status) const
```

```
void MPI::Comm::Sendrecv_replace(void* buf, int count, const
   MPI::Datatype& datatype, int dest, int sendtag, int source,
   int recvtag) const
```

MPI_SENDRECV_REPLACE executes a blocking send and receive. The same buffer is used both for the send and for the receive, so that the message sent is replaced by the message received.

The example below shows the main loop of the parallel Jacobi code, reimplemented using send-receive.

Example 2.15   Main loop of Jacobi code—version using send-receive.

```
...
! Main loop
DO WHILE(.NOT.converged)
   ! Compute
   DO j=1,m
      DO i=1,n
         B(i,j) = 0.25*(A(i-1,j)+A(i+1,j)+A(i,j-1)+A(i,j+1))
      END DO
   END DO
   DO j=1,m
      DO i=1,n
         A(i,j) = B(i,j)
      END DO
   END DO

   ! Communicate
   ! Right wave
   IF (myrank.EQ.0) THEN
      CALL MPI_SEND(B(1,m), n, MPI_REAL, myrank+1, tag, &
                        comm, ierr)
   ELSE IF (myrank.EQ.p-1) THEN
      CALL MPI_RECV(A(1,0), n, MPI_REAL, myrank-1, tag, &
                        comm, status, ierr)
   ELSE
```

```
            CALL MPI_SENDRECV(B(1,m), n, MPI_REAL, myrank+1, tag, &
                              A(1,0), n, MPI_REAL, myrank-1, tag, comm, &
                              status, ierr)
        END IF


        ! Left wave
        IF (myrank.EQ.0) THEN
           CALL MPI_RECV(A(1,m+1), n, MPI_REAL, myrank+1, tag, &
                             comm, status, ierr)
        ELSE IF (myrank.EQ.p-1) THEN
           CALL MPI_SEND(B(1,1), n, MPI_REAL, myrank-1, tag, &
                             comm, ierr)
        ELSE
           CALL MPI_SENDRECV(B(1,1), n, MPI_REAL, myrank-1, tag, &
                             A(1,m+1), n, MPI_REAL, myrank+1, tag, comm, &
                             status, ierr)
        END IF


     ...
     END DO
```

This code is safe. Communication occurs in two "waves". In the first one one data is shifted right, and in the second one data is shifted left.

Advice to implementors.   Additional, intermediate buffering is needed for the replace variant. Only a fixed amount of buffer space should be used, otherwise send-receive will not be more robust then the equivalent pair of blocking send and receive calls. ☐

2.7 Null Processes

In many instances, it is convenient to specify a "dummy" source or destination for communication.

In the Jacobi example, this will avoid special handling of boundary processes. This also simplifies handling of boundaries in the case of a non-circular shift, when used in conjunction with the functions described in Chapter 6.

The special value MPI_PROC_NULL (MPI::PROC_NULL, in C++) can be used instead of a rank wherever a source or a destination argument is required in a communication function. A communication with process MPI_PROC_NULL has no effect. A send to MPI_PROC_NULL succeeds and returns as soon as possible. A receive from MPI_PROC_NULL succeeds and returns as soon as possible with no modifications to the receive buffer. When a receive with source = MPI_PROC_NULL is executed then the status object returns source = MPI_PROC_NULL, tag = MPI_ANY_TAG and count = 0.

We take advantage of null processes to further simplify the parallel Jacobi code.

Example 2.16   Jacobi code—version of parallel code using sendrecv and null processes.

```
...
REAL, DIMENSION(:,:), ALLOCATABLE :: A, B
...
! Compute number of processes and myrank
CALL MPI_COMM_SIZE(comm, p, ierr)
CALL MPI_COMM_RANK(comm, myrank, ierr)

! Compute size of local block
m = n/p
IF (myrank.LT.(n-p*m)) THEN
   m = m+1
END IF

! Compute neighbors
IF (myrank.EQ.0) THEN
   left = MPI_PROC_NULL
ELSE
   left = myrank -1
END IF
IF (myrank.EQ.p-1) THEN
   right = MPI_PROC_NULL
ELSE
   right = myrank+1
END IF
```

```
! Allocate local arrays
ALLOCATE (A(0:n+1,0:m+1), B(n,m))
...
! Main loop
DO WHILE(.NOT. converged)
   ! Compute
   DO j=1,m
      DO i=1,n
         B(i,j) = 0.25*(A(i-1,j)+A(i+1,j)+A(i,j-1)+A(i,j+1))
      END DO
   END DO
   DO j=1,m
      DO i=1,n
         A(i,j) = B(i,j)
      END DO
   END DO

   ! Communicate
   CALL MPI_SENDRECV(B(1,m), n, MPI_REAL, right, tag, A(1,0), n, &
                     MPI_REAL, left, tag, comm, status, ierr)
   CALL MPI_SENDRECV(B(1,1), n, MPI_REAL, left, tag, A(1,m+1), n, &
                     MPI_REAL, right, tag, comm, status, ierr)
...
END DO
```

The boundary test that was previously executed inside the loop has been effectively moved outside the loop. Although this is not expected to change performance significantly, the code is simplified.

In this code, each process first sends to its right neighbor and receives from its left neighbor (right shift), next sends to its left neighbor and receives from its right nighbor (left shift). The order in which sends and receives are executed is important. Suppose that the code was slightly modified, so that each processor first sends to and receives from its left neighbor (MPI_SENDRECV(..., left, ..., left, ...)), next sends to and receives from its right neighbor (MPI_SENDRECV(..., right, ..., right, ...)). The code would still be correct, but communications would be serialized: process 0 communicates with process 1, next process 1 communicates with process 2, and so on.

2.8   Nonblocking Communication

One can improve performance on many systems by overlapping communication and computation. This is especially true on systems where communication can be executed autonomously by an intelligent communication controller. Multithreading is one mechanism for achieving such overlap. While one thread is blocked, waiting for a communication to complete, another thread may execute on the same processor. This mechanism is efficient if the system supports light-weight threads that are integrated with the communication subsystem. An alternative mechanism that often gives better performance is to use **nonblocking communication**. A nonblocking **post-send** initiates a send operation, but does not complete it. The post-send may return before the message is copied out of the send buffer. A separate **complete-send** call is needed to verify that the send operation has completed, that is, to verify that the data has been copied out of the send buffer. With suitable hardware, the transfer of data out of the sender memory may proceed concurrently with computations done at the sender after the send was initiated and before it completed. Similarly, a nonblocking **post-receive** initiates a receive operation, but does not complete it. The call may return before a message is stored into the receive buffer. A separate **complete-receive** is needed to verify that the receive operation has completed, that is, to verify that the data has been received into the receive buffer.

A nonblocking send can be posted whether a matching receive has been posted or not. The post-send call is local: it returns immediately, irrespective of the status of other processes. If the call causes some system resource to be exhausted, then it will fail and return an error code. Quality implementations of MPI should ensure that this happens only in "pathological" cases. That is, an MPI implementation should be able to support a large number of pending nonblocking operations.

The complete-send returns when data has been copied out of the send buffer. The complete-send is non-local. The call may return before a matching receive is posted, if the message is buffered. On the other hand, the complete-send may not return until a matching receive is posted.

There is compatibility between blocking and nonblocking communication functions. Nonblocking sends can be matched with blocking receives, and vice-versa.

Advice to users.   The use of nonblocking sends allows the sender to proceed ahead of the receiver, so that the computation is more tolerant of fluctuations in the speeds of the two processes.

The MPI message-passing model fits a "push" model, where communication is initiated by the sender. The communication will generally have lower overhead if a receive buffer is already posted when the sender initiates the communication. The use of nonblocking receives allows one to post receives "early" and so achieve lower communication overheads without blocking the receiver while it waits for the send. ▢

2.8.1 Request Objects

Nonblocking communications use **request** objects to identify communication operations and link the posting operation with the completion operation. Request objects are allocated by MPI and reside in MPI "system" memory. The request object is opaque in the sense that the type and structure of the object is not visible to users. The application program can only manipulate handles to request objects, not the objects themselves. The system may use the request object to identify various properties of a communication operation, such as the communication buffer that is associated with it, or to store information about the status of the pending communication operation. The user may access request objects through various MPI calls to inquire about the status of pending communication operations.

The special value MPI_REQUEST_NULL (MPI::REQUEST_NULL, in C++) is used to indicate an invalid request handle. Operations that deallocate request objects set the request handle to this value.

2.8.2 Posting Operations

Calls that post send or receive operations have the same names as the corresponding blocking calls, except that an additional prefix of I (for immediate) indicates that the call is nonblocking.

MPI_ISEND(buf, count, datatype, dest, tag, comm, request)

IN	buf	initial address of send buffer (choice)
IN	count	number of entries in send buffer (integer)
IN	datatype	datatype of each send buffer entry (handle)
IN	dest	rank of destination (integer)
IN	tag	message tag (integer)
IN	comm	communicator (handle)
OUT	request	request handle (handle)

```
int MPI_Isend(void* buf, int count, MPI_Datatype datatype, int dest,
    int tag, MPI_Comm comm, MPI_Request *request)
```

```
MPI_ISEND(BUF, COUNT, DATATYPE, DEST, TAG, COMM, REQUEST, IERROR)
    <type> BUF(*)
    INTEGER COUNT, DATATYPE, DEST, TAG, COMM, REQUEST, IERROR
```

```
MPI::Request MPI::Comm::Isend(const void* buf, int count, const
    MPI::Datatype& datatype, int dest, int tag) const
```

MPI_ISEND posts a standard-mode, nonblocking send.

MPI_IRECV(buf, count, datatype, source, tag, comm, request)

OUT	buf	initial address of receive buffer (choice)
IN	count	number of entries in receive buffer (integer)
IN	datatype	datatype of each receive buffer entry (handle)
IN	source	rank of source (integer)
IN	tag	message tag (integer)
IN	comm	communicator (handle)
OUT	request	request handle (handle)

```
int MPI_Irecv(void* buf, int count, MPI_Datatype datatype,
    int source, int tag, MPI_Comm comm, MPI_Request *request)
```

```
MPI_IRECV(BUF, COUNT, DATATYPE, SOURCE, TAG, COMM, REQUEST, IERROR)
    <type> BUF(*)
    INTEGER COUNT, DATATYPE, SOURCE, TAG, COMM, REQUEST, IERROR
```

```
MPI::Request MPI::Comm::Irecv(void* buf, int count, const
    MPI::Datatype& datatype, int source, int tag) const
```

MPI_IRECV posts a nonblocking receive.

These calls allocate a request object and return a handle to it in request. The request is used to query the status of the communication or wait for its completion.

A nonblocking post-send call indicates that the system may start copying data out of the send buffer. The sender must not access any part of the send buffer (neither for loads nor for stores) after a nonblocking send operation is posted, until the complete-send returns.

A nonblocking post-receive indicates that the system may start writing data into the receive buffer. The receiver must not access any part of the receive buffer after a nonblocking receive operation is posted, until the complete-receive returns.

Rationale. We prohibit read accesses to a send buffer while it is being used, even though the send operation is not supposed to alter the content of this buffer.

This may seem more stringent than necessary, and this additional restriction causes some loss of functionality. For example, if the same data has to be sent to several destinations (multicast), the send operations cannot be concurrent, if they use the same communication buffer, one has either to serialize the send operations, or to create multiple copies of the send buffer. On the other hand, this restriction allows better performance on some systems. Consider the case where data transfer is done by a separate DMA engine. With this restriction, it is possible to unmap pages that are totally contained inside the communication buffer from the application address space, while they are been accessed by the DMA engine. □

2.8.3 Completion Operations

The functions MPI_WAIT and MPI_TEST are used to complete nonblocking send and receive request. The completion of a send requests indicates that the associated send operation has completed, so that data have been copied out of the send buffer. The sender is now free to access the send buffer. The completion of a receive request indicates that the receive operation has completed, so that the receive buffer contains the message. The receiver is now free to access the receive buffer.

MPI_WAIT(request, status)

| INOUT | request | request handle (handle) |
| OUT | status | status object (Status) |

```
int MPI_Wait(MPI_Request *request, MPI_Status *status)
```

```
MPI_WAIT(REQUEST, STATUS, IERROR)
    INTEGER REQUEST, STATUS(MPI_STATUS_SIZE), IERROR
```

```
void MPI::Request::Wait(MPI::Status& status)
```

```
void MPI::Request::Wait()
```

A call to MPI_WAIT returns when the operation identified by request is complete. If the system object pointed to by request was originally created by a nonblocking send or receive, then the object is deallocated by MPI_WAIT and request is set to MPI_REQUEST_NULL. The status object is set to contain information on the completed operation (unless MPI_STATUS_IGNORE was used for status). MPI_WAIT is non-local.

MPI_WAIT, and other functions with a request argument, can return the error code MPI_ERR_REQUEST (MPI::ERR_REQUEST, in C++) to indicate an invalid request argument.

MPI_TEST(request, flag, status)

INOUT	request	request handle (handle)
OUT	flag	true if operation completed (logical)
OUT	status	status object (Status)

```
int MPI_Test(MPI_Request *request, int *flag, MPI_Status *status)
```

```
MPI_TEST(REQUEST, FLAG, STATUS, IERROR)
    LOGICAL FLAG
    INTEGER REQUEST, STATUS(MPI_STATUS_SIZE), IERROR
```

```
bool MPI::Request::Test(MPI::Status& status)
```

```
bool MPI::Request::Test()
```

A call to MPI_TEST returns flag = true if the operation identified by request is complete. In this case, the status object is set to contain information on the completed operation (unless MPI_STATUS_IGNORE was passed in). If the system object pointed to by request was originally created by a nonblocking send or receive, then the object is deallocated by MPI_TEST and request is set to MPI_REQUEST_-NULL. The call returns flag = false, otherwise. In this case, the value of the status object is undefined. MPI_TEST is local.

For both MPI_WAIT and MPI_TEST, information on the completed operation is returned in status. The content of the status object for a receive operation is accessed as described in Section 2.2.8. The fields in a status object returned by a call to MPI_WAIT, MPI_TEST, or any of the other derived functions (MPI_-{TEST|WAIT}{ALL|SOME|ANY}), where the request corresponds to a send call, are undefined, with two exceptions: the error status field will contain valid information if the wait or test call returned with MPI_ERR_IN_STATUS (Section 2.9), and the returned status can be queried by the call MPI_TEST_CANCELLED (Section 2.10).

Advice to users. The use of MPI_TEST allows one to schedule alternative activities within a single thread of execution. □

Rationale. MPI_WAIT and MPI_TEST are defined so that MPI_TEST returns successfully (with flag = true) exactly in those situation where MPI_WAIT returns.

In those cases, both return the same information in status. This allows one to replace a blocking call to MPI_WAIT with a nonblocking call to MPI_TEST with few changes in the program. The same design logic will be followed for the multi-completion operations of Section 2.9. □

2.8.4 Examples

We illustrate the use of nonblocking communication for the same Jacobi computation used in previous examples (Example 2.12–2.16). To achieve maximum overlap between computation and communication, communications should be started as soon as possible and completed as late as possible. That is, sends should be posted as soon as the data to be sent is available; receives should be posted as soon as the receive buffer can be reused; sends should be completed just before the send buffer is to be reused; and receives should be completed just before the data in the receive buffer is to be used. Sometimes, the overlap can be increased by reordering computations.

Example 2.17   Use of nonblocking communications in Jacobi computation.

```
...
REAL, DIMENSION(:,:), ALLOCATABLE :: A, B
INTEGER req(4)
INTEGER status(MPI_STATUS_SIZE,4)
...
! Compute number of processes and myrank
CALL MPI_COMM_SIZE(comm, p, ierr)
CALL MPI_COMM_RANK(comm, myrank, ierr)

! Compute size of local block
m = n/p
IF (myrank.LT.(n-p*m)) THEN
   m = m+1
END IF

! Compute neighbors
IF (myrank.EQ.0) THEN
   left = MPI_PROC_NULL
ELSE
   left = myrank -1
```

```
END IF
IF (myrank.EQ.p-1) THEN
   right = MPI_PROC_NULL
ELSE
   right = myrank+1
ENDIF

! Allocate local arrays
ALLOCATE (A(0:n+1,0:m+1), B(n,m))
...
! Main loop
DO WHILE(.NOT.converged)

   ! Compute boundary columns
   DO i=1,n
      B(i,1) = 0.25*(A(i-1,1)+A(i+1,1)+A(i,0)+A(i,2))
      B(i,m) = 0.25*(A(i-1,m)+A(i+1,m)+A(i,m-1)+A(i,m+1))
   END DO

   ! Start communication
   CALL MPI_IRECV(A(1,0), n, MPI_REAL, left, tag, comm, req(3), ierr)
   CALL MPI_IRECV(A(1,m+1), n, MPI_REAL, right, tag, comm, req(4), &
                  ierr)
   CALL MPI_ISEND(B(1,1), n, MPI_REAL, left, tag, comm, req(1), ierr)
   CALL MPI_ISEND(B(1,m), n, MPI_REAL, right, tag, comm, req(2), &
                  ierr)

   ! Compute interior
   DO j=2,m-1
      DO i=1,n
         B(i,j) = 0.25*(A(i-1,j)+A(i+1,j)+A(i,j-1)+A(i,j+1))
      END DO
   END DO
   DO j=1,m
      DO i=1,n
         A(i,j) = B(i,j)
      END DO
   END DO
```

```
  ! Complete communication
  DO i=1,4
     CALL MPI_WAIT(req(i), status(1,i), ierr)
  END DO
...
END DO
```

The communication calls use the leftmost and rightmost columns of local array B and set the leftmost and rightmost columns of local array A. The send buffers are made available early by separating the update of the leftmost and rightmost columns of B from the update of the interior of B. Since this is also where the leftmost and rightmost columns of A are used, the communication can be started immediately after these columns are updated and can be completed just before the next iteration.

The next example shows a multiple-producer, single-consumer code. The last process in the group consumes messages sent by the other processes.

Example 2.18   Multiple-producer, single-consumer code using nonblocking communication.

```
...
typedef struct {
  char data[MAXSIZE];
  int datasize;
  MPI_Request req;
} Buffer;
Buffer *buffer;
MPI_Status status;
...

MPI_Comm_rank(comm, &rank);
MPI_Comm_size(comm, &size);
if (rank != size-1) {  /* producer code  */
  /* initialization - producer allocates one buffer */
  buffer = (Buffer *)malloc(sizeof(Buffer));
  while(1) {  /* main loop */
    /* producer fills data buffer and returns
       number of bytes stored in buffer */
```

```
      produce( buffer->data, &buffer->datasize);
      /* send data */
      MPI_Send(buffer->data, buffer->datasize, MPI_CHAR,
              size-1, tag, comm);
   }
}
else { /* rank == size-1; consumer code */
  /* initialization - consumer allocates one buffer
     per producer */
  buffer = (Buffer *)malloc(sizeof(Buffer)*(size-1));
  for(i=0;  i< size-1; i++)
    /* post a receive from each producer */
    MPI_Irecv(buffer[i].data, MAXSIZE, MPI_CHAR, i, tag,
            comm, &(buffer[i].req));

  for(i=0; ; i=(i+1)%(size-1)) { /* main loop */
    MPI_Wait(&(buffer[i].req), &status);
    /* find number of bytes actually received */
    MPI_Get_count(&status, MPI_CHAR, &(buffer[i].datasize));
    /* consume empties data buffer */
    consume(buffer[i].data, buffer[i].datasize);
    /* post new receive */
    MPI_Irecv(buffer[i].data, MAXSIZE, MPI_CHAR, i, tag,
            comm, &(buffer[i].req));
  }
}
```

Each producer runs an infinite loop where it repeatedly produces one message and sends it. The consumer serves each producer in turn, by receiving its message and consuming it.

The example imposes a strict round-robin discipline, since the consumer receives one message from each producer, in turn. In some cases it is preferable to use a "first-come-first-served" discipline. This is achieved by using MPI_TEST, rather than MPI_WAIT, as shown below. Note that MPI can only offer an approximation to first-come-first-served, since messages do not necessarily arrive in the order they were sent.

Example 2.19   Multiple-producer, single-consumer code, modified to use test calls.

```
typedef struct {
  char data[MAXSIZE];
  int datasize;
  MPI_Request req;
} Buffer;
Buffer *buffer;
MPI_Status status;
...
MPI_Comm_rank(comm, &rank);
MPI_Comm_size(comm, &size);
if (rank != size-1) {  /* producer code */
  buffer = (Buffer *)malloc(sizeof(Buffer));
  while(1) {  /* main loop */
    produce( buffer->data, &buffer->datasize);
    MPI_Send(buffer->data, buffer->datasize, MPI_CHAR,
             size-1, tag, comm);
  }
}
else { /* rank == size-1; consumer code */
  buffer = (Buffer *)malloc(sizeof(Buffer)*(size-1));
  for (i=0;  i< size-1; i++)
    MPI_Irecv(buffer[i].data, MAXSIZE, MPI_CHAR, i, tag,
              comm, &buffer[i].req);
  i = 0;
  while(1) { /* main loop */
    for (flag=0; !flag; i= (i+1)%(size-1)) {
      /* busy-wait for completed receive */
      MPI_Test(&(buffer[i].req), &flag, &status);
    }
    MPI_Get_count(&status, MPI_CHAR, &buffer[i].datasize);
    consume(buffer[i].data, buffer[i].datasize);
    MPI_Irecv(buffer[i].data, MAXSIZE, MPI_CHAR, i, tag,
              comm, &buffer[i].req);
  }
}
```

If there is no message pending from a producer, then the consumer process skips to the next producer. A more efficient implementation that does not require multiple test calls and busy-waiting will be presented in Section 2.9.

2.8.5   Freeing Requests

A request object is deallocated automatically by a successful call to MPI_WAIT or MPI_TEST. In addition, a request object can be explicitly deallocated by using the following operation.

MPI_REQUEST_FREE(request)

   INOUT   request   request handle (handle)

```
int MPI_Request_free(MPI_Request *request)
```

```
MPI_REQUEST_FREE(REQUEST, IERROR)
    INTEGER REQUEST, IERROR
```

```
void MPI::Request::Free()
```

MPI_REQUEST_FREE marks the request object for deallocation and sets request to MPI_REQUEST_NULL. An ongoing communication associated with the request will be allowed to complete. The request becomes unavailable after it is deallocated, as the handle is reset to MPI_REQUEST_NULL. However, the request object itself need not be deallocated immediately. If the communication associated with this object is still ongoing, and the object is required for its correct completion, then MPI will not deallocate the object until after its completion.

MPI_REQUEST_FREE cannot be used for cancelling an ongoing communication. For that purpose, one should use MPI_CANCEL, described in Section 2.10. One should use MPI_REQUEST_FREE when the logic of the program is such that a nonblocking communication is known to have terminated and, therefore, a call to MPI_WAIT or MPI_TEST is superfluous. For example, the program could be such that a send command generates a reply from the receiver. If the reply has been successfully received, then the send is known to be complete.

Example 2.20   An example using MPI_REQUEST_FREE.

```
CALL MPI_COMM_RANK(MPI_COMM_WORLD, rank, ierr)
IF(rank.EQ.0) THEN
    DO i=1, n
```

```
            CALL MPI_ISEND(outval, 1, MPI_REAL, 1, 0, comm, req, ierr)
            CALL MPI_REQUEST_FREE(req, ierr)
            CALL MPI_IRECV(inval, 1, MPI_REAL, 1, 0, comm, req, ierr)
            CALL MPI_WAIT(req, status, ierr)
        END DO
ELSE IF (rank.EQ.1) THEN
        CALL MPI_IRECV(inval, 1, MPI_REAL, 0, 0, comm, req, ierr)
        CALL MPI_WAIT(req, status, ierr)
        DO i=1, n-1
            CALL MPI_ISEND(outval, 1, MPI_REAL, 0, 0, comm, req, ierr)
            CALL MPI_REQUEST_FREE(req, ierr)
            CALL MPI_IRECV(inval, 1, MPI_REAL, 0, 0, comm, req, ierr)
            CALL MPI_WAIT(req, status, ierr)
        END DO
        CALL MPI_ISEND(outval, 1, MPI_REAL, 0, 0, comm, req, ierr)
        CALL MPI_WAIT(req, status, ierr)
END IF
```

Advice to users.   Requests should not be freed explicitly unless the communication is known to complete. Receive requests should never be freed without a call to MPI_-WAIT or MPI_TEST, since only such a call can guarantee that a nonblocking receive operation has completed. This is explained in Section 2.8.7. If an error occurs during a communication after the request object has been freed, then an error code cannot be returned to the user (the error code would normally be returned to the MPI_TEST or MPI_WAIT request). Therefore, such an error will be treated by MPI as fatal. □

2.8.6 Nondestructive Test of status

It is sometimes useful to access the status information associated with a request, without freeing the request, as a call to MPI_WAIT or MPI_TEST would do. This allows one to layer libraries more conveniently, since multiple layers of software may access the same completed request and extract from it the status information.

MPI_REQUEST_GET_STATUS(request, flag, status)

IN	request	request (handle) (handle)
OUT	flag	boolean flag, same as from MPI_TEST (logical)
OUT	status	MPI_STATUS object if flag is true (Status)

```
int MPI_Request_get_status(MPI_Request request, int *flag,
    MPI_Status *status)
```

```
MPI_REQUEST_GET_STATUS( REQUEST, FLAG, STATUS, IERROR)
    INTEGER REQUEST, STATUS(MPI_STATUS_SIZE), IERROR
    LOGICAL FLAG
```

```
bool MPI::Request::Get_status(MPI::Status& status) const
```

```
bool MPI::Request::Get_status() const
```

MPI_REQUEST_GET_STATUS sets flag=true if the operation is complete, and, if so, returns in status the request status. However, unlike test or wait, it does not deallocate or deactivate the request; a subsequent call to test, wait or free should be executed with that request. It sets flag=false if the operation is not complete.

Note that a call to MPI_REQUEST_GET_STATUS(request, flag, MPI_STATUS_IGNORE) can be used to test whether an operation completed, without accessing its status and without freeing request.

2.8.7 Semantics of Nonblocking Communications

The semantics of nonblocking communication is defined by suitably extending the definitions in Section 2.4.

Order Nonblocking communication operations are ordered according to the execution order of the posting calls. The non-overtaking requirement of Section 2.4 is extended to nonblocking communication.

Example 2.21 Message ordering for nonblocking operations.

```
MPI::Intracomm comm;
float *a, *b;
MPI::Request r1, r2;
MPI::Status status;
...
int rank = comm.Get_rank();
if (rank == 0) {
  r1 = comm.Isend(a, 1, MPI::FLOAT, 1, 0);
  r2 = comm.Isend(b, 1, MPI::FLOAT, 1, 0);
} else if (rank == 1) {
  r1 = comm.Irecv(a, 1, MPI::FLOAT, 0, 0);
```

```
    r2 = comm.Irecv(b, 1, MPI::FLOAT, 0, 0);
}
r2.Wait(status);
r1.Wait(status);
```

The first send of process zero will match the first receive of process one, even if
both messages are sent before process one executes either receive.

   The order requirement specifies how post-send calls are matched to post-receive
calls. There are no restrictions on the order in which operations complete. Consider
the code in Example 2.22.

Example 2.22   Order of completion for nonblocking communications.

```
MPI::Intracomm comm;
int n;
float *a, *b;
MPI::Request r1, r2;
bool flag1 = false, flag2 = false;
...
int rank = comm.Get_rank();
if (rank == 0) {
  r1 = comm.Isend(a, n, MPI::FLOAT, 1, 0);
  r2 = comm.Isend(b, 1, MPI::FLOAT, 1, 0);
} else if (rank == 1) {
  r1 = comm.Irecv(a, n, MPI::FLOAT, 0, 0);
  r2 = comm.Irecv(b, 1, MPI::FLOAT, 0, 0);
}
while (!(flag1 && flag2)) {
  if (!flag1) flag1 = r1.Test();
  if (!flag2) flag2 = r2.Test();
}
```

As in Example 2.21, the first send of process zero will match the first receive of
process one. However, the second receive may complete ahead of the first receive,
and the second send may complete ahead of the first send, especially if the first
communication involves more data than the second.

Since the completion of a receive can take an arbitrary amount of time, there is no way to infer that the receive operation completed, short of executing a complete-receive call. On the other hand, the completion of a send operation can be inferred indirectly from the completion of a matching receive.

Progress   A communication is *enabled* once a send and a matching receive have been posted by two processes. The progress rule requires that once a communication is enabled, then either the send or the receive will proceed to completion (they might not both complete as the send might be matched by another receive or the receive might be matched by another send). Thus, a call to MPI_WAIT that completes a receive will eventually return if a matching send has been started, unless the send is satisfied by another receive. In particular, if the matching send is nonblocking, then the receive completes even if no complete-send call is made on the sender side.

Similarly, a call to MPI_WAIT that completes a send eventually returns if a matching receive has been started, unless the receive is satisfied by another send, and even if no complete-receive call is made on the receiving side.

Example 2.23   An illustration of progress semantics.

```
MPI::Intracomm comm;
float *a, *b;
int count;
...
int rank = comm.Get_rank();
if (rank == 0) {
  comm.Send(a, count, MPI::FLOAT, 1, 0);
  comm.Send(b, count, MPI::FLOAT, 1, 0);
} else if (rank == 1) {
  MPI::Request r = comm.Irecv(a, 1, MPI::FLOAT, 0, 0);
  comm.Recv(b, count, MPI::FLOAT, 0, 0);
  r.Wait();
}
```

This program is safe and should not deadlock. The first send of process zero must complete after process one posts the matching (nonblocking) receive even if process one has not yet reached the call to MPI_WAIT. Thus, process zero will continue and execute the second send, allowing process one to complete execution.

If a call to MPI_TEST that completes a receive is repeatedly made with the same arguments, and a matching send has been started, then the call will eventually return flag = true, unless the send is satisfied by another receive. If a call to MPI_TEST that completes a send is repeatedly made with the same arguments, and a matching receive has been started, then the call will eventually return flag = true, unless the receive is satisfied by another send.

Fairness   The statement made in Section 2.4 concerning fairness applies to non-blocking communications. Namely, MPI does not guarantee fairness.

Buffering and resource limitations   The use of nonblocking communication alleviates the need for buffering, since a sending process may progress after it has posted a send. Therefore, the constraints of safe programming can be relaxed. However, some amount of storage is consumed by a pending communication. At a minimum, the communication subsystem needs to copy the parameters of a posted send or receive before the call returns. If this storage is exhausted, then a call that posts a new communication will fail, since post-send or post-receive calls are not allowed to block. A high-quality implementation will consume only a fixed amount of storage per posted, nonblocking communication, thus supporting a large number of pending communications. The failure of a parallel program that exceeds the bounds on the number of pending nonblocking communications, like the failure of a sequential program that exceeds the bound on stack size, should be seen as a pathological case, due either to a pathological program or a pathological MPI implementation.

Example 2.24   An illustration of buffering for nonblocking messages.

```
MPI::Intracomm comm;
float *sendbuf, *recvbuf;
int count, tag;
MPI::Request req;
...
int rank = comm.Get_rank();
if (rank == 0) {
  req = comm.Isend(sendbuf, count, MPI::FLOAT, 1, tag);
  comm.Recv(recvbuf, count, MPI::FLOAT, 1, tag);
} else { // rank == 1
  req = comm.Isend(sendbuf, count, MPI::FLOAT, 0, tag);
```

```
  comm.Recv(recvbuf, count, MPI::FLOAT, 0, tag);
}
req.Wait();
```

This program is similar to the program shown in Example 2.10, page 51: two
processes exchange messages, by first executing a send, next a receive. However,
unlike Example 2.10, a nonblocking send is used. This program is safe, since it is
not necessary to buffer any of the messages data.

Example 2.25   Out of order communication with nonblocking messages.

```
MPI::Intracomm comm;
float *sendbuf1, *sendbuf2;
float *recvbuf1, *recvbuf2;
int count;
MPI::Request req1, req2;
...
int rank = comm.Get_rank();
if (rank == 0) {
  req1 = comm.Isend(sendbuf1, count, MPI::FLOAT, 1, 1);
  comm.Recv(recvbuf1, count, MPI::FLOAT, 1, 2);
  req1.Wait();
} else { // rank == 1
  req2 = comm.Isend(sendbuf2, count, MPI::FLOAT, 0, 2);
  comm.Recv(recvbuf2, count, MPI::FLOAT, 0, 1);
  req2.Wait();
}
```

In this program process zero sends two messages to process one, while process one
receives these two messages in the reverse order. If blocking send and receive operations were used, the program would be unsafe: the first message has to be copied
and buffered before the second send can proceed; the first receive can complete
only after the second send executes. However, since we used nonblocking receive
operations, the program is safe. The MPI implementation will store a small, fixed
amount of information about the first receive call before it proceeds to the second
receive call. Once the second post-receive call occurred at process one and the first
(blocking) send occurred at process zero then the transfer of buffer **sendbuf1** is

enabled and is guaranteed to complete. At that point, the second send at process zero is started, and is also guaranteed to complete.

The approach illustrated in the last two examples can be used, in general, to transform unsafe programs into safe ones. Assume that the program consists of successive communication phases, where processes exchange data, followed by computation phases. The communication phase should be rewritten as two sub-phases, the first where each process posts all its communication, and the second where the process waits for the completion of all its communications. The order in which the communications are posted is not important, as long as the total number of messages sent or received at any node is moderate. This is further discussed in Section 9.2.

2.8.8   Comments on Semantics of Nonblocking Communications

Advice to users.   Typically, a posted send will consume storage both at the sending and at the receiving process. The sending process has to keep track of the posted send, and the receiving process needs the message envelope, so as to be able to match it to posted receives. Thus, storage for pending communications can be exhausted not only when any one node executes a large number of post-send or post-receive calls, but also when any one node is the destination of a large number of messages. In a large system, such a "hot-spot" may occur even if each individual process has only a small number of pending posted sends or receives, if the communication pattern is very unbalanced.   ◻

Advice to implementors.   In most MPI implementations, sends and receives are matched at the receiving process node. This is because the receive may specify a wildcard source parameter. When a post-send returns, the MPI implementation must guarantee not only that it has stored the parameters of the call, but also that it can forward the envelope of the posted message to the destination. Otherwise, no progress might occur on the posted send, even though a matching receive was posted. This imposes restrictions on implementations strategies for MPI.

Assume, for example, that each pair of communicating processes is connected by one ordered, flow-controlled channel. A naïve MPI implementation may eagerly send down the channel any posted send message; the back pressure from the flow-control mechanism will prevent loss of data and will throttle the sender if the receiver is not ready to receive the incoming data. Unfortunately, with this *short protocol*, a long message sent by a nonblocking send operation may fill the channel, and prevent moving to the receiver any information on subsequently posted sends. This might

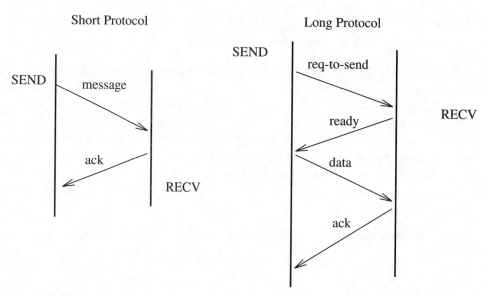

Figure 2.5
Message passing protocols.

occur, for example, with the program in Example 2.25, page 84. The data sent by the first send call might clog the channel, and prevent process zero from informing process one that the second send was posted.

The problem can be remedied by using a *long protocol*: when a send is posted, it is only the message envelope that is sent to the receiving process. The receiving process buffers the fixed-size envelope. When a matching receive is posted, it sends back a "ready-to-receive" message to the sender. The sender can now transmit the message data, without clogging the communication channel. The two protocols are illustrated in Figure 2.5.

While safer, this protocol requires two additional transactions, as compared to the simpler, eager protocol. A possible compromise is to use the short protocol for short messages, and the long protocol for long messages. An early-arriving short message is buffered at the destination. The amount of storage consumed per pending communication is still bounded by a (reasonably small) constant and the hand-shaking overhead can be amortized over the transfer of larger amounts of data. ☐

Rationale.   When a process runs out of space and cannot handle a new post-send operation, would it not be better to block the sender, rather than declare failure? If one merely blocks the post-send, then it is possible that the messages that clog the communication subsystem will be consumed, allowing the computation to proceed. Thus, blocking would allow more programs to run successfully.

The counterargument is that, in a well-designed system, the large majority of programs that exceed the system bounds on the number of pending communications do so because of program errors. Rather then artificially prolonging the life of a program that is doomed to fail, and then have it fail in an obscure deadlock mode, it may be better to cleanly terminate it, and have the programmer correct the program. Also, when programs run close to the system limits, they "thrash" and waste resources, as processes repeatedly block. Finally, the claim of a more lenient behavior should not be used as an excuse for a deficient implementation that cannot support a large number of pending communications.

A different line of argument against the current design is that MPI should not force implementors to use more complex communication protocols, in order to support out-of-order receives with a large number of pending communications. Rather, users should be encouraged to order their communications so that, for each pair of communicating processes, receives are posted in the same order as the matching sends.

This argument is made by implementors, not users. Many users perceive this ordering restriction as too constraining. The design of MPI encourages virtualization of communication, as one process can communicate through several, separate communication spaces. One can expect that users will increasingly take advantage of this feature, especially on multithreaded systems. A process may support multiple threads, each with its own separate communication domain. The communication subsystem should provide robust multiplexing of these communications, and minimize the chances that one thread is blocked because of communications initiated by another thread, in another communication domain.

Users should be aware that different MPI implementations differ not only in their bandwidth or latency, but also in their ability to support out-of-order delivery of messages. □

2.9   Multiple Completions

It is convenient and efficient to complete in one call a list of multiple pending
communication operations, rather than completing only one. MPI_WAITANY or
MPI_TESTANY are used to complete one out of several operations. MPI_WAITALL
or MPI_TESTALL are used to complete all operations in a list. MPI_WAITSOME or
MPI_TESTSOME are used to complete all enabled operations in a list. The behavior
of these functions is described in this section and in Section 2.12.

MPI_WAITANY(count, array_of_requests, index, status)

IN	count	list length (integer)
INOUT	array_of_requests	array of request handles (array of handles)
OUT	index	index of request handle that completed (integer)
OUT	status	status object (Status)

```
int MPI_Waitany(int count, MPI_Request *array_of_requests,
    int *index, MPI_Status *status)
```

```
MPI_WAITANY(COUNT, ARRAY_OF_REQUESTS, INDEX, STATUS, IERROR)
    INTEGER COUNT, ARRAY_OF_REQUESTS(*), INDEX,
    STATUS(MPI_STATUS_SIZE), IERROR
```

```
static int MPI::Request::Waitany(int count,
    MPI::Request array_of_requests[], MPI::Status& status)
```

```
static int MPI::Request::Waitany(int count,
    MPI::Request array_of_requests[])
```

MPI_WAITANY blocks until one of the communication operations associated with
requests in the array has completed. If more then one operation can be completed,
MPI_WAITANY arbitrarily picks one and completes it. MPI_WAITANY returns in
index the array location of the completed request and returns in status the status
of the completed communication (unless MPI_STATUS_IGNORE was passed in). The
request object is deallocated and the request handle is set to MPI_REQUEST_NULL.
MPI_WAITANY is non-local.

MPI_TESTANY(count, array_of_requests, index, flag, status)

IN	count	list length (integer)
INOUT	array_of_requests	array of request handles (array of handles)

OUT	index	index of request handle that completed (integer)
OUT	flag	true if one has completed (logical)
OUT	status	status object (Status)

```
int MPI_Testany(int count, MPI_Request *array_of_requests,
    int *index, int *flag, MPI_Status *status)
```

```
MPI_TESTANY(COUNT, ARRAY_OF_REQUESTS, INDEX, FLAG, STATUS, IERROR)
    LOGICAL FLAG
    INTEGER COUNT, ARRAY_OF_REQUESTS(*), INDEX,
    STATUS(MPI_STATUS_SIZE), IERROR
```

```
static bool MPI::Request::Testany(int count,
    MPI::Request array_of_requests[], int& index,
    MPI::Status& status)
```

```
static bool MPI::Request::Testany(int count,
    MPI::Request array_of_requests[], int& index)
```

MPI_TESTANY tests for completion of the communication operations associated with requests in the array. MPI_TESTANY is local.

If an operation has completed, it returns flag = true, returns in index the array location of the completed request, and returns in status the status of the completed communication. The request is deallocated and the handle is set to MPI_REQUEST_-NULL.

If no operation has completed, it returns flag = false, returns MPI_UNDEFINED in index and status is undefined.

The execution of MPI_Testany(count, array_of_requests, &index, &flag, &status) has the same effect as the execution of MPI_Test(&array_of_requests[i], &flag, &status), for i=0, 1 ,..., count-1, in some arbitrary order, until one call returns flag = true, or all fail. In the former case, index is set to the last value of i, and in the latter case, it is set to MPI_UNDEFINED.

Example 2.26   Producer-consumer code using waitany.

```
...
typedef struct {
  char data[MAXSIZE];
  int datasize;
} Buffer;
```

```
Buffer *buffer;
MPI_Request *req;
MPI_Status status;
...

MPI_Comm_rank(comm, &rank);
MPI_Comm_size(comm, &size);
if (rank != size-1) { /* producer code */
  buffer = (Buffer *)malloc(sizeof(Buffer));
  while(1) { /* main loop */
    produce( buffer->data, &buffer->datasize);
    MPI_Send(buffer->data, buffer->datasize, MPI_CHAR,
             size-1, tag, comm);
  }
}
else { /* rank == size-1; consumer code */
  buffer = (Buffer *)malloc(sizeof(Buffer)*(size-1));
  req = (MPI_Request *)malloc(sizeof(MPI_Request)*(size-1));
  for(i=0;  i< size-1; i++)
    MPI_Irecv(buffer[i].data, MAXSIZE, MPI_CHAR, i, tag, comm,
              &req[i]);
  while(1) { /* main loop */
    MPI_Waitany(size-1, req, &i, &status);
    MPI_Get_count(&status, MPI_CHAR, &buffer[i].datasize);
    consume(buffer[i].data, buffer[i].datasize);
    MPI_Irecv(buffer[i].data, MAXSIZE, MPI_CHAR, i, tag, comm,
              &req[i]);
  }
}
```

This program implements the same producer-consumer protocol as the program in Example 2.19, page 77. The use of MPI_WAIT_ANY avoids the execution of multiple tests to find a communication that completed, resulting in more compact and more efficient code. However, this code, unlike the code in Example 2.19, does not prevent starvation of producers. It is possible that the consumer repeatedly consumes messages sent from process zero, while ignoring messages sent by the other processes. Example 2.28 below shows how to implement a fair server, using MPI_WAITSOME.

MPI_WAITALL(count, array_of_requests, array_of_statuses)

IN	count	list length (integer)
INOUT	array_of_requests	array of request handles (array of handles)
OUT	array_of_statuses	array of status objects (array of Statuses)

```
int MPI_Waitall(int count, MPI_Request *array_of_requests,
    MPI_Status *array_of_statuses)
```

```
MPI_WAITALL(COUNT, ARRAY_OF_REQUESTS, ARRAY_OF_STATUSES, IERROR)
    INTEGER COUNT, ARRAY_OF_REQUESTS(*)
    INTEGER ARRAY_OF_STATUSES(MPI_STATUS_SIZE,*), IERROR
```

```
static void MPI::Request::Waitall(int count,
    MPI::Request array_of_requests[],
    MPI::Status array_of_statuses[])
```

```
static void MPI::Request::Waitall(int count,
    MPI::Request array_of_requests[])
```

MPI_WAITALL blocks until all communications, associated with requests in the array, complete. The i-th entry in array_of_statuses is set to the return status of the i-th operation. All request objects are deallocated and the corresponding handles in the array are set to MPI_REQUEST_NULL. MPI_WAITALL is non-local.

The execution of MPI_Waitall(count, array_of_requests, array_of_statuses) has the same effect as the execution of MPI_Wait(&array_of_requests[i],&array_of_statuses[i]), for i=0 ,..., count-1, in some arbitrary order.

If there is no need for the returned statuses, then the argument MPI_STATUSES_IGNORE can be passed to array_of_statuses. MPI_WAITALL will recognize this special value and will not attempt to return any status information. The same effect is achieved in C++ by calling MPI::Request::Waitany with no status argument: the function has two bindings, with and without this argument. The same optimization applies to all functions that return an array_of_statuses.

MPI_STATUSES_IGNORE is a reference constant (see Section 1.9, page 14) and cannot be used in Fortran, other than as an argument to functions that return an array_of_statuses.

When one or more of the communications completed by a call to MPI_WAITALL fail, MPI_WAITALL will return the error code MPI_ERR_IN_STATUS (MPI::ERR_IN_STATUS, in C++) and will set the error field of each status to a specific error code. This code will be MPI_SUCCESS (MPI::SUCCESS, in C++), if the specific communication completed; it will be another specific error code, if it failed; or it will be MPI_ERR_PENDING (MPI::ERR_PENDING, in C++) if it has not failed nor completed. The function MPI_WAITALL will return MPI_SUCCESS if it completed successfully, or will return another error code if it failed for other reasons (such as invalid arguments). MPI_WAITALL updates the error fields of the status objects only when it returns MPI_ERR_IN_STATUS.

Rationale. This design streamlines error handling in the application. The application code need only test the (single) function result to determine if an error has occurred. It needs to check individual statuses only when an error occurred. ▯

Advice to users. If the user passed in MPI_STATUSES_IGNORE, or, in C++, called MPI_WAITALL with no array_of_statuses argument, then, if an error occurs, the call cannot return information about the communication that caused the error. The call will return MPI_ERR_IN_STATUS, even though there is no status to put the error information in. ▯

MPI_TESTALL(count, array_of_requests, flag, array_of_statuses)

IN	count	list length (integer)
INOUT	array_of_requests	array of request handles (array of handles)
OUT	flag	true if all have completed (logical)
OUT	array_of_statuses	array of status objects (array of Statuses)

```
int MPI_Testall(int count, MPI_Request *array_of_requests, int *flag,
    MPI_Status *array_of_statuses)
```

```
MPI_TESTALL(COUNT, ARRAY_OF_REQUESTS, FLAG, ARRAY_OF_STATUSES,
    IERROR)
    LOGICAL FLAG
    INTEGER COUNT, ARRAY_OF_REQUESTS(*),
    ARRAY_OF_STATUSES(MPI_STATUS_SIZE,*), IERROR
```

```
static bool MPI::Request::Testall(int count,
    MPI::Request array_of_requests[],
    MPI::Status array_of_statuses[])
```

```
static bool MPI::Request::Testall(int count,
    MPI::Request array_of_requests[])
```

MPI_TESTALL tests for completion of all communications associated with requests in the array. MPI_TESTALL is local.

If all operations have completed, it returns flag = true, sets the corresponding entries in status (unless MPI_STATUSES_IGNORE was passed in), deallocates all requests and sets all request handles to MPI_REQUEST_NULL.

If some operation has not completed, flag = false is returned, no request is modified and the values of the status entries are undefined.

Errors that occurred during the execution of MPI_TEST_ALL are handled in the same way as errors in MPI_WAIT_ALL.

Example 2.27   Main loop of Jacobi computation using waitall.

```fortran
...
! Main loop
DO WHILE(.NOT. converged)
   ! Compute boundary columns
   DO i=1,n
      B(i,1) = 0.25*(A(i-1,1)+A(i+1,1)+A(i,0)+A(i,2))
      B(i,m) = 0.25*(A(i-1,m)+A(i+1,m)+A(i,m-1)+A(i,m+1))
   END DO

   ! Start communication
   CALL MPI_ISEND(B(1,1), n, MPI_REAL, left, tag, comm, req(1), ierr)
   CALL MPI_ISEND(B(1,m), n, MPI_REAL, right, tag, comm, req(2), &
                  ierr)
   CALL MPI_IRECV(A(1,0), n, MPI_REAL, left, tag, comm, req(3), ierr)
   CALL MPI_IRECV(A(1,m+1), n, MPI_REAL, right, tag, comm, req(4), &
                  ierr)

   ! Compute interior
   DO j=2,m-1
      DO i=1,n
         B(i,j) = 0.25*(A(i-1,j)+A(i+1,j)+A(i,j-1)+A(i,j+1))
      END DO
   END DO
   DO j=1,m
      DO i=1,n
         A(i,j) = B(i,j)
      END DO
```

```
        END DO

        ! Complete communication
        CALL MPI_WAITALL(4, req, status, ierr)
...
     END DO
```

This code solves the same problem as the code in Example 2.17, page 73. We replaced four calls to MPI_WAIT by one call to MPI_WAITALL. This saves function calls and context switches.

MPI_WAITSOME(incount, array_of_requests, outcount, array_of_indices,
    array_of_statuses)

IN	incount	length of array_of_requests (integer)
INOUT	array_of_requests	array of request handles (array of handles)
OUT	outcount	number of completed requests (integer)
OUT	array_of_indices	array of indices of completed operations (array of integers)
OUT	array_of_statuses	array of status objects for completed operations (array of Statuses)

```
int MPI_Waitsome(int incount, MPI_Request *array_of_requests,
    int *outcount, int *array_of_indices,
    MPI_Status *array_of_statuses)
```

```
MPI_WAITSOME(INCOUNT, ARRAY_OF_REQUESTS, OUTCOUNT, ARRAY_OF_INDICES,
    ARRAY_OF_STATUSES, IERROR)
    INTEGER INCOUNT, ARRAY_OF_REQUESTS(*), OUTCOUNT,
    ARRAY_OF_INDICES(*), ARRAY_OF_STATUSES(MPI_STATUS_SIZE,*), IERROR
```

```
static int MPI::Request::Waitsome(int incount,
    MPI::Request array_of_requests[], int array_of_indices[],
    MPI::Status array_of_statuses[])
```

```
static int MPI::Request::Waitsome(int incount,
    MPI::Request array_of_requests[], int array_of_indices[])
```

MPI_WAITSOME waits until at least one of the communications, associated with requests in the array, completes. MPI_WAITSOME returns in outcount the number of completed requests. The first outcount locations of the array array_of_indices are set to the indices of these operations. The first outcount locations of the array array_of_statuses are set to the status for these completed operations (unless MPI_STATUSES_IGNORE was passed in). Each request that completed is deallocated, and the associated handle is set to MPI_REQUEST_NULL. MPI_WAITSOME is non-local.

If one or more of the communications completed by MPI_WAITSOME fail then the arguments outcount, array_of_indices and array_of_statuses will be adjusted to indicate completion of all communications that have succeeded or failed. The call will return the error code MPI_ERR_IN_STATUS and the error field of each status returned will be set to indicate success or to indicate the specific error that occurred. The call will return MPI_SUCCESS if it succeeded, and will return another error code if it failed for for other reasons (such as invalid arguments). MPI_WAITSOME updates the status fields of the request objects only when it returns MPI_ERR_IN_STATUS.

MPI_TESTSOME(incount, array_of_requests, outcount, array_of_indices,
    array_of_statuses)

IN	incount	length of array_of_requests (integer)
INOUT	array_of_requests	array of request handles (array of handles)
OUT	outcount	number of completed requests (integer)
OUT	array_of_indices	array of indices of completed operations (array of integers)
OUT	array_of_statuses	array of status objects for completed operations (array of Statuses)

```
int MPI_Testsome(int incount, MPI_Request *array_of_requests,
    int *outcount, int *array_of_indices,
    MPI_Status *array_of_statuses)
```

```
MPI_TESTSOME(INCOUNT, ARRAY_OF_REQUESTS, OUTCOUNT, ARRAY_OF_INDICES,
    ARRAY_OF_STATUSES, IERROR)
    INTEGER INCOUNT, ARRAY_OF_REQUESTS(*), OUTCOUNT,
    ARRAY_OF_INDICES(*), ARRAY_OF_STATUSES(MPI_STATUS_SIZE,*), IERROR
```

```
static int MPI::Request::Testsome(int incount,
    MPI::Request array_of_requests[], int array_of_indices[],
    MPI::Status array_of_statuses[])
```

```
static int MPI::Request::Testsome(int incount,
    MPI::Request array_of_requests[], int array_of_indices[])
```

MPI_TESTSOME behaves like MPI_WAITSOME, except that it returns immediately. If no operation has completed it returns outcount = 0. MPI_TESTSOME is local.

Errors that occur during the execution of MPI_TESTSOME are handled as for MPI_WAIT_SOME.

Both MPI_WAITSOME and MPI_TESTSOME fulfill a fairness requirement: if a request for a receive repeatedly appears in a list of requests passed to MPI_WAITSOME or MPI_TESTSOME, and a matching send has been posted, then the receive will eventually complete, unless the send is satisfied by another receive. A similar fairness requirement holds for send requests.

Error codes belonging to the error class MPI_ERR_IN_STATUS should be returned only by the MPI completion functions that take arrays of MPI_STATUS. For the functions (MPI_TEST, MPI_TESTANY, MPI_WAIT, MPI_WAITANY) that return a single MPI_STATUS value, the normal MPI error return process should be used (not the MPI_ERROR field in the MPI_STATUS argument).

Example 2.28   A client-server code where starvation is prevented.

```
...
typedef struct {
  char data[MAXSIZE];
  int datasize;
} Buffer;
Buffer *buffer;
MPI_Request *req;
MPI_Status *status;
int *index;
...

MPI_Comm_rank(comm, &rank);
MPI_Comm_size(comm, &size);
if(rank != size-1) {  /* producer code  */
  buffer = (Buffer *)malloc(sizeof(Buffer));
  while(1) {  /* main loop */
    produce( buffer->data, &buffer->datasize);
    MPI_Send(buffer->data, buffer->datasize, MPI_CHAR, size-1, tag,
          comm);
  }
}
```

```
else { /* rank == size-1; consumer code */
  buffer = (Buffer *)malloc(sizeof(Buffer)*(size-1));
  req = (MPI_Request *)malloc(sizeof(MPI_Request)*(size-1));
  status = (MPI_Status *)malloc(sizeof(MPI_Status)*(size-1));
  index = (int *)malloc(sizeof(int)*(size-1));
  for(i=0;  i< size-1; i++)
    MPI_Irecv(buffer[i].data, MAXSIZE, MPI_CHAR, i, tag, comm,
              &req[i]);
  while(1) { /* main loop */
    MPI_Waitsome(size-1, req, &count, index, status);
    for(i=0; i < count; i++) {
      j = index[i];
      MPI_Get_count(&status[i], MPI_CHAR, &(buffer[j].datasize));
      consume(buffer[j].data, buffer[j].datasize);
      MPI_Irecv(buffer[j].data, MAXSIZE, MPI_CHAR, j, tag,comm,
                &req[j]);
    }
  }
}
```

This code solves the starvation problem of the code in Example 2.26, page 89. We replaced the consumer call to MPI_WAITANY by a call to MPI_WAITSOME. This achieves two goals. The number of communication calls is reduced, since one call now can complete multiple communications. Secondly, the consumer will not starve any of the consumers, since it will receive any posted send.

Advice to implementors.   MPI_WAITSOME and MPI_TESTSOME should complete as many pending communications as possible. It is expected that both will complete all receive operations for which information on matching sends has reached the receiver node. This will ensure that they satisfy their fairness requirement. □

2.10   Probe and Cancel

MPI_PROBE and MPI_IPROBE allow polling of incoming messages without actually receiving them. The application can then decide how to receive them, based on the information returned by the probe (in a status variable). For example, the application might allocate memory for the receive buffer according to the length of the probed message.

MPI_CANCEL allows pending communications to be cancelled. This is required for cleanup in some situations. Suppose an application has posted nonblocking sends or receives and then determines that these operations will not complete. Posting a send or a receive ties up application resources (send or receive buffers), and a cancel allows these resources to be freed.

MPI_IPROBE(source, tag, comm, flag, status)

IN	source	rank of source (integer)
IN	tag	message tag (integer)
IN	comm	communicator (handle)
OUT	flag	true if there is a message (logical)
OUT	status	status object (Status)

```
int MPI_Iprobe(int source, int tag, MPI_Comm comm, int *flag,
    MPI_Status *status)
```

```
MPI_IPROBE(SOURCE, TAG, COMM, FLAG, STATUS, IERROR)
    LOGICAL FLAG
    INTEGER SOURCE, TAG, COMM, STATUS(MPI_STATUS_SIZE), IERROR
```

```
bool MPI::Comm::Iprobe(int source, int tag, MPI::Status& status)
    const
```

```
bool MPI::Comm::Iprobe(int source, int tag) const
```

MPI_IPROBE is a nonblocking operation that returns flag = true if there is a message that can be received and that matches the message envelope specified by source, tag, and comm. The call matches the same message that would have been received by a call to MPI_RECV (with these arguments) executed at the same point in the program, and returns in status the same value. Otherwise, the call returns flag = false, and leaves status undefined. MPI_IPROBE is local.

If MPI_IPROBE(source, tag, comm, flag, status) returns flag = true, then the first, subsequent receive executed with the communicator comm, and with the source and tag returned in status, will receive the message that was matched by the probe, if no other intervening receive occurs after the probe, and the send is not successfully cancelled before the receive.

The argument source can be MPI_ANY_SOURCE, and tag can be MPI_ANY_TAG, so that one can probe for messages from an arbitrary source and/or with an arbitrary tag. However, a specific communicator must be provided in comm.

It is not necessary to receive a message immediately after it has been probed for, and the same message may be probed for several times before it is received.

MPI_PROBE(source, tag, comm, status)

IN	source	rank of source (integer)
IN	tag	message tag (integer)
IN	comm	communicator (handle)
OUT	status	status object (Status)

```
int MPI_Probe(int source, int tag, MPI_Comm comm, MPI_Status *status)
```

```
MPI_PROBE(SOURCE, TAG, COMM, STATUS, IERROR)
    INTEGER SOURCE, TAG, COMM, STATUS(MPI_STATUS_SIZE), IERROR
```

```
void MPI::Comm::Probe(int source, int tag, MPI::Status& status)
    const
```

```
void MPI::Comm::Probe(int source, int tag) const
```

MPI_PROBE behaves like MPI_IPROBE except that it blocks and returns only after a matching message has been found. MPI_PROBE is non-local.

The semantics of MPI_PROBE and MPI_IPROBE guarantee progress, in the same way as a corresponding receive executed at the same point in the program. If a call to MPI_PROBE has been issued by a process, and a send that matches the probe has been initiated by some process, then the call to MPI_PROBE will return, unless the message is received by another, concurrent receive operation, irrespective of other activities in the system. Similarly, if a process busy waits with MPI_IPROBE and a matching message has been issued, then the call to MPI_IPROBE will eventually return flag = true unless the message is received by another concurrent receive operation, irrespective of other activities in the system.

Example 2.29   Use a blocking probe to wait for an incoming message.

```
CALL MPI_COMM_RANK(comm, rank, ierr)
IF (rank.EQ.0) THEN
   CALL MPI_SEND(i, 1, MPI_INTEGER, 2, 0, comm, ierr)
ELSE IF (rank.EQ.1) THEN
```

```
    CALL MPI_SEND(x, 1, MPI_REAL, 2, 0, comm, ierr)
ELSE IF (rank.EQ.2) THEN
    DO i=1, 2
        CALL MPI_PROBE(MPI_ANY_SOURCE, 0, comm, status, ierr)
        IF (status(MPI_SOURCE) .eq. 0) THEN
            CALL MPI_RECV(i, 1, MPI_INTEGER, 0, 0, comm, status, ierr)
        ELSE
            CALL MPI_RECV(x, 1, MPI_REAL, 1, 0, comm, status, ierr)
        END IF
    END DO
END IF
```

Each message is received with the right type.

Example 2.30   A similar program to the previous example, but with a problem.

```
CALL MPI_COMM_RANK(comm, rank, ierr)
IF (rank.EQ.0) THEN
    CALL MPI_SEND(i, 1, MPI_INTEGER, 2, 0, comm, ierr)
ELSE IF (rank.EQ.1) THEN
    CALL MPI_SEND(x, 1, MPI_REAL, 2, 0, comm, ierr)
ELSE IF (rank.EQ.2) THEN
    DO i=1, 2
        CALL MPI_PROBE(MPI_ANY_SOURCE, 0, &
                       comm, status, ierr)
        IF (status(MPI_SOURCE) .eq. 0) THEN
            CALL MPI_RECV(i, 1, MPI_INTEGER, MPI_ANY_SOURCE, &
                      0, comm, status, ierr)
        ELSE
            CALL MPI_RECV(x, 1, MPI_REAL, MPI_ANY_SOURCE, &
                      0, comm, status, ierr)
        END IF
    END DO
END IF
```

We slightly modified example 2.29, using MPI_ANY_SOURCE as the source argument in the two receive calls in statements labeled 100 and 200. The program now has different behavior: the receive operation may receive a message that is distinct from the message probed.

Advice to implementors.   A call to MPI_PROBE(source, tag, comm, status) will match the message that would have been received by a call to MPI_RECV(..., source, tag, comm, status) executed at the same point. Suppose that this message has source s, tag t and communicator c. If the tag argument in the probe call has value MPI_ANY_TAG then the message probed will be the earliest pending message from source s with communicator c and any tag; in any case, the message probed will be the earliest pending message from source s with tag t and communicator c (this is the message that would have been received, so as to preserve message order). This message continues as the earliest pending message from source s with tag t and communicator c, until it is received. The first receive operation subsequent to the probe that uses the same communicator as the probe and uses the tag and source values returned by the probe, must receive this message. ☐

MPI_CANCEL(request)

| IN | request | request handle (handle) |

```
int MPI_Cancel(MPI_Request *request)
```

```
MPI_CANCEL(REQUEST, IERROR)
    INTEGER REQUEST, IERROR
```

```
void MPI::Request::Cancel() const
```

MPI_CANCEL marks for cancellation a pending, nonblocking communication operation (send or receive). MPI_CANCEL is local. It returns immediately, possibly before the communication is actually cancelled. After this, it is still necessary to complete a communication that has been marked for cancellation, using a call to MPI_REQUEST_FREE, MPI_WAIT, MPI_TEST or one of the functions in Section 2.9. If the communication was not cancelled (that is, if the communication happened to start before the cancellation could take effect), then the completion call will complete the communication, as usual. If the communication was successfully cancelled, then the completion call will deallocate the request object and will return in status the information that the communication was cancelled. The application should then call MPI_TEST_CANCELLED, using status as input, to test whether the communication was actually cancelled.

Either the cancellation succeeds, and no communication occurs, or the communication completes, and the cancellation fails. If a send is marked for cancellation, then it must be the case that either the send completes normally, and the message sent is received at the destination process, or that the send is successfully cancelled, and no part of the message is received at the destination. If a receive is marked for cancellation, then it must be the case that either the receive completes normally, or that the receive is successfully cancelled, and no part of the receive buffer is altered.

If a communication is marked for cancellation, then a completion call for that communication is guaranteed to return, irrespective of the activities of other processes. In this case, MPI_WAIT behaves as a local function. Similarly, if MPI_TEST is repeatedly called in a busy wait loop for a cancelled communication, then MPI_TEST will eventually succeed.

MPI_TEST_CANCELLED(status, flag)

IN	status	status object (Status)
OUT	flag	true if cancelled (logical)

```
int MPI_Test_cancelled(MPI_Status *status, int *flag)
```

```
MPI_TEST_CANCELLED(STATUS, FLAG, IERROR)
    LOGICAL FLAG
    INTEGER STATUS(MPI_STATUS_SIZE), IERROR
```

```
bool MPI::Status::Is_cancelled() const
```

MPI_TEST_CANCELLED is used to test whether the communication operation was actually cancelled by MPI_CANCEL. It returns flag = true if the communication associated with the status object was cancelled successfully. In this case, all other fields of status are undefined. It returns flag = false, otherwise.

Example 2.31   Code using MPI_CANCEL

```
MPI_Comm_rank(comm, &rank);
if (rank == 0) {
  MPI_Send(a, 1, MPI_CHAR, 1, tag, comm);
}
else if (rank==1) {
  MPI_Irecv(a, 1, MPI_CHAR, 0, tag, comm, &req);
  MPI_Cancel(&req);
  MPI_Wait(&req, &status);
  MPI_Test_cancelled(&status, &flag);
```

```
  if (flag) { /* cancel succeeded -- need to post new receive */
    MPI_Irecv(a, 1, MPI_CHAR, 0, tag, comm, &req);
  }
}
```

Advice to users.   MPI_CANCEL can be an expensive operation that should be used only exceptionally. ▯

Advice to implementors.   A communication operation cannot be cancelled once the receive buffer has been partly overwritten. In this situation, the communication should be allowed to complete. In general, a communication may be allowed to complete, if send and receive have already been matched. The implementation should take care of the possible race between cancellation and matching.

The cancellation of a send operation will internally require communication with the intended receiver, if information on the send operation has already been forwarded to the destination. Note that, while communication may be needed to implement MPI_CANCEL, this is still a local operation, since its completion does not depend on the application code executed by other processes. ▯

2.11   Persistent Communication Requests

Often a communication with the same argument list is repeatedly executed within the inner loop of a parallel computation. In such a situation, it may be possible to optimize the communication by binding the list of communication arguments to a **persistent** communication request once and then, repeatedly, using the request to initiate and complete messages. A persistent request can be thought of as a communication port or a "half-channel." It does not provide the full functionality of a conventional channel, since there is no binding of the send port to the receive port. This construct allows reduction of the overhead for communication between the process and communication controller, but not of the overhead for communication between one communication controller and another.

It is not necessary that messages sent with a persistent request be received by a receive operation using a persistent request, or vice-versa. Persistent communication requests are associated with nonblocking send and receive operations.

A persistent communication request is created using the following functions. They involve no communication and thus are local.

MPI_SEND_INIT(buf, count, datatype, dest, tag, comm, request)

IN	buf	initial address of send buffer (choice)
IN	count	number of entries to send (integer)
IN	datatype	datatype of each entry (handle)
IN	dest	rank of destination (integer)
IN	tag	message tag (integer)
IN	comm	communicator (handle)
OUT	request	request handle (handle)

```
int MPI_Send_init(void* buf, int count, MPI_Datatype datatype,
    int dest, int tag, MPI_Comm comm, MPI_Request *request)
```

```
MPI_SEND_INIT(BUF, COUNT, DATATYPE, DEST, TAG, COMM, REQUEST, IERROR)
    <type> BUF(*)
    INTEGER REQUEST, COUNT, DATATYPE, DEST, TAG, COMM, REQUEST,
    IERROR
```

```
MPI::Prequest MPI::Comm::Send_init(const void* buf, int count, const
    MPI::Datatype& datatype, int dest, int tag) const
```

MPI_SEND_INIT creates a persistent communication request for a standard-mode, nonblocking send operation, and binds to it all the arguments of a send operation.

MPI_RECV_INIT(buf, count, datatype, source, tag, comm, request)

OUT	buf	initial address of receive buffer (choice)
IN	count	max number of entries to receive (integer)
IN	datatype	datatype of each entry (handle)
IN	source	rank of source (integer)
IN	tag	message tag (integer)
IN	comm	communicator (handle)
OUT	request	request handle (handle)

```
int MPI_Recv_init(void* buf, int count, MPI_Datatype datatype,
    int source, int tag, MPI_Comm comm, MPI_Request *request)
```

```
MPI_RECV_INIT(BUF, COUNT, DATATYPE, SOURCE, TAG, COMM, REQUEST,
    IERROR)
    <type> BUF(*)
    INTEGER COUNT, DATATYPE, SOURCE, TAG, COMM, REQUEST, IERROR
```

```
MPI::Prequest MPI::Comm::Recv_init(void* buf, int count, const
    MPI::Datatype& datatype, int source, int tag) const
```

MPI_RECV_INIT creates a persistent communication request for a nonblocking receive operation. The argument buf is marked as OUT because the application gives permission to write on the receive buffer.

Persistent communication requests are created by the preceding functions, but they are, so far, inactive. They are activated, and the associated communication operations started, by MPI_START or MPI_STARTALL.

MPI_START(request)

    INOUT   request   request handle (handle)

```
int MPI_Start(MPI_Request *request)
```

```
MPI_START(REQUEST, IERROR)
    INTEGER REQUEST, IERROR
```

```
void MPI::Prequest::Start()
```

MPI_START activates request (which should be persistent) and initiates the associated communication. Since all persistent requests are associated with nonblocking communications, MPI_START is local. The semantics of communications done with persistent requests are identical to the corresponding operations without persistent requests. That is, a call to MPI_START with a request created by MPI_SEND_INIT starts a communication in the same manner as a call to MPI_ISEND; a call to MPI_START with a request created by MPI_RECV_INIT starts a communication in the same manner as a call to MPI_IRECV.

A send operation initiated with MPI_START can be matched with any receive operation (including MPI_PROBE) and a receive operation initiated with MPI_START can receive messages generated by any send operation.

MPI_STARTALL(count, array_of_requests)

    IN   count   list length (integer)
    INOUT array_of_requests   array of request handles (array of handles)

```
int MPI_Startall(int count, MPI_Request *array_of_requests)
```

```
MPI_STARTALL(COUNT, ARRAY_OF_REQUESTS, IERROR)
    INTEGER COUNT, ARRAY_OF_REQUESTS(*), IERROR
```

```
static void MPI::Prequest::Startall(int count,
    MPI::Prequest array_of_requests[])
```

MPI_STARTALL starts all communications associated with persistent requests in array_of_requests. A call to MPI_STARTALL(count, array_of_requests) has the same effect as calls to MPI_START(array_of_requests[i]), executed for i=0 ,..., count-1, in some arbitrary order.

A communication started with a call to MPI_START or MPI_STARTALL is completed by a call to MPI_WAIT, MPI_TEST, or one of the other completion functions described in Section 2.9. The persistent request becomes inactive after the completion of such a call, but it is not deallocated and it can be re-activated by another MPI_START or MPI_STARTALL.

Persistent requests are explicitly deallocated by a call to MPI_REQUEST_FREE (Section 2.8.5). The call to MPI_REQUEST_FREE can occur at any point in the program after the persistent request was created. However, the request will be deallocated only after it becomes inactive. Active receive requests should not be freed. Otherwise, it will not be possible to check that the receive has completed.

MPI_CANCEL can be used to cancel a communication that uses a persistent request, in the same way it is used for nonpersistent requests. A successful cancellation cancels the active communication, but does not deallocate the request. After the call to MPI_CANCEL and the subsequent call to MPI_WAIT or MPI_TEST (or other completion function), the request becomes inactive and can be activated for a new communication.

Example 2.32   Jacobi computation, using persistent requests.

```
...
REAL, DIMENSION(:,:), ALLOCATABLE :: A, B
INTEGER req(4)
INTEGER status(MPI_STATUS_SIZE,4)
...
! Compute number of processes and myrank
CALL MPI_COMM_SIZE(comm, p, ierr)
CALL MPI_COMM_RANK(comm, myrank, ierr)

! Compute size of local block
m = n/p
```

```
IF (myrank.LT.(n-p*m)) THEN
   m = m+1
END IF


! Compute neighbors
IF (myrank.EQ.0) THEN
   left = MPI_PROC_NULL
ELSE
   left = myrank -1
END IF
IF (myrank.EQ.p-1) THEN
   right = MPI_PROC_NULL
ELSE
   right = myrank+1
ENDIF


! Allocate local arrays
ALLOCATE (A(n,0:m+1), B(n,m))
...
! Create persistent requests
CALL MPI_SEND_INIT(B(1,1), n, MPI_REAL, left, tag, comm, req(1), &
                   ierr)
CALL MPI_SEND_INIT(B(1,m), n, MPI_REAL, right, tag, comm, req(2), &
                   ierr)
CALL MPI_RECV_INIT(A(1,0), n, MPI_REAL, left, tag, comm, req(3), &
                   ierr)
CALL MPI_RECV_INIT(A(1,m+1), n, MPI_REAL, right, tag, comm, req(4), &
                   ierr)
....


! Main loop
DO WHILE(.NOT.converged)

   ! Compute boundary columns
   DO i=1,n
      B(i,1) = 0.25*(A(i-1,1)+A(i+1,1)+A(i,0)+A(i,2))
      B(i,m) = 0.25*(A(i-1,m)+A(i+1,m)+A(i,m-1)+A(i,m+1))
   END DO
```

```
! Start communication
CALL MPI_STARTALL(4, req, ierr)

! Compute interior
DO j=2,m-1
   DO i=1,n
      B(i,j) = 0.25*(A(i-1,j)+A(i+1,j)+A(i,j-1)+A(i,j+1))
   END DO
END DO
DO j=1,m
   DO i=1,n
      A(i,j) = B(i,j)
   END DO
END DO

! Complete communication
   CALL MPI_WAITALL(4, req, status, ierr)
...
END DO
```

We come back (for a last time!) to our Jacobi example (Example 2.13, page 58). The communication calls in the main loop are reduced to two: one to start all four communications and one to complete all four communications.

2.12   Communication-Complete Calls with Null Request Handles

Normally, an invalid handle to an MPI object is not a valid argument for a call that expects an object. There is one exception to this rule: communication-complete calls can be passed request handles with value MPI_REQUEST_NULL. A communication complete call with such an argument is a "no-op": the null handles are ignored. The same rule applies to persistent handles that are not associated with an active communication operation.

We shall use the following terminology. A **null** request handle is a handle with value MPI_REQUEST_NULL. A handle to a persistent request is **inactive** if the request is not currently associated with an ongoing communication. A handle is **active**, if it is neither null nor inactive. An **empty** status is a status that is set to tag = MPI_ANY_TAG, source = MPI_ANY_SOURCE, error = MPI_SUCCESS, and is also internally configured so that calls to MPI_GET_COUNT and MPI_GET_ELEMENT return count = 0 and MPI_TEST_CANCELLED returns false. We set a status variable to empty in cases when the value returned is not significant. Status is set this way to prevent errors due to access of stale information.

A call to MPI_WAIT with a null or inactive request argument returns immediately with an empty status.

A call to MPI_TEST with a null or inactive request argument returns immediately with flag = true and an empty status.

The list of requests passed to MPI_WAITANY may contain null or inactive requests. If some of the requests are active, then the call returns when an active request has completed. If all the requests in the list are null or inactive then the call returns immediately, with index = MPI_UNDEFINED and an empty status.

The list of requests passed to MPI_TESTANY may contain null or inactive requests. The call returns flag = false if there are active requests in the list, and none have completed. It returns flag = true if an active request has completed, or if all the requests in the list are null or inactive. In the later case, it returns index = MPI_UNDEFINED and an empty status.

The list of requests passed to MPI_WAITALL may contain null or inactive requests. The call returns as soon as all active requests have completed. The call sets to empty each status associated with a null or inactive request.

The list of requests passed to MPI_TESTALL may contain null or inactive requests. The call returns flag = true if all active requests have completed. In this case, the call sets to empty each status associated with a null or inactive request. Otherwise, the call returns flag = false.

The list of requests passed to MPI_WAITSOME may contain null or inactive requests. If the list contains active requests, then the call returns when some of the active requests have completed. If all requests were null or inactive, then the call returns immediately, with outcount = MPI_UNDEFINED.

The list of requests passed to MPI_TESTSOME may contain null or inactive requests. If the list contains active requests and some have completed, then the call returns in outcount the number of completed request. If it contains active requests, and none have completed, then it returns outcount = 0. If the list contains no active requests, then it returns outcount = MPI_UNDEFINED.

In all these cases, null or inactive request handles are not modified by the call.

Example 2.33   Starvation-free producer-consumer code

```
...
typedef struct {
```

```
    char data[MAXSIZE];
    int datasize;
} Buffer;
Buffer *buffer;
MPI_Request *req;
MPI_Status status;
...

MPI_Comm_rank(comm, &rank);
MPI_Comm_size(comm, &size);
if(rank != size-1)  {  /* producer code  */
  buffer = (Buffer *)malloc(sizeof(Buffer));
  while(1) {  /* main loop */
    produce(buffer->data, &buffer->datasize);
    MPI_Send(buffer->data, buffer->datasize, MPI_CHAR,
             size-1, tag, comm);
  }
}
else { /* rank == size-1; consumer code */
  buffer = (Buffer *)malloc(sizeof(Buffer)*(size-1));
  req = (MPI_Request *)malloc(sizeof(MPI_Request)*(size-1));
  for (i=0; i<size-1; i++)
    req[i] = MPI_REQUEST_NULL;
  while (1) { /* main loop */
    MPI_Waitany(size-1, req, &i, &status);
    if (i == MPI_UNDEFINED) { /* no pending receive left */
      for(j=0;  j< size-1; j++)
        MPI_Irecv(buffer[j].data, MAXSIZE, MPI_CHAR, j, tag,
                  comm, &req[j]);
    }
    else {
      MPI_Get_count(&status, MPI_CHAR, &buffer[i].datasize);
      consume(buffer[i].data, buffer[i].datasize);
    }
  }
}
```

This is our last remake of the producer-consumer code from Example 2.18, page 75. As in Example 2.18, the computation proceeds in phases, where at each phase the consumer consumes one message from each producer. Unlike Example 2.18, messages need not be consumed in order within each phase but, rather, can be consumed as soon as arrived.

Rationale.   The acceptance of null or inactive requests in communication-complete calls facilitate the use of multiple completion calls (Section 2.9). As in the example above, the user need not delete each request from the list as soon as it has completed, but can reuse the same list until all requests in the list have completed. Checking for null or inactive requests is not expected to add a significant overhead, since quality implementations will check parameters, anyhow. However, most implementations will suffer some performance loss if they often traverse mostly empty request lists, looking for active requests.

The behavior of the multiple completion calls was defined with the following structure.

• Test returns with flag = true whenever Wait would return; both calls return same information in this case.

• A call to Wait, Waitany, Waitsome or Waitall will return if all requests in the list are null or inactive, thus avoiding deadlock.

• The information returned by a Test, Testany, Testsome or Testall call distinguishes between the case "no operation completed" and the case "there is no operation to complete."

                                                                                         ⬜

2.13   Communication Modes

The send call described in Section 2.2.1 used the **standard** communication mode. In this mode, it is up to MPI to decide whether outgoing messages will be buffered. MPI may buffer outgoing messages. In such a case, the send operation may complete before a matching receive is invoked. On the other hand, buffer space may be unavailable, or MPI may choose not to buffer outgoing messages, for performance reasons. In this case, the send operation will not complete until a matching receive has been posted, and the data has been moved to the receiver.

Thus, a send operation in standard mode can be started whether or not a matching receive has been posted. It may complete before a matching receive is posted.

The standard-mode send is non-local, since successful completion of the send operation may depend on the occurrence of a matching receive.

A **buffered**-mode send operation can be started whether or not a matching receive has been posted. It may complete before a matching receive is posted. Buffered-mode send is local: its completion does not depend on the occurrence of a matching receive. In order to complete the operation, it may be necessary to buffer the outgoing message locally. For that purpose, buffer space is provided by the application (Section 2.13.4). An error will occur if a buffered-mode send is called and there is insufficient buffer space. The buffer space occupied by the message is freed when the message is transferred to its destination or when the buffered send is cancelled.

A **synchronous**-mode send operation can be started whether or not a matching receive was posted. However, the send will complete successfully only if a matching receive is posted, and the receive operation has started to receive the message sent by the synchronous send. Thus, the completion of a synchronous send not only indicates that the send buffer can be reused, but also indicates that the receiver has reached a certain point in its execution, namely that it has started executing the matching receive. Synchronous mode provides synchronous communication semantics: a communication does not complete at either end before both processes rendezvous at the communication. A synchronous-mode send is non-local.

A **ready**-mode send operation may be started *only* if the matching receive has already been posted. Otherwise, the operation is erroneous and its outcome is undefined. On some systems, this allows the removal of a hand-shake operation and results in improved performance. A ready-mode send has the same semantics as a standard-mode send. In a correct program, therefore, a ready-mode send could be replaced by a standard-mode send with no effect on the behavior of the program other than performance.

Three additional send functions are provided for the three additional communication modes. The communication mode is indicated by a one letter prefix: B for buffered, S for synchronous, and R for ready. There is only one receive mode and it matches any of the send modes.

All send and receive operations use the buf, count, datatype, source, dest, tag, comm, status and request arguments in the same way as the standard-mode send and receive operations.

2.13.1 Blocking Calls

MPI_BSEND(buf, count, datatype, dest, tag, comm)

IN	buf	initial address of send buffer (choice)
IN	count	number of entries in send buffer (integer)
IN	datatype	datatype of each send buffer entry (handle)
IN	dest	rank of destination (integer)
IN	tag	message tag (integer)
IN	comm	communicator (handle)

```
int MPI_Bsend(void* buf, int count, MPI_Datatype datatype, int dest,
    int tag, MPI_Comm comm)
```

```
MPI_BSEND(BUF, COUNT, DATATYPE, DEST, TAG, COMM, IERROR)
    <type> BUF(*)
    INTEGER COUNT, DATATYPE, DEST, TAG, COMM, IERROR
```

```
void MPI::Comm::Bsend(const void* buf, int count, const
    MPI::Datatype& datatype, int dest, int tag) const
```

MPI_BSEND performs a buffered-mode, blocking send.

MPI_SSEND(buf, count, datatype, dest, tag, comm)

IN	buf	initial address of send buffer (choice)
IN	count	number of entries in send buffer (integer)
IN	datatype	datatype of each send buffer entry (handle)
IN	dest	rank of destination (integer)
IN	tag	message tag (integer)
IN	comm	communicator (handle)

```
int MPI_Ssend(void* buf, int count, MPI_Datatype datatype, int dest,
    int tag, MPI_Comm comm)
```

```
MPI_SSEND(BUF, COUNT, DATATYPE, DEST, TAG, COMM, IERROR)
    <type> BUF(*)
    INTEGER COUNT, DATATYPE, DEST, TAG, COMM, IERROR
```

```
void MPI::Comm::Ssend(const void* buf, int count, const
    MPI::Datatype& datatype, int dest, int tag) const
```

MPI_SSEND performs a synchronous-mode, blocking send.

MPI_RSEND(buf, count, datatype, dest, tag, comm)

IN	buf	initial address of send buffer (choice)
IN	count	number of entries in send buffer (integer)
IN	datatype	datatype of each send buffer entry (handle)
IN	dest	rank of destination (integer)
IN	tag	message tag (integer)
IN	comm	communicator (handle)

```
int MPI_Rsend(void* buf, int count, MPI_Datatype datatype, int dest,
     int tag, MPI_Comm comm)
```

```
MPI_RSEND(BUF, COUNT, DATATYPE, DEST, TAG, COMM, IERROR)
     <type> BUF(*)
     INTEGER COUNT, DATATYPE, DEST, TAG, COMM, IERROR
```

```
void MPI::Comm::Rsend(const void* buf, int count, const
     MPI::Datatype& datatype, int dest, int tag) const
```

MPI_RSEND performs a ready-mode, blocking send.

2.13.2   Nonblocking Calls

We use the same naming conventions as for blocking communication: a prefix of B, S, or R is used for buffered, synchronous or ready mode. In addition, a prefix of I (for immediate) indicates that the call is nonblocking. There is only one nonblocking receive call, MPI_IRECV. Nonblocking send operations are completed with the same Wait and Test calls as for standard-mode send.

MPI_IBSEND(buf, count, datatype, dest, tag, comm, request)

IN	buf	initial address of send buffer (choice)
IN	count	number of elements in send buffer (integer)
IN	datatype	datatype of each send buffer element (handle)
IN	dest	rank of destination (integer)
IN	tag	message tag (integer)
IN	comm	communicator (handle)
OUT	request	request handle (handle)

```
int MPI_Ibsend(void* buf, int count, MPI_Datatype datatype, int dest,
     int tag, MPI_Comm comm, MPI_Request *request)
```

```
MPI_IBSEND(BUF, COUNT, DATATYPE, DEST, TAG, COMM, REQUEST, IERROR)
```

```
<type> BUF(*)
INTEGER COUNT, DATATYPE, DEST, TAG, COMM, REQUEST, IERROR
```

```
MPI::Request MPI::Comm::Ibsend(const void* buf, int count, const
    MPI::Datatype& datatype, int dest, int tag) const
```

MPI_IBSEND posts a buffered-mode, nonblocking send.

MPI_ISSEND(buf, count, datatype, dest, tag, comm, request)

IN	buf	initial address of send buffer (choice)
IN	count	number of elements in send buffer (integer)
IN	datatype	datatype of each send buffer element (handle)
IN	dest	rank of destination (integer)
IN	tag	message tag (integer)
IN	comm	communicator (handle)
OUT	request	request handle (handle)

```
int MPI_Issend(void* buf, int count, MPI_Datatype datatype, int dest,
    int tag, MPI_Comm comm, MPI_Request *request)
```

```
MPI_ISSEND(BUF, COUNT, DATATYPE, DEST, TAG, COMM, REQUEST, IERROR)
    <type> BUF(*)
    INTEGER COUNT, DATATYPE, DEST, TAG, COMM, REQUEST, IERROR
```

```
MPI::Request MPI::Comm::Issend(const void* buf, int count, const
    MPI::Datatype& datatype, int dest, int tag) const
```

MPI_ISSEND posts a synchronous-mode, nonblocking send.

MPI_IRSEND(buf, count, datatype, dest, tag, comm, request)

IN	buf	initial address of send buffer (choice)
IN	count	number of elements in send buffer (integer)
IN	datatype	datatype of each send buffer element (handle)
IN	dest	rank of destination (integer)
IN	tag	message tag (integer)
IN	comm	communicator (handle)
OUT	request	request handle (handle)

```
int MPI_Irsend(void* buf, int count, MPI_Datatype datatype, int dest,
    int tag, MPI_Comm comm, MPI_Request *request)
```

```
MPI_IRSEND(BUF, COUNT, DATATYPE, DEST, TAG, COMM, REQUEST, IERROR)
    <type> BUF(*)
    INTEGER COUNT, DATATYPE, DEST, TAG, COMM, REQUEST, IERROR
```

```
MPI::Request MPI::Comm::Irsend(const void* buf, int count, const
    MPI::Datatype& datatype, int dest, int tag) const
```

MPI_IRSEND posts a ready-mode, nonblocking send.

2.13.3 Persistent Requests

MPI_BSEND_INIT(buf, count, datatype, dest, tag, comm, request)

IN	buf	initial address of send buffer (choice)
IN	count	number of entries to send (integer)
IN	datatype	datatype of each entry (handle)
IN	dest	rank of destination (integer)
IN	tag	message tag (integer)
IN	comm	communicator (handle)
OUT	request	request handle (handle)

```
int MPI_Bsend_init(void* buf, int count, MPI_Datatype datatype,
    int dest, int tag, MPI_Comm comm, MPI_Request *request)
```

```
MPI_BSEND_INIT(BUF, COUNT, DATATYPE, DEST, TAG, COMM, REQUEST,
    IERROR)
    <type> BUF(*)
    INTEGER REQUEST, COUNT, DATATYPE, DEST, TAG, COMM, REQUEST,
    IERROR
```

```
MPI::Prequest MPI::Comm::Bsend_init(const void* buf, int count,
    const MPI::Datatype& datatype, int dest, int tag) const
```

MPI_BSEND_INIT creates a persistent communication request for a buffered-mode, nonblocking send, and binds to it all the arguments of a send operation.

MPI_SSEND_INIT(buf, count, datatype, dest, tag, comm, request)

IN	buf	initial address of send buffer (choice)
IN	count	number of entries to send (integer)
IN	datatype	datatype of each entry (handle)
IN	dest	rank of destination (integer)
IN	tag	message tag (integer)

IN	comm	communicator (handle)
OUT	request	request handle (handle)

```
int MPI_Ssend_init(void* buf, int count, MPI_Datatype datatype,
    int dest, int tag, MPI_Comm comm, MPI_Request *request)
```

```
MPI_SSEND_INIT(BUF, COUNT, DATATYPE, DEST, TAG, COMM, REQUEST,
    IERROR)
    <type> BUF(*)
    INTEGER COUNT, DATATYPE, DEST, TAG, COMM, REQUEST, IERROR
```

```
MPI::Prequest MPI::Comm::Ssend_init(const void* buf, int count,
    const MPI::Datatype& datatype, int dest, int tag) const
```

MPI_SSEND_INIT creates a persistent communication object for a synchronous-mode, nonblocking send, and binds to it all the arguments of a send operation.

MPI_RSEND_INIT(buf, count, datatype, dest, tag, comm, request)

IN	buf	initial address of send buffer (choice)
IN	count	number of entries to send (integer)
IN	datatype	datatype of each entry (handle)
IN	dest	rank of destination (integer)
IN	tag	message tag (integer)
IN	comm	communicator (handle)
OUT	request	request handle (handle)

```
int MPI_Rsend_init(void* buf, int count, MPI_Datatype datatype,
    int dest, int tag, MPI_Comm comm, MPI_Request *request)
```

```
MPI_RSEND_INIT(BUF, COUNT, DATATYPE, DEST, TAG, COMM, REQUEST,
    IERROR)
    <type> BUF(*)
    INTEGER COUNT, DATATYPE, DEST, TAG, COMM, REQUEST, IERROR
```

```
MPI::Prequest MPI::Comm::Rsend_init(const void* buf, int count,
    const MPI::Datatype& datatype, int dest, int tag) const
```

MPI_RSEND_INIT creates a persistent communication object for a ready-mode, nonblocking send, and binds to it all the arguments of a send operation.

Example 2.34   Use of ready-mode and synchronous-mode

```
INTEGER req(2), status(MPI_STATUS_SIZE,2), comm, ierr, rank
REAL buff(1000,2)
...
CALL MPI_COMM_RANK(comm, rank, ierr)
IF (rank.EQ.0) THEN
   CALL MPI_IRECV(buff(1,1), 1000, MPI_REAL, 1, 1, comm, req(1), &
                  ierr)
   CALL MPI_IRECV(buff(1,2), 1000, MPI_REAL, 1, 2, comm, req(2), &
                  ierr)
   CALL MPI_WAITALL(2, req, status, ierr)
ELSE IF (rank.EQ.1) THEN
   CALL MPI_SSEND(buff(1,2), 1000, MPI_REAL, 0, 2, comm, ierr)
   CALL MPI_RSEND(buff(1,1), 1000, MPI_REAL, 0, 1, comm, ierr)
END IF
```

The first, synchronous-mode send of process one matches the second receive of process zero. This send operation will complete only after the second receive of process zero has started, and after the completion of the first post-receive of process zero. Therefore, the second, ready-mode send of process one starts, correctly, after a matching receive is posted.

2.13.4   Buffer Allocation and Usage

An application must specify a buffer to be used for buffering messages sent in buffered mode. Buffering is done by the sender.

MPI_BUFFER_ATTACH(buffer, size)

IN	buffer	initial buffer address (choice)
IN	size	buffer size, in bytes (integer)

```
int MPI_Buffer_attach( void* buffer, int size)
```

```
MPI_BUFFER_ATTACH( BUFFER, SIZE, IERROR)
    <type> BUFFER(*)
    INTEGER SIZE, IERROR
```

```
void MPI::Attach_buffer(void* buffer, int size)
```

MPI_BUFFER_ATTACH provides to MPI a buffer in the application's memory to be used for buffering outgoing messages. The buffer is used only by messages sent in buffered mode. Only one buffer can be attached at a time (per process).

MPI_BUFFER_DETACH(buffer, size)

OUT	buffer	initial buffer address (choice)
OUT	size	buffer size, in bytes (integer)

```
int MPI_Buffer_detach( void* buffer, int* size)
```

```
MPI_BUFFER_DETACH( BUFFER, SIZE, IERROR)
    <type> BUFFER(*)
    INTEGER SIZE, IERROR
```

```
int MPI::Detach_buffer(void*& buffer)
```

MPI_BUFFER_DETACH detaches the buffer currently associated with MPI. The call returns the address and the size of the detached buffer. This operation will block until all messages currently in the buffer have been transmitted. Upon return of this function, the user may reuse or deallocate the space taken by the buffer.

Example 2.35   Calls to attach and detach buffers.

```
#define BUFFSIZE 10000
int size;
char *buff;
buff = (char *)malloc(BUFFSIZE);
MPI_Buffer_attach(buff, BUFFSIZE);
/* a buffer of 10000 bytes can now be used by MPI_Bsend */
MPI_Buffer_detach( &buff, &size);
/* Buffer size reduced to zero */
MPI_Buffer_attach( buff, size);
/* Buffer of 10000 bytes available again */
```

Advice to users.   Even though the C functions MPI_Buffer_attach and MPI_Buffer_detach both have a first argument of type void*, these arguments are used differently: A pointer to the buffer is passed to MPI_Buffer_attach; the address of the pointer is passed to MPI_Buffer_detach, so that this call can return the pointer value. □

Rationale.   Both arguments are defined to be of type void* (rather than void* and void**, respectively), so as to avoid complex type casts. E.g., in the last example, &buff, which is of type char**, can be passed as an argument to MPI_Buffer_detach without type casting. If the formal parameter had type void** then one would need a type cast before and after the call. ▢

Now the question arises: how is the attached buffer to be used? The answer is that MPI must behave *as if* outgoing message data were buffered by the sending process, in the specified buffer space, using a circular, contiguous-space allocation policy. We outline below a model implementation that defines this policy. MPI may provide more buffering, and may use a better buffer allocation algorithm than described below. On the other hand, MPI may signal an error whenever the simple buffering allocator described below would run out of space.

2.13.5   Model Implementation of Buffered Mode

The model implementation uses the packing and unpacking functions described in Section 3.12 and the nonblocking communication functions described in Section 2.8.

We assume that a circular queue of pending message entries (PME) is maintained. Each entry contains a communication request that identifies a pending nonblocking send, a pointer to the next entry and the packed message data. The entries are stored in successive locations in the buffer. Free space is available between the queue tail and the queue head.

A buffered send call results in the execution of the following algorithm.

• Traverse sequentially the PME queue from head towards the tail, deleting all entries for communications that have completed, up to the first entry with an uncompleted request; update queue head to point to that entry.

• Compute the number, n, of bytes needed to store entries for the new message. An upper bound on n can be computed as follows: A call to the function MPI_PACK_SIZE(count, datatype, comm, size), with the count, datatype and comm arguments used in the MPI_BSEND call, returns an upper bound on the amount of space needed to buffer the message data (see Section 3.12). The MPI constant MPI_BSEND_OVERHEAD (MPI::BSEND_OVERHEAD, in C++) provides an upper bound on the additional space consumed by the entry (e.g., for pointers or envelope information).

• Find the next contiguous, empty space of n bytes in buffer (space following queue tail, or space at start of buffer if queue tail is too close to end of buffer). If space is not found then raise buffer overflow error.

- Copy request, next pointer and packed message data into empty space; MPI-PACK is used to pack data. Set pointers so that this entry is at tail of PME queue.
- Post nonblocking send (standard mode) for packed data.
- Return

2.13.6 Comments on Communication Modes

Advice to users.   When should one use each mode?

Most of the time, it is preferable to use the standard-mode send: implementors are likely to provide the best and most robust performance for this mode.

Users that do not trust the buffering policy of standard-mode may use the buffered-mode, and control buffer allocation themselves. With this authority comes responsibility: it is the user responsibility to ensure that buffers never overflow.

The synchronous mode is convenient in cases where an acknowledgment would be otherwise required, e.g., when communication with rendezvous semantics is desired. Also, use of the synchronous-mode is a hint to the system that buffering should be avoided, since the sender cannot progress anyhow, even if the data is buffered.

The ready-mode is error prone and should be used with care. □

Advice to implementors.   Since a synchronous-mode send cannot complete before a matching receive is posted, one will not normally buffer messages sent by such an operation.

It is usually preferable to choose buffering over blocking the sender, for standard-mode sends. The programmer can get the non-buffered protocol by using synchronous mode.

A possible choice of communication protocols for the various communication modes is outlined below.

standard-mode send: Short protocol is used for short messages, and long protocol is used for long messages (see Figure 2.5, page 86).

ready-mode send: The message is sent with the short protocol (that is, ready-mode messages are always "short").

synchronous-mode send: The long protocol is used (that is, synchronous-mode messages are always "long").

buffered-mode send: The send copies the message into the application-provided buffer and then sends it with a standard-mode, nonblocking send.

Ready-mode send can be implemented as a standard-mode send. In this case there will be no performance advantage (or disadvantage) for the use of ready-mode send.

A standard-mode send could be implemented as a synchronous-mode send, so that no data buffering is needed. This is consistent with the MPI specification. However, many users would be surprised by this choice, since standard-mode is the natural place for system-provided buffering. ☐

3 User-Defined Datatypes and Packing

In this chapter we discuss the powerful capability in MPI to send noncontiguous memory locations in a single communication. This is achieved by generalizing the datatypes presented into ones that can be defined by the user. We present the functions from the simplest to the most complex so the easiest method can be used for a given task. We give the array datatype constructions which are generally used with the MPI-2 I/O capability. We present another MPI mechanism for noncontiguous memory communication, pack and unpack, and conclude by comparing the two mechanisms.

3.1 Introduction

The MPI communication mechanisms introduced in the previous chapter can be used to send or receive a sequence of identical elements that are contiguous in memory. It is often desirable to send data that is not homogeneous, such as a structure, or that is not contiguous in memory, such as an array section. This would amortize the fixed overhead of sending and receiving a message over the transmittal of many elements, even in these more general circumstances. MPI provides two mechanisms to achieve this.

- The user can define **derived datatypes** that specify more general data layouts. User-defined datatypes can be used in MPI communication functions in place of the basic, **predefined datatypes**.
- A sending process can explicitly pack noncontiguous data into a contiguous buffer, and next send it; a receiving process can explicitly unpack data received in a contiguous buffer and store in noncontiguous locations.

The construction and use of derived datatypes is described in Section 3.2–3.11. The use of Pack and Unpack functions is described in Section 3.12. It is often possible to achieve the same data transfer using either mechanisms. We discuss the pros and cons of each approach at the end of this chapter.

3.2 Introduction to User-Defined Datatypes

All MPI communication functions take a datatype argument. In the simplest case this will be a **predefined** datatype, such as MPI_INT or MPI_FLOAT. An important and powerful generalization results by allowing user-defined **derived datatypes** wherever the predefined datatypes can occur. These are not "types" as far as the programming language is concerned. They are only "types" in that MPI is made aware of them through the use of type-constructor functions, and they describe the layout, in memory, of sets of primitive types. Through user-defined types, MPI supports the communication of complex data structures such as array sections and structures containing combinations of primitive types. Example 3.1 shows how a user-defined datatype is used to send the upper-triangular part of a matrix, and Figure 3.1 diagrams the memory layout represented by the user-defined datatype.

Example 3.1   MPI code that sends an upper triangular matrix.

```
double a[100][100];
int disp[100],blocklen[100],i,dest,tag;
MPI_Datatype upper;
...
/* compute start and size of each row */
for (i=0; i<100; ++i) {
  disp[i] = 100 * i + i;
  blocklen[i] = 100 - i;
}
/* create datatype for upper triangular part */
MPI_Type_indexed(100, blocklen, disp, MPI_DOUBLE, &upper);
MPI_Type_commit(&upper);
/* .. and send it */
MPI_Send(a, 1, upper, dest, tag, MPI_COMM_WORLD);
```

Derived datatypes are constructed from predefined datatypes using the constructors described in Section 3.4. The constructors can be applied recursively.

A **derived datatype** is an opaque object that specifies two things:

- A sequence of primitive types and,
- A sequence of integer (byte) displacements.

The displacements are not required to be positive, distinct, or in increasing order. Therefore, the order of items need not coincide with their order in memory, and an item may appear more than once. We call such a pair of sequences (or sequence of pairs) a **type map**. The sequence of primitive types (displacements ignored) is the **type signature** of the datatype.

Let

$$Typemap = \{(type_0, disp_0), \ldots, (type_{n-1}, disp_{n-1})\},$$

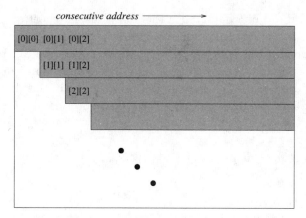

Figure 3.1
A diagram of the memory cells represented by the user-defined datatype **upper**. The shaded cells are the locations of the array that will be sent.

be such a type map, where $type_i$ are primitive types, and $disp_i$ are displacements. Let

$$Typesig = \{type_0, \ldots, type_{n-1}\}$$

be the associated type signature. This type map, together with a base address *buf*, specifies a communication buffer: the communication buffer that consists of n entries, where the i-th entry is at address $buf + disp_i$ and has type $type_i$. A message assembled from a single type of this sort will consist of n values, of the types defined by $Typesig$.

A handle to a derived datatype can appear as an argument in a send or receive operation, instead of a predefined datatype argument. The operation MPI_SEND(buf, 1, datatype,...) will use the send buffer defined by the base address buf and the derived datatype associated with datatype. It will generate a message with the type signature determined by the datatype argument. MPI_RECV(buf, 1, datatype,...) will use the receive buffer defined by the base address buf and the derived datatype associated with datatype.

Derived datatypes can be used in all send and receive operations including collective. We discuss, in Section 3.5.3, the case where the second argument count has value > 1.

The predefined datatypes presented in Section 2.2.2 are special cases of a derived datatype. Thus, MPI_INT is a predefined handle to a datatype with type map $\{(int, 0)\}$, with one entry of type int and displacement zero. The other predefined datatypes are similar.

The **lower bound** of a datatype is the lowest displacement of an entry in this datatype, that is, the relative address of the first byte occupied by entries in this datatype. Normally, this is 0, but as we shall see latter, one can build datatypes with a lower bound that is distinct from zero. The **upper bound** of a datatype is the relative address of the last byte occupied by entries in this datatype, rounded up to satisfy alignment requirements. The **extent** of a datatype is defined to be the span from the lower bound to the upper bound.

That is, if

$$Typemap = \{(type_0, disp_0), \ldots, (type_{n-1}, disp_{n-1})\},$$

then

$$lower\_bound(Typemap) \quad = \quad \min_j disp_j,$$

$$upper\_bound(Typemap) \quad = \quad \max_j(disp_j + sizeof(type_j)) + \epsilon, \text{ and}$$

$$extent(Typemap) \quad = \quad upper\_bound(Typemap) - lower\_bound(Typemap),$$

where $j = 0, \ldots, n - 1$. If $type_i$ requires alignment to a byte address that is a multiple of k_i, then ϵ is the least nonnegative increment needed to round $extent(Typemap)$ to the next multiple of $\max_i k_i$. (The definition of extent is expanded in Section 3.7.)

Example 3.2   Assume that $Type = \{(\text{double}, 0), (\text{char}, 8)\}$ (a double at displacement zero, followed by a char at displacement eight). Assume, furthermore, that doubles have to be strictly aligned at addresses that are multiples of eight. Then, the extent of this datatype is 16 (9 rounded to the next multiple of 8). A datatype that consists of a character immediately followed by a double will also have an extent of 16.

Rationale.   The rounding term that appears in the definition of upper bound is to facilitate the definition of datatypes that correspond to arrays of structures. The extent of a datatype defined to describe a structure will be the extent of memory a compiler will normally allocate for this structure entry in an array.

More explicit control of the extent is described in Section 3.7. Such explicit control is needed in cases where this assumption does not hold, for example, where the compiler offers different alignment options for structures. □

Advice to implementors.   Implementors should provide information on the "default" alignment option used by the MPI library to define upper bound and extent. This should match, whenever possible, the "default" alignment option of the compiler. □

We present in the following sections the functions available for accessing and constructing derived datatypes. Some of these functions belong to MPI-2 and replace deprecated MPI-1 functions (see Section 1.9.1 for the status of deprecated functions). We list in Section 3.11 the old MPI-1 functions. These are still part of the MPI standard, but the new functions should preferably be used.

3.3   Datatype Accessors

The following functions return information on datatypes.

MPI_TYPE_GET_EXTENT(datatype, lb, extent)

IN	datatype	datatype to get information on (handle)
OUT	lb	lower bound of datatype (integer)
OUT	extent	extent of datatype (integer)

```
int MPI_Type_get_extent(MPI_Datatype datatype, MPI_Aint *lb,
    MPI_Aint *extent)
```

```
MPI_TYPE_GET_EXTENT(DATATYPE, LB, EXTENT, IERROR)
    INTEGER DATATYPE, IERROR
    INTEGER(KIND = MPI_ADDRESS_KIND) LB, EXTENT
```

```
void MPI::Datatype::Get_extent(MPI::Aint& lb, MPI::Aint& extent)
    const
```

MPI_TYPE_GET_EXTENT returns the lower bound and the extent of datatype. The upper bound can be computed from these two returned values, since upper_bound = lower_bound + extent.

Rationale.   A derived datatype can describe an arbitrary layout in memory. Therefore, address-sized integers are used for the two returned values. ☐

Advice to users.   Since datatypes in MPI are opaque handles, it is important to use the function MPI_TYPE_GET_EXTENT to determine the "size" of the datatype. As an example, it may be tempting (in C) to use sizeof(datatype), e.g., sizeof(MPI_DOUBLE). However, this will return the size of the opaque handle, which is most likely the size of a pointer, and usually a different value than sizeof(double). ☐

MPI_TYPE_SIZE(datatype, size)

   IN   datatype   datatype (handle)
   OUT   size   datatype size (integer)

```
int MPI_Type_size(MPI_Datatype datatype, int *size)
```

```
MPI_TYPE_SIZE(DATATYPE, SIZE, IERROR)
    INTEGER DATATYPE, SIZE, IERROR
```

```
int MPI::Datatype::Get_size() const
```

MPI_TYPE_SIZE returns the total size, in bytes, of the entries in the type signature associated with datatype; that is, the total size of the data in a message that would be created with this datatype. Entries that occur multiple times in the datatype are counted with their multiplicity. For predefined datatypes, this function returns the same extent information as MPI_TYPE_GET_EXTENT.

Example 3.3   Let datatype have the Type map *Type* defined in Example 3.2 on page 126. Then a call to MPI_TYPE_GET_EXTENT(datatype, lb, extent) will return extent = 16; a call to MPI_TYPE_SIZE(datatype, size) will return size = 9.

3.4   Datatype Constructors

This section presents the MPI functions for constructing derived datatypes. The functions are presented in an order from simplest to most complex.

3.4.1   Dup

MPI_TYPE_DUP(oldtype, newtype)
   IN   oldtype   datatype (handle)
   OUT   newtype   copy of **type** (handle)

```
int MPI_Type_dup(MPI_Datatype oldtype, MPI_Datatype *newtype)
```

```
MPI_TYPE_DUP(OLDTYPE, NEWTYPE, IERROR)
    INTEGER OLDTYPE, NEWTYPE, IERROR
```

```
MPI::Datatype MPI::Datatype::Dup() const
```

MPI_TYPE_DUP returns in newtype a copy of type. The datatypes are distinct objects, but have both the same type map and the same committed state. Datatype commit is discussed in Section 3.5.

The state of cached information is determined by the copy callback function associated with the particular key. Caching on datatypes is discussed in Section II-6.7.

Advice to users.   There is normally no good reason to duplicate a datatype. However, the facility is useful for library writers, when a library function needs to duplicate in persistent storage a datatype parameter. ▯

3.4.2   Contiguous

MPI_TYPE_CONTIGUOUS(count, oldtype, newtype)

IN	count	replication count (integer)
IN	oldtype	old datatype (handle)
OUT	newtype	new datatype (handle)

```
int MPI_Type_contiguous(int count, MPI_Datatype oldtype,
    MPI_Datatype *newtype)
```

```
MPI_TYPE_CONTIGUOUS(COUNT, OLDTYPE, NEWTYPE, IERROR)
    INTEGER COUNT, OLDTYPE, NEWTYPE, IERROR
```

```
MPI::Datatype MPI::Datatype::Create_contiguous(int count) const
```

MPI_TYPE_CONTIGUOUS constructs a typemap consisting of the replication of a datatype into contiguous locations. The argument newtype is the datatype obtained by concatenating count copies (nonnegative) of oldtype. Concatenation is defined using *extent(oldtype)* as the size of the concatenated copies. The action of the Contiguous constructor is represented schematically in Figure 3.2.

Example 3.4   Let oldtype have type map $\{(double, 0), (char, 8)\}$, with extent 16, and let count $= 3$. The type map of the datatype returned by newtype is

$$\{(double, 0), (char, 8), (double, 16), (char, 24), (double, 32), (char, 40)\},$$

that is, alternating double and char elements, with displacements $0, 8, 16, 24, 32, 40$.

In general, assume that the type map of oldtype is

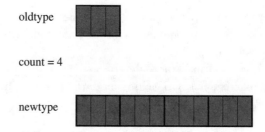

Figure 3.2
Effect of datatype constructor MPI_TYPE_CONTIGUOUS.

$$\{(type_0, disp_0), \ldots, (type_{n-1}, disp_{n-1})\},$$

with extent ex. Then newtype has a type map with count $\cdot\, n$ entries defined by:

$$\{(type_0, disp_0), \ldots, (type_{n-1}, disp_{n-1}),$$

$$(type_0, disp_0 + ex), \ldots, (type_{n-1}, disp_{n-1} + ex),$$

$$\ldots, (type_0, disp_0 + ex \cdot (\mathsf{count} - 1)), \ldots, (type_{n-1}, disp_{n-1} + ex \cdot (\mathsf{count} - 1))\}.$$

3.4.3   Vector

MPI_TYPE_VECTOR(count, blocklength, stride, oldtype, newtype)

IN	count	number of blocks (integer)
IN	blocklength	number of elements in each block (integer)
IN	stride	spacing between start of each block, measured as number of elements (integer)
IN	oldtype	old datatype (handle)
OUT	newtype	new datatype (handle)

```
int MPI_Type_vector(int count, int blocklength, int stride,
    MPI_Datatype oldtype, MPI_Datatype *newtype)
```

```
MPI_TYPE_VECTOR(COUNT, BLOCKLENGTH, STRIDE, OLDTYPE, NEWTYPE, IERROR)
    INTEGER COUNT, BLOCKLENGTH, STRIDE, OLDTYPE, NEWTYPE, IERROR
```

```
MPI::Datatype MPI::Datatype::Create_vector(int count,
    int blocklength, int stride) const
```

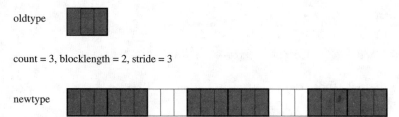

Figure 3.3
Datatype constructor MPI_TYPE_VECTOR.

MPI_TYPE_VECTOR is a constructor that allows replication of a datatype into locations that consist of equally spaced blocks. Each block is obtained by concatenating the same number of copies of the old datatype. The spacing between blocks is a multiple of the extent of the old datatype. A total of count blocks (nonnegative) are used. The action of the Vector constructor is represented schematically in Figure 3.3.

Example 3.5   As before, let oldtype have type map $\{(\text{double}, 0), (\text{char}, 8)\}$, with extent 16. A call to MPI_TYPE_VECTOR(2, 3, 4, oldtype, newtype) will create the datatype with type map

$$\{(\text{double}, 0), (\text{char}, 8), (\text{double}, 16), (\text{char}, 24), (\text{double}, 32), (\text{char}, 40),$$

$$(\text{double}, 64), (\text{char}, 72), (\text{double}, 80), (\text{char}, 88), (\text{double}, 96), (\text{char}, 104)\}.$$

That is, two blocks with three copies each of the old type, with a stride of 4 elements $(4 \times 16$ bytes$)$ between the blocks.

Example 3.6   A call to MPI_TYPE_VECTOR(3, 1, -2, oldtype, newtype) will create the datatype with type map

$$\{(\text{double}, 0), (\text{char}, 8), (\text{double}, -32), (\text{char}, -24), (\text{double}, -64), (\text{char}, -56)\}.$$

In general, assume that oldtype has type map

$$\{(type_0, disp_0), \ldots, (type_{n-1}, disp_{n-1})\},$$

with extent ex. Let bl be the blocklength. The new datatype has a type map with count $\cdot$ bl $\cdot$ n entries:

$$\{(type_0, disp_0), \ldots, (type_{n-1}, disp_{n-1}),$$

$$(type_0, disp_0 + ex), \ldots, (type_{n-1}, disp_{n-1} + ex), \ldots,$$

$$(type_0, disp_0 + (\mathsf{bl} - 1) \cdot ex), \ldots, (type_{n-1}, disp_{n-1} + (\mathsf{bl} - 1) \cdot ex),$$

$$(type_0, disp_0 + \mathsf{stride} \cdot ex), \ldots, (type_{n-1}, disp_{n-1} + \mathsf{stride} \cdot ex), \ldots,$$

$$(type_0, disp_0 + (\mathsf{stride} + \mathsf{bl} - 1) \cdot ex), \ldots, (type_{n-1}, disp_{n-1} + (\mathsf{stride} + \mathsf{bl} - 1) \cdot ex),$$

$$\ldots, (type_0, disp_0 + \mathsf{stride} \cdot (\mathsf{count} - 1) \cdot ex), \ldots,$$

$$(type_{n-1}, disp_{n-1} + \mathsf{stride} \cdot (\mathsf{count} - 1) \cdot ex), \ldots,$$

$$(type_0, disp_0 + (\mathsf{stride} \cdot (\mathsf{count} - 1) + \mathsf{bl} - 1) \cdot ex), \ldots,$$

$$(type_{n-1}, disp_{n-1} + (\mathsf{stride} \cdot (\mathsf{count} - 1) + \mathsf{bl} - 1) \cdot ex)\}.$$

A call to MPI_TYPE_CONTIGUOUS(count, oldtype, newtype) is equivalent to a call to MPI_TYPE_VECTOR(count, 1, 1, oldtype, newtype), or to a call to MPI_TYPE_VECTOR(1, count, num, oldtype, newtype), with num arbitrary.

3.4.4 Hvector

The Vector type constructor assumes that the stride between successive blocks is a multiple of the oldtype extent. This avoids, most of the time, the need for computing stride in bytes. Sometimes it is useful to relax this assumption and allow a stride which consists of an arbitrary number of bytes. The Hvector type constructor below achieves this purpose. The usage of both Vector and Hvector is illustrated in Examples 3.7–3.10.

MPI_TYPE_CREATE_HVECTOR(count, blocklength, stride, oldtype, newtype)

IN	count	number of blocks (integer)
IN	blocklength	number of elements in each block (integer)
IN	stride	number of bytes between start of each block (integer)
IN	oldtype	old datatype (handle)
OUT	newtype	new datatype (handle)

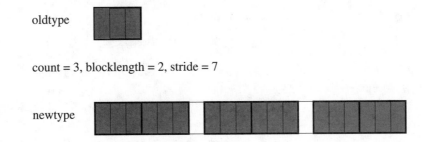

count = 3, blocklength = 2, stride = 7

Figure 3.4
Datatype constructor MPI_TYPE_HVECTOR.

```
int MPI_Type_create_hvector(int count, int blocklength,
    MPI_Aint stride, MPI_Datatype oldtype, MPI_Datatype *newtype)
```

```
MPI_TYPE_CREATE_HVECTOR(COUNT, BLOCKLENGTH, STIDE, OLDTYPE, NEWTYPE,
    IERROR)
    INTEGER COUNT, BLOCKLENGTH, OLDTYPE, NEWTYPE, IERROR
    INTEGER(KIND=MPI_ADDRESS_KIND) STRIDE
```

```
MPI::Datatype MPI::Datatype::Create_hvector(int count, int
    blocklength, MPI::Aint stride) const
```

MPI_TYPE_CREATE_HVECTOR is identical to MPI_TYPE_VECTOR, except that stride is given in bytes, rather than in elements. (H stands for "heterogeneous"). The action of the Hvector constructor is represented schematically in Figure 3.4.

Example 3.7   Consider a call to MPI_TYPE_CREATE_HVECTOR, using the same arguments as in the call to MPI_TYPE_VECTOR in Example 3.5. As before, assume that oldtype has type map $\{(\text{double}, 0), (\text{char}, 8)\}$, with extent 16.

A call to MPI_TYPE_CREATE_HVECTOR(2, 3, 4, oldtype, newtype) will create the datatype with type map

$$\{(\text{double}, 0), (\text{char}, 8), (\text{double}, 16), (\text{char}, 24), (\text{double}, 32), (\text{char}, 40),$$

$$(\text{double}, 4), (\text{char}, 12), (\text{double}, 20), (\text{char}, 28), (\text{double}, 36), (\text{char}, 44)\}.$$

This derived datatype specifies overlapping entries. Since a DOUBLE cannot start both at displacement zero and at displacement four, the use of this datatype in a send operation will cause a type match error. In order to define the same type map as in Example 3.5 on page 131, one would use here stride = 64 (4×16).

In general, assume that oldtype has type map

$$\{(type_0, disp_0), \ldots, (type_{n-1}, disp_{n-1})\},$$

with extent ex. Let bl be the blocklength. The new datatype has a type map with count $\cdot$ bl $\cdot$ n entries:

$$\{(type_0, disp_0), \ldots, (type_{n-1}, disp_{n-1}),$$

$$(type_0, disp_0 + ex), \ldots, (type_{n-1}, disp_{n-1} + ex), \ldots,$$

$$(type_0, disp_0 + (\text{bl} - 1) \cdot ex), \ldots, (type_{n-1}, disp_{n-1} + (\text{bl} - 1) \cdot ex),$$

$$(type_0, disp_0 + \text{stride}), \ldots, (type_{n-1}, disp_{n-1} + \text{stride}), \ldots,$$

$$(type_0, disp_0 + \text{stride} + (\text{bl} - 1) \cdot ex), \ldots,$$

$$(type_{n-1}, disp_{n-1} + \text{stride} + (\text{bl} - 1) \cdot ex), \ldots,$$

$$(type_0, disp_0 + \text{stride} \cdot (\text{count} - 1)), \ldots, (type_{n-1}, disp_{n-1} + \text{stride} \cdot (\text{count} - 1)), \ldots,$$

$$(type_0, disp_0 + \text{stride} \cdot (\text{count} - 1) + (\text{bl} - 1) \cdot ex), \ldots,$$

$$(type_{n-1}, disp_{n-1} + \text{stride} \cdot (\text{count} - 1) + (\text{bl} - 1) \cdot ex)\}.$$

Example 3.8   Send and receive a section of a 2D array. The layout of the 2D array section is shown in Fig 3.5. The first call to MPI_TYPE_VECTOR defines a datatype that describes one column of the section: the 1D array section (1:6:2) which consists of three REAL's, spaced two apart. The second call to MPI_TYPE_CREATE_- HVECTOR defines a datatype that describes the 2D array section (1:6:2, 1:5:2): three copies of the previous 1D array section, with a stride of 12*sizeofreal; the stride is not a multiple of the extent of the 1D section, which is 5*sizeofreal. The usage of MPI_TYPE_COMMIT is explained later, in Section 3.5.

```
REAL a(6,5), e(3,3)
INTEGER oneslice, twoslice, lb, sizeofreal, myrank, ierr
INTEGER status(MPI_STATUS_SIZE)

!     extract the section a(1:6:2,1:5:2) and store it in e(:,:).
```

Figure 3.5
Memory layout of 2D array section for Example 3.8. The shaded blocks are sent.

```
CALL MPI_COMM_RANK(MPI_COMM_WORLD, myrank, ierr)

CALL MPI_TYPE_GET_EXTENT(MPI_REAL, lb, sizeofreal, ierr)

!    create datatype for a 1D section
CALL MPI_TYPE_VECTOR(3, 1, 2, MPI_REAL, oneslice, ierr)

!    create datatype for a 2D section
CALL MPI_TYPE_CREATE_HVECTOR(3, 1, 12*sizeofreal, oneslice, &
                            twoslice, ierr)

CALL MPI_TYPE_COMMIT(twoslice, ierr)

!    send and recv on same process
CALL MPI_SENDRECV(a(1,1), 1, twoslice, myrank, 0, e, 9, MPI_REAL, &
             myrank, 0, MPI_COMM_WORLD, status, ierr)
```

Example 3.9   Transpose a matrix. To do so, we create a datatype that describes the matrix layout in row-major order; we send the matrix with this datatype and receive the matrix in natural, column-major order.

```fortran
REAL a(100,100), b(100,100)
INTEGER row, xpose, lb, sizeofreal, myrank, ierr
INTEGER status(MPI_STATUS_SIZE)

!   transpose matrix a into b

CALL MPI_COMM_RANK(MPI_COMM_WORLD, myrank, ierr)

CALL MPI_TYPE_GET_EXTENT(MPI_REAL, lb, sizeofreal, ierr)

!   create datatype for one row
!   (vector with 100 real entries and stride 100)
CALL MPI_TYPE_VECTOR(100, 1, 100, MPI_REAL, row, ierr)

!   create datatype for matrix in row-major order
!   (one hundred copies of the row datatype, strided one word
!   apart; the successive row datatypes are interleaved)
CALL MPI_TYPE_CREATE_HVECTOR(100, 1, sizeofreal, row, xpose, ierr)

CALL MPI_TYPE_COMMIT(xpose, ierr)

!   send matrix in row-major order and receive in column major order
CALL MPI_SENDRECV(a, 1, xpose, myrank, 0, b, 100*100, MPI_REAL, &
                  myrank, 0, MPI_COMM_WORLD, status, ierr)
```

Example 3.10   Each entry in the array particle is a structure which contains several fields. One of these fields consists of six coordinates (location and velocity). One needs to extract the first three (location) coordinates of all particles and send them in one message. The relative displacement between successive triplets of coordinates may not be a multiple of sizeof(double); therefore, the Hvector datatype constructor is used.

```c
struct Partstruct
{
  char   class;  /* particle class */
  double d[6];   /* particle coordinates */
  char   b[7];   /* some additional information */
};
```

```
void SendParticles( MPI_Comm comm )
{
struct Partstruct    particle[1000];
int                  dest, tag;
MPI_Datatype Locationtype;  /* datatype for locations */

MPI_Type_create_hvector(1000, 3, sizeof(struct Partstruct),
                        MPI_DOUBLE, &Locationtype);
MPI_Type_commit(&Locationtype);

MPI_Send(particle[0].d, 1, Locationtype, dest, tag, comm);
```

...

Rationale.   The reader may have noticed that the naming scheme for datatype constructors is not consistent: some functions are named MPI_TYPE_{CONTIGUOUS|INDEXED|...} and some are named MPI_TYPE_CREATE_{HINDEXED|STRUCT|...}. MPI-1 consistently used names of the form MPI_TYPE_{CONTIGUOUS|INDEXED|...}. When some of the constructors were deprecated and replaced by new functions in MPI-2, new names were needed. The new functions were named MPI_TYPE_CREATE_{HINDEXED|STRUCT|...}. This is consistent with the C++ binding. It might have been preferable to create new synonyms for all datatype constructors, to avoid the confusion. □

3.4.5 Indexed

The Indexed constructor allows one to specify a noncontiguous data layout where displacements between successive blocks need not be equal. This allows gathering of arbitrary entries from an array and sending them in one message, or receiving one message and scattering the received entries into arbitrary locations in an array.

MPI_TYPE_INDEXED(count, array_of_blocklengths, array_of_displacements, oldtype, newtype)

IN	count	number of blocks (integer)
IN	array_of_blocklengths	number of elements per block (array of integers)
IN	array_of_displacements	displacement for each block, measured as number of elements (array of integers)
IN	oldtype	old datatype (handle)
OUT	newtype	new datatype (handle)

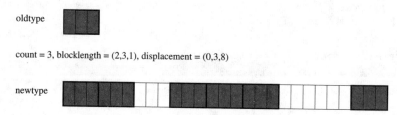

oldtype

count = 3, blocklength = (2,3,1), displacement = (0,3,8)

newtype

Figure 3.6
Datatype constructor MPI_TYPE_INDEXED.

```
int MPI_Type_indexed(int count, int *array_of_blocklengths,
    int *array_of_displacements, MPI_Datatype oldtype,
    MPI_Datatype *newtype)
```

```
MPI_TYPE_INDEXED(COUNT, ARRAY_OF_BLOCKLENGTHS, ARRAY_OF_DISPLACEMENTS,
    OLDTYPE, NEWTYPE, IERROR)
    INTEGER COUNT, ARRAY_OF_BLOCKLENGTHS(*),
    ARRAY_OF_DISPLACEMENTS(*), OLDTYPE, NEWTYPE, IERROR
```

```
MPI::Datatype MPI::Datatype::Create_indexed(int count,
    const int array_of_blocklengths[],
    const int array_of_displacements[]) const
```

MPI_TYPE_INDEXED allows replication of an old datatype into a sequence of blocks (each block is a concatenation of the old datatype), where each block can contain a different number of copies of oldtype and have a different displacement. All block displacements are measured in units of the oldtype extent. A total of count blocks (nonnegative) are used. The action of the Indexed constructor is represented schematically in Figure 3.6.

Example 3.11   Let oldtype have type map
   $\{(double, 0), (char, 8)\}$,
with extent 16. Let B = (3, 1) and let D = (4, 0). A call to MPI_TYPE_INDEXED(2, B, D, oldtype, newtype) returns a datatype with type map

$\{(double, 64), (char, 72), (double, 80), (char, 88), (double, 96), (char, 104),$

$(double, 0), (char, 8)\}$.

That is, three copies of the old type starting at displacement $4 \times 16 = 64$, and one copy starting at displacement 0.

In general, assume that oldtype has type map

$$\{(type_0, disp_0), \ldots, (type_{n-1}, disp_{n-1})\},$$

with extent ex. Let B be the array_of_blocklengths argument and D be the array_of_displacements argument. The new datatype has a type map with $n \cdot \sum_{i=0}^{count-1} B[i]$ entries:

$$\{(type_0, disp_0 + D[0] \cdot ex), \ldots, (type_{n-1}, disp_{n-1} + D[0] \cdot ex), \ldots,$$

$$(type_0, disp_0 + (D[0] + B[0] - 1) \cdot ex), \ldots,$$

$$(type_{n-1}, disp_{n-1} + (D[0] + B[0] - 1) \cdot ex), \ldots,$$

$$(type_0, disp_0 + D[count-1] \cdot ex), \ldots, (type_{n-1}, disp_{n-1} + D[count-1] \cdot ex), \ldots,$$

$$(type_0, disp_0 + (D[count-1] + B[count-1] - 1) \cdot ex), \ldots,$$

$$(type_{n-1}, disp_{n-1} + (D[count-1] + B[count-1] - 1) \cdot ex)\}.$$

A call to MPI_TYPE_VECTOR(count, blocklength, stride, oldtype, newtype) is equivalent to a call to MPI_TYPE_INDEXED(count, B, D, oldtype, newtype) where

$$D[j] = j \cdot stride, \quad j = 0, \ldots, count - 1,$$

and

$$B[j] = blocklength, \quad j = 0, \ldots, count - 1.$$

The use of the MPI_TYPE_INDEXED function was illustrated in Example 3.1 on page 124; the function was used to transfer the upper triangular part of a square matrix.

3.4.6   Block Indexed

MPI_TYPE_INDEXED is most often called with blocks all of the same length (usually, one). The following convenience function allows for constant blocksize and arbitrary displacements.

MPI_TYPE_CREATE_INDEXED_BLOCK(count, blocklength, array_of_displacements, oldtype, newtype)

IN	count	length of array of displacements (integer)
IN	blocklength	size of block (integer)
IN	array_of_displacements	array of displacements (array of integers)
IN	oldtype	old datatype (handle)
OUT	newtype	new datatype (handle)

```
int MPI_Type_create_indexed_block(int count, int blocklength,
    int *array_of_displacements, MPI_Datatype oldtype,
    MPI_Datatype *newtype)
```

```
MPI_TYPE_CREATE_INDEXED_BLOCK(COUNT, BLOCKLENGTH,
    ARRAY_OF_DISPLACEMENTS, OLDTYPE, NEWTYPE, IERROR)
    INTEGER COUNT, BLOCKLENGTH, ARRAY_OF_DISPLACEMENTS(*), OLDTYPE,
    NEWTYPE, IERROR
```

```
MPI::Datatype MPI::Datatype::Create_indexed_block( int count,
    int blocklength, const int array_of_displacements[]) const
```

A call to MPI_TYPE_INDEXED_BLOCK(count, blen, disps, oldtype, newtype) is equivalent to a call to MPI_TYPE_INDEXED_BLOCK(count, blens, disps, oldtype, newtype) with blens[i] = blen, $i = 0, \ldots, \text{count} - 1$.

3.4.7   Hindexed

As with the Vector and Hvector constructors, it is usually convenient to measure displacements in multiples of the extent of the oldtype, but sometimes necessary to allow for arbitrary displacements. The Hindexed constructor satisfies the later need.

MPI_TYPE_CREATE_HINDEXED(count, array_of_blocklengths, array_of_displacements, oldtype, newtype)

IN	count	number of blocks (integer)
IN	array_of_blocklengths	number of elements in each block (array of integers)
IN	array_of_displacements	byte displacement of each block (array of integers)
IN	oldtype	old datatype (handle)
OUT	newtype	new datatype (handle)

```
int MPI_Type_create_hindexed(int count, int *array_of_blocklengths,
    MPI_Aint *array_of_displacements, MPI_Datatype oldtype,
    MPI_Datatype *newtype)
```

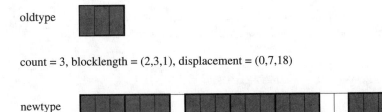

Figure 3.7
Datatype constructor MPI_TYPE_CREATE_HINDEXED.

```
MPI_TYPE_CREATE_HINDEXED(COUNT, ARRAY_OF_BLOCKLENGTHS,
    ARRAY_OF_DISPLACEMENTS, OLDTYPE, NEWTYPE, IERROR)
    INTEGER COUNT, ARRAY_OF_BLOCKLENGTHS(*), OLDTYPE, NEWTYPE, IERROR
    INTEGER(KIND=MPI_ADDRESS_KIND) ARRAY_OF_DISPLACEMENTS(*)
```

```
MPI::Datatype MPI::Datatype::Create_hindexed(int count,
    const int array_of_blocklengths[],
    const MPI::Aint array_of_displacements[]) const
```

MPI_TYPE_CREATE_HINDEXED is identical to MPI_TYPE_INDEXED, except that block displacements in array_of_displacements are specified in bytes, rather than in multiples of the oldtype extent. The action of the Hindexed constructor is represented schematically in Figure 3.7.

Example 3.12   We use the same arguments as for MPI_TYPE_INDEXED, in Example 3.11. Thus, oldtype has type map, $\{(\text{double}, 0), (\text{char}, 8)\}$, with extent 16; B = (3, 1), and D = (4, 0). A call to MPI_TYPE_CREATE_HINDEXED(2, B, D, oldtype, newtype) returns a datatype with type map

$$\{(\text{double}, 4), (\text{char}, 12), (\text{double}, 20), (\text{char}, 28), (\text{double}, 36), (\text{char}, 44),$$

$$(\text{double}, 0), (\text{char}, 8)\}.$$

The partial overlap between the entries of type DOUBLE implies that a type matching error will occur if this datatype is used in a send operation. To get the same datatype as in Example 3.11 on page 138, the call would have D = (64, 0).

In general, assume that oldtype has type map

$$\{(type_0, disp_0), \ldots, (type_{n-1}, disp_{n-1})\},$$

with extent ex. Let B be the array_of_blocklength argument and D be the array_of_-displacements argument. The new datatype has a type map with $n \cdot \sum_{i=0}^{\text{count}-1} \text{B[i]}$ entries:

$$\{(type_0, disp_0 + \text{D[0]}), \ldots, (type_{n-1}, disp_{n-1} + \text{D[0]}), \ldots,$$

$$(type_0, disp_0 + \text{D[0]} + (\text{B[0]} - 1) \cdot ex), \ldots,$$

$$(type_{n-1}, disp_{n-1} + \text{D[0]} + (\text{B[0]} - 1) \cdot ex), \ldots,$$

$$(type_0, disp_0 + \text{D[count-1]}), \ldots, (type_{n-1}, disp_{n-1} + \text{D[count-1]}), \ldots,$$

$$(type_0, disp_0 + \text{D[count-1]} + (\text{B[count-1]} - 1) \cdot ex), \ldots,$$

$$(type_{n-1}, disp_{n-1} + \text{D[count-1]} + (\text{B[count-1]} - 1) \cdot ex)\}.$$

3.4.8   Struct

MPI_TYPE_CREATE_STRUCT(count, array_of_blocklengths, array_of_displacements, array_of_types, newtype)

IN	count	number of blocks (integer)
IN	array_of_blocklengths	number of elements in each block (array of integers)
IN	array_of_displacements	byte displacement of each block (array of integers)
IN	array_of_types	type of elements in each block (array of handles)
OUT	newtype	new datatype (handle)

```
int MPI_Type_create_struct(int count, int *array_of_blocklengths,
    MPI_Aint *array_of_displacements, MPI_Datatype *array_of_types,
    MPI_Datatype *newtype)
```

```
MPI_TYPE_CREATE_STRUCT(COUNT, ARRAY_OF_BLOCKLENGTHS,
    ARRAY_OF_DISPLACEMENTS, ARRAY_OF_TYPES, NEWTYPE, IERROR)
    INTEGER COUNT, ARRAY_OF_BLOCKLENGTHS(*), ARRAY_OF_TYPES(*),
    NEWTYPE, IERROR
    INTEGER(KIND=MPI_ADDRESS_KIND) ARRAY_OF_DISPLACEMENTS(*)
```

```
static MPI::Datatype MPI::Datatype::Create_struct(int count,
    const int array_of_blocklengths[], const MPI::Aint
    array_of_displacements[], const MPI::Datatype array_of_types[])
```

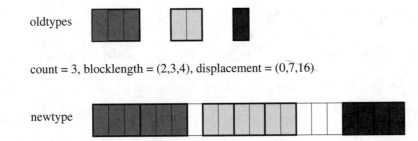

oldtypes

count = 3, blocklength = (2,3,4), displacement = (0,7,16)

newtype

Figure 3.8
Datatype constructor MPI_TYPE_CREATE_STRUCT.

MPI_TYPE_CREATE_STRUCT is the most general type constructor. It further generalizes MPI_TYPE_CREATE_HINDEXED in that it allows each block to consist of replications of different datatypes. The intent is to allow descriptions of arrays of structures, as a single datatype. The action of the Struct constructor is represented schematically in Figure 3.8.

Example 3.13   Let type1 have type map
   {(double, 0), (char, 8)},
with extent 16. Let B = (2, 1, 3), D = (0, 16, 26), and T = (MPI_FLOAT, type1, MPI_CHAR). Then a call to MPI_TYPE_CREATE_STRUCT(3, B, D, T, newtype) returns a datatype with type map

{(float, 0), (float, 4), (double, 16), (char, 24), (char, 26), (char, 27), (char, 28)}.

That is, two copies of MPI_FLOAT starting at 0, followed by one copy of type1 starting at 16, followed by three copies of MPI_CHAR, starting at 26. (We assume that a float occupies four bytes.)

In general, let T be the array_of_types argument, where T[i] is a handle to,

$$typemap_i = \{(type^i_0, disp^i_0), \ldots, (type^i_{n_i-1}, disp^i_{n_i-1})\},$$

with extent ex_i. Let B be the array_of_blocklength argument and D be the array_of_displacements argument. Let c be the count argument. Then the new datatype has a type map with $\sum_{i=0}^{c-1} B[i] \cdot n_i$ entries:

$$\{(type^0_0, disp^0_0 + D[0]), \ldots, (type^0_{n_0}, disp^0_{n_0} + D[0]), \ldots,$$

$$(type^0_0, disp^0_0 + D[0] + (B[0] - 1) \cdot ex_0), \ldots,$$

$$(type_{n_0}^0, disp_{n_0}^0 + \text{D[0]} + (\text{B[0]-1}) \cdot ex_0), \dots,$$

$$(type_0^{C-1}, disp_0^{C-1} + \text{D[c-1]}), \dots, (type_{n_{C-1}-1}^{C-1}, disp_{n_{C-1}-1}^{C-1} + \text{D[c-1]}), \dots,$$

$$(type_0^{C-1}, disp_0^{C-1} + \text{D[c-1]} + (\text{B[c-1]} - 1) \cdot ex_{C-1}), \dots,$$

$$(type_{n_{C-1}-1}^{C-1}, disp_{n_{C-1}-1}^{C-1} + \text{D[c-1]} + (\text{B[c-1]-1}) \cdot ex_{C-1})\}.$$

A call to MPI_TYPE_CREATE_HINDEXED(count, B, D, oldtype, newtype) is equivalent to a call to MPI_TYPE_CREATE_STRUCT(count, B, D, T, newtype), where each entry of T is equal to oldtype.

Example 3.14   Sending an array of structures.

```
struct Partstruct
{
  char    class;    /* particle class */
  double  d[6];     /* particle coordinates */
  char    b[7];     /* some additional information */
};

struct Partstruct    particle[1000];
int                  dest, tag;
MPI_Comm      comm;

/* build datatype describing structure */

MPI_Datatype Particletype;
MPI_Datatype type[3] = {MPI_CHAR, MPI_DOUBLE, MPI_CHAR};
int          blocklen[3] = {1, 6, 7};
MPI_Aint     disp[3] = {0, sizeof(double), 7*sizeof(double)};

MPI_Type_create_struct(3, blocklen, disp, type, &Particletype);
MPI_Type_commit(&Particletype);

/* send the array */
MPI_Send(particle, 1000, Particletype, dest, tag, comm);
```

The array disp was initialized assuming that a double is double-word aligned. If double's are single-word aligned, then disp should be initialized to (0, sizeof(int), sizeof(int)+6*sizeof(double)). We show in Example 3.21 on page 153, how to avoid this machine dependence.

Example 3.15   A more complex example, using the same array of structures as in Example 3.14: process zero sends a message that consists of all particles of class zero. Process one receives these particles in contiguous locations.

```
struct Partstruct
{
  char    class;   /* particle class */
  double d[6];     /* particle coordinates */
  char    b[7];    /* some additional information */
};


void SendParticles( MPI_Comm comm )
{
struct Partstruct     particle[1000];
int                   i, j, myrank;
MPI_Status            status;
MPI_Datatype Particletype;
MPI_Datatype type[3] = {MPI_CHAR, MPI_DOUBLE, MPI_CHAR};
int          blocklen[3] = {1, 6, 7};
MPI_Aint     disp[3] = {0, sizeof(double), 7*sizeof(double)};
MPI_Datatype Zparticles;    /* datatype describing all particles
                               with class zero (needs to be recomputed
                               if classes change) */
int          *zdisp;
int          *zblocklen;

MPI_Type_create_struct(3, blocklen, disp, type, &Particletype);
MPI_Comm_rank(comm, &myrank);

if (myrank == 0) {

  /* send message consisting of all class zero particles */

  /* allocate data structures for datatype creation */
```

```
zdisp = (int*)malloc(1000*sizeof(int));
zblocklen = (int*)malloc(1000*sizeof(int));

/* compute displacements of class zero particles */
j = 0;
for (i=0; i < 1000; i++) {
  if (particle[i].class==0) {
    zdisp[j] = i;
    zblocklen[j] = 1;
    j++;
  }
}

/* create datatype for class zero particles  */
MPI_Type_indexed(j, zblocklen, zdisp, Particletype, &Zparticles);
MPI_Type_commit(&Zparticles);

/* send */
MPI_Send(particle, 1, Zparticles, 1, 0, comm);
}
else if (myrank == 1) {
  /* receive class zero particles in contiguous locations */
  MPI_Recv(particle, 1000, Particletype, 0, 0, comm, &status);

}

...
```

Example 3.16   An optimization for the last example: rather than handling each class zero particle as a separate block, it may be more efficient to compute largest consecutive blocks of class zero particles and use these blocks in the call to MPI_Type_indexed. The modified loop that computes zblock and zdisp is shown below.

```
...
j=0;
for (i=0; i < 1000; i++) {
  if (particle[i].class==0) {
    for (k=i+1; (k < 1000)&&(particle[k].class == 0); k++);
    zdisp[j] = i;
```

```
    zblocklen[j] = k-i;
    j++;
    i = k;
  }
}
MPI_Type_indexed(j, zblocklen, zdisp, Particletype, &Zparticles);
...
```

3.5   Use of Derived Datatypes

3.5.1   Commit

A derived datatype must be **committed** before it can be used in a communication. A committed datatype can continue to be used as an input argument in datatype constructors (so that other datatypes can be derived from the committed datatype). There is no need to commit predefined datatypes.

MPI_TYPE_COMMIT(datatype)

   INOUT   datatype   datatype that is to be committed (handle)

```
int MPI_Type_commit(MPI_Datatype *datatype)
```

```
MPI_TYPE_COMMIT(DATATYPE, IERROR)
    INTEGER DATATYPE, IERROR
```

```
void MPI::Datatype::Commit()
```

MPI_TYPE_COMMIT commits the datatype. Commit should be thought of as a possible "flattening" or "compilation" of the formal description of a type map into an efficient representation. Commit does not imply that the datatype is bound to the current content of a communication buffer. After a datatype has been committed, it can be repeatedly reused to communicate different data.

All datatype constructors return uncommitted datatypes, that must be committed before they can be used in a communication. There is one exception to this rule: MPI_TYPE_DUP(oldtype, newtype) returns a in newtype a datatype with the same commit status as oldtype.

MPI_TYPE_COMMIT can be called with a datatype which is already committed, in which case, it is equivalent to a no-op.

Advice to implementors. The system may "compile" at commit time an internal representation for the datatype that facilitates communication. □

3.5.2 Deallocation

A datatype object is deallocated by a call to MPI_TYPE_FREE.

MPI_TYPE_FREE(datatype)

  INOUT datatype   datatype to be freed (handle)

```
int MPI_Type_free(MPI_Datatype *datatype)

MPI_TYPE_FREE(DATATYPE, IERROR)
    INTEGER DATATYPE, IERROR

void MPI::Datatype::Free()
```

MPI_TYPE_FREE marks the datatype object associated with datatype for deallocation and sets datatype to MPI_DATATYPE_NULL (MPI::DATATYPE_NULL, in C++). Any communication that is currently using this datatype will complete normally. Derived datatypes that were defined from the freed datatype are not affected.

Advice to implementors. An implementation may keep a reference count of active communications that use the datatype, in order to decide when to free it. Also, one may implement constructors of derived datatypes so that they keep pointers to their datatype arguments, rather then copying them. In this case, one needs to keep track of active datatype definition references in order to know when a datatype object can be freed. □

Example 3.17 The following code fragment gives examples of using MPI_TYPE-_COMMIT and MPI_TYPE_FREE.

```
MPI::Datatype type1 = MPI::FLOAT.Create_contiguous(5); // create new
                                                        //type object
type1.Commit(); // now type1 can be used for communication
MPI::Datatype type2 = type1; // type2 can be used for communication
                             // (it is a handle to same object as
                             // type1)
type1 = MPI::FLOAT.Create_vector(3, 5, 4); // create new uncommitted
```

```
                                               // type object
type1.Commit(); // type1 can be used anew for communication
type2.Free();   // free before overwriting handle
type2 = type1;  // type2 can be used
type2.Free();   // both type1 and type2 are unavailable
                // type2 has value MPI::DATATYPE_NULL
                // and type1 is undefined
```

3.5.3   Relation to count

A call of the form MPI_SEND(buf, count, datatype , ...), where count > 1, is interpreted as if the call was passed a new datatype which is the concatenation of count copies of datatype. Thus, MPI_SEND(buf, count, datatype, dest, tag, comm) is equivalent to,

```
MPI_TYPE_CONTIGUOUS(count, datatype, newtype)
MPI_TYPE_COMMIT(newtype)
MPI_SEND(buf, 1, newtype, dest, tag, comm).
```

Similar statements apply to all other communication functions that have a count and datatype argument.

3.5.4   Type Matching

Suppose that a send operation MPI_SEND(buf, count, datatype, dest, tag, comm) is executed, where datatype has type map
$\{(type_0, disp_0), \ldots, (type_{n-1}, disp_{n-1})\}$,
and extent $extent$. The send operation sends $n \cdot$count entries, where entry (i, j) is at location $addr_{i,j} = $ buf $+ extent \cdot i + disp_j$ and has type $type_j$, for $i = 0, \ldots, $count$-1$ and $j = 0, \ldots, n-1$. The variable stored at address $addr_{i,j}$ in the calling program should be of a type that matches $type_j$, where type matching is defined as in Section 2.3.1.

Similarly, suppose that a receive operation MPI_RECV(buf, count, datatype, source, tag, comm, status) is executed. The receive operation receives up to $n \cdot$count entries, where entry (i, j) is at location buf $+ extent \cdot i + disp_j$ and has type $type_j$. Type matching is defined according to the type signature of the corresponding datatypes, that is, the sequence of primitive type components. Type matching does not depend on other aspects of the datatype definition, such as the displacements (layout in memory) or the intermediate types used to define the datatypes.

For sends, a datatype may specify overlapping entries. This is not true for receives. If the datatype used in a receive operation specifies overlapping entries then the call is erroneous.

Example 3.18   This example shows that type matching is defined only in terms of the primitive types that constitute a derived type.

```
...
CALL MPI_TYPE_CONTIGUOUS(2, MPI_REAL, type2, ...)
CALL MPI_TYPE_CONTIGUOUS(4, MPI_REAL, type4, ...)
CALL MPI_TYPE_CONTIGUOUS(2, type2, type22, ...)
...
CALL MPI_SEND(a, 4, MPI_REAL, ...)
CALL MPI_SEND(a, 2, type2, ...)
CALL MPI_SEND(a, 1, type22, ...)
CALL MPI_SEND(a, 1, type4, ...)
...
CALL MPI_RECV(a, 4, MPI_REAL, ...)
CALL MPI_RECV(a, 2, type2, ...)
CALL MPI_RECV(a, 1, type22, ...)
CALL MPI_RECV(a, 1, type4, ...)
```

Each of the sends matches *any* of the receives.

3.5.5   Message Length

If a message was received using a user-defined datatype, then a subsequent call to MPI_GET_COUNT(status, datatype, count) (Section 2.2.8) will return the number of "copies" of datatype received (count). That is, if the receive operation was MPI_RECV(buff, count,datatype,...) then MPI_GET_COUNT may return any integer value k, where $0 \leq k \leq$ count. If MPI_GET_COUNT returns k, then the number of primitive elements received is $n \cdot k$, where n is the number of primitive elements in the type map of datatype. The received message need not fill an integral number of "copies" of datatype. If the number of primitive elements received is not a multiple of n, that is, if the receive operation has not received an integral number of datatype "copies," then MPI_GET_COUNT returns the value MPI_UNDEFINED. The datatype argument should match the argument provided by the receive call that set the status variable.

The function MPI_GET_ELEMENTS below can be used to determine the number of primitive elements received.

MPI_GET_ELEMENTS(status, datatype, count)

IN	status	status of receive (Status)
IN	datatype	datatype used by receive operation (handle)
OUT	count	number of primitive elements received (integer)

```
int MPI_Get_elements(MPI_Status *status, MPI_Datatype datatype,
    int *count)
```

```
MPI_GET_ELEMENTS(STATUS, DATATYPE, COUNT, IERROR)
    INTEGER STATUS(MPI_STATUS_SIZE), DATATYPE, COUNT, IERROR
```

```
int MPI::Status::Get_elements(const MPI::Datatype& datatype) const
```

Example 3.19   Usage of MPI_GET_COUNT and MPI_GET_ELEMENT.

```
MPI::Intracomm comm;
MPI::Status status;
...
MPI::Datatype type2 = MPI::FLOAT.Create_contiguous(2);
type2.Commit();
...
if (comm.Get_rank() == 0) {
  comm.Send(a, 2, MPI::FLOAT, 1, 0);
  comm.Send(a, 3, MPI::FLOAT, 1, 1);
} else {
  comm.Recv(a, 2, type2, 0, 0, status);
  i = status.Get_count(type2); // i gets 1
  i = status.Get_elements(type2); // i gets 2
  comm.Recv(a, 2, type2, 0, 1, status);
  i = status.Get_count(type2); // i gets MPI::UNDEFINED
  i = status.Get_elements(type2); // i gets 3
}
```

The function MPI_GET_ELEMENTS can also be used after a probe to find the number of primitive elements in the probed message. Note that the two functions MPI_GET_COUNT and MPI_GET_ELEMENTS return the same values when they are used with predefined datatypes.

Rationale. The definition of MPI_GET_COUNT is consistent with the use of the count argument in the receive call: the function returns the value of the count argument, when the receive buffer is filled. Sometimes datatype represents a basic unit of data one wants to transfer. One should be able to find out how many components were received without bothering to divide by the number of elements in each component. The MPI_GET_COUNT is used in such cases. However, on other occasions, datatype is used to define a complex layout of data in the receiver memory, and does not represent a basic unit of data for transfers. In such cases, one must use MPI_GET_ELEMENTS. ☐

Advice to implementors. Structures often contain padding space used to align entries correctly. Assume that data is moved from a send buffer that describes a structure into a receive buffer that describes an identical structure on another process. In such a case, it is probably advantageous to copy the structure, together with the padding, as one contiguous block. The user can "force" this optimization by explicitly including padding as part of the message. The implementation is free to do this optimization when it does not impact the outcome of the computation. However, it may be hard to detect when this optimization applies, since data sent from a structure may be received into a set of disjoint variables. Also, padding will differ when data is communicated in a heterogeneous environment, or even on the same architecture, when different compiling options are used. This problem was considered by the MPI-2 Forum, but no satisfactory solution was found. ☐

3.6 Address Function

As shown in Example 3.14 on page 144, one sometimes needs to be able to find the displacement, in bytes, of a structure component relative to the structure start. In C, one can use the sizeof operator to find the size of C objects; and one will be tempted to use the & operator to compute addresses and then displacements. However, the C standard does not require that (int)&v be the byte address of variable v: the mapping of pointers to integers is implementation-dependent. Some systems may have "word" pointers and "byte" pointers; other systems may have a segmented, noncontiguous address space. Therefore, a portable mechanism has to be provided by MPI to compute the "address" of a variable. Such a mechanism is certainly needed in Fortran, which has no address-of operator.

MPI_GET_ADDRESS(location, address)

IN	location	location in caller memory (choice)
OUT	address	address of location (integer)

```
int MPI_Get_address(void *location, MPI_Aint *address)
```

```
MPI_GET_ADDRESS(LOCATION, ADDRESS, IERROR)
    <type> LOCATION(*)
    INTEGER IERROR
    INTEGER(KIND=MPI_ADDRESS_KIND) ADDRESS
```

```
MPI::Aint MPI::Get_address(void* location)
```

MPI_GET_ADDRESS is used to find the address of a location in memory. It returns the byte address of location.

Example 3.20   Using MPI_GET_ADDRESS for an array. The value of DIFF is set to 909*sizeofreal, while the values of I1 and I2 are implementation-dependent.

```
REAL A(100,100)
INTEGER(KIND=MPI_ADDRESS_KIND) I1, I2, DIFF
CALL MPI_GET_ADDRESS(A(1,1), I1, IERR)
CALL MPI_GET_ADDRESS(A(10,10), I2, IERR)
DIFF = I2 - I1
```

Example 3.21   We modify the code in Example 3.14, page 144, so as to avoid architectural dependencies. Calls to MPI_GET_ADDRESS are used to compute the displacements of the structure components.

```
struct Partstruct
{
  char    class;   /* particle class */
  double  d[6];    /* particle coordinates */
  char    b[7];    /* some additional information */
};
struct Partstruct    particle[1000];
int           i, dest, tag;
MPI_Comm      comm;
MPI_Datatype Particletype;
```

```
MPI_Datatype type[3] = {MPI_CHAR, MPI_DOUBLE, MPI_CHAR};
int          blocklen[3] = {1, 6, 7};
MPI_Aint     disp[3];

/* compute displacements */
MPI_Get_address(&particle[0].class, &disp[0]);
MPI_Get_address(&particle[0].d, &disp[1]);
MPI_Get_address(&particle[0].b, &disp[2]);

for (i=2; i >= 0; i--) disp[i] -= disp[0];

/* build datatype */
MPI_Type_create_struct(3, blocklen, disp, type, &Particletype);
MPI_Type_commit(&Particletype);
...
/*  send the entire array */
MPI_Send(particle, 1000, Particletype, dest, tag, comm);
...
```

3.7 Datatype Resizing

Sometimes it is necessary to override the definition of extent given in Section 3.2. Consider, for example, the code in Example 3.21 in the previous section. Assume that a double occupies 8 bytes and must be double-word aligned. There will be 7 bytes of padding after the first field and one byte of padding after the last field of the structure Partstruct, and the structure will occupy 64 bytes. If, on the other hand, a double can be word aligned only, then there will be only 3 bytes of padding after the first field, and Partstruct will occupy 60 bytes. The MPI library will follow the alignment rules used on the target systems so that the extent of datatype Particletype equals the amount of storage occupied by Partstruct. The catch is that different alignment rules may be specified, on the same system, using different compiler options. An even more difficult problem is that some compilers allow the use of pragmas in order to specify different alignment rules for different structures within the same program. (Many architectures can correctly handle misaligned values, but with lower performance; different alignment rules trade speed of access for storage density.) The MPI library will assume the default alignment rules. However, the user should be able to overrule this assumption if structures are packed otherwise. Also, it is sometimes convenient to define an artificial extent to a datatype, before it is used as an argument in a datatype constructor: this provides more flexibility in assembling such datatypes. This will be illustrated in Example 3.24. The following datatype constructor provides this capability.

MPI_TYPE_CREATE_RESIZED(oldtype, lb, extent, newtype)

IN	oldtype	input datatype (handle)
IN	lb	new lower bound of datatype (integer)
IN	extent	new extent of datatype (integer)
OUT	newtype	output datatype (handle)

```
int MPI_Type_create_resized(MPI_Datatype oldtype, MPI_Aint lb,
    MPI_Aint extent, MPI_Datatype *newtype)
```

```
MPI_TYPE_CREATE_RESIZED(OLDTYPE, LB, EXTENT, NEWTYPE, IERROR)
    INTEGER OLDTYPE, NEWTYPE, IERROR
    INTEGER(KIND=MPI_ADDRESS_KIND) LB, EXTENT
```

```
MPI::Datatype MPI::Datatype::Resized(const MPI::Aint lb,
    const MPI::Aint extent) const
```

MPI_TYPE_CREATE_RESIZED returns in newtype a new datatype that is identical to oldtype, except that the lower bound of this new datatype is set to be lb, and its upper bound is set to be lb + extent. The call is erroneous if extent is negative.

One can think that MPI provides two additional predefined "pseudo-datatypes," MPI_LB and MPI_UB (MPI::LB and MPI::UB, in C++), that can be used, respectively, to mark the lower bound or the upper bound of a datatype. These pseudo-datatypes occupy no space ($extent(\text{MPI\_LB}) = extent(\text{MPI\_UB}) = 0$). They do not affect the size or count of a datatype, and do not contribute any additional data to a message created with this datatype. However, MPI_LB changes the starting point of the datatype and, therefore, displaces the data layout indicated by the datatype, relative to the starting address of the communication buffer. Furthermore, the extent of the datatype is taken to be the span from MPI_LB to MPI_UB. This affects the outcome of a replication of this datatype by a datatype constructor, or of the implicit replication effected by the count argument of a communication operation.

Formally, let oldtype have type map

$$Oldtypemap = \{(type_0, disp_0), \ldots, (type_{n-1}, disp_{n-1})\},$$

Let datatype newtype be returned by a call to MPI_TYPE_CREATE-
RESIZED(oldtype, lb, extent, newtype). Then the type map $Newtypemap$ of newtype
is computed as follows: First delete any entry with type MPI_LB or MPI_UB from
$Oldtypemap$, thus obtaining the sequence

$$Oldtypemap = \{(type_{i_0}, disp_{i_0}), \ldots, (type_{i_k}, disp_{i_k})\},$$

Then

$$Newtypemap = \{(\text{lb}, \text{lb}), (\text{ub}, \text{lb} + \text{extent}), (type_{i_0}, disp_{i_0}), \ldots, (type_{i_k}, disp_{i_k})\};$$

We can now update the definitions of lower bound, upper bound and extent given
on page 126. In general, if

$$Typemap = \{(type_0, disp_0), \ldots, (type_{n-1}, disp_{n-1})\},$$

then the lower bound of $Typemap$ is defined to be

$$lower\_bound(Typemap) = \begin{cases} \min_j disp_j & \text{if no entry has basic type lb} \\ \min_j\{disp_j \text{ such that } type_j = \text{lb}\} & \text{otherwise} \end{cases}$$

Similarly, the upper bound of $Typemap$ is defined to be

$$upper\_bound(Typemap) = \begin{cases} \max_j disp_j + sizeof(type_j) + \epsilon & \text{if no entry has} \\ & \text{basic type ub} \\ \max_j\{disp_j \text{ such that } type_j = \text{ub}\} & \text{otherwise} \end{cases}$$

And

$$extent(Typemap) = upper\_bound(Typemap) - lower\_bound(Typemap)$$

If $type_i$ requires alignment to a byte address that is a multiple of k_i, then ϵ is the
least nonnegative increment needed to round $extent(Typemap)$ to the next multiple
of $\max_i k_i$.

The formal definitions given for the various datatype constructors continue to apply, with the amended definition of extent. Also, MPI_TYPE_GET_EXTENT returns
the above as its values for lower bound and extent.

Example 3.22   Let type0 have type map

$$Typemap0 = \{(0, \text{MPI\_CHAR}), (32, \text{MPI\_INT})\},$$

where ints occupy 4 bytes. Consider the sequence of calls

```
MPI_Type_create_resized(type0, -4, 8, &type1);
MPI_Type_contiguous(2, type1, &type2);
MPI_Type_create_resized(type2, 0, 64, &type3);
```

Then, type0 has lower bound 0, upper bound 36 and extent 36.

type1 has type map

$$Typemap1 = \{(-4, \mathsf{lb}), (8, \mathsf{ub}), (0, \mathsf{char}), (32, \mathsf{int})\},$$

the lower bound is -4, the upper bound is 8, and the extent is 12.

type2 has type map

$$Typemap2 = \{(-4, \mathsf{lb}), (8, \mathsf{ub}), (0, \mathsf{char}), (32, \mathsf{int}), (8, \mathsf{lb}), (20, \mathsf{ub}), (12, \mathsf{char}), (44, \mathsf{int})\},$$

the lower bound is -4, the upper bound is 20, and the extent is 24.

type3 has type map

$$Typemap3 = \{(0, \mathsf{lb}), (64, \mathsf{ub}), (0, \mathsf{char}), (32, \mathsf{int}), (12, \mathsf{char}), (44, \mathsf{int})\},$$

the lower bound is 0, the upper bound is 64, and the extent is 64.

Example 3.23   We modify Example 3.21, page 153, so that the code explicitly sets the extent of Particletype to the right value, rather than trusting MPI to compute fills correctly.

```
struct Partstruct
{
  char    class;  /* particle class */
  double  d[6];   /* particle coordinates */
  char    b[7];   /* some additional information */
};

void SendParticle( MPI_Comm comm )
{
struct Partstruct    particle[1000];
int           i, dest, tag;
MPI_Datatype Particletype, ptype;
MPI_Datatype type[3] = {MPI_CHAR, MPI_DOUBLE, MPI_CHAR};
int           blocklen[3] = {1, 6, 7};
MPI_Aint     disp[3];

/* compute displacements of structure components */
MPI_Get_address(&particle[0].class, &disp[0]);
MPI_Get_address(&particle[0].d, &disp[1]);
MPI_Get_address(&particle[0].b, &disp[2]);
```

```
for (i=2; i >= 0; i--) disp[i] -= disp[0];

/* resize */
MPI_Type_create_struct(3, blocklen, disp, type, &ptype);

/* build datatype for structure */
MPI_Type_create_resized(ptype, 0, sizeof(struct Partstruct),
                        &Particletype);
MPI_Type_commit(&Particletype);

/* send the entire array */
MPI_Send(particle, 1000, Particletype, dest, tag, comm);
```

...

Example 3.24 We modify Example 3.9, page 135, using datatype resizing, rather then the hvector constructor.

```
REAL a(100,100), b(100,100)
INTEGER row, row1, lb, sizeofreal, myrank, ierr
INTEGER status(MPI_STATUS_SIZE)

!    transpose matrix a into b

CALL MPI_COMM_RANK(MPI_COMM_WORLD, myrank, ierr)

CALL MPI_TYPE_GET_EXTENT(MPI_REAL, lb, sizeofreal, ierr)

!    create datatype for one row
CALL MPI_TYPE_VECTOR(100, 1, 100, MPI_REAL, row, ierr)

!    resize row datatype to the extent of one matrix entry
CALL MPI_TYPE_CREATE_RESIZED(row, 0, sizeofreal, row, row1, ierr)

CALL MPI_TYPE_COMMIT(row1, ierr)

!    send matrix in row-major order and receive in column major order
CALL MPI_SENDRECV(a, 100, row1, myrank, 0, b, 100*100, &
                  MPI_REAL, myrank, 0, MPI_COMM_WORLD, status, ierr)
```

3.7.1 True Extent of Datatypes

The capability of associating "artificial" extents to datatypes is very convenient, as shown in the previous examples. It has, however, one undesirable consequence. When only "natural" extents are used (no lower and upper bound markers) a memory area of size extent(datatype) is sufficient to hold a copy of the communication buffer described by datatype. This is not true with artificial extents. This complicates the implementation of communication libraries that require the allocation of buffer space. The following function solves this problem:

MPI_TYPE_GET_TRUE_EXTENT(datatype, true_lb, true_extent)

IN	datatype	datatype to get information on (handle)
OUT	true_lb	true lower bound of datatype (integer)
OUT	true_extent	true size of datatype (integer)

```
int MPI_Type_get_true_extent(MPI_Datatype datatype, MPI_Aint *true_lb,
    MPI_Aint *true_extent)
```

```
MPI_TYPE_GET_TRUE_EXTENT(DATATYPE, TRUE_LB, TRUE_EXTENT, IERROR)
    INTEGER DATATYPE, IERROR
    INTEGER(KIND = MPI_ADDRESS_KIND) TRUE_LB, TRUE_EXTENT
```

```
void MPI::Datatype::Get_true_extent(MPI::Aint& true_lb,
    MPI::Aint& true_extent) const
```

true_lb returns the offset of the lowest unit of store which is addressed by the datatype, i.e., the lower bound of the corresponding type map, ignoring MPI_LB markers. true_extent returns the true size of the datatype, i.e., the extent of the corresponding type map, ignoring MPI_LB and MPI_UB markers, and performing no rounding for alignment. If the type map associated with datatype is

$$Typemap = \{(type_0, disp_0), \ldots, (type_{n-1}, disp_{n-1})\}$$

then

$$true\_lb(Typemap) = min_j\{disp_j \ : \ type_j \neq \mathsf{lb}, \mathsf{ub}\},$$

$$true\_ub(Typemap) = max_j\{disp_j + sizeof(type_j) \ : \ type_j \neq \mathsf{lb}, \mathsf{ub}\},$$

and

$true\_extent(Typemap) = true\_ub(Typemap) - true\_lb(typemap).$

(Readers should compare this with the definitions on page 156.)

Advice to users.   A memory area of size extent, as returned by a call to MPI_
TYPE_GET_TRUE_EXTENT(type, lb, extent), is sufficient to store a copy of the
communication buffer described by type. However, the actual size of the data in
the communication buffer may be much smaller than extent, if the datatype is not
contiguous. One can easily construct (using the MPI_GET_ADDRESS and MPI_
TYPE_CREATE_STRUCT functions) a datatype with a true extent that spans the
entire application space, but contains only two data items, at the bottom and the
top of this space. In order to identify the locations of the gaps in a communication
buffer and compress the data, it is necessary to decode the datatype that describes
it, using the functions in Section II-6.6. ☐

3.8   Absolute Addresses

Consider Example 3.21 on page 153. One computes the "absolute address" of
the structure components, using calls to MPI_GET_ADDRESS, then subtracts the
starting address of the array to compute relative displacements. When the send
operation is executed, the starting address of the array is added back, in order to
compute the send buffer location. These superfluous arithmetics could be avoided
if "absolute" addresses were used in the derived datatype, and "address zero" was
passed as the buffer argument in the send call.

MPI supports the use of such "absolute" addresses in derived datatypes. The
displacement arguments used in datatype constructors can be "absolute addresses", i.e., addresses returned by calls to MPI_GET_ADDRESS. "Address zero"
is indicated to communication functions by passing the constant MPI_BOTTOM
(MPI::BOTTOM, in C++) as the buffer argument.

Example 3.25   The code in Example 3.21 on page 153 is modified to use absolute
addresses, rather than relative displacements.

```
struct Partstruct
{
  char   class;  /* particle class */
  double d[6];   /* particle coordinates */
  char   b[7];   /* some additional information */
};
```

```
struct Partstruct    particle[1000];
int                  dest, tag;
MPI_Comm     comm;

/* build datatype describing structure */

MPI_Datatype Particletype;
MPI_Datatype type[3] = {MPI_CHAR, MPI_DOUBLE, MPI_CHAR};
int          blocklen[3] = {1, 6, 7};
MPI_Aint     disp[3];

/* compute addresses of components in 1st structure*/
MPI_Get_address(particle, disp);
MPI_Get_address(particle[0].d, disp+1);
MPI_Get_address(particle[0].b, disp+2);

/* build datatype for 1st structure */
MPI_Type_create_struct(3, blocklen, disp, type, &Particletype);
MPI_Type_commit(&Particletype);

/*  send the entire array */
MPI_Send(MPI_BOTTOM, 1000, Particletype, dest, tag, comm);
```

MPI_BOTTOM is a reference constant (see Section 1.9, page 14. It cannot be used in Fortran, except as a buffer argument.

Advice to users.   MPI_BOTTOM is not necessarily equal to zero. It is incorrect to pass 0 or NULL, instead of MPI_BOTTOM. Similarly, in Fortran MPI_BOTTOM cannot be replaced by 0. □

3.9   Array Datatype Constructors

The two datatype constructors introduced in this section are convenience functions that facilitate common array manipulations: The extraction of a subarray from an array, and the distribution of an array on a processor grid.

MPI_TYPE_CREATE_SUBARRAY(ndims, array_of_sizes, array_of_subsizes,
    array_of_starts, order, oldtype, newtype)

IN	ndims	number of array dimensions (integer)
IN	array_of_sizes	number of elements in each array dimension (array of integers)
IN	array_of_subsizes	number of elements subarray dimension (array of integers)
IN	array_of_starts	starting coordinates of subarray (array of integers)
IN	order	array storage order flag (state)
IN	oldtype	array element datatype (handle)
OUT	newtype	new datatype (handle)

```
int MPI_Type_create_subarray(int ndims, int *array_of_sizes,
    int *array_of_subsizes, int *array_of_starts, int order,
    MPI_Datatype oldtype, MPI_Datatype *newtype)
```

```
MPI_TYPE_CREATE_SUBARRAY(NDIMS, ARRAY_OF_SIZES, ARRAY_OF_SUBSIZES,
    ARRAY_OF_STARTS, ORDER, OLDTYPE, NEWTYPE, IERROR)
    INTEGER NDIMS, ARRAY_OF_SIZES(*), ARRAY_OF_SUBSIZES(*),
    ARRAY_OF_STARTS(*), ORDER, OLDTYPE, NEWTYPE, IERROR
```

```
MPI::Datatype MPI::Datatype::Create_subarray(int ndims,
    const int array_of_sizes[], const int array_of_subsizes[],
    const int array_of_starts[], int order) const
```

The subarray type constructor creates an MPI datatype describing an n-dimensional contiguous subarray of an n-dimensional array. The subarray may be situated anywhere within the full array, and may be of any size. This type constructor facilitates extracting and sending or receiving a subarray from an array.

This type constructor can handle arrays with an arbitrary number of dimensions and works for both C and Fortran ordered matrices (i.e., row-major or column-major). Note that a C program may use Fortran order and a Fortran program may use C order.

The ndims parameter specifies the number of dimensions in the full data array and gives the number of elements in array_of_sizes, array_of_subsizes, and array_of_starts.

The number of elements in each dimension of the n-dimensional array and the requested subarray are specified by array_of_sizes and array_of_subsizes, respectively. For any dimension i, it is erroneous to specify array_of_subsizes[i] < 1 or array_of_subsizes[i] > array_of_sizes[i].

The array_of_starts contains the starting coordinates of the subarray in the array. Arrays are assumed to be indexed starting from zero. For any dimension i, it is erroneous to specify array_of_starts[i] < 0 or array_of_starts[i] > (array_of_sizes[i] − array_of_subsizes[i]).

Advice to users. In a Fortran program with arrays indexed starting from 1, if the starting coordinate of a particular dimension of the subarray is n, then the entry in array_of_starts for that dimension is n-1. ☐

The order argument specifies the storage order for the subarray as well as the full array. It must be set to one of the following:

MPI_ORDER_C The ordering used by C arrays, (i.e., row-major order)

MPI_ORDER_FORTRAN The ordering used by Fortran arrays, (i.e., column-major order)

(The C++ constants are MPI::ORDER_C and MPI::ORDER_FORTRAN.)

A ndims-dimensional subarray (newtype) with no extra padding can be defined by the function Subarray() as follows:

$$
\begin{aligned}
\textsf{newtype} \quad = \quad & \text{Subarray}(ndims, \{size_0, size_1, \ldots, size_{ndims-1}\}, \\
& \{subsize_0, subsize_1, \ldots, subsize_{ndims-1}\}, \\
& \{start_0, start_1, \ldots, start_{ndims-1}\}, \textsf{oldtype})
\end{aligned}
$$

Let the typemap of oldtype have the form:

$$
\{(type_0, disp_0), (type_1, disp_1), \ldots, (type_{n-1}, disp_{n-1})\}
$$

where $type_i$ is a predefined MPI datatype, and let ex be the extent of oldtype. Then we define the Subarray() function recursively using the following three equations. Equation 3.9.1 defines the base step. Equation 3.9.2 defines the recursion step when order = MPI_ORDER_FORTRAN, and Equation 3.9.3 defines the recursion step when order = MPI_ORDER_C.

$$
\begin{aligned}
& \text{Subarray}(1, \{size_0\}, \{subsize_0\}, \{start_0\}, \tag{3.9.1} \\
& \qquad \{(type_0, disp_0), (type_1, disp_1), \ldots, (type_{n-1}, disp_{n-1})\}) \\
= \ & \{(\textsf{MPI\_LB}, 0), \\
& (type_0, disp_0 + start_0 \times ex), \ldots, (type_{n-1}, disp_{n-1} + start_0 \times ex), \\
& (type_0, disp_0 + (start_0 + 1) \times ex), \ldots, (type_{n-1}, \\
& \qquad disp_{n-1} + (start_0 + 1) \times ex), \ldots \\
& (type_0, disp_0 + (start_0 + subsize_0 - 1) \times ex), \ldots, \\
& \qquad (type_{n-1}, disp_{n-1} + (start_0 + subsize_0 - 1) \times ex), \\
& (\textsf{MPI\_UB}, size_0 \times ex)\}
\end{aligned}
$$

$$\text{Subarray}(ndims, \{size_0, size_1, \ldots, size_{ndims-1}\}, \tag{3.9.2}$$
$$\{subsize_0, subsize_1, \ldots, subsize_{ndims-1}\},$$
$$\{start_0, start_1, \ldots, start_{ndims-1}\}, \textsf{oldtype})$$
$$= \quad \text{Subarray}(ndims-1, \{size_1, size_2, \ldots, size_{ndims-1}\},$$
$$\{subsize_1, subsize_2, \ldots, subsize_{ndims-1}\},$$
$$\{start_1, start_2, \ldots, start_{ndims-1}\},$$
$$\text{Subarray}(1, \{size_0\}, \{subsize_0\}, \{start_0\}, \textsf{oldtype}))$$

$$\text{Subarray}(ndims, \{size_0, size_1, \ldots, size_{ndims-1}\}, \tag{3.9.3}$$
$$\{subsize_0, subsize_1, \ldots, subsize_{ndims-1}\},$$
$$\{start_0, start_1, \ldots, start_{ndims-1}\}, \textsf{oldtype})$$
$$= \quad \text{Subarray}(ndims-1, \{size_0, size_1, \ldots, size_{ndims-2}\},$$
$$\{subsize_0, subsize_1, \ldots, subsize_{ndims-2}\},$$
$$\{start_0, start_1, \ldots, start_{ndims-2}\},$$
$$\text{Subarray}(1, \{size_{ndims-1}\}, \{subsize_{ndims-1}\},$$
$$\{start_{ndims-1}\}, \textsf{oldtype}))$$

For an example use of MPI_TYPE_CREATE_SUBARRAY in the context of I/O see Section II-7.9.3.

MPI_TYPE_CREATE_DARRAY(size, rank, ndims, array_of_gsizes, array_of_distribs, array_of_dargs, array_of_psizes, order, oldtype, newtype)

IN	size	size of process group (integer)
IN	rank	rank in process group (integer)
IN	ndims	number of array dimensions (integer)
IN	array_of_gsizes	number of array elements in each dimension (array of integers)
IN	array_of_distribs	distribution of array in each dimension (array of states)
IN	array_of_dargs	distribution argument in each dimension (array of integers)
IN	array_of_psizes	size of process grid in each dimension (array of integers)
IN	order	array storage order (state)
IN	oldtype	type of each element (handle)
OUT	newtype	new datatype (handle)

```
int MPI_Type_create_darray(int size, int rank, int ndims,
    int *array_of_gsizes, int *array_of_distribs, int *array_of_dargs,
    int *array_of_psizes, int order, MPI_Datatype oldtype,
    MPI_Datatype *newtype)
```

```
MPI_TYPE_CREATE_DARRAY(SIZE, RANK, NDIMS, ARRAY_OF_GSIZES,
    ARRAY_OF_DISTRIBS, ARRAY_OF_DARGS, ARRAY_OF_PSIZES, ORDER,
    OLDTYPE, NEWTYPE, IERROR)
    INTEGER SIZE, RANK, NDIMS, ARRAY_OF_GSIZES(*),
    ARRAY_OF_DISTRIBS(*), ARRAY_OF_DARGS(*), ARRAY_OF_PSIZES(*),
    ORDER, OLDTYPE, NEWTYPE, IERROR
```

```
MPI::Datatype MPI::Datatype::Create_darray(int size, int rank,
    int ndims, const int array_of_gsizes[],
    const int array_of_distribs[], const int array_of_dargs[],
    const int array_of_psizes[], int order) const
```

MPI_TYPE_CREATE_DARRAY helps with arrays that are distributed HPF-like [25] on Cartesian process grids. However, unlike in HPF, the storage order may be specified for C arrays as well as for Fortran arrays. The functions can be used to generate the datatypes corresponding to the subarrays to be stored on each process. This can be used to distribute an array, or to assemble it back. The call generates a datatype that describes one subarray, corresponding to one process in the process grid.

The total size of the process grid is specified by the argument size.

The call computes a datatype that describes the subarray for the process with rank rank. It must be $0 \leq$ rank $<$ size. The ordering of processes in the process grid is assumed to be row-major, as in the case for virtual Cartesian process topologies in MPI.

ndims is the number of array and process grid dimensions.

The array array_of_gsizes has ndims elements that specify the number of elements of the array in each dimension.

The array array_of_psizes has ndims elements that specify the number of elements of the process grid in each dimension. For a call to MPI_TYPE_CREATE_DARRAY to be correct, the equation $\prod_{i=0}^{ndims-1} array\_of\_psizes[i] = size$ must be satisfied.

The array array_of_distribs has ndims elements that specify the type of distribution for each array dimension. Each dimension of the array can be distributed in one of three ways, specified by the following special values.

- MPI_DISTRIBUTE_BLOCK - Block distribution
- MPI_DISTRIBUTE_CYCLIC - Cyclic distribution
- MPI_DISTRIBUTE_NONE - Dimension not distributed.

(The C++ constants are MPI::DISTRIBUTE_BLOCK, MPI::DISTRIBUTE_CYCLIC, and MPI::DISTRIBUTE_NONE, respectively.)

The array array_of_dargs has ndims elements that specify the distribution argument for each dimension. The special value MPI_DISTRIBUTE_DFLT_DARG (MPI::-DISTRIBUTE_DFLT_DARG, in C++) can be used to specify default distribution. Thus, if array_of_disribs[i] = MPI_DISTRIBUTE_BLOCK and array_of_dargs[i] = k then the i-th dimension of the array is distributed with a BLOCK(k) HPF distribution. If array_of_dargs[i] = MPI_DISTRIBUTE_DFLT_DARG then the i-th dimension of the array is distributed with a BLOCK HPF distribution. And, similarly, for cyclic.

The distribution argument for a dimension that is not distributed is ignored.

For any dimension i in which the distribution is MPI_DISTRIBUTE_BLOCK, it is erroneous to specify array_of_dargs[i] * array_of_psizes[i] < array_of_gsizes[i].

The order argument is used as in MPI_TYPE_CREATE_SUBARRAY to specify the storage order. Therefore, arrays described by this type constructor may be stored in Fortran (column-major) or C (row-major) order. Valid values for order are MPI_ORDER_FORTRAN and MPI_ORDER_C.

This routine creates a new MPI datatype with a typemap defined in terms of a function called "cyclic()" (see below).

Without loss of generality, it suffices to define the typemap for the MPI_DISTRIBUTE_CYCLIC case where MPI_DISTRIBUTE_DFLT_DARG is not used.

MPI_DISTRIBUTE_BLOCK and MPI_DISTRIBUTE_NONE can be reduced to the MPI_DISTRIBUTE_CYCLIC case for dimension i as follows.

MPI_DISTRIBUTE_BLOCK with array_of_dargs[i] equal to MPI_DISTRIBUTE_DFLT_DARG is equivalent to MPI_DISTRIBUTE_CYCLIC with array_of_dargs[i] set to

(array_of_gsizes[i] + array_of_psizes[i] − 1)/array_of_psizes[i].

If array_of_dargs[i] is not MPI_DISTRIBUTE_DFLT_DARG, then MPI_DISTRIBUTE_BLOCK and MPI_DISTRIBUTE_CYCLIC are equivalent.

MPI_DISTRIBUTE_NONE is equivalent to MPI_DISTRIBUTE_CYCLIC with array_of_dargs[i] set to array_of_gsizes[i].

Finally, MPI_DISTRIBUTE_CYCLIC with array_of_dargs[i] equal to MPI_DISTRIBUTE_DFLT_DARG is equivalent to MPI_DISTRIBUTE_CYCLIC with array_of_dargs[i] set to 1.

For MPI_ORDER_FORTRAN, an ndims-dimensional distributed array (newtype) is defined by the following code fragment:

```
type[0] = oldtype;
for ( i = 0; i < ndims; i++ ) {
   type[i+1] = cyclic(array_of_dargs[i],
                      array_of_gsizes[i],
                      r[i],
                      array_of_psizes[i],
                      type[i]);
}
newtype = type[ndims];
```

For MPI_ORDER_C, the code is:

```
type[0] = oldtype;
for ( i = 0; i < ndims; i++ ) {
   type[i + 1] = cyclic(array_of_dargs[ndims - i - 1],
                        array_of_gsizes[ndims - i - 1],
                        r[ndims - i - 1],
                        array_of_psizes[ndims - i - 1],
                        type[i]);
}
newtype = type[ndims];
```

where $r[i]$ is the position of the process (with rank rank) in the process grid at dimension i. The values of $r[i]$ are given by the following code fragment:

```
t_rank = rank;
t_size = 1;
for (i = 0; i < ndims; i++)
        t_size *= array_of_psizes[i];
for (i = 0; i < ndims; i++) {
    t_size = t_size / array_of_psizes[i];
    r[i] = t_rank / t_size;
    t_rank = t_rank % t_size;
}
```

Let the typemap of oldtype have the form:

$$\{(type_0, disp_0), (type_1, disp_1), \ldots, (type_{n-1}, disp_{n-1})\}$$

where $type_i$ is a predefined MPI datatype, and let ex be the extent of oldtype.

Given the above, the function cyclic() is defined as follows:

cyclic($darg, gsize, r, psize,$ oldtype)

$= \quad \{(\text{MPI\_LB}, 0),$

$\quad (type_0, disp_0 + r \times darg \times ex), \ldots,$

$\qquad\qquad (type_{n-1}, disp_{n-1} + r \times darg \times ex),$

$\quad (type_0, disp_0 + (r \times darg + 1) \times ex), \ldots,$

$\qquad\qquad (type_{n-1}, disp_{n-1} + (r \times darg + 1) \times ex),$

$\quad \ldots$

$\quad (type_0, disp_0 + ((r + 1) \times darg - 1) \times ex), \ldots,$

$\qquad\qquad (type_{n-1}, disp_{n-1} + ((r + 1) \times darg - 1) \times ex),$

$\quad (type_0, disp_0 + r \times darg \times ex + psize \times darg \times ex), \ldots,$

$\qquad\qquad (type_{n-1}, disp_{n-1} + r \times darg \times ex + psize \times darg \times ex),$

$\quad (type_0, disp_0 + (r \times darg + 1) \times ex + psize \times darg \times ex), \ldots,$

$\qquad\qquad (type_{n-1}, disp_{n-1} + (r \times darg + 1) \times ex + psize \times darg \times ex),$

$\quad \ldots$

$\quad (type_0, disp_0 + ((r + 1) \times darg - 1) \times ex + psize \times darg \times ex), \ldots,$

$\qquad\qquad (type_{n-1}, disp_{n-1} + ((r + 1) \times darg - 1) \times ex + psize \times darg \times ex),$

$\qquad\qquad \vdots$

$\quad (type_0, disp_0 + r \times darg \times ex + psize \times darg \times ex \times (count - 1)), \ldots,$

$\qquad\qquad (type_{n-1}, disp_{n-1} + r \times darg \times ex$

$\qquad\qquad + psize \times darg \times ex \times (count - 1)),$

$\quad (type_0, disp_0 + (r \times darg + 1) \times ex + psize \times darg \times ex \times (count - 1)), \ldots,$

$\qquad\qquad (type_{n-1}, disp_{n-1} + (r \times darg + 1) \times ex$

$\qquad\qquad\qquad + psize \times darg \times ex \times (count - 1)),$

$\quad \ldots$

$\quad (type_0, disp_0 + (r \times darg + darg_{last} - 1) \times ex$

$\qquad\qquad\qquad + psize \times darg \times ex \times (count - 1)), \ldots,$

$\qquad\qquad (type_{n-1}, disp_{n-1} + (r \times darg + darg_{last} - 1) \times ex$

$$+psize \times darg \times ex \times (count - 1)),$$
$$(\text{MPI\_UB}, gsize * ex)\}$$

where *count* is defined by this code fragment:

```
nblocks = (gsize + (darg - 1)) / darg;
count = nblocks / psize;
left_over = nblocks - count * psize;
if (r < left_over)
    count = count + 1;
```

Here, *nblocks* is the number of blocks that must be distributed among the processors. Finally, $darg_{last}$ is defined by this code fragment:

```
if ((num_in_last_cyclic = gsize % (psize * darg)) == 0)
    darg_last = darg;
else
    darg_last = num_in_last_cyclic - darg * r;
    if (darg_last > darg)
            darg_last = darg;
    if (darg_last <= 0)
            darg_last = darg;
```

Example 3.26   Consider generating the types corresponding to the HPF distribution:

```
    REAL ARRAY(100, 200, 300)
!HPF$ PROCESSORS PROCESSES(2, 3)
!HPF$ DISTRIBUTE ARRAY(CYCLIC(10), *, BLOCK) ONTO PROCESSES
```

This can be achieved by the following Fortran code, assuming there will be six processes attached to the run:

```
ndims = 3
array_of_gsizes(1) = 100
array_of_distribs(1) = MPI_DISTRIBUTE_CYCLIC
array_of_dargs(1) = 10
array_of_gsizes(2) = 200
array_of_distribs(2) = MPI_DISTRIBUTE_NONE
```

```
array_of_dargs(2) = 0
array_of_gsizes(3) = 300
array_of_distribs(3) = MPI_DISTRIBUTE_BLOCK
array_of_dargs(3) = MPI_DISTRIBUTE_DFLT_ARG
array_of_psizes(1) = 2
array_of_psizes(2) = 1
array_of_psizes(3) = 3
call MPI_COMM_SIZE(MPI_COMM_WORLD, size, ierr)
call MPI_COMM_RANK(MPI_COMM_WORLD, rank, ierr)
call MPI_TYPE_CREATE_DARRAY(size, rank, ndims,               &
     array_of_gsizes, array_of_distribs, array_of_dargs,     &
     array_of_psizes, MPI_ORDER_FORTRAN, oldtype, newtype,   &
     ierr)
```

3.10   Portability of Datatypes

Example 3.27   Consider the following two datatype

```
MPI_Datatype type1, type2;
MPI_Type_contiguous(2, MPI_INT, &type1);
MPI_Type_create_hvector(2, 1, 8, MPI_INT, &type2);
```

Assume that an int takes 8 bytes of storage. Then both type1 and type2 have the same typemap, namely (0, int), (8, int), and both describe the same data layout in memory. On the other hand, the two datatypes would describe different data layouts on a machine where ints take 4 bytes: in the first case, it would be (0, int), (4, int) while in the second case it would be (0, int), (8, int). The first datatype will fit an array with two ints in both environments. The second datatypes fits such an array only on systems where ints take 8 bytes. This simple example shows that care has to be exercised when using derived datatypes with byte displacements in a heterogeneous environment.

A datatype is **portable** if it is a predefined datatype or is derived from a portable datatype using only the type constructors MPI_TYPE_CREATE_CONTIGUOUS, MPI_TYPE_CREATE_VECTOR, MPI_TYPE_CREATE_INDEXED, MPI_-TYPE_CREATE_INDEXED_BLOCK, MPI_TYPE_CREATE_SUBARRAY, MPI_TYPE_-DUP, and MPI_TYPE_CREATE_DARRAY. Such a datatype is portable because all displacements in the datatype are in terms of extents of one predefined datatype. Therefore, if such a datatype fits a data layout in one memory, it will fit the corresponding data layout in another memory if the same declarations were used, even if the two systems have different architectures. On the other hand, if a datatype was constructed using MPI_TYPE_CREATE_HINDEXED, MPI_TYPE_CREATE_-HVECTOR or MPI_TYPE_CREATE_STRUCT, then the datatype contains explicit byte displacements (e.g., providing padding to meet alignment restrictions). These displacements are unlikely to be chosen correctly if they fit data layout on one memory, but are used for data layouts on another process running on a processor with a different architecture.

3.11   Deprecated Functions

MPI-2 replaced some of the constructor and accessor functions defined in MPI-1 for the following two reasons.

• The Fortran binding of the MPI-1 functions used INTEGERs for addresses and byte displacements. This caused problems on systems that use 64 bit addresses but 32 bit INTEGERs. Datatypes could not span more than 2 GB of address space, and the use of absolute addresses was restricted to the lower 2 GB of the application address space. This was a serious problem. Even if an application uses less than 2 GB of memory, the memory it uses usually consists of several segments (stack, heap, etc.) that need not be contiguous in virtual memory. Byte displacements and absolute addresses may span more than 2 GB. The replacement MPI-2 functions use address-sized addresses and byte displacements, thus solving this problem.

• MPI-1 supported the explicit control of datatype bounds and extent by providing the two predefined datatypes MPI_LB and MPI_UB. Users could create datatypes that contain these markers, using the MPI_TYPE_CREATE_STRUCT function. This was an awkward mechanism. More importantly, MPI-1 did not provide a mechanism for erasing upper bound and lower bound markers. As a result, once a datatype was resized, and its type map contained upper bound and lower bound markers, the lower bound could be extended downward, but never upward; the upper bound could be extended upward, but not downward; the extent could be increased, but not decreased. This problem is solved by MPI_TYPE_CREATE_RESIZED.

We list below the deprecated MPI-1 functions and constants, with their C and Fortran bindings, followed by their replacement. As usual, deprecated functions continue to be part of the MPI standard, but users are strongly encouraged to use the new functions, whenever available (see Section 1.9.1 for the status of deprecated functions).

MPI_TYPE_EXTENT(datatype, extent)

```
int MPI_Type_extent(MPI_Datatype datatype, MPI_Aint *extent)
```

```
MPI_TYPE_EXTENT(DATATYPE, EXTENT, IERROR)
    INTEGER DATATYPE, EXTENT, IERROR
```

MPI_TYPE_LB(datatype, displacement)

```
int MPI_Type_lb(MPI_Datatype datatype, MPI_Aint* displacement)
```

```
MPI_TYPE_LB(DATATYPE, DISPLACEMENT, IERROR)
    INTEGER DATATYPE, DISPLACEMENT, IERROR
```

MPI_TYPE_UB(datatype, displacement)

```
int MPI_Type_ub(MPI_Datatype datatype, MPI_Aint* displacement)
```

```
MPI_TYPE_UB(DATATYPE, DISPLACEMENT, IERROR)
    INTEGER DATATYPE, DISPLACEMENT, IERROR
```

These three functions are replaced by the one function MPI_TYPE_GET_EXTENT(datatype, extent, lb). The new function returns in one call the lower bound and the extent of the datatype, from which the upper bound can be computed; MPI-1 had each of these three parameters returned by a separate call. Furthermore, the Fortran binding of the old functions specify that the returned values are of type INTEGER, whereas the new function returns arguments of type INTEGER(KIND=MPI_- ADDRESS_KIND).

MPI_TYPE_HVECTOR(count, blocklength, stride, oldtype, newtype)

```
int MPI_Type_hvector(int count, int blocklength, MPI_Aint stride,
    MPI_Datatype oldtype, MPI_Datatype *newtype)
```

```
MPI_TYPE_HVECTOR(COUNT, BLOCKLENGTH, STRIDE, OLDTYPE, NEWTYPE,
    IERROR)
    INTEGER COUNT, BLOCKLENGTH, STRIDE, OLDTYPE, NEWTYPE, IERROR
```

Replaced by MPI_TYPE_CREATE_HVECTOR(count, blocklength, stride, oldtype, newtype). The language-neutral definition and the C binding are the same. The Fortran binding differ in that the old function used an INTEGER STRIDE argument, whereas the new function uses an argument of type INTEGER(KIND=MPI_ADDRESS_- KIND).

MPI_TYPE_HINDEXED(count, array_of_blocklengths, array_of_displacements, old-type, newtype)

```
int MPI_Type_hindexed(int count, int *array_of_blocklengths,
    MPI_Aint *array_of_displacements, MPI_Datatype oldtype,
    MPI_Datatype *newtype)
```

```
MPI_TYPE_HINDEXED(COUNT, ARRAY_OF_BLOCKLENGTHS,
    ARRAY_OF_DISPLACEMENTS, OLDTYPE, NEWTYPE, IERROR)
    INTEGER COUNT, ARRAY_OF_BLOCKLENGTHS(*),
    ARRAY_OF_DISPLACEMENTS(*), OLDTYPE, NEWTYPE, IERROR
```

Replaced by MPI_TYPE_CREATE_HINDEXED(count, array_of_blocklengths, array_of_displacements, oldtype, newtype). The language-neutral definition and the C binding are the same. The Fortran binding differ in that the old function used an INTEGER ARRAY_OF_DISPLACEMENTS(*) argument, whereas the new function uses an argument of type INTEGER(KIND=MPI_ADDRESS_KIND).

MPI_TYPE_STRUCT(count, array_of_blocklengths, array_of_displacements, array_-of_types, newtype)

```
int MPI_Type_struct(int count, int *array_of_blocklengths,
    MPI_Aint *array_of_displacements, MPI_Datatype *array_of_types,
    MPI_Datatype *newtype)
```

```
MPI_TYPE_STRUCT(COUNT, ARRAY_OF_BLOCKLENGTHS, ARRAY_OF_DISPLACEMENTS,
    ARRAY_OF_TYPES, NEWTYPE, IERROR)
    INTEGER COUNT, ARRAY_OF_BLOCKLENGTHS(*),
    ARRAY_OF_DISPLACEMENTS(*), ARRAY_OF_TYPES(*), NEWTYPE, IERROR
```

Replaced by MPI_TYPE_CREATE_STRUCT(count, array_of_blocklengths, array_of_-displacements, array_of_types, newtype). The language neutral definition and the C ARRAY_OF_DISPLACEMENTS(*) binding are the same. The Fortran binding differ in that the old function used an INTEGER ARRAY_OF_DISPLACEMENTS(*) argument, whereas the new function uses an argument of type INTEGER(KIND=MPI_-ADDRESS_KIND).

MPI_ADDRESS(location, address)

```
int MPI_Address(void* location, MPI_Aint *address)
```

```
MPI_ADDRESS(LOCATION, ADDRESS, IERROR)
    <type> LOCATION(*)
    INTEGER ADDRESS, IERROR
```

Replaced by MPI_GET_ADDRESS(location, address). The language neutral definition and the C binding are the same. The Fortran binding differ in that the old function used an INTEGER ADDRESS argument, whereas the new function uses an argument of type INTEGER(KIND=MPI_ADDRESS_KIND).

The use of the two "pseudo-datatypes," MPI_LB and MPI_UB, is replaced by calls to MPI_TYPE_CREATE_RESIZED.

Example 3.28   Consider the sequence of calls in Example 3.22, page 156. Then the the first call can be replaced by the following equivalent (MPI-1) code.

```
MPI_Datatype types[3];
MPI_Aint disps[3];
int blens[3];

types[0] = MPI_LB;
types[1] = MPI_UB;
types[2] = type0;

disps[0] = -4;
disps[1] = 8;
disps[2] = 0;

blens[0] = blens[1] = blens[2] = 1;

MPI_Type_struct(3, blens, disps, types, &type1);
```

There is no MPI-1 code that is equivalent to the second call to MPI_TYPE_-CREATE_RESIZED. This because this call moves an existing MPI_LB marker up – this cannot be done in MPI-1.

If MPI_ADDRESS is used, in Fortran, to access an address, then the address may be truncated (the least significant part of the variable is returned, with the sign extended). Also, the displacement returned by a call to MPI_GET_EXTENT, MPI_-GET_LB, or MPI_GET_UB may be truncated, if the displacement was created by "new style" datatype constructors. Conversely, if one of the deprecated datatype constructor is used in Fortran, then the input INTEGER address argument will be converted to an address-sized value.

3.12   Pack and Unpack

Some existing communication libraries, such as PVM [33] and Parmacs [3], provide pack and unpack functions for sending noncontiguous data. In these, the application explicitly packs data into a contiguous buffer before sending it, and unpacks it from a contiguous buffer after receiving it. Derived datatypes, described in the previous sections of this chapter, allow one, in most cases, to avoid explicit packing and unpacking. The application specifies the layout of the data to be sent or received, and MPI directly accesses a noncontiguous buffer when derived datatypes are used. The pack/unpack routines are provided for compatibility with previous libraries. Also, they provide some functionality that is not otherwise available in MPI. For instance, a message can be received in several parts, where the receive operation done on a later part may depend on the content of a former part. Another use is that the availability of pack and unpack operations facilitates the development of additional communication libraries layered on top of MPI.

MPI_PACK(inbuf, incount, datatype, outbuf, outsize, position, comm)

IN	inbuf	input buffer (choice)
IN	incount	number of input components (integer)
IN	datatype	datatype of each input component (handle)
OUT	outbuf	output buffer (choice)
IN	outsize	output buffer size, in bytes (integer)
INOUT	position	current position in buffer, in bytes (integer)
IN	comm	communicator for packed message (handle)

```
int MPI_Pack(void* inbuf, int incount, MPI_Datatype datatype,
    void *outbuf, int outsize, int *position, MPI_Comm comm)
```

```
MPI_PACK(INBUF, INCOUNT, DATATYPE, OUTBUF, OUTSIZE, POSITION, COMM,
    IERROR)
    <type> INBUF(*), OUTBUF(*)
    INTEGER INCOUNT, DATATYPE, OUTSIZE, POSITION, COMM, IERROR
```

```
void MPI::Datatype::Pack(const void* inbuf, int incount,
    void* outbuf, int outsize, int& position, const MPI::Comm &comm)
    const
```

MPI_PACK packs a message specified by inbuf, incount, datatype, comm into the buffer space specified by outbuf and outsize. The input buffer can be any communication buffer allowed in MPI_SEND. The output buffer is a contiguous storage area containing outsize bytes, starting at the address outbuf.

The input value of position is the first position in the output buffer (relative to buffer start) to be used for packing. The argument position is incremented by the size of the packed message so that it can be used as input to a subsequent call to MPI_PACK. The comm argument is the communicator that will be subsequently used for sending the packed message.

MPI_UNPACK(inbuf, insize, position, outbuf, outcount, datatype, comm)

IN	inbuf	input buffer (choice)
IN	insize	size of input buffer, in bytes (integer)
INOUT	position	current position in bytes (integer)
OUT	outbuf	output buffer (choice)
IN	outcount	number of components to be unpacked (integer)
IN	datatype	datatype of each output component (handle)
IN	comm	communicator for packed message (handle)

```
int MPI_Unpack(void* inbuf, int insize, int *position, void *outbuf,
    int outcount, MPI_Datatype datatype, MPI_Comm comm)
```

```
MPI_UNPACK(INBUF, INSIZE, POSITION, OUTBUF, OUTCOUNT, DATATYPE,
    COMM, IERROR)
    <type> INBUF(*), OUTBUF(*)
    INTEGER INSIZE, POSITION, OUTCOUNT, DATATYPE, COMM, IERROR
```

```
void MPI::Datatype::Unpack(const void* inbuf, int insize,
    void* outbuf, int outcount, int& position,
    const MPI::Comm& comm) const
```

MPI_UNPACK unpacks a message into the receive buffer specified by outbuf, outcount, datatype from the buffer space specified by inbuf and insize. The output buffer can be any communication buffer allowed in MPI_RECV. The input buffer is a contiguous storage area containing insize bytes, starting at address inbuf. The input value of position is the relative position in the input buffer where one wishes the unpacking to begin. The output value of position is incremented by the size of the packed message, so that it can be used as input to a subsequent call to MPI_UNPACK. The argument comm was the communicator used to receive the packed message.

Rationale. The Pack and Unpack calls have a communicator argument in order to facilitate data conversion at the source in a heterogeneous environment. That is, this will allow for an implementation that uses the XDR format for packed data in a heterogeneous communication domain, and performs no data conversion if the communication domain is homogeneous. If no communicator was provided, the implementation would always use XDR. If the destination was provided, in addition to the communicator, then one would be able to format the pack buffer specifically for that destination. But, then, one loses the ability to pack a buffer once and send it to multiple destinations. ☐

Advice to users. Note the difference between MPI_RECV and MPI_UNPACK: in MPI_RECV, the count argument specifies the maximum number of components that can be received. In MPI_UNPACK, the count argument specifies the actual number of components that are unpacked. The reason for that change is that, for a regular receive, the incoming message size determines the number of components that will be received. With MPI_UNPACK, it is up to the user to specify how many components he or she wants to unpack, since one may want to unpack only part of the message. ☐

The MPI_PACK/MPI_UNPACK calls relate to message passing as the sprintf/sscanf calls in C relate to file I/O, or internal Fortran files relate to external units. Basically, the MPI_PACK function allows one to "send" a message into a memory buffer; the MPI_UNPACK function allows one to "receive" a message from a memory buffer.

Several communication buffers can be successively packed into one **packing unit**. This is effected by several, successive **related** calls to MPI_PACK, where the first call provides position = 0, and each successive call inputs the value of position that was output by the previous call, and the same values for outbuf, outcount and comm. This packing unit now contains the equivalent information that would have been stored in a message by one send call with a send buffer that is the "concatenation" of the individual send buffers.

A packing unit must be sent using type MPI_PACKED (MPI::PACKED, in C++). Any point-to-point or collective communication function can be used. The message sent is identical to the message that would be sent by a send operation with a datatype argument describing the concatenation of the send buffer(s) used in the

Pack calls. The message can be received with any datatype that matches this send datatype.

Example 3.29   The following two programs generate identical messages.
   Derived datatype is used:

```
int i;
char c[100];
MPI_Aint disp[2];
int blocklen[2] = {1, 100};
MPI_Datatype type[2] = {MPI_INT, MPI_CHAR};
MPI_Datatype Type;

/* create datatype */
MPI_Get_address(&i, &(disp[0]));
MPI_Get_address(c, &(disp[1]));
MPI_Type_create_struct(2, blocklen, disp, type, &Type);
MPI_Type_commit(&Type);

/* send */
MPI_Send(MPI_BOTTOM, 1, Type, 1, 0, MPI_COMM_WORLD);
```

   Packing is used:

```
int i;
char c[100];

char buffer[110];
int position = 0;

/* pack */
MPI_Pack(&i, 1, MPI_INT, buffer, 110,&position, MPI_COMM_WORLD);
MPI_Pack(c, 100, MPI_CHAR, buffer, 110, &position, MPI_COMM_WORLD);

/* send */
MPI_Send(buffer, position, MPI_PACKED, 1, 0, MPI_COMM_WORLD);
```

Any message can be received in a point-to-point or collective communication using the type MPI_PACKED. Such a message can then be unpacked by calls to

MPI_UNPACK. The message can be unpacked by several, successive calls to MPI_-UNPACK, where the first call provides position = 0, and each successive call inputs the value of position that was output by the previous call, and the same values for inbuf, insize and comm.

Example 3.30   Any of the following two programs can be used to receive the message sent in Example 3.29. The outcome will be identical.

Derived datatype is used:

```
char c[100];
MPI_Status status;
int i;
MPI_Aint disp[2];
int blocklen[2] = {1, 100};
MPI_Datatype type[2] = {MPI_INT, MPI_CHAR};
MPI_Datatype Type;

/* create datatype */
MPI_Get_address(&i, &(disp[0]));
MPI_Get_address(c, &(disp[1]));
MPI_Type_create_struct(2, blocklen, disp, type, &Type);
MPI_Type_commit(&Type);

/* receive */
MPI_Recv(MPI_BOTTOM, 1, Type, 0, 0, MPI_COMM_WORLD, &status);
```

Unpacking is used:

```
int i;
char c[100];

MPI_Status status;

char buffer[110];
int position = 0;

/* receive */
MPI_Recv(buffer, 110, MPI_PACKED, 1, 0, MPI_COMM_WORLD, &status);

/* unpack */
```

```
MPI_Unpack(buffer, 110, &position, &i, 1, MPI_INT, MPI_COMM_WORLD);
MPI_Unpack(buffer, 110, &position, c, 100, MPI_CHAR, MPI_COMM_WORLD);
```

Advice to users. A packing unit may contain, in addition to data, metadata. For example, it may contain in a header, information on the encoding used to represent data; or information on the size of the unit for error checking. Therefore, such a packing unit must be treated as an "atomic" entity which can only be sent using type MPI_PACKED. One cannot concatenate two such packing units and send the result in one send operation (however, a collective communication operation can be used to send multiple packing units in one operation, to the same extent it can be used to send multiple regular messages). Also, one cannot split a packing unit and then unpack the two halves separately (however, a collective communication operation can be used to receive multiple packing units, to the same extent it can be used to receive multiple regular messages). □

MPI_PACK_SIZE(incount, datatype, comm, size)

IN	incount	count argument to packing call (integer)
IN	datatype	datatype argument to packing call (handle)
IN	comm	communicator argument to packing call (handle)
OUT	size	upper bound on size of packed message, in bytes (integer)

```
int MPI_Pack_size(int incount, MPI_Datatype datatype, MPI_Comm comm,
    int *size)
```

```
MPI_PACK_SIZE(INCOUNT, DATATYPE, COMM, SIZE, IERROR)
    INTEGER INCOUNT, DATATYPE, COMM, SIZE, IERROR
```

```
int MPI::Datatype::Pack_size(int incount, const MPI::Comm& comm)
    const
```

MPI_PACK_SIZE allows the application to find out how much space is needed to pack a message and, thus, manage space allocation for buffers. The function returns, in size, an upper bound on the increment in position that would occur in a call to MPI_PACK with the same values for incount, datatype, and comm.

Rationale. The MPI_PACK_SIZE call returns an upper bound, rather than an exact bound, since the exact amount of space needed to pack the message may depend on the position of the message in the packing unit (for example, the first message packed in a packing unit may contain additional metadata). □

Example 3.31   We return to the problem of Example 3.15 on page 145. Process zero sends to process one a message containing all class zero particles. Process one receives and stores these structures in contiguous locations. Process zero uses calls to MPI_PACK to gather class zero particles, whereas process one uses a regular receive.

```
struct Partstruct
{
  char   class;  /* particle class */
  double d[6];   /* particle coordinates */
  char   b[7];   /* some additional information */
};
struct Partstruct   particle[1000];
int         i, size, position, myrank;
char        *buffer; /* pack buffer */
MPI_Status  status;
MPI_Comm    comm;

/* variables used to create datatype for particle */
MPI_Datatype Particletype;
MPI_Datatype type[3] = {MPI_CHAR, MPI_DOUBLE, MPI_CHAR};
int          blocklen[3] = {1, 6, 7};
MPI_Aint     disp[3] = {0, sizeof(double), 7*sizeof(double)};

/* define datatype for one particle */
MPI_Type_create_struct( 3, blocklen, disp, type, &Particletype);
MPI_Type_commit( &Particletype);
MPI_Comm_rank(comm, &myrank);

if (myrank == 0) {
  /* send message that consists of class zero particles */

  /* allocate pack buffer */
  MPI_Pack_size(1000, Particletype, comm, &size);
  buffer = (char*)malloc(size);
```

```
/* pack class zero particles */
position  = 0;
for(i=0;  i < 1000;  i++)
  if (particle[i].class == 0)
    MPI_Pack(&particle[i], 1, Particletype, buffer,
             size, &position, comm);

/* send */
MPI_Send(buffer, position, MPI_PACKED, 1, 0, comm);
}
else if (myrank == 1) {
  /* receive class zero particles in contiguous locations in
     array particle */
  MPI_Recv(particle, 1000, Particletype, 0, 0, comm, &status);
}
```

Example 3.32   This is a variant on the previous example, where the class zero particles have to be received by process one in array **particle** at the same locations where they are in the array of process zero. Process zero packs the entry index with each entry it sends. Process one uses this information to move incoming data to the right locations. As a further optimization, we avoid the transfer of the **class** field, which is known to be zero. (We have ignored in this example the computation of a tight bound on the size of the pack/unpack buffer. One could be rigorous and define an additional derived datatype for the purpose of computing such an estimate. Or one can use an approximate estimate.)

```
struct Partstruct
{
  char    class;  /* particle class */
  double d[6];    /* particle coordinates */
  char    b[7];   /* some additional information */
};
struct Partstruct    particle[1000];
int          i, myrank;
int          position = 0;
MPI_Status   status;
char         buffer[BUFSIZE]; /* pack-unpack buffer */
```

```
/* variables used to create datatype for particle,
   not including class field */

MPI_Datatype Particletype;
MPI_Datatype type[2] = {MPI_DOUBLE, MPI_CHAR};
int          blocklen[2] = {6, 7};
MPI_Aint     disp[2] = {0, 6*sizeof(double)};

/* define datatype */
MPI_Type_create_struct(2, blocklen, disp, type, &Particletype);
MPI_Type_commit(&Particletype);

MPI_Comm_rank(MPI_COMM_WORLD, &myrank);

if (myrank == 0) {
  /* send message that consists of class zero particles */

  /* pack class zero particles and their index */
  for(i=0; i < 1000; i++)
    if (particle[i].class == 0) {
      MPI_Pack(&i, 1, MPI_INT, buffer, BUFSIZE,
              &position, MPI_COMM_WORLD); /* pack index */
      MPI_Pack(particle[i].d, 1, Particletype, buffer, BUFSIZE,
              &position, MPI_COMM_WORLD); /* pack struct */
    }
  /* pack negative index as end of list marker */
  i = -1;
  MPI_Pack(&i, 1, MPI_INT, buffer, BUFSIZE, &position,
          MPI_COMM_WORLD);

  /* send */
  MPI_Send(buffer, position, MPI_PACKED, 1, 0, MPI_COMM_WORLD);
}
else if (myrank == 1) {
  /* receive class zero particles at original locations */

  /* receive */
  MPI_Recv(buffer, BUFSIZE, MPI_PACKED, 0, 0, MPI_COMM_WORLD,
```

```
              &status);

    /* unpack */
    while (MPI_Unpack(buffer, BUFSIZE, &position, &i, 1, MPI_INT,
                      MPI_COMM_WORLD) >= 0) {   /* unpack index */
       MPI_Unpack(buffer, BUFSIZE, &position, particle[i].d,
                  1, Particletype, MPI_COMM_WORLD); /* unpack struct */
       particle[i].class = 0;
    }
}
```

3.12.1   Canonical MPI_PACK and MPI_UNPACK

The design of the pack and unpack functions leaves up to the implementation to select a data format for packed data. It is sometimes desirable to specify explicitly the data format, e.g., when data is exchanged between distinct MPI implementations, or is stored into a file. The following functions read/write data to/from the buffer in the **external32** data format specified below, and calculate the size needed for packing.

The external32 format is defined as follows. Data packed with this format is stored contiguously, with no header in front of the data, and no padding spaces (byte alignment). The size of the code for each MPI type is specified in Table 3.1.

For Fortran LOGICAL and C++ bool, 0 implies false and nonzero implies true.

Characters are in ISO 8859-1 format [24].

Wide characters (of type MPI_WCHAR) are in Unicode format [34].

All signed numerals (e.g., MPI_INT, MPI_REAL) have the sign bit at the most significant bit. MPI_COMPLEX and MPI_DOUBLE_COMPLEX have the sign bit of the real and imaginary parts at the most significant bit of each part.

All floating point values are in big-endian IEEE format [23] of the appropriate size.

Floating point values are represented by one of three IEEE formats. These are the IEEE "Single," "Double," and "Double Extended" formats, requiring 4, 8, and 16 bytes of storage, respectively.

For the IEEE "Double Extended" formats, MPI specifies a Format Width of 16 bytes, with 15 exponent bits, bias = +10383, 112 fraction bits, and an encoding analogous to the "Double" format. All integral values are in two's complement big-endian format. Big-endian means that the most significant byte is the one with the lowest address.

Table 3.1
Size of the code for MPI types

Type	Length
MPI_PACKED	1
MPI_BYTE	1
MPI_CHAR	1
MPI_UNSIGNED_CHAR	1
MPI_SIGNED_CHAR	1
MPI_WCHAR	2
MPI_SHORT	2
MPI_UNSIGNED_SHORT	2
MPI_INT	4
MPI_UNSIGNED	4
MPI_LONG	4
MPI_UNSIGNED_LONG	4
MPI_FLOAT	4
MPI_DOUBLE	8
MPI_LONG_DOUBLE	16
MPI_CHARACTER	1
MPI_LOGICAL	4
MPI_INTEGER	4
MPI_REAL	4
MPI_DOUBLE_PRECISION	8
MPI_COMPLEX	2*4
MPI_DOUBLE_COMPLEX	2*8
MPI_INTEGER1	1
MPI_INTEGER2	2
MPI_INTEGER4	4
MPI_INTEGER8	8
MPI_LONG_LONG	8
MPI_UNSIGNED_LONG_LONG	8
MPI_REAL4	4
MPI_REAL8	8
MPI_REAL16	16

Fortran COMPLEX and DOUBLE COMPLEX are represented by a pair of floating point format values for the real and imaginary components.

According to IEEE specifications [23], the "NaN" (not a number) is system dependent. It should not be interpreted within MPI as anything other than "NaN."

The types MPI_PACKED and MPI_BYTE are not converted.

Datatypes listed in this section need not be supported if they are not required to be supported by other parts of MPI (e.g., MPI_INTEGER2 on a machine that does not support 2-byte integers).

Advice to implementors. When converting a larger size integer to a smaller size integer, only the less significant bytes are moved. Care must be taken to preserve the sign bit value. This allows no conversion errors if the data range is within the range of the smaller size integer.

The MPI treatment of "NaN" is similar to the approach used in XDR (see

`ftp://ds.internic.net/rfc/rfc1832.txt`).

All bytes of LOGICAL and bool must be checked to determine the value. □

MPI_PACK_EXTERNAL(datarep, inbuf, incount, datatype, outbuf, outsize, position)

IN	datarep	data representation (string)
IN	inbuf	input buffer start (choice)
IN	incount	number of input data items (integer)
IN	datatype	datatype of each input data item (handle)
OUT	outbuf	output buffer start (choice)
IN	outsize	output buffer size, in bytes (integer)
INOUT	position	current position in buffer, in bytes (integer)

```
int MPI_Pack_external(char *datarep, void *inbuf, int incount,
    MPI_Datatype datatype, void *outbuf, MPI_Aint outsize,
    MPI_Aint *position)
```

```
MPI_PACK_EXTERNAL(DATAREP, INBUF, INCOUNT, DATATYPE, OUTBUF, OUTSIZE,
    POSITION, IERROR)
    INTEGER INCOUNT, DATATYPE, IERROR
    INTEGER(KIND=MPI_ADDRESS_KIND) OUTSIZE, POSITION
    CHARACTER*(*) DATAREP
    <type> INBUF(*), OUTBUF(*)
```

```
void MPI::Datatype::Pack_external(const char* datarep, const
    void* inbuf, int incount, void* outbuf, MPI::Aint outsize,
    MPI::Aint& position) const
```

MPI_UNPACK_EXTERNAL(datarep, inbuf, incount, datatype, outbuf, outsize, position)

IN	datarep	data representation (string)
IN	inbuf	input buffer start (choice)
IN	insize	input buffer size, in bytes (integer)
INOUT	position	current position in buffer, in bytes (integer)
OUT	outbuf	output buffer start (choice)
IN	outcount	number of output data items (integer)
IN	datatype	datatype of output data item (handle)

```
int MPI_Unpack_external(char *datarep, void *inbuf, MPI_Aint insize,
    MPI_Aint *position, void *outbuf, int outcount,
    MPI_Datatype datatype)
```

```
MPI_UNPACK_EXTERNAL(DATAREP, INBUF, INSIZE, POSITION, OUTBUF,
    OUTCOUNT, DATATYPE, IERROR)
    INTEGER OUTCOUNT, DATATYPE, IERROR
    INTEGER(KIND=MPI_ADDRESS_KIND) INSIZE, POSITION
    CHARACTER*(*) DATAREP
    <type> INBUF(*), OUTBUF(*)
```

```
void MPI::Datatype::Unpack_external(const char* datarep,
    const void* inbuf, MPI::Aint insize, MPI::Aint& position,
    void* outbuf, int outcount) const
```

MPI_PACK_EXTERNAL_SIZE(datarep, incount, datatype, size)

IN	datarep	data representation (string)
IN	incount	number of input data items (integer)
IN	datatype	datatype of each input data item (handle)
OUT	size	output buffer size, in bytes (integer)

```
int MPI_Pack_external_size(char *datarep, int incount,
    MPI_Datatype datatype, MPI_Aint *size)
```

```
MPI_PACK_EXTERNAL_SIZE(DATAREP, INCOUNT, DATATYPE, SIZE, IERROR)
    INTEGER INCOUNT, DATATYPE, IERROR
    INTEGER(KIND=MPI_ADDRESS_KIND) SIZE
    CHARACTER*(*) DATAREP
```

```
MPI::Aint MPI::Datatype::Pack_external_size(const char* datarep,
    int incount) const
```

These three functions behave as MPI_PACK, MPI_UNPACK and MPI_PACK_SIZE, respectively, except that the data is packed using the data format specified by the datarep argument, and no additional header is put in the front of the data.

The datarep arguments specify the data format. The only valid value in the current version of MPI is external32. The argument is provided for future extensibility (e.g., to "external64"),

Rationale. The MPI-2 Forum had a long discussion on the advisability of an "external64" format. The desire to have one (and only one) standard data representation outweighed the added convenience of an additional format. The "external32" format was chosen, rather than a 64-bit oriented format, because in many usages of external formats it is important to reduce the size of the encoded data. □

3.12.2 Derived Datatypes versus Pack/Unpack

A comparison between Example 3.15 on page 145 and Example 3.31 in the previous section is instructive. There are three salient issues that we compare: programing convenience, storage use, and compute time.

With regard to programming convenience, it is somewhat less tedious to pack the class zero particles in the loop that locates them, rather then defining in this loop the datatype that will later collect them. On the other hand, it would be very tedious (and inefficient) to pack separately the components of each structure entry in the array. Defining a datatype is more convenient when this definition depends only on declarations; packing may be more convenient when the communication buffer layout is data dependent.

With regard to storage use, the packing code uses at least 56,000 bytes for the pack buffer, e.g., up to 1000 copies of the structure (1 char, 6 doubles, and 7 char is $1 + 8 \times 6 + 7 = 56$ bytes). The derived datatype code uses 12,000 bytes for the three, 1,000 long, integer arrays used to define the derived datatype. It also probably uses a similar amount of storage for the internal datatype representation. The difference is likely to be larger in realistic codes. The use of packing requires additional storage for a *copy* of the data, whereas the use of derived datatypes requires additional storage for a *description* of the data layout.

Finally, regarding compute time, the packing code executes a function call for each packed item whereas the derived datatype code executes only a fixed number of function calls. The packing code is likely to require one additional memory to memory copy of the data, as compared to the derived-datatype code. One may expect, on most implementations, to achieve better performance with the derived datatype code.

Both codes send the same size message, so that there is no difference in communication time. However, if the buffer described by the derived datatype is not contiguous in memory, it may take longer to access.

Example 3.32 above illustrates another advantage of pack/unpack; namely the receiving process may use information in part of an incoming message in order to decide how to handle subsequent data in the message. In order to achieve the same outcome without pack/unpack, one would have to send two messages: the first with the list of indices, to be used to construct a derived datatype that is then used to receive the particle entries sent in a second message.

The use of derived datatypes will often lead to improved performance: data copying can be avoided, and information on data layout can be reused, when the same communication buffer is reused. On the other hand, the definition of derived datatypes for complex layouts can be more tedious than explicit packing. Derived datatypes should be used whenever data layout is defined by program declarations (e.g., structures), or is regular (e.g., array sections). Packing might be considered for complex, dynamic, data-dependent layouts. Packing may result in more efficient code in situations where the sender has to communicate to the receiver information that affects the layout of the receive buffer.

4 Collective Communications

In this chapter we present the MPI capabilities to communicate between multiple processes simultaneously. We discuss the vast array of collective communication capabilities including broadcasting, spreading, and collecting data. We also present the MPI ability to perform reduction and scan operations including ones defined by the user. The variants which control which process or processes receive the result are given.

4.1 Introduction and Overview

This chapter describes collective communications that transmit data among all processes in a group specified by an intracommunicator object. (Collective communication with intercommunicators is described in Chapter II-5.) One function, the barrier, serves to synchronize processes without passing data.

MPI provides the following collective communication functions.

- Barrier synchronization across all group members (Section 4.4).
- Global communication functions, which are illustrated in Figure 4.1, for intracommunicators. They include:
  - Broadcast from one member to all members of a group (Section 4.6).
  - Gather data from all group members to one member (Section 4.7).
  - Scatter data from one member to all members of a group (Section 4.8).
  - A variation on Gather where all members of the group receive the result (Section 4.9). This is shown as "allgather" in Figure 4.1.
  - Scatter/Gather data from all members to all members of a group (also called complete exchange or all-to-all) (Section 4.10). This is shown as "alltoall" in Figure 4.1.
- Global reduction operations such as sum, max, min, or user-defined functions. They are illustrated in Figure 4.11, for intracommunicators.
  - Reduction where the result is returned to all group members and a variation where the result is returned to only one member (Section 4.11).
  - A combined reduction and scatter operation (Section 4.11.5).
  - Scan across all members of a group (also called prefix) (Section 4.12).

The syntax and semantics of the MPI collective functions was designed to be consistent with point-to-point communications. However, to keep the number of functions and their argument lists to a reasonable level of complexity, the MPI Forum made collective functions more restrictive than the point-to-point functions, in several ways. One restriction is that, in contrast to point-to-point communication, the amount of data sent must exactly match the amount of data specified by the receiver.

Collective functions do not use a `tag` argument. Thus, within each intragroup communication domain, collective calls are matched strictly according to the order of execution.

A major simplification is that collective functions come in blocking versions only.

A final simplification of collective functions concerns modes. Collective functions come in only one mode, and this mode may be regarded as analogous to the standard mode of point-to-point. Specifically, the semantics are as follows. A collective function invocation on a given process can return as soon as its participation in the overall communication is complete. As usual, the completion indicates that the caller is now free to access and modify locations in the communication buffer(s). It does not indicate that other processes have completed, or even started, the operation. The invocation may not be able to complete its participation in the collective communication until matching invocations occurred at some, or all other participating processes. Thus, a collective communication may, or may not, have the effect of synchronizing all calling processes. The barrier, of course, is the exception to this statement.

This choice of semantics was made so as to allow a variety of implementations.

The user of MPI must keep these issues in mind. For example, even though a particular implementation of MPI may provide a broadcast with the side-effect of synchronization (the standard allows this), the standard does not *require* this, and hence, any program that relies on the synchronization will be non-portable. On the other hand, a correct and portable program must allow a collective function to be synchronizing. Though one should not rely on synchronization side-effects, one must program so as to allow for it. See Section 4.14 for further details.

Though these issues and statements may seem unusually obscure, they are merely a consequence of the desire of MPI to:

- allow efficient implementations on a variety of architectures; and,
- be clear about exactly what is, and what is not, guaranteed by the standard.

Rationale.   The MPI Forum had long arguments about possible designs for non-blocking collective functions. In principle, such functions could support the overlap of computation and collective communication. This is important, as collective communications are often time consuming. However, many implementors felt that support for general nonblocking collective communications would slow down regular communications, and that the desired overlap would not be achieved on most systems. Restricted forms of nonblocking collective functions could be implemented efficiently, but the syntax and semantics of these functions was not consistent with nonblocking point-to-point communication. □

4.2   Operational Details

A collective operation is executed by having all processes in the group call the communication routine, with matching arguments. The syntax and semantics of the collective operations are defined to be consistent with the syntax and semantics of the point-to-point operations. Thus, user-defined datatypes are allowed and must match between sending and receiving processes as specified in Chapter 3. One of the key arguments is an intracommunicator that defines the group of participating processes and provides a communication domain for the operation. In calls where a unique root process is defined, some arguments are specified as "significant only at root," and are ignored for all participants except the root. The reader is referred to Chapter 2 for information concerning communication buffers and type matching rules, to Chapter 3 for user-defined datatypes, and to Chapter 5 for information on how to define groups and create communicators.

The type-matching conditions for the collective operations are stricter than the corresponding conditions between sender and receiver in point-to-point. Namely, for collective operations, the amount of data sent must exactly match the amount of data specified by the receiver. Distinct type maps (the layout in memory, see Section 3.2) between sender and receiver are still allowed.

Collective communication calls may use the same communicators as point-to-point communication; MPI guarantees that messages generated on behalf of collective communication calls will not be confused with messages generated by point-to-point communication. A more detailed discussion of correct use of collective routines is found in Section 4.14.

Rationale.   The equal-data restriction (on type matching) was made so as to avoid the complexity of providing a facility analogous to the status argument of MPI_RECV for discovering the amount of data sent. Some of the collective routines would require an array of status values. This restriction also simplifies implementation. □

Advice to users.   As described in Section 4.1, it is dangerous to rely on syn-chronization side-effects of the collective operations for program correctness. These issues are discussed further in Section 4.14. ☐

Advice to implementors.   While vendors may write optimized collective routines matched to their architectures, a complete library of the collective communication routines can be written entirely using the MPI point-to-point communication functions and a few auxiliary functions. If implementing on top of point-to-point, a hidden, special communicator must be created for the collective operation so as to avoid interference with any on-going point-to-point communication at the time of the collective call. This is discussed further in Section 4.14.

Although collective communications are described in terms of messages sent directly from sender(s) to receiver(s), implementations may use a communication pattern where data is forwarded through intermediate nodes. Thus, one could use a logarithmic depth tree to implement broadcast, rather then sending data directly from the root to each other process. Messages can be forwarded to intermediate nodes and split (for scatter) or concatenated (for gather). An optimal implementation of collective communication will take advantage of the specifics of the underlying communication network (such as support for multicast, which can be used for MPI broadcast), and will use different algorithms, according to the number of participating processes and the amounts of data communicated. See, e.g. [4]. ☐

4.3   Communicator Argument

The key concept of the collective functions is to have a "group" of participating processes. The routines do not have a group identifier as an explicit argument. Instead, there is a communicator argument. For the purposes of this chapter, communicators are intracommunicators, that can be thought of as a group identifier linked with a communication domain. These will have type `MPI::Intracomm`, or a type derived from `MPI::Intracomm`, in C++. Collective communication with intercommunicators, that is, communicators that span two groups, is described in Chapter II-5.

In C++, functions for collective communication are members of the MPI::Comm class. However, since the collective operations do not make sense on the base class (since an MPI::Comm is neither an intercommunicator nor an intracommunicator), the functions are all pure virtual. See II-8.1.7 for further information.

4.4 Barrier Synchronization

Group synchronization is achieved through

MPI_BARRIER(comm)

   IN   comm   communicator (handle)

```
int MPI_Barrier(MPI_Comm comm)
```

```
MPI_BARRIER(COMM, IERROR)
    INTEGER COMM, IERROR
```

```
void MPI::Comm::Barrier() const = 0
```

MPI_BARRIER blocks the caller until all group members have called it. The call
returns at any process only after all group members have entered the call.

4.5 Global Communication Functions

Figure 4.1 gives a pictorial representation of the global communication functions.
All these functions (broadcast excepted) come in two variants: the simple variant,
where all communicated items are messages of the same size, and the "vector"
variant, where each item can be of a different size. In addition, in the simple variant,
multiple items originating from the same process or received at the same process, are
contiguous in memory; the vector variant allows the call to pick the distinct items
from non-contiguous locations. The all-to-all function has an additional variant,
where each item can have an arbitrary layout in memory.

Some of these functions, such as broadcast or gather, have a single origin or a
single receiving process. Such a process is called the **root**. Global communication
functions basically come in three patterns:

- Root sends data to all processes (itself included): broadcast and scatter.
- Root receives data from all processes (itself included): gather.
- Each process communicates with each process (itself included): allgather and
alltoall.

All these functions, with the exception of broadcast, have separate send and
receive arguments, which must be disjoint. The send arguments are significant
only at the root for scatter; the receive arguments are significant only at the root

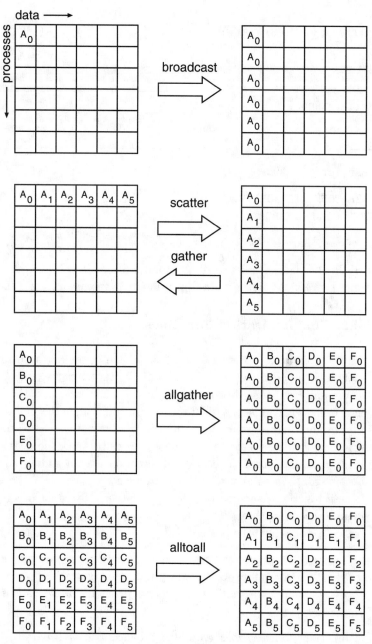

Figure 4.1
Collective move functions illustrated for a group of six processes. In each case, each row of boxes represents data locations in one process. Thus, in the broadcast, initially just the first process contains the item A_0, but after the broadcast all processes contain it.

for gather. With each of these two functions, data has to be copied from the send buffer of the root to the receive buffer of the root.

It is sometimes preferable to have "in place" communication, where the same communication buffer is used both for sending and for receiving data. This is specified by providing a special argument value, MPI_IN_PLACE (MPI::IN_PLACE, in C++), instead of the send buffer or receive buffer argument.

MPI_IN_PLACE is a reference constant (see Section 1.9). It cannot be used in Fortran, except as a buffer argument to those collective communication functions that have an "in place" option.

Rationale.   The "in place" operations are provided to reduce unnecessary memory usage and superfluous data motion. Note that the alternative of allowing the input and output buffers to overlap does not work, for two reasons: First, there is no simple way for MPI to identify that the buffers overlap (the buffer addresses would not be equal, in many cases). Second, Fortran explicitly prohibits aliasing of arguments. The approach of using a special value to denote an "in place" operation eliminates these difficulties. ☐

Advice to implementors.   By allowing the "in place" option, the receive buffer in many of the collective calls becomes an INOUT argument. A Fortran binding that includes INTENT must mark these as INOUT, not OUT. ☐

4.6   Broadcast

MPI_BCAST(buffer, count, datatype, root, comm)

INOUT	buffer	starting address of buffer (choice)
IN	count	number of entries in buffer (integer)
IN	datatype	data type of buffer (handle)
IN	root	rank of broadcast root (integer)
IN	comm	communicator (handle)

```
int MPI_Bcast(void* buffer, int count, MPI_Datatype datatype,
    int root, MPI_Comm comm )
```

```
MPI_BCAST(BUFFER, COUNT, DATATYPE, ROOT, COMM, IERROR)
    <type> BUFFER(*)
    INTEGER COUNT, DATATYPE, ROOT, COMM, IERROR
```

```
void MPI::Comm::Bcast(void* buffer, int count, const MPI::Datatype&
    datatype, int root) const = 0
```

MPI_BCAST broadcasts a message from the process with rank root to all processes of the group, itself included. The argument root must have identical values on all processes, and comm must represent the same intragroup communication domain. On return, the contents of root's communication buffer has been copied to all processes.

General, derived datatypes are allowed for datatype. The type signature of count and datatype on any process must be equal to the type signature of count and datatype at the root. This implies that the amount of data sent must be equal to the amount received, pairwise between each process and the root. MPI_BCAST and all other data-movement collective routines make this restriction. Distinct type maps between sender and receiver are still allowed.

MPI_BCAST and other functions with a root argument may return the error code MPI_ERR_ROOT (MPI::ERR_ROOT, in C++) to indicate an invalid root argument.

There is no "in place" option for broadcast. (Broadcast is already "in place", as data is not moved at the root.)

4.6.1   An Example Using MPI_BCAST

Example 4.1   Broadcast 100 ints from process 0 to every process in the group.

```
MPI_Comm comm;
int array[100];
int root=0;
...
MPI_Bcast( array, 100, MPI_INT, root, comm);
```

Rationale.   MPI does not support a *multicast* function, where a broadcast executed by a root can be matched by regular receives at the remaining processes. Such a function is easy to implement if the root directly sends data to each receiving process. However, there is little to be gained, as compared to executing multiple send operations. An implementation where processes are used as intermediate nodes in a broadcast tree is hard, since only the root executes a call that identifies the operation as a multicast. In contrast, in a collective call to MPI_BCAST all processes are aware that they participate in a broadcast. □

4.7 Gather

MPI_GATHER(sendbuf, sendcount, sendtype, recvbuf, recvcount, recvtype, root,
    comm)

IN	sendbuf	starting address of send buffer (choice)
IN	sendcount	number of elements in send buffer (integer)
IN	sendtype	data type of send buffer elements (handle)
OUT	recvbuf	address of receive buffer (choice)
IN	recvcount	number of elements for any single receive (integer)
IN	recvtype	data type of recv buffer elements (handle)
IN	root	rank of receiving process (integer)
IN	comm	communicator (handle)

```
int MPI_Gather(void* sendbuf, int sendcount, MPI_Datatype sendtype,
    void* recvbuf, int recvcount, MPI_Datatype recvtype, int root,
    MPI_Comm comm)
```

```
MPI_GATHER(SENDBUF, SENDCOUNT, SENDTYPE, RECVBUF, RECVCOUNT,
    RECVTYPE, ROOT, COMM, IERROR)
    <type> SENDBUF(*), RECVBUF(*)
    INTEGER SENDCOUNT, SENDTYPE, RECVCOUNT, RECVTYPE, ROOT, COMM,
    IERROR
```

```
void MPI::Comm::Gather(const void* sendbuf, int sendcount, const
    MPI::Datatype& sendtype, void* recvbuf, int recvcount,
    const MPI::Datatype& recvtype, int root) const = 0
```

Each process (root process included) sends the contents of its send buffer to the
root process. The root process receives the messages and stores them in rank order.
The outcome is *as if* each of the n processes in the group (including the root process) had executed a call to MPI_Send(sendbuf, sendcount, sendtype, root , ...), and
the root had executed n calls to MPI_Recv(recvbuf+i · recvcount · extent(recvtype),
recvcount, recvtype, i ,...), where extent(recvtype) is the type extent obtained from
a call to MPI_Type_get_extent().

An alternative description is that the n messages sent by the processes in the
group are concatenated in rank order, and the resulting message is received by the
root as if by a call to MPI_RECV(recvbuf, recvcount·n, recvtype, ...).

The receive buffer is ignored for all non-root processes.

General, derived datatypes are allowed for both sendtype and recvtype. The type
signature of sendcount and sendtype on process i must be equal to the type signature

of recvcount and recvtype at the root. This implies that the amount of data sent must be equal to the amount of data received, pairwise between each process and the root. Distinct type maps between sender and receiver are still allowed.

All arguments to the function are significant on process root, while on other processes, only arguments sendbuf, sendcount, sendtype, root, and comm are significant. The argument root must have identical values on all processes and comm must represent the same intragroup communication domain.

The specification of counts and types should not cause any location on the root to be written more than once. Such a call is erroneous.

Note that the recvcount argument at the root indicates the number of items it receives from *each* process, not the total number of items it receives.

The "in place" option is specified by passing MPI_IN_PLACE as the value of sendbuf at the root. In such a case, sendcount and sendtype are ignored at the root, and the contribution of the root to the gathered vector is already assumed to be in the correct place in the receive buffer.

4.7.1   Examples Using MPI_GATHER

Example 4.2   Gather 100 ints from every process in group to root. See Figure 4.2.

```
MPI_Comm comm;
int gsize,sendarray[100];
int root, *rbuf;
...
MPI_Comm_size(comm, &gsize);
rbuf = (int *)malloc(gsize*100*sizeof(int));
MPI_Gather(sendarray, 100, MPI_INT, rbuf, 100, MPI_INT, root, comm);
```

Example 4.3   Previous example modified – only the root allocates memory for the receive buffer.

```
MPI_Comm comm;
int gsize,sendarray[100];
int root, myrank, *rbuf;
...
MPI_Comm_rank(comm, &myrank);
if (myrank == root) {
  MPI_Comm_size(comm, &gsize);
  rbuf = (int *)malloc(gsize*100*sizeof(int));
```

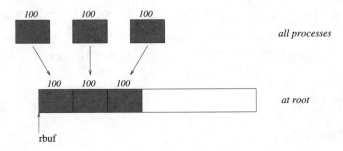

Figure 4.2
The root process gathers 100 `ints` from each process in the group.

```
}
MPI_Gather(sendarray, 100, MPI_INT, rbuf, 100, MPI_INT, root, comm);
```

Example 4.4 Previous example modified – using "in place" gather at the root.

```
MPI_Comm comm;
int gsize;
int root, myrank, *rbuf, *sbuf;

MPI_Comm_rank(comm, &myrank);

if (myrank == root) {
  MPI_Comm_size(comm, &gsize);
  rbuf = (int *)malloc(gsize*100*sizeof(int));
  sbuf = rbuf + 100*myrank;
}
else {
  sbuf = (int *)malloc(100*sizeof(int));
}
...

if (myrank == root)
  MPI_Gather(MPI_IN_PLACE, 100, MPI_INT, rbuf, 100, MPI_INT,
             root, comm);
else
  MPI_Gather(sbuf, 100, MPI_INT, 0, 0, 0, root, comm);
```

Example 4.5   Do the same as the Example 4.3, but use a derived datatype. Note that the type cannot be the entire set of `gsize*100` ints since type matching is defined pairwise between the root and each process in the gather.

```
MPI_Comm comm;
int gsize,sendarray[100];
int root, *rbuf;
MPI_Datatype rtype;
...
MPI_Comm_size(comm, &gsize);
MPI_Type_contiguous(100, MPI_INT, &rtype );
MPI_Type_commit(&rtype);
rbuf = (int *)malloc(gsize*100*sizeof(int));
MPI_Gather(sendarray, 100, MPI_INT, rbuf, 1, rtype, root, comm);
```

4.7.2   Gather, Vector Variant

MPI_GATHERV(sendbuf, sendcount, sendtype, recvbuf, recvcounts, displs, recvtype, root, comm)

IN	sendbuf	starting address of send buffer (choice)
IN	sendcount	number of elements in send buffer (integer)
IN	sendtype	data type of send buffer elements (handle)
OUT	recvbuf	address of receive buffer (choice)
IN	recvcounts	integer array (array of integers)
IN	displs	integer array of displacements (array of integers)
IN	recvtype	data type of recv buffer elements (handle)
IN	root	rank of receiving process (integer)
IN	comm	communicator (handle)

```
int MPI_Gatherv(void* sendbuf, int sendcount, MPI_Datatype sendtype,
    void* recvbuf, int *recvcounts, int *displs,
    MPI_Datatype recvtype, int root, MPI_Comm comm)
```

```
MPI_GATHERV(SENDBUF, SENDCOUNT, SENDTYPE, RECVBUF, RECVCOUNTS,
    DISPLS, RECVTYPE, ROOT, COMM, IERROR)
    <type> SENDBUF(*), RECVBUF(*)
    INTEGER SENDCOUNT, SENDTYPE, RECVCOUNTS(*), DISPLS(*), RECVTYPE,
    ROOT, COMM, IERROR
```

```
void MPI::Comm::Gatherv(const void* sendbuf, int sendcount, const
    MPI::Datatype& sendtype, void* recvbuf, const int recvcounts[],
    const int displs[], const MPI::Datatype& recvtype, int root)
    const = 0
```

MPI_GATHERV extends the functionality of MPI_GATHER by allowing a varying count of data from each process, since recvcounts is now an array. It also allows more flexibility as to where the data is placed on the root, by providing the new argument, displs.

The outcome is *as if* each process, including the root process, sends a message to the root, MPI_Send(sendbuf, sendcount, sendtype, root, ...) and the root executes n receives, MPI_Recv(recvbuf+disp[i]· extent(recvtype), recvcounts[i], recvtype, i, ...).

The data sent from process j is placed in the jth portion of the receive buffer recvbuf on process root. The jth portion of recvbuf begins at offset displs[j] elements (in terms of recvtype) into recvbuf.

The receive buffer is ignored for all non-root processes.

The type signature implied by sendcount and sendtype on process i must be equal to the type signature implied by recvcounts[i] and recvtype at the root. This implies that the amount of data sent must be equal to the amount of data received, pairwise between each process and the root. Distinct type maps between sender and receiver are still allowed, as illustrated in Example 4.7.

All arguments to the function are significant on process root, while on other processes, only arguments sendbuf, sendcount, sendtype, root, and comm are significant. The argument root must have identical values on all processes, and comm must represent the same intragroup communication domain.

The specification of counts, types, and displacements should not cause any location on the root to be written more than once. Such a call is erroneous. On the other hand, the successive displacements in the array disps need not be a monotonic sequence.

The "in place" option is specified by passing MPI_IN_PLACE as the value of sendbuf at the root. In such a case, sendcount and sendtype are ignored at the root, and the contribution of the root to the gathered vector is assumed to be already in the correct place in the receive buffer.

4.7.3   Examples Using MPI_GATHERV

Example 4.6   Have each process send 100 ints to root, but place each set (of 100) *stride* ints apart at receiving end. Use MPI_GATHERV and the displs argument to achieve this effect. Assume *stride* $\geq$ 100. See Figure 4.3.

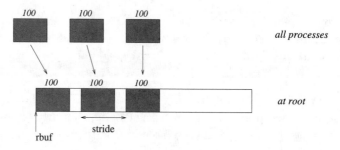

Figure 4.3
The root process gathers 100 ints from each process in the group, each set is placed **stride** ints apart.

```
MPI_Comm comm;
int gsize,sendarray[100];
int root, *rbuf, stride;
int *displs,i,*rcounts;
...
MPI_Comm_size(comm, &gsize);
rbuf = (int *)malloc(gsize*stride*sizeof(int));
displs = (int *)malloc(gsize*sizeof(int));
rcounts = (int *)malloc(gsize*sizeof(int));
for (i=0; i<gsize; ++i) {
  displs[i]  = i*stride;
  rcounts[i] = 100;
}
MPI_Gatherv(sendarray, 100, MPI_INT, rbuf, rcounts, displs, MPI_INT,
            root, comm);
```

Note that the program is erroneous if $-100 < stride < 100$.

Example 4.7   Same as Example 4.6 on the receiving side, but send the 100 ints from the 0th column of a 100×150 int array, in C. See Figure 4.4.

```
MPI_Comm comm;
int gsize,sendarray[100][150];
int root, *rbuf, stride;
MPI_Datatype stype;
int *displs,i,*rcounts;
```

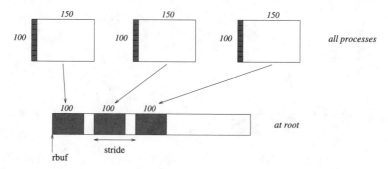

Figure 4.4
The root process gathers column 0 of a 100×150 C array, and each set is placed **stride** ints apart.

```
...
MPI_Comm_size(comm, &gsize);
rbuf = (int *)malloc(gsize*stride*sizeof(int));
displs = (int *)malloc(gsize*sizeof(int));
rcounts = (int *)malloc(gsize*sizeof(int));
for (i=0; i<gsize; ++i) {
  displs[i] = i*stride;
  rcounts[i] = 100;
}
/* Create datatype for 1 column of array */
MPI_Type_vector(100, 1, 150, MPI_INT, &stype);
MPI_Type_commit(&stype);
MPI_Gatherv(sendarray, 1, stype, rbuf, rcounts, displs, MPI_INT,
            root, comm);
```

Example 4.8   Process i sends (100-i) ints from the ith column of a 100×150 int array, in C. It is received into a buffer with stride, as in the previous two examples. See Figure 4.5.

```
MPI_Comm comm;
int gsize,sendarray[100][150],*sptr;
int root, *rbuf, stride, myrank;
MPI_Datatype stype;
int *displs,i,*rcounts;
...
```

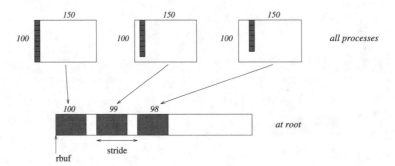

Figure 4.5
The root process gathers 100-i ints from column i of a 100×150 C array, and each set is placed `stride` ints apart.

```
MPI_Comm_size(comm, &gsize);
MPI_Comm_rank(comm, &myrank);
rbuf = (int *)malloc(gsize*stride*sizeof(int));
displs = (int *)malloc(gsize*sizeof(int));
rcounts = (int *)malloc(gsize*sizeof(int));
for (i=0; i<gsize; ++i) {
  displs[i] = i*stride;
  rcounts[i] = 100-i;    /* note change from previous example */
}
/* Create datatype for the column we are sending */
MPI_Type_vector(100-myrank, 1, 150, MPI_INT, &stype);
MPI_Type_commit(&stype);
/* sptr is the address of start of "myrank" column */
sptr = &sendarray[0][myrank];
MPI_Gatherv(sptr, 1, stype, rbuf, rcounts, displs, MPI_INT,
            root, comm);
```

Note that a different amount of data is received from each process.

Example 4.9   Same as Example 4.8, but done in a different way at the sending end. We create a datatype that causes the correct striding at the sending end so that that we read a column of a C array.

```
MPI_Comm comm;
int gsize,sendarray[100][150],*sptr;
```

```
int root, *rbuf, stride, myrank, blocklen[2];
MPI_Aint disp[2];
MPI_Datatype stype,type[2];
int *displs,i,*rcounts;
...
MPI_Comm_size(comm, &gsize);
MPI_Comm_rank(comm, &myrank);
rbuf = (int *)malloc(gsize*stride*sizeof(int));
displs = (int *)malloc(gsize*sizeof(int));
rcounts = (int *)malloc(gsize*sizeof(int));
for (i=0; i<gsize; ++i) {
  displs[i] = i*stride;
  rcounts[i] = 100-i;
}
/* Create datatype for one int, with extent of entire row */
disp[0] = 0;       disp[1] = 150*sizeof(int);
type[0] = MPI_INT; type[1] = MPI_UB;
blocklen[0] = 1;    blocklen[1] = 1;
MPI_Type_create_struct(2, blocklen, disp, type, &stype);
MPI_Type_commit(&stype);
sptr = &sendarray[0][myrank];
MPI_Gatherv(sptr, 100-myrank, stype, rbuf, rcounts, displs, MPI_INT,
            root, comm);
```

Example 4.10   Same as Example 4.8 at sending side, but at receiving side we
make the stride between received blocks vary from block to block. See Figure 4.6.

```
MPI_Comm comm;
int gsize,sendarray[100][150],*sptr;
int root, *rbuf, *stride, myrank, bufsize;
MPI_Datatype stype;
int *displs,i,*rcounts,offset;
...
MPI_Comm_size(comm, &gsize);
MPI_Comm_rank(comm, &myrank);

stride = (int *)malloc(gsize*sizeof(int));
...
```

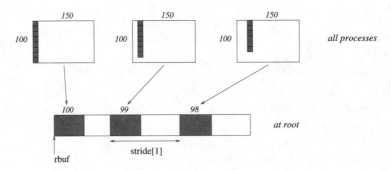

Figure 4.6
The root process gathers 100-i ints from column i of a 100×150 C array, and each set is placed
`stride[i]` ints apart (a varying stride).

```
/* stride[i] for i = 0 to gsize-1 is set somehow */

/* set up displs and rcounts vectors first */
displs = (int *)malloc(gsize*sizeof(int));
rcounts = (int *)malloc(gsize*sizeof(int));
offset = 0;
for (i=0; i<gsize; ++i) {
  displs[i] = offset;
  offset += stride[i];
  rcounts[i] = 100-i;
}
/* the required buffer size for rbuf is now easily obtained */
bufsize = displs[gsize-1]+rcounts[gsize-1];
rbuf = (int *)malloc(bufsize*sizeof(int));
/* Create datatype for the column we are sending */
MPI_Type_vector(100-myrank, 1, 150, MPI_INT, &stype);
MPI_Type_commit(&stype);
sptr = &sendarray[0][myrank];
MPI_Gatherv(sptr, 1, stype, rbuf, rcounts, displs, MPI_INT,
            root, comm);
```

Example 4.11   Process i sends `num` ints from the ith column of a 100×150 int
array, in C. The complicating factor is that the various values of `num` are not known

to **root**, so a separate gather must first be run to find these out. The data is placed contiguously at the receiving end.

```
MPI_Comm comm;
int gsize,sendarray[100][150],*sptr;
int root, *rbuf, myrank, blocklen[2];
MPI_Aint disp[2];
MPI_Datatype stype,types[2];
int *displs,i,*rcounts,num;
...
MPI_Comm_size(comm, &gsize);
MPI_Comm_rank(comm, &myrank);

/* First, gather nums to root */
rcounts = (int *)malloc(gsize*sizeof(int));
MPI_Gather(&num, 1, MPI_INT, rcounts, 1, MPI_INT, root, comm);
/* root now has correct rcounts, using these we set displs[] so that
 * data is placed contiguously (or concatenated) at receive end */
displs = (int *)malloc(gsize*sizeof(int));
displs[0] = 0;
for (i=1; i<gsize; ++i) {
  displs[i] = displs[i-1]+rcounts[i-1];
}
/* And, create receive buffer */
rbuf = (int *)malloc(gsize*(displs[gsize-1]+rcounts[gsize-1])
                     *sizeof(int));
/* Create datatype for one int, with extent of entire row */
disp[0] = 0;        disp[1] = 150*sizeof(int);
types[0] = MPI_INT; types[1] = MPI_UB;
blocklen[0] = 1;    blocklen[1] = 1;
MPI_Type_create_struct(2, blocklen, disp, types, &stype);
MPI_Type_commit(&stype);
sptr = &sendarray[0][myrank];
MPI_Gatherv(sptr, num, stype, rbuf, rcounts, displs, MPI_INT,
            root, comm);
```

4.8 Scatter

MPI_SCATTER(sendbuf, sendcount, sendtype, recvbuf, recvcount, recvtype, root, comm)

IN	sendbuf	address of send buffer (choice)
IN	sendcount	number of elements sent to each process (integer)
IN	sendtype	data type of send buffer elements (handle)
OUT	recvbuf	address of receive buffer (choice)
IN	recvcount	number of elements in receive buffer (integer)
IN	recvtype	data type of receive buffer elements (handle)
IN	root	rank of sending process (integer)
IN	comm	communicator (handle)

```
int MPI_Scatter(void* sendbuf, int sendcount, MPI_Datatype sendtype,
    void* recvbuf, int recvcount, MPI_Datatype recvtype, int root,
    MPI_Comm comm)
```

```
MPI_SCATTER(SENDBUF, SENDCOUNT, SENDTYPE, RECVBUF, RECVCOUNT,
    RECVTYPE, ROOT, COMM, IERROR)
    <type> SENDBUF(*), RECVBUF(*)
    INTEGER SENDCOUNT, SENDTYPE, RECVCOUNT, RECVTYPE, ROOT, COMM,
    IERROR
```

```
void MPI::Comm::Scatter(const void* sendbuf, int sendcount, const
    MPI::Datatype& sendtype, void* recvbuf, int recvcount,
    const MPI::Datatype& recvtype, int root) const = 0
```

MPI_SCATTER is the inverse operation to MPI_GATHER.

The outcome is *as if* the root executed n send operations, MPI_Send(sendbuf+i · sendcount · extent(sendtype), sendcount, sendtype, i,...), i = 0 to n - 1. and each process executed a receive, MPI_Recv(recvbuf, recvcount, recvtype, root,...).

An alternative description is that the root sends a message with MPI_Send(sendbuf, sendcount·n, sendtype, ...). This message is split into n equal segments, the ith segment is sent to the ith process in the group, and each process receives this message as above.

The type signature associated with sendcount and sendtype at the root must be equal to the type signature associated with recvcount and recvtype at all processes. This implies that the amount of data sent must be equal to the amount of data received, pairwise between each process and the root. Distinct type maps between sender and receiver are still allowed.

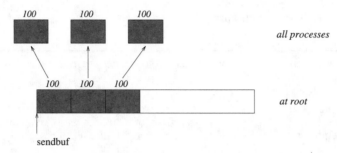

Figure 4.7
The root process scatters sets of 100 `ints` to each process in the group.

All arguments to the function are significant on process root, while on other processes, only arguments recvbuf, recvcount, recvtype, root, comm are significant. The argument root must have identical values on all processes and comm must represent the same intragroup communication domain. The send buffer is ignored for all non-root processes.

The "in place" option is specified by passing MPI_IN_PLACE as the value of recvbuf at the root. In such a case, recvcount and recvtype are ignored at the root, and root "sends" no data to itself. The scattered vector is still assumed to contain n segments, where n is the group size; the *root*-th segment, which root should "send to itself," is not moved.

4.8.1   An Example Using MPI_SCATTER

Example 4.12   The reverse of Example 4.2, page 200. Scatter sets of 100 ints from the root to each process in the group. See Figure 4.7.

```
MPI::Intracomm comm;
int root, rbuf[100];
...
const int gsize = comm.Get_size();
int *sendbuf = new int [gsize * 100 * sizeof(int)];
...
comm.Scatter(sendbuf, 100, MPI::INT, rbuf, 100, MPI::INT, root);
```

4.8.2   Scatter: Vector Variant

MPI_SCATTERV(sendbuf, sendcounts, displs, sendtype, recvbuf, recvcount, recvtype,
    root, comm)

IN	sendbuf	address of send buffer (choice)
IN	sendcounts	integer array (array of integers)
IN	displs	integer array of displacements (array of integers)
IN	sendtype	data type of send buffer elements (handle)
OUT	recvbuf	address of receive buffer (choice)
IN	recvcount	number of elements in receive buffer (integer)
IN	recvtype	data type of receive buffer elements (handle)
IN	root	rank of sending process (integer)
IN	comm	communicator (handle)

```
int MPI_Scatterv(void* sendbuf, int *sendcounts, int *displs,
    MPI_Datatype sendtype, void* recvbuf, int recvcount,
    MPI_Datatype recvtype, int root, MPI_Comm comm)
```

```
MPI_SCATTERV(SENDBUF, SENDCOUNTS, DISPLS, SENDTYPE, RECVBUF,
    RECVCOUNT, RECVTYPE, ROOT, COMM, IERROR)
    <type> SENDBUF(*), RECVBUF(*)
    INTEGER SENDCOUNTS(*), DISPLS(*), SENDTYPE, RECVCOUNT, RECVTYPE,
    ROOT, COMM, IERROR
```

```
void MPI::Comm::Scatterv(const void* sendbuf,
    const int sendcounts[], const int displs[],
    const MPI::Datatype& sendtype, void* recvbuf, int recvcount,
    const MPI::Datatype& recvtype, int root) const = 0
```

MPI_SCATTERV is the inverse operation to MPI_GATHERV.

MPI_SCATTERV extends the functionality of MPI_SCATTER by allowing a varying count of data to be sent to each process, since sendcounts is now an array. It also allows more flexibility as to where the data is taken from on the root by providing the new argument displs.

The outcome is as if the root executed n send operations, MPI_-Send(sendbuf+displs[i] · extent(sendtype), sendcounts[i], sendtype, i,...), i = 0 to n - 1, and each process executed a receive, MPI_Recv(recvbuf, recvcount, recvtype, root,...).

The type signature implied by sendcount[i] and sendtype at the root must be equal to the type signature implied by recvcount and recvtype at process i. This implies that the amount of data sent must be equal to the amount of data received, pairwise between each process and the root. Distinct type maps between sender and receiver are still allowed.

All arguments to the function are significant on process root, while on other processes, only arguments recvbuf, recvcount, recvtype, root, comm are significant. The arguments root must have identical values on all processes, and comm must represent the same intragroup communication domain. The send buffer is ignored for all non-root processes.

The specification of counts, types, and displacements should not cause any location on the root to be read more than once.

Rationale.   Though not essential, the last restriction is imposed so as to achieve symmetry with MPI_GATHER, where the corresponding restriction (a multiple-write restriction) is necessary. □

The "in place" option is specified by passing MPI_IN_PLACE as the value of recvbuf at the root. In such a case, recvcount and recvtype are ignored at the root, and root "sends" no data to itself. The scattered vector is still assumed to contain n segments, where n is the group size; the *root*-th segment, which root should "send to itself," is not moved.

4.8.3   Examples Using MPI_SCATTERV

Example 4.13   The reverse of Example 4.6, page 203. The root process scatters sets of 100 ints to the other processes, but the sets of 100 are *stride* ints apart in the sending buffer, where $stride \geq 100$. This requires use of MPI_SCATTERV. See Figure 4.8.

```
MPI_Comm comm;
int gsize,*sendbuf;
int root, stride, rbuf[100], i, *displs, *scounts;
...
MPI_Comm_size(comm, &gsize);
sendbuf = (int *)malloc(gsize*stride*sizeof(int));
...
displs = (int *)malloc(gsize*sizeof(int));
scounts = (int *)malloc(gsize*sizeof(int));
for (i=0; i<gsize; ++i) {
  displs[i] = i*stride;
  scounts[i] = 100;
```

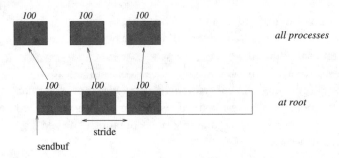

Figure 4.8
The root process scatters sets of 100 ints, moving by `stride` ints from send to send in the scatter.

```
}
MPI_Scatterv(sendbuf, scounts, displs, MPI_INT, rbuf, 100, MPI_INT,
             root, comm);
```

Example 4.14   The reverse of Example 4.10. We have a varying stride between blocks at sending (root) side, at the receiving side we receive $100 - i$ elements into the ith column of a 100×150 C array at process i. See Figure 4.9.

```
MPI_Comm comm;
int gsize,recvarray[100][150],*rptr;
int root, *sendbuf, myrank, *stride;
MPI_Datatype rtype;
int i, *displs, *scounts, offset;
...
MPI_Comm_size(comm, &gsize);
MPI_Comm_rank(comm, &myrank);

stride = (int *)malloc(gsize*sizeof(int));
...
/* stride[i] for i = 0 to gsize-1 is set somehow
 * sendbuf comes from elsewhere */
...
displs = (int *)malloc(gsize*sizeof(int));
scounts = (int *)malloc(gsize*sizeof(int));
offset = 0;
for (i=0; i<gsize; ++i) {
```

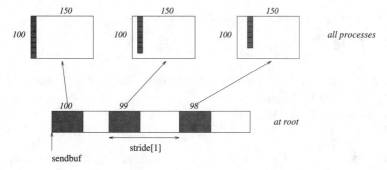

Figure 4.9
The root scatters blocks of 100-i ints into column i of a 100×150 C array. At the sending side,
the blocks are `stride[i]` ints apart.

```
    displs[i] = offset;
    offset += stride[i];
    scounts[i] = 100 - i;
}
/* Create datatype for the column we are receiving */
MPI_Type_vector(100-myrank, 1, 150, MPI_INT, &rtype);
MPI_Type_commit(&rtype);
rptr = &recvarray[0][myrank];
MPI_Scatterv(sendbuf, scounts, displs, MPI_INT, rptr, 1, rtype,
             root, comm);
```

4.9   Gather to All

MPI_ALLGATHER(sendbuf, sendcount, sendtype, recvbuf, recvcount, recvtype,
    comm)

IN	sendbuf	starting address of send buffer (choice)
IN	sendcount	number of elements in send buffer (integer)
IN	sendtype	data type of send buffer elements (handle)
OUT	recvbuf	address of receive buffer (choice)
IN	recvcount	number of elements received from any process (integer)
IN	recvtype	data type of receive buffer elements (handle)
IN	comm	communicator (handle)

```
int MPI_Allgather(void* sendbuf, int sendcount,
    MPI_Datatype sendtype, void* recvbuf, int recvcount,
    MPI_Datatype recvtype, MPI_Comm comm)
```

```
MPI_ALLGATHER(SENDBUF, SENDCOUNT, SENDTYPE, RECVBUF, RECVCOUNT,
    RECVTYPE, COMM, IERROR)
    <type> SENDBUF(*), RECVBUF(*)
    INTEGER SENDCOUNT, SENDTYPE, RECVCOUNT, RECVTYPE, COMM, IERROR
```

```
void MPI::Comm::Allgather(const void* sendbuf, int sendcount, const
    MPI::Datatype& sendtype, void* recvbuf, int recvcount,
    const MPI::Datatype& recvtype) const = 0
```

MPI_ALLGATHER can be thought of as MPI_GATHER, except all processes receive the result, instead of just the root. The block of data sent from the jth process is received by every process and placed in the jth block of the buffer recvbuf.

The type signature associated with sendcount and sendtype at a process must be equal to the type signature associated with recvcount and recvtype at all processes.

The outcome of a call to MPI_ALLGATHER(...) is as if all processes executed **n** calls to MPI_GATHER(sendbuf,sendcount,sendtype,recvbuf,recvcount, recvtype,root, comm), for root = 0 , ..., n-1. The rules for correct usage of MPI_ALLGATHER are easily found from the corresponding rules for MPI_GATHER.

The "in place" option is specified by passing the value MPI_IN_PLACE to the argument sendbuf at all processes. sendcount and sendtype are ignored. Then the input data of each process is assumed to be in the area where that process would receive its own contribution to the receive buffer. Specifically, the outcome of a call to MPI_ALLGATHER in the "in place" case is as if all processes executed n calls to MPI_GATHER(MPI_IN_PLACE, 0, MPI_DATATYPE_NULL, recvbuf, recvcount, recvtype, root, comm) for root = 0, ..., n - 1.

4.9.1   An Example Using MPI_ALLGATHER

Example 4.15   The all-gather version of Example 4.2, page 200. Using MPI_ALLGATHER, we will gather 100 ints from every process in the group to every process.

```
MPI::Intracomm comm;
int sendarray[100];
...
const int gsize = comm.Get_size();
int *rbuf = new int [gsize * 100 * sizeof(int)];
```

```
...
comm.Allgather(sendarray, 100, MPI::INT, rbuf, 100, MPI::INT);
```

After the call, every process has the group-wide concatenation of the sets of data.

4.9.2 Gather to All: Vector Variant

MPI_ALLGATHERV(sendbuf, sendcount, sendtype, recvbuf, recvcounts, displs,
    recvtype, comm)

IN	sendbuf	starting address of send buffer (choice)
IN	sendcount	number of elements in send buffer (integer)
IN	sendtype	data type of send buffer elements (handle)
OUT	recvbuf	address of receive buffer (choice)
IN	recvcounts	integer array (array of integers)
IN	displs	integer array of displacements (array of integers)
IN	recvtype	data type of receive buffer elements (handle)
IN	comm	communicator (handle)

```
int MPI_Allgatherv(void* sendbuf, int sendcount,
    MPI_Datatype sendtype, void* recvbuf, int *recvcounts,
    int *displs, MPI_Datatype recvtype, MPI_Comm comm)
```

```
MPI_ALLGATHERV(SENDBUF, SENDCOUNT, SENDTYPE, RECVBUF, RECVCOUNTS,
    DISPLS, RECVTYPE, COMM, IERROR)
    <type> SENDBUF(*), RECVBUF(*)
    INTEGER SENDCOUNT, SENDTYPE, RECVCOUNTS(*), DISPLS(*), RECVTYPE,
    COMM, IERROR
```

```
void MPI::Comm::Allgatherv(const void* sendbuf, int sendcount, const
    MPI::Datatype& sendtype, void* recvbuf, const int recvcounts[],
    const int displs[], const MPI::Datatype& recvtype) const = 0
```

MPI_ALLGATHERV can be thought of as MPI_GATHERV, except all processes receive the result, instead of just the root. The jth block of data sent from each process is received by every process and placed in the jth block of the buffer recvbuf. These blocks need not all be the same size.

The type signature associated with sendcount and sendtype at process j must be equal to the type signature associated with recvcounts[j] and recvtype at all processes.

The outcome is as if all processes executed calls to MPI_GATHERV(sendbuf, send-count,sendtype,recvbuf,recvcounts,displs,recvtype,root,comm), for root = 0 , ..., n-1. The rules for correct usage of MPI_ALLGATHERV are easily found from the corresponding rules for MPI_GATHERV.

The "in place" option is specified by passing the value MPI_IN_PLACE to the argument sendbuf at all processes. sendcount and sendtype are ignored. Then the input data of each process is assumed to be in the area where that process would receive its own contribution to the receive buffer. Specifically, the outcome of a call to MPI_ALLGATHER in the "in place" case is as if all processes executed n calls to MPI_GATHERV(MPI_IN_PLACE, 0, MPI_DATATYPE_NULL, recvbuf, recvcounts, displs, recvtype, root, comm) for root = 0, ..., n - 1.

4.10   All to All Scatter/Gather

MPI_ALLTOALL(sendbuf, sendcount, sendtype, recvbuf, recvcount, recvtype, comm)

IN	sendbuf	starting address of send buffer (choice)
IN	sendcount	number of elements sent to each process (integer)
IN	sendtype	data type of send buffer elements (handle)
OUT	recvbuf	address of receive buffer (choice)
IN	recvcount	number of elements received from any process (integer)
IN	recvtype	data type of receive buffer elements (handle)
IN	comm	communicator (handle)

```
int MPI_Alltoall(void* sendbuf, int sendcount, MPI_Datatype sendtype,
    void* recvbuf, int recvcount, MPI_Datatype recvtype,
    MPI_Comm comm)
```

```
MPI_ALLTOALL(SENDBUF, SENDCOUNT, SENDTYPE, RECVBUF, RECVCOUNT,
    RECVTYPE, COMM, IERROR)
    <type> SENDBUF(*), RECVBUF(*)
    INTEGER SENDCOUNT, SENDTYPE, RECVCOUNT, RECVTYPE, COMM, IERROR
```

```
void MPI::Comm::Alltoall(const void* sendbuf, int sendcount, const
    MPI::Datatype& sendtype, void* recvbuf, int recvcount,
    const MPI::Datatype& recvtype) const = 0
```

MPI_ALLTOALL is an extension of MPI_ALLGATHER to the case where each process sends distinct data to each of the receivers. The jth block sent from process i is received by process j and is placed in the ith block of recvbuf.

The type signature associated with sendcount and sendtype at a process must be equal to the type signature associated with recvcount and recvtype at any other process. This implies that the amount of data sent must be equal to the amount of data received, pairwise between every pair of processes. As usual, however, the type maps may be different.

The outcome is as if each process executed a send to each process (itself included) with a call to, MPI_Send(sendbuf+i · sendcount · extent(sendtype),sendcount,sendtype,i, ...), and a receive from every other process with a call to, MPI_Recv(recvbuf+i · recvcount ·t extent(recvtype),recvcount,i,...), where i = 0, ···, n - 1.

All arguments on all processes are significant. The argument comm must represent the same intragroup communication domain on all processes.

Rationale.   The definition of MPI_ALLTOALL gives as much flexibility as one would achieve by specifying at each process 2n independent, point-to-point communications, where the process sends a message to each process and receives a message from each process; this with two exceptions: all messages use the same datatype, and messages are scattered from (or gathered to) sequential storage. ☐

4.10.1   All to All: Vector Variant

MPI_ALLTOALLV(sendbuf, sendcounts, sdispls, sendtype, recvbuf, recvcounts, rdispls, recvtype, comm)

IN	sendbuf	starting address of send buffer (choice)
IN	sendcounts	integer array (array of integers)
IN	sdispls	integer array of send displacements (array of integers)
IN	sendtype	data type of send buffer elements (handle)
OUT	recvbuf	address of receive buffer (choice)
IN	recvcounts	integer array (array of integers)
IN	rdispls	integer array of receive displacements (array of integers)
IN	recvtype	data type of receive buffer elements (handle)
IN	comm	communicator (handle)

```
int MPI_Alltoallv(void* sendbuf, int *sendcounts, int *sdispls,
    MPI_Datatype sendtype, void* recvbuf, int *recvcounts,
    int *rdispls, MPI_Datatype recvtype, MPI_Comm comm)
```

```
MPI_ALLTOALLV(SENDBUF, SENDCOUNTS, SDISPLS, SENDTYPE, RECVBUF,
    RECVCOUNTS, RDISPLS, RECVTYPE, COMM, IERROR)
    <type> SENDBUF(*), RECVBUF(*)
    INTEGER SENDCOUNTS(*), SDISPLS(*), SENDTYPE, RECVCOUNTS(*),
    RDISPLS(*), RECVTYPE, COMM, IERROR
```

```
void MPI::Comm::Alltoallv(const void* sendbuf,
    const int sendcounts[], const int sdispls[],
    const MPI::Datatype& sendtype, void* recvbuf,
    const int recvcounts[], const int rdispls[],
    const MPI::Datatype& recvtype) const = 0
```

MPI_ALLTOALLV adds flexibility to MPI_ALLTOALL in that the location of data for the send is specified by sdispls and the location of the placement of the data on the receive side is specified by rdispls.

The jth block sent from process i is received by process j and is placed in the ith block of recvbuf. These blocks need not all have the same size.

The type signature associated with sendcount[j] and sendtype at process i must be equal to the type signature associated with recvcount[i] and recvtype at process j. This implies that the amount of data sent must be equal to the amount of data received, pairwise between every pair of processes. Distinct type maps between sender and receiver are still allowed.

The outcome is as if each process sent a message to every other process with, MPI_Send(sendbuf + displs[i] · extent(sendtype), sendcounts[i], sendtype, i, ...), and received a message from every other process with a call to, MPI_Recv(recvbuf + displs[i] · extent(recvtype), recvcounts[i], recvtype, i, ...), where i = 0 ⋯ n - 1. (Here, and in the remainder of this chapter, expressions of the form buf + a should be interpreted as if buf is byte-sized, so that buf + a points a bytes ahead of buf.)

All arguments on all processes are significant. The argument comm must specify the same intragroup communication domain on all processes.

The specification of counts, types, and displacements should not cause any location on the root to be written more than once. Such a call is erroneous.

Rationale.   The definition of MPI_ALLTOALLV gives as much flexibility as one would achieve by specifying at each process n independent, point-to-point communications, with the exception that all messages use the same datatype.

The "in-place" option is not available for all-to-all communication because it would not be possible, in general, to perform the communication without copying the data a process sends to itself. □

4.10.2   All to All: Generalized Function

MPI_ALLTOALLW(sendbuf, sendcounts, sdispls, sendtypes, recvbuf, recvcounts, rdispls, recvtypes, comm)

IN	sendbuf	starting address of send buffer (choice)
IN	sendcounts	integer array (integer)
IN	sdispls	integer array of send displacements (array of integers)
IN	sendtypes	array of send datatypes (array of handles)
OUT	recvbuf	address of receive buffer (choice)
IN	recvcounts	integer array (array of integers)
IN	rdispls	integer array of receive displacements (array of integers)
IN	recvtypes	array of receive datatypes (array of handles)
IN	comm	communicator (handle)

```
int MPI_Alltoallw(void *sendbuf, int *sendcounts, int *sdispls,
    MPI_Datatype *sendtypes, void *recvbuf, int *recvcounts,
    int *rdispls, MPI_Datatype *recvtypes, MPI_Comm comm)
```

```
MPI_ALLTOALLW(SENDBUF, SENDCOUNTS, SDISPLS, SENDTYPES, RECVBUF,
    RECVCOUNTS, RDISPLS, RECVTYPES, COMM, IERROR)
    <type> SENDBUF(*), RECVBUF(*)
    INTEGER SENDCOUNTS(*), SENDTYPES(*), RECVCOUNTS(*),
    RECVTYPES(*), COMM, IERROR
    INTEGER SDISPLS(*), RDISPLS(*)
```

```
void MPI::Comm::Alltoallw(const void* sendbuf, const int
    sendcounts[], const int sdispls[], const MPI::Datatype
    sendtypes[], void* recvbuf, const int recvcounts[], const int
    rdispls[], const MPI::Datatype recvtypes[]) const = 0
```

MPI_ALLTOALLW is the most general form of All-to-all. It allows separate specification of count, byte displacement and datatype for each block.

The j-th block sent from process i is received by process j and is placed in the i-th block of recvbuf. These blocks need not all have the same size or datatype.

The type signature associated with sendcounts[j], sendtypes[j] at process i must be equal to the type signature associated with recvcounts[i], recvtypes[i] at process j. This implies that the amount of data sent must be equal to the amount of data received, pairwise between every pair of processes. Distinct type maps between sender and receiver are still allowed.

The outcome is as if each process sent a message to every other process with MPI_-Send(sendbuf+sdispls[i], sendcounts[i], sendtypes[i], i, ...), and received a message from every other process with a call to MPI_Recv(recvbuf+rdispls[i], recvcounts[i], recvtypes[i], i, ...).

All arguments on all processes are significant. The argument comm must describe the same communicator on all processes.

The specification of counts, types, and displacements should not cause any location on the root to be written more than once. Such a call is erroneous.

A call to MPI_ALLTOALLW has as much flexibility as one would achieve by specifying at each process **2n** independent, point-to-point communications, where the process sends a message to each process and receives a message from each process.

Rationale. The "W" in MPI_ALLTOALLW was chosen unimaginatively to indicate that this is an extension to MPI_ALLTOALLV. A similar extension could be made for all other "vector" forms of collective communication. However, all these functions can be obtained by specializing MPI_ALLTOALLW. For example, by making all but one process have `sendcounts[i] = 0`, one obtains an `MPI_SCATTERW` function. □

4.10.3   An Example Using MPI_ALLTOALLW

Example 4.16   Using MPI_ALLTOALLW, we will transpose a block distributed matrix. We do not assume that the matrix is square, nor do we assume that all blocks are of equal size: the number of processes need not evenly divide the leading matrix dimension. The data movement executed by such a transpose is illustrated in Figure 4.10

```
void Transpose(float *localA, float *localB, int M, int N,
               MPI_Comm comm)
/* transpose MxN matrix A that is block distributed on
   processes of comm onto block distributed matrix B  */
{
  int i, j, extent, myrank, p, *scounts, *rcounts, n[2], m[2];
```

```
int lasti, lastj;
int sendcounts[MAX_SIZE], recvcounts[MAX_SIZE];
int *sdispls, *rdispls;
MPI_Datatype xtype[2][2], stype[2][2], *sendtypes, *recvtypes;

/* compute parameters */
MPI_Comm_size(comm, &p);
MPI_Comm_rank(comm, &myrank);
extent = sizeof(float);

/* allocate arrays */
scounts = (int *)malloc(p*sizeof(int));
sdispls = (int *)malloc(p*sizeof(int));
rcounts = (int *)malloc(p*sizeof(MPI_Aint));
rdispls = (int *)malloc(p*sizeof(int));
sendtypes = (MPI_Datatype *)malloc(p*sizeof(MPI_Datatype));
recvtypes = (MPI_Datatype *)malloc(p*sizeof(MPI_Datatype));

/* compute block sizes */
m[0] = M/p;
m[1] = M - (p-1)*(M/p);
n[0] = N/p;
n[1] = N - (p-1)*(N/p);

/* compute types */
for (i=0; i <= 1; i++)
  for (j=0; j <= 1; j++) {
    xtype[i][j] = transpose_type(m[i], n[j], MPI_FLOAT);
    stype[i][j] = submatrix_type(M, m[i], n[j], MPI_FLOAT);
  }

/* prepare collective operation arguments */
lasti = myrank == p-1;
for (j=0;  j < p; j++) {
  lastj = j == p-1;
  sendcounts[j] = 1;
  sdispls[j] = j*n[0]*extent;
  sendtypes[j] = xtype[lasti][lastj];
```

```
    recvcounts[j] = 1;
    rdispls[j] = j*m[0]*extent;
    recvtypes[j] = stype[lastj][lasti];
  }

  /* communicate */
  MPI_Alltoallw(&localA, sendcounts, sdispls, sendtypes,
                &localB, recvcounts, rdispls, recvtypes, comm);
}



MPI_Datatype submatrix_type(int N, int m, int n, MPI_Datatype type)
/* computes a datatype for an mxn submatrix within an MxN matrix
   with entries of type type */
{
  MPI_Datatype subrow, submatrix;

  MPI_Type_contiguous(n, type, &subrow);
  MPI_Type_vector(m, 1, N, subrow, &submatrix);
  MPI_Type_commit(&submatrix);
  return(submatrix);
}



MPI_Datatype transpose_type(int m, int n, MPI_Datatype type)
/* computes a datatype for the transpose of an mxn matrix
   with entries of type type */
{
  MPI_Datatype subrow, subrow1, submatrix;
  MPI_Aint lb, extent;

  MPI_Type_vector(m, 1, n, type, &subrow);
  MPI_Type_get_extent(type, &lb, &extent);
  MPI_Type_create_resized(subrow, 0, extent, &subrow1);
  MPI_Type_contiguous(n, subrow1, &submatrix);
  MPI_Type_commit(&submatrix);
  return(submatrix);
}
```

4.11   Global Reduction Operations

The functions in this section perform a global reduce operation (such as sum, max, logical AND, etc.) across all the members of a group. The reduction operation can be either one from a predefined list of operations, or a user-defined operation. The global reduction functions come in several flavors: a reduce that returns the result of the reduction at one node, an all-reduce that returns this result at all nodes, and a scan (parallel prefix) operation. In addition, a reduce-scatter operation combines the functionality of a reduce and a scatter operation. In order to improve performance, the functions can be passed an array of values; one call will perform a sequence of element-wise reductions on the arrays of values. Figure 4.11 gives a pictorial representation of these operations.

"In place" variants of the three reduce functions are obtained by passing MPI_-IN_PLACE as a send buffer argument. The input to the reduction is then taken from the receive buffer argument, which is updated in place.

4.11.1   Reduce

MPI_REDUCE(sendbuf, recvbuf, count, datatype, op, root, comm)

IN	sendbuf	address of send buffer (choice)
OUT	recvbuf	address of receive buffer (choice)
IN	count	number of elements in send buffer (integer)
IN	datatype	data type of elements of send buffer (handle)
IN	op	reduce operation (handle)
IN	root	rank of root process (integer)
IN	comm	communicator (handle)

```
int MPI_Reduce(void* sendbuf, void* recvbuf, int count,
    MPI_Datatype datatype, MPI_Op op, int root, MPI_Comm comm)
```

```
MPI_REDUCE(SENDBUF, RECVBUF, COUNT, DATATYPE, OP, ROOT, COMM,
    IERROR)
    <type> SENDBUF(*), RECVBUF(*)
    INTEGER COUNT, DATATYPE, OP, ROOT, COMM, IERROR
```

```
void MPI::Comm::Reduce(const void* sendbuf, void* recvbuf,
    int count, const MPI::Datatype& datatype, const MPI::Op& op,
    int root) const = 0
```

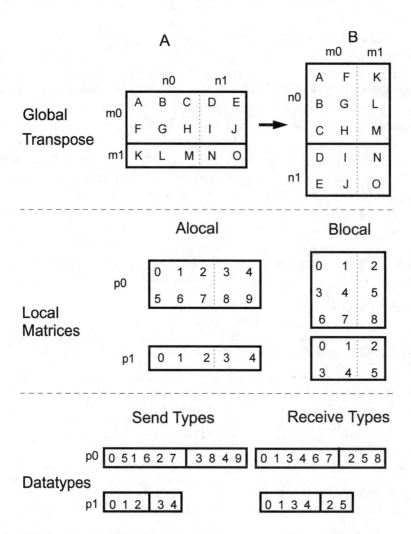

Figure 4.10
Transpose of a 5x3 matrix that is block distributed on 2 processes.

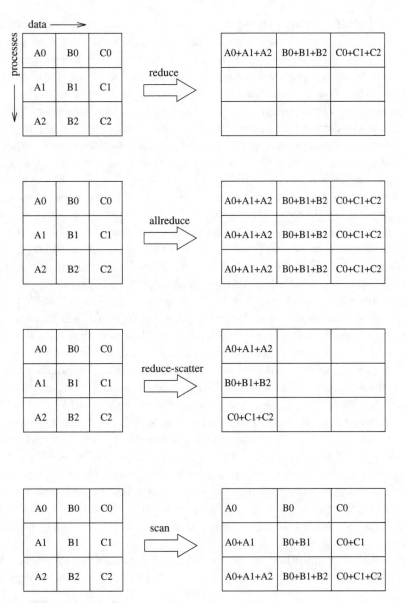

Figure 4.11
Reduce functions illustrated for a group of three processes. In each case, each row of boxes represents data items in one process. Thus, in the reduce, initially each process has three items; after the reduce the root process has three sums.

MPI_REDUCE combines the elements provided in the input buffer of each process in the group, using the operation op, and returns the combined value in the output buffer of the process with rank root. The input buffer is defined by the arguments sendbuf, count and datatype. The output buffer is defined by the arguments recvbuf, count and datatype. Both have the same number of elements with the same type. The arguments count, op and root must have identical values at all processes, the datatype arguments should match, and comm should represent the same intragroup communication domain. Thus, all processes provide input buffers and output buffers of the same length, with elements of the same type. Each process can provide one element, or a sequence of elements, in which case the combine operation is executed element-wise on each entry of the sequence. For example, if the operation is MPI_MAX (MPI::MAX, in C++) and the send buffer contains two elements that are floating point numbers (count = 2 and datatype = MPI_FLOAT), then recvbuf(0) = global max(sendbuf(0)) and recvbuf(1) = global max(sendbuf(1)). Overlapping datatypes are permitted in "send" buffers. Overlapping datatypes in "receive" buffers are erroneous and may give unpredictable results.

The "in place" option is specified by passing the value MPI_IN_PLACE to the argument sendbuf at the root. In such a case, the input data is taken at the root from the receive buffer, where it will be replaced by the output data.

Section 4.11.2 lists the set of predefined operations provided by MPI. That section also enumerates the allowed datatypes for each operation. In addition, users may define their own operations that can be overloaded to operate on several datatypes, either basic or derived. This is further explained in Section 4.13.

The operation op is always assumed to be associative. All predefined operations are also commutative. Users may define operations that are assumed to be associative, but not commutative. The "canonical" evaluation order of a reduction is determined by the ranks of the processes in the group. However, the implementation can take advantage of associativity, or associativity and commutativity to change the order of evaluation. This may change the result of the reduction for operations that are not strictly associative and commutative, such as floating point addition.

MPI_REDUCE and other functions with an op argument may return the error code MPI_ERR_OP (MPI::ERR_OP, in C++) to indicate an invalid op argument.

Advice to implementors.   It is strongly recommended that MPI_REDUCE be implemented so that the same result be obtained whenever the function is applied on the same arguments, appearing in the same order. Note that this may prevent optimizations that take advantage of the physical location of processors. □

The datatype argument of MPI_REDUCE must be compatible with op. Predefined operators work only with the MPI types listed in Section 4.11.2 and Section 4.11.3. Furthermore, the datatype and op given for predefined operators must be the same on all processes. User-defined operators may operate on general, derived datatypes. In this case, each argument that the reduce operation is applied to is one element described by such a datatype, which may contain several basic values. Note that it is possible for users to supply different user-defined operations to MPI_REDUCE in each process. Even if the operations are defined at all processes by the same text, their effect may not be identical, in a heterogeneous environment. Each process invokes its local operation, but MPI does not define which process computes each of the reduction operations.

Advice to users.   Users should make no assumptions about how MPI_REDUCE is implemented. It is safest to ensure that the same function is passed to MPI_REDUCE by each process. □

User-defined operators are further explained in Section 4.13.

4.11.2   Predefined Reduce Operations

The following predefined operations are supplied for MPI_REDUCE and related functions MPI_ALLREDUCE, MPI_REDUCE_SCATTER, and MPI_SCAN. These operations are invoked by placing the following in op.

Name	Meaning
MPI_MAX	maximum
MPI_MIN	minimum
MPI_SUM	sum
MPI_PROD	product
MPI_LAND	logical and
MPI_BAND	bit-wise and
MPI_LOR	logical or
MPI_BOR	bit-wise or
MPI_LXOR	logical xor
MPI_BXOR	bit-wise xor
MPI_MAXLOC	max value and location
MPI_MINLOC	min value and location

The C++ binding for these constants is

Name	Meaning
MPI::MAX	maximum
MPI::MIN	minimum
MPI::SUM	sum
MPI::PROD	product
MPI::LAND	logical and
MPI::BAND	bitwise and
MPI::LOR	logical or
MPI::BOR	bit-wise or
MPI::LXOR	logical xor
MPI::BXOR	bit-wise xor
MPI::MAXLOC	max value and location
MPI::MINLOC	min value and location

The two operations MPI_MINLOC and MPI_MAXLOC are discussed separately in Section 4.11.3. For the other predefined operations, we enumerate below the allowed combinations of op and datatype arguments. First, define groups of MPI basic datatypes in the following way.

C integer:	MPI_SIGNED_CHAR, MPI_UNSIGNED_CHAR, MPI_INT, MPI_LONG, MPI_SHORT, MPI_UNSIGNED_SHORT, MPI_UNSIGNED, MPI_UNSIGNED_LONG
C++ integer:	MPI::SIGNED_CHAR, MPI::UNSIGNED_CHAR, MPI::SHORT, MPI::INT, MPI::UNSIGNED, MPI::UNSIGNED_SHORT, MPI::LONG, MPI::UNSIGNED_LONG
Fortran integer:	MPI_INTEGER
Floating point:	MPI_FLOAT, MPI_DOUBLE, MPI_LONG_DOUBLE MPI_REAL, MPI_DOUBLE_PRECISION, MPI::FLOAT, MPI::DOUBLE, MPI::LONG_DOUBLE
Logical:	MPI_LOGICAL, MPI::BOOL
Complex:	MPI_COMPLEX, MPI::COMPLEX, MPI::DOUBLE_COMPLEX, MPI::LONG_DOUBLE_COMPLEX

Byte: MPI_BYTE

Now, the valid datatypes for each option is specified below.

Op	Allowed Types
MPI_MAX, MPI_MIN	C integer, Fortran integer, Floating point
MPI_SUM, MPI_PROD	C integer, Fortran integer, Floating point, Complex
MPI_LAND, MPI_LOR, MPI_LXOR	C integer, Logical
MPI_BAND, MPI_BOR, MPI_BXOR	C++ integer, C integer, Fortran integer, Byte

Datatype MPI_SIGNED_CHAR is an MPI-2 addition. The cross-language datatypes (e.g., MPI::REAL) are also allowed and follow the native language rules. Note that reductions are not allowed with datatype MPI_CHAR. This is consistent with the intended usage of these two datatypes: MPI_CHAR should be used when the corresponding C variable represents a character, while type MPI_SIGNED_CHAR should be used when the corresponding C variable represents a (very short) integer.

Example 4.17   A routine that computes the dot product of two vectors that are distributed across a group of processes and returns the answer at node zero.

```fortran
SUBROUTINE PAR_BLAS1(m, a, b, c, comm)
USE MPI
REAL a(m), b(m)        ! local slice of array
REAL c                 ! result (at node zero)
REAL sum
INTEGER m, comm, i, ierr

! local sum
sum = 0.0
DO i = 1, m
   sum = sum + a(i)*b(i)
END DO

! global sum
CALL MPI_REDUCE(sum, c, 1, MPI_REAL, MPI_SUM, 0, comm, ierr)
RETURN
END
```

Example 4.18   A routine that computes the product of a vector and an array that are distributed across a group of processes and returns the answer at node zero. The distribution of vector **a** and matrix **b** is illustrated in Figure 4.12.

```fortran
SUBROUTINE PAR_BLAS2(m, n, a, b, c, comm)
USE MPI
REAL a(m), b(m,n)    ! local slice of array
REAL c(n)            ! result
REAL sum(n)
INTEGER m, n, comm, i, j, ierr

! local sum
DO j= 1, n
  sum(j) = 0.0
  DO i = 1, m
    sum(j) = sum(j) + a(i)*b(i,j)
  END DO
END DO

! global sum
CALL MPI_REDUCE(sum, c, n, MPI_REAL, MPI_SUM, 0, comm, ierr)

! return result at node zero (and garbage at the other nodes)
RETURN
END
```

4.11.3   MINLOC and MAXLOC

The operator MPI_MINLOC is used to compute a global minimum and also an index attached to the minimum value.   MPI_MAXLOC similarly computes a global maximum and index. One application of these is to compute a global minimum (maximum) and the rank of the process containing this value.

The operation that defines MPI_MAXLOC is:

$$\begin{pmatrix} u \\ i \end{pmatrix} \circ \begin{pmatrix} v \\ j \end{pmatrix} = \begin{pmatrix} w \\ k \end{pmatrix} \text{ where } w = \max(u,v) \text{ and } k = \begin{cases} i & \text{if } u > v \\ \min(i,j) & \text{if } u = v \\ j & \text{if } u < v \end{cases}$$

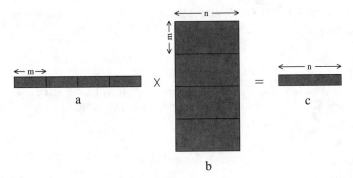

Figure 4.12
Vector-matrix product. Vector **a** and matrix **b** are distributed in one dimension. The distribution is illustrated for four processes. The slices need not be all of the same size: each process may have a different value for **m**.

MPI_MINLOC is defined similarly:

$$\begin{pmatrix} u \\ i \end{pmatrix} \circ \begin{pmatrix} v \\ j \end{pmatrix} = \begin{pmatrix} w \\ k \end{pmatrix} \text{ where } w = \min(u,v) \text{ and } k = \begin{cases} i & \text{if } u < v \\ \min(i,j) & \text{if } u = v \\ j & \text{if } u > v \end{cases}$$

Both operations are associative and commutative. Note that if MPI_MAXLOC is applied to reduce a sequence of pairs $(u_0, 0), (u_1, 1), \ldots, (u_{n-1}, n-1)$, then the value returned is (u, r), where $u = \max_i u_i$ and r is the index of the first global maximum in the sequence. Thus, if each process supplies a value and its rank within the group, then a reduce operation with op = MPI_MAXLOC will return the maximum value and the rank of the first process with that value. Similarly, MPI_MINLOC can be used to return a minimum and its index. More generally, MPI_MINLOC computes a *lexicographic minimum*, where elements are ordered according to the first component of each pair, and ties are resolved according to the second component.

The reduce operation is defined to operate on arguments that consist of a pair: value and index. In order to use MPI_MINLOC and MPI_MAXLOC in a reduce operation, one must provide a **datatype** argument that represents a pair (value and index). MPI provides pairs for predefined datatypes. In C, the index is an **int** and the value can be a short or long **int**, a **float**, or a **double**. The potentially mixed-type nature of such arguments is a problem in Fortran. The problem is circumvented, for Fortran, by having the MPI-provided type consist of a pair of the same type as value, and coercing the index to this type.

The operations MPI_MAXLOC and MPI_MINLOC can be used with each of the following datatypes.

Fortran:

Name	Description
MPI_2REAL	pair of REALs
MPI_2DOUBLE_PRECISION	pair of DOUBLE PRECISION variables
MPI_2INTEGER	pair of INTEGERs

C:

Name	Description
MPI_FLOAT_INT	float and int
MPI_DOUBLE_INT	double and int
MPI_LONG_INT	long and int
MPI_2INT	pair of int
MPI_SHORT_INT	short and int
MPI_LONG_DOUBLE_INT	long double and int
MPI_2REAL	pair of Fortran REALs
MPI_2DOUBLE_PRECISION	pair of Fortran DOUBLE PRECISION variables
MPI_2INTEGER	pair of Fortran INTEGERs

C++:

Name	Description
MPI::FLOAT_INT	float and int
MPI::DOUBLE_INT	double and int
MPI::LONG_INT	long and int
MPI::TWOINT	pair of int
MPI::SHORT_INT	short and int
MPI::LONG_DOUBLE_INT	long double and int
MPI::TWOREAL	pair of Fortran REALs
MPI::TWODOUBLE_PRECISION	pair of Fortran DOUBLE PRECISION variables
MPI::TWOINTEGER	pair of Fortran INTEGERs

The datatype MPI_2REAL is *as if* defined by the following (see Section 3.4).

```
CALL MPI_TYPE_CONTIGUOUS(2, MPI_REAL, MPI_2REAL, IERR)
```

Similar statements apply for MPI_2INTEGER, MPI_2DOUBLE_PRECISION, and MPI_2INT.

The datatype MPI_FLOAT_INT is *as if* defined by the following sequence of instructions.

```
type[0] = MPI_FLOAT;
type[1] = MPI_INT;
disp[0] = 0;
disp[1] = sizeof(float);
block[0] = 1;
block[1] = 1;
MPI_Type_create_struct(2, block, disp, type, &MPI_FLOAT_INT);
```

Similar statements apply for the other mixed types in C.

Example 4.19   Each process has an array of 30 doubles, in C. For each of the 30 locations, compute the value and rank of the process containing the largest value.

```
...
/* each process has an array of 30 doubles: ain[30] */
double ain[30], aout[30];
int   ind[30];
struct {
  double val;
  int    rank;
} in[30], out[30];
int i, myrank, root;

MPI_Comm_rank(MPI_COMM_WORLD, &myrank);
for (i=0; i<30; i++) {
  in[i].val = ain[i];
  in[i].rank = myrank;
}
MPI_Reduce(in, out, 30, MPI_DOUBLE_INT, MPI_MAXLOC, root, comm);
/* At this point, the answer resides on process root */
if (myrank == root) {
  /* read ranks out */
  for (i=0; i<30; i++) {
    aout[i] = out[i].val;
    ind[i] = out[i].rank;
  }
}
```

Example 4.20   Same example, in Fortran.

```
...
! each process has an array of 30 doubles: ain(30)

DOUBLE PRECISION ain(30), aout(30)
INTEGER ind(30);
DOUBLE PRECISION in(2,30), out(2,30)
INTEGER i, comm, myrank, root, ierr;

call MPI_COMM_RANK(MPI_COMM_WORLD, myrank, ierr)
DO i=1, 30
   in(1,i) = ain(i)
   in(2,i) = myrank        ! myrank is coerced to a double
END DO

call MPI_REDUCE(in, out, 30, MPI_2DOUBLE_PRECISION, MPI_MAXLOC, &
            root, comm, ierr)
! At this point, the answer resides on process root

IF (myrank .EQ. root) THEN
    ! read ranks out
    DO I= 1, 30
       aout(i) = out(1,i)
       ind(i) = out(2,i)  ! rank is coerced back to an integer
    END DO
END IF
```

Example 4.21   Same example, in C++.

```
...
// Each process has an array of 30 doubles: ain[30]
double ain[30], aout[30];
int ind[30];
struct {
  double val;
  int    rank;
} in[30], out[30];
```

```
int i, root;
...
const int myrank = MPI::COMM_WORLD.Get_rank();
for (i = 0; i < 30; i++) {
  in[i].val = ain[i];
  in[i].rank = myrank;
}
comm.Reduce(in, out, 30, MPI::DOUBLE_INT, MPI::MAXLOC, root);
// At this point, the answer resides on process root
if (myrank == root) {
  // Read ranks out
  for (i = 0; i < 30; i++) {
    aout[i] = out[i].val;
    ind[i] = out[i].rank;
  }
}
```

Example 4.22   Each process has a non-empty array of values. Find the minimum global value, the rank of the process that holds it and its index on this process.

```
#define  LEN    1000

float val[LEN];        /* local array of values */
int count;             /* local number of values */
int myrank, minrank, minindex;
float minval;

struct {
  float value;
  int index;
} in, out;

/* local minloc */
in.value = val[0];
in.index = 0;
for (i=1; i < count; i++) {
  if (in.value > val[i]) {
```

```
      in.value = val[i];
      in.index = i;
    }
}


/* global minloc */
MPI_Comm_rank(MPI_COMM_WORLD, &myrank);
in.index = myrank*LEN + in.index;
MPI_Reduce( &in, &out, 1, MPI_FLOAT_INT, MPI_MINLOC, root, comm );
/* At this point, the answer resides on process root */
if (myrank == root) {
  /* read answer out */
  minval = out.value;
  minrank = out.index / LEN;
  minindex = out.index % LEN;
}
```

Rationale.   The definition of MPI_MINLOC and MPI_MAXLOC given here has the
advantage that it does not require any special-case handling of these two operations:
they are handled like any other reduce operation. A programmer can provide
his or her own definition of MPI_MAXLOC and MPI_MINLOC, if so desired. The
disadvantage is that values and indices have to be first interleaved, and that indices
and values have to be coerced to the same type, in Fortran. □

4.11.4   All Reduce

MPI includes variants of each of the reduce operations where the result is returned
to all processes in the group. MPI requires that all processes participating in these
operations receive identical results.

MPI_ALLREDUCE(sendbuf, recvbuf, count, datatype, op, comm)

IN	sendbuf	starting address of send buffer (choice)
OUT	recvbuf	starting address of receive buffer (choice)
IN	count	number of elements in send buffer (integer)
IN	datatype	data type of elements of send buffer (handle)
IN	op	operation (handle)
IN	comm	communicator (handle)

```
int MPI_Allreduce(void* sendbuf, void* recvbuf, int count,
    MPI_Datatype datatype, MPI_Op op, MPI_Comm comm)
```

```
MPI_ALLREDUCE(SENDBUF, RECVBUF, COUNT, DATATYPE, OP, COMM, IERROR)
    <type> SENDBUF(*), RECVBUF(*)
    INTEGER COUNT, DATATYPE, OP, COMM, IERROR
```

```
void MPI::Comm::Allreduce(const void* sendbuf, void* recvbuf,
    int count, const MPI::Datatype& datatype, const MPI::Op& op)
    const = 0
```

Same as MPI_REDUCE except that the result appears in the receive buffer of all the group members.

The "in place" option is specified by passing the value MPI_IN_PLACE to the argument sendbuf at all processes. In such case, the input data is taken at each process from the receive buffer, where it will be replaced by the output data.

Advice to users. When the "in-place" option is specified, users may pass MPI_IN_PLACE as the argument sendbuf at all processes. This usage is encouraged, since it is consistent with the current standard and seems more consistent with the handling of "in-place" in other cases. ⬚

Advice to implementors. The all-reduce operations can be implemented as a reduce, followed by a broadcast. However, a direct implementation can lead to better performance. In this case care must be taken to make sure that all processes receive the same result. ⬚

Example 4.23 A routine that computes the product of a vector and an array that are distributed across a group of processes and returns the answer at all nodes (see also Example 4.18).

```
void
par_blas2(int m, int n, double *a, double **b, double *c,
         MPI::Intracomm &comm)
{
  double *sum = new double [n];
  for (int j = 0; j < n; j++) {
    double tmp = 0.0;
    for (int i = 0; i < m; i++)
      tmp += a[i] * b[j][i];
    sum[j] = tmp;
```

```
      }
      comm.Allreduce(sum, c, n, MPI::REAL, MPI::SUM);
      delete [] sum;
}
```

4.11.5 Reduce-Scatter

MPI includes variants of each of the reduce operations where the result is scattered to all processes in the group on return.

MPI_REDUCE_SCATTER(sendbuf, recvbuf, recvcounts, datatype, op, comm)

IN	sendbuf	starting address of send buffer (choice)
OUT	recvbuf	starting address of receive buffer (choice)
IN	recvcounts	integer array (array of integers)
IN	datatype	data type of elements of input buffer (handle)
IN	op	operation (handle)
IN	comm	communicator (handle)

```
int MPI_Reduce_scatter(void* sendbuf, void* recvbuf, int *recvcounts,
    MPI_Datatype datatype, MPI_Op op, MPI_Comm comm)
```

```
MPI_REDUCE_SCATTER(SENDBUF, RECVBUF, RECVCOUNTS, DATATYPE, OP, COMM,
    IERROR)
    <type> SENDBUF(*), RECVBUF(*)
    INTEGER RECVCOUNTS(*), DATATYPE, OP, COMM, IERROR
```

```
void MPI::Comm::Reduce_scatter(const void* sendbuf, void* recvbuf,
    int recvcounts[], const MPI::Datatype& datatype,
    const MPI::Op& op) const = 0
```

MPI_REDUCE_SCATTER acts as if it first does an element-wise reduction on vector of $count = \sum_i recvcounts[i]$ elements in the send buffer defined by sendbuf, count and datatype. Next, the resulting vector of results is split into n disjoint segments, where n is the number of processes in the group of comm. Segment i contains recvcounts[i] elements. The ith segment is sent to process i and stored in the receive buffer defined by recvbuf, recvcounts[i] and datatype.

The "in place" option is specified by passing MPI_IN_PLACE in the sendbuf argument at all processes. In this case, the input data is taken from the top of the receive buffer. Note that the area occupied by the input data may be either longer or shorter than the data filled by the output data.

Example 4.24   A routine that computes the product of a vector and an array that are distributed across a group of processes and returns the answer in a distributed array. The distribution of vectors a and c and matrix b is illustrated in Figure 4.13.

```fortran
SUBROUTINE PAR_BLAS2(m, n, k, a, b, c, comm)
USE MPI
REAL a(m), b(m,n), c(k)      ! local slice of array
REAL, ALLOCATABLE :: sum(:)
INTEGER m, n, k, comm, i, j, gsize, ierr
INTEGER, ALLOCATABLE :: recvcounts(:)

! distribute to all processes the sizes of the slices of
! array c (in real life, this would be precomputed)
CALL MPI_COMM_SIZE(comm, gsize, ierr)
ALLOCATE (recvcounts(gsize))
CALL MPI_ALLGATHER(k, 1, MPI_INTEGER, recvcounts, 1, &
                   MPI_INTEGER, comm, ierr)

ALLOCATE (sum(n))
! local sum
DO j= 1, n
  sum(j) = 0.0
  DO i = 1, m
    sum(j) = sum(j) + a(i)*b(i,j)
  END DO
END DO

! global sum and distribution of vector c
CALL MPI_REDUCE_SCATTER(sum, c, recvcounts, MPI_REAL, &
                        MPI_SUM, comm, ierr)
DEALLOCATE(sum,recvcounts)
! return result in distributed vector
RETURN
END
```

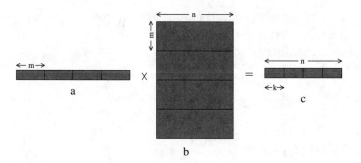

Figure 4.13
Vector-matrix product. All vectors and matrices are distributed. The distribution is illustrated for four processes. Each process may have a different value for m and k.

Advice to implementors. The MPI_REDUCE_SCATTER routine is functionally equivalent to: An MPI_REDUCE operation with count equal to the sum of recv-counts[i] followed by MPI_SCATTERV with sendcounts equal to recvcounts. However, a direct implementation may run faster. □

4.12   Scan Operations

4.12.1   Inclusive Scan

MPI_SCAN(sendbuf, recvbuf, count, datatype, op, comm)
IN	sendbuf	starting address of send buffer (choice)
OUT	recvbuf	starting address of receive buffer (choice)
IN	count	number of elements in input buffer (integer)
IN	datatype	data type of elements of input buffer (handle)
IN	op	operation (handle)
IN	comm	communicator (handle)

```
int MPI_Scan(void* sendbuf, void* recvbuf, int count,
    MPI_Datatype datatype, MPI_Op op, MPI_Comm comm )

MPI_SCAN(SENDBUF, RECVBUF, COUNT, DATATYPE, OP, COMM, IERROR)
    <type> SENDBUF(*), RECVBUF(*)
    INTEGER COUNT, DATATYPE, OP, COMM, IERROR
```

```
void MPI::Intracomm::Scan(const void* sendbuf, void* recvbuf,
    int count, const MPI::Datatype& datatype, const MPI::Op& op)
    const
```

MPI_SCAN is used to perform an inclusive prefix reduction on data distributed across the group. The operation returns, in the receive buffer of the process with rank i, the reduction of the values in the send buffers of processes with ranks $0,\ldots,i$ (inclusive). The type of operations supported, their semantics, and the constraints on send and receive buffers are as for MPI_REDUCE.

The "in place" option is specified by passing MPI_IN_PLACE in the sendbuf argument at all processes. In this case, the input data is taken from the receive buffer, and replaced by the output data.

4.12.2 Exclusive Scan

MPI_EXSCAN(sendbuf, recvbuf, count, datatype, op, comm)

IN	sendbuf	starting address of send buffer (choice)
OUT	recvbuf	starting address of receive buffer (choice)
IN	count	number of elements in input buffer (integer)
IN	datatype	data type of elements of input buffer (handle)
IN	op	operation (handle)
IN	comm	Communicator (handle)

```
int MPI_Exscan(void *sendbuf, void *recvbuf, int count,
    MPI_Datatype datatype, MPI_Op op, MPI_Comm comm)
```

```
MPI_EXSCAN(SENDBUF, RECVBUF, COUNT, DATATYPE, OP, COMM, IERROR)
    <type> SENDBUF(*), RECVBUF(*)
    INTEGER COUNT, DATATYPE, OP, COMM, IERROR
```

```
void MPI::Intracomm::Exscan(const void* sendbuf, void* recvbuf, int
    count, const MPI::Datatype& datatype, const MPI::Op& op) const
```

MPI_EXSCAN is used to perform an exclusive prefix reduction on data distributed across the group. The value in recvbuf on the process with rank 0 is undefined, and recvbuf is not significant on process 0. The value in recvbuf on the process with rank 1 is defined as the value in sendbuf on the process with rank 0. For processes with rank $i > 1$, the operation returns, in the receive buffer of the process with rank i, the reduction of the values in the send buffers of processes with ranks $0,\ldots,i-1$

(inclusive). The type of operations supported, their semantics, and the constraints on send and receive buffers, are as for MPI_REDUCE.

No "in place" option is supported.

Advice to users.   MPI does not specify which process computes which operation. In particular, both process 0 and process 1 may participate in the computation, even though no value is returned at process 0, and process 1 merely returns the value provided to process 0. All processes, even the processes with ranks zero and one, must provide the same op. ☐

Rationale.   Both exclusive scan and inclusive scan are useful operations. The exclusive scan function is more general than the inclusive scan, in the following sense: The inclusive scan can always be computed from the exclusive scan with no additional communication; for non-invertible operations such as max and min, communication is required to compute the exclusive scan from the inclusive scan.

Nevertheless, the MPI-1 Forum chose an inclusive scan operation, and the exclusive scan was only added in MPI-2. This is because the definition of MPI_EXSCAN is unsatisfactory from a mathematical viewpoint. There is no reason the have an undefined output at process 0; the "mathematically correct" output for process 0 is the unit element of the reduction operation. Thus, we have $out_i = out_{i-1} \theta in_{i-1}$, for $i = 1, \ldots, n - 1$. (See, for example, the definition of array prefix and suffix functions in High Performance Fortran [25]) But such a definition of exclusive scan would not work with user-defined functions: how does MPI "know" the unit value for a user-defined operation? ☐

4.13   User-Defined Operations for Reduce and Scan

MPI_OP_CREATE(function, commute, op)

IN	function	user defined function (function)
IN	commute	true if commutative; false otherwise. (logical)
OUT	op	operation (handle)

```
int MPI_Op_create(MPI_User_function *function, int commute,
    MPI_Op *op)
```

```
MPI_OP_CREATE( FUNCTION, COMMUTE, OP, IERROR)
    EXTERNAL FUNCTION
```

```
LOGICAL COMMUTE
INTEGER OP, IERROR
```

```
void MPI::Op::Init(MPI::User_function* function, bool commute)
```

MPI_OP_CREATE binds a user-defined global operation to an op handle that can subsequently be used in MPI_REDUCE, MPI_ALLREDUCE, MPI_REDUCE-SCATTER, MPI_SCAN, and MPI_EXSCAN. The user-defined operation is assumed to be associative. If commute = true, then the operation should be both commutative and associative. If commute = false, the order of operations is then fixed and is defined to be in ascending, process rank order, beginning with process zero. The order of evaluation can be changed to take advantage of the associativity of the operation. If commute = true then the order of evaluation can be changed to take advantage of commutativity and associativity.

function is the user-defined function, which must have the following four arguments: invec, inoutvec, len and datatype.

The ISO C prototype for the function is the following:

```
typedef void MPI_User_function( void *invec, void *inoutvec,
                                int *len, MPI_Datatype *datatype);
```

The Fortran declaration of the user-defined function appears below:

```
FUNCTION USER_FUNCTION( INVEC, INOUTVEC, LEN, TYPE)
<type> INVEC(LEN), INOUTVEC(LEN)
 INTEGER LEN, TYPE
```

The C++ prototype for the function is the following:

```
typedef void MPI_User_function(const void *invec, void* inoutvec,
                               int len, const Datatype& datatype);
```

The datatype argument is a handle to the data type that was passed into the call to MPI_REDUCE. The user reduce function should be written such that the following holds: Let u[0], ... , u[len-1] be the len elements in the communication buffer described by the arguments invec, len and datatype when the function is invoked; let v[0], ... , v[len-1] be len elements in the communication buffer described by the arguments inoutvec, len and datatype when the function is invoked; let w[0], ... , w[len-1] be len elements in the communication buffer described by the arguments inoutvec, len and datatype. When the function returns w[i] = u[i]∘v[i], for i=0 , ... , len-1, where ∘ is the reduce operation that the function computes.

Informally, we can think of invec and inoutvec as arrays of len elements that function is combining. The result of the reduction over-writes values in inoutvec, hence the name. Each invocation of the function results in the pointwise evaluation of the reduce operator on len elements, i.e, the function returns in inoutvec[i] the value invec[i] ∘ inoutvec[i], for $i = 0, \ldots, \text{count} - 1$, where ∘ is the combining operation computed by the function.

Rationale.   The len argument allows MPI_REDUCE to avoid calling the function for each element in the input buffer. Rather, the system can choose to apply the function to chunks of input. In C and C++, it is respectively passed in as a pointer and reference for reasons of compatibility with Fortran.

By internally comparing the value of the datatype argument to known, global handles, it is possible to overload the use of a single user-defined function for several different data types. □

General datatypes may be passed to the user function. However, use of datatypes that are not contiguous is likely to lead to inefficiencies.

No MPI communication function may be called inside the user function. MPI_ABORT may be called inside the function in case of an error.

Advice to users.   The Fortran version of MPI_REDUCE will invoke a user-defined reduce function using the Fortran calling conventions and will pass a Fortran-type datatype argument; the C version will use C calling convention and the C representation of a datatype handle. Users who plan to mix languages should define their reduction functions accordingly. □

Advice to implementors.   We outline below a naive and inefficient implementation of MPI_REDUCE.

```
if (rank > 0) {
    MPI_Recv(tempbuf, count, datatype, rank-1,...);
    User_reduce( tempbuf, sendbuf, &count, &datatype );
}
if (rank < groupsize-1) {
    MPI_Send( sendbuf, count, datatype, rank+1, ...);
}
/* answer now resides in process groupsize-1.
   now send to root */
if (rank == groupsize-1) {
```

```
            MPI_Send( sendbuf, count, datatype, root, ...);
       }
       if (rank == root) {
            MPI_Recv(recvbuf, count, datatype, groupsize-1,...);
       }
```

The reduction computation proceeds sequentially from process 0 to process groupsize-1. This order is chosen so as to respect the order of a possibly non-commutative operator defined by the function User_reduce(). A more efficient implementation is achieved by taking advantage of associativity and using a logarithmic tree reduction. Commutativity can be used to advantage for those cases in which the commute argument to MPI_OP_CREATE is true. Also, the amount of temporary buffer required can be reduced, and communication can be pipelined with computation, by transferring and reducing the elements in chunks of size len < count.

The predefined reduce operations can be implemented as a library of user-defined operations. However, better performance might be achieved if MPI_REDUCE handles these functions as a special case. □

MPI_OP_FREE(op)

   INOUT op   operation (handle)

```
int MPI_op_free( MPI_Op *op)
```

```
MPI_OP_FREE( OP, IERROR)
    INTEGER OP, IERROR
```

```
void MPI::Op::Free()
```

Marks a user-defined reduction operation for deallocation and sets op to MPI_OP_NULL (MPI::OP_NULL, in C++).

Example of User-defined Reduce It is time for an example of a user-defined reduction.

Example 4.25   Compute the product of an array of complex numbers, in C.

```c
typedef struct {
  double real,imag;
} Complex;

/* the user-defined function */
void myProd(Complex *in, Complex *inout, int *len,
            MPI_Datatype *dptr)
{
  int i;
  Complex c;

  for (i=0; i< *len; ++i) {
    c.real = inout->real*in->real - inout->imag*in->imag;
    c.imag = inout->real*in->imag + inout->imag*in->real;
    *inout = c;
    in++; inout++;
  }
}


/* and, to call it.. */
...
/* each process has an array of 100 Complexes */
Complex a[100], answer[100];
MPI_Op myOp;
MPI_Datatype ctype;

/* explain to MPI how type Complex is defined */
MPI_Type_contiguous(2, MPI_DOUBLE, &ctype);
MPI_Type_commit(&ctype);
/* create the complex-product user-op */
MPI_Op_create((MPI_User_function*)myProd, True, &myOp);

MPI_Reduce(a, answer, 100, ctype, myOp, root, comm);

/* At this point, the answer, which consists of 100 Complexes,
 * resides on process root */
```

Example of User-defined Op for Segmented Scan

Example 4.26   This example uses a user-defined operation to produce a *segmented scan*. A segmented scan takes, as input, a set of values and a set of logicals, where the logicals delineate the various segments of the scan. For example:

values	v_1	v_2	v_3	v_4	v_5	v_6	v_7	v_8
logicals	0	0	1	1	1	0	0	1
result	v_1	$v_1 + v_2$	v_3	$v_3 + v_4$	$v_3 + v_4 + v_5$	v_6	$v_6 + v_7$	v_8

The operator that produces this effect is,

$$\begin{pmatrix} u \\ i \end{pmatrix} \circ \begin{pmatrix} v \\ j \end{pmatrix} = \begin{pmatrix} w \\ j \end{pmatrix},$$

where,

$$w = \begin{cases} u + v & \text{if } i = j \\ v & \text{if } i \neq j \end{cases}.$$

Note that this is a non-commutative operator. C code that implements it is given below.

```
typedef struct {
  double val;
  int log;
} SegScanPair;

/* the user-defined function */
void segScan(SegScanPair *in, SegScanPair *inout, int *len,
            MPI_Datatype *dptr)
{
  int i;
  SegScanPair c;

  for (i=0; i< *len; ++i) {
    if ( in->log == inout->log )
      c.val = in->val + inout->val;
    else
      c.val = inout->val;
    c.log = inout->log;
    *inout = c;
    in++; inout++;
  }
}
```

```
/* Note that the inout argument to the user-defined
 * function corresponds to the right-hand operand of the
 * operator.  When using this operator, we must be careful
 * to specify that it is non-commutative, as in the following.
 */

int i,base;
SegScanPair  a, answer;
MPI_Op       myOp;
MPI_Datatype type[2] = {MPI_DOUBLE, MPI_INT};
MPI_Aint     disp[2];
int          blocklen[2] = { 1, 1};
MPI_Datatype sspair;

/* explain to MPI how type SegScanPair is defined */
MPI_Get_address(&a, disp);
MPI_Get_address(&a.log, disp+1);
base = disp[0];
for (i=0; i<2; ++i) disp[i] -= base;
MPI_Type_create_struct(2, blocklen, disp, type, &sspair);
MPI_Type_commit(&sspair);
/* create the segmented-scan user-op */
MPI_Op_create((MPI_User_function*)segScan, False, &myOp);
...
MPI_Scan(&a, &answer, 1, sspair, myOp, comm);
```

4.14   The Semantics of Collective Communications

A correct, portable program must invoke collective communications so that dead-lock will not occur, whether collective communications are synchronizing or not. The following examples illustrate dangerous use of collective routines.

Example 4.27   The following is erroneous.

```
switch(rank) {
case 0:
  MPI_Bcast(buf1, count, type, 0, comm);
  MPI_Bcast(buf2, count, type, 1, comm);
```

```
  break;
case 1:
  MPI_Bcast(buf2, count, type, 1, comm);
  MPI_Bcast(buf1, count, type, 0, comm);
  break;
}
```

We assume that the group of comm is {0,1}. Two processes execute two broadcast operations in reverse order. MPI may match the first broadcast call of each process resulting in an error since the calls do not specify the same root. Alternatively, if MPI matches the calls correctly, then a deadlock will occur if the the operation is synchronizing.

Collective operations must be executed in the same order at all members of the communication group.

Example 4.28   The following is erroneous.

```
switch(rank) {
case 0:
  MPI_Bcast(buf1, count, type, 0, comm0);
  MPI_Bcast(buf2, count, type, 2, comm2);
  break;
case 1:
  MPI_Bcast(buf1, count, type, 1, comm1);
  MPI_Bcast(buf2, count, type, 0, comm0);
  break;
case 2:
  MPI_Bcast(buf1, count, type, 2, comm2);
  MPI_Bcast(buf2, count, type, 1, comm1);
  break;
}
```

Assume that the group of comm0 is {0,1}, of comm1 is {1, 2} and of comm2 is {2,0}. If the broadcast is a synchronizing operation, then there is a cyclic dependency: the broadcast in comm2 completes only after the broadcast in comm0; the broadcast in comm0 completes only after the broadcast in comm1; and the broadcast in comm1 completes only after the broadcast in comm2. Thus, the code will deadlock.

Collective operations must be executed in an order so that no cyclic dependencies occur.

Example 4.29   The following is erroneous.

```
switch(rank) {
case 0:
  MPI_Bcast(buf1, count, type, 0, comm);
  MPI_Send(buf2, count, type, 1, tag, comm);
  break;
case 1:
  MPI_Recv(buf2, count, type, 0, tag, comm,&status);
  MPI_Bcast(buf1, count, type, 0, comm);
  break;
}
```

Process zero executes a broadcast followed by a blocking send operation. Process one first executes a blocking receive that matches the send followed by broadcast call that matches the broadcast of process zero. This program may deadlock. The broadcast call on process zero *may* block until process one executes the matching broadcast call, so that the send is not executed. Process one will definitely block on the receive and so, in this case, never executes the broadcast.

The relative order of execution of collective operations and point-to-point operations should be such that even if the collective operations and the point-to-point operations are synchronizing no deadlock will occur.

Example 4.30   A correct, but non-deterministic program.

```
switch(rank) {
case 0:
  MPI_Bcast(buf1, count, type, 0, comm);
  MPI_Send(buf2, count, type, 1, tag, comm);
  break;
case 1:
  MPI_Recv(buf2, count, type, MPI_ANY_SOURCE, tag, comm, &status);
  MPI_Bcast(buf1, count, type, 0, comm);
  MPI_Recv(buf2, count, type, MPI_ANY_SOURCE, tag, comm, &status);
  break;
case 2:
```

```
  MPI_Send(buf2, count, type, 1, tag, comm);
  MPI_Bcast(buf1, count, type, 0, comm);
  break;
}
```

All three processes participate in a broadcast. Process 0 sends a message to process 1 after the broadcast, and process 2 sends a message to process 1 before the broadcast. Process 1 receives before and after the broadcast, with a wildcard source argument.

Two possible executions of this program, with different matchings of sends and receives, are illustrated in Figure 4.14. Note that the second execution has the peculiar effect that a send executed after the broadcast is received at another node before the broadcast. This example illustrates the fact that one should not rely on collective communication functions to have particular synchronization effects. A program that works correctly only when the first execution occurs (only when broadcast is synchronizing) is erroneous.

Finally, in multithreaded implementations, one can have more than one, concurrently executing, collective communication calls at a process. This is discussed in Section II-2.1

Advice to implementors.   Assume that broadcast is implemented using point-to-point MPI communication. Suppose the following two rules are followed.

1. All receives specify their source explicitly (no wildcards).

2. Each process sends all messages that pertain to one collective call before sending any message that pertain to a subsequent collective call.

Then, messages belonging to successive broadcasts cannot be confused, as the order of point-to-point messages is preserved.

It is the implementor's responsibility to ensure that point-to-point messages are not confused with collective messages. One way to accomplish this is, whenever a communicator is created, to also create a "hidden communicator" for collective communication. One could achieve a similar effect more cheaply, for example, by using a hidden tag or context bit to indicate whether the communicator is used for point-to-point or collective communication. □

First Execution

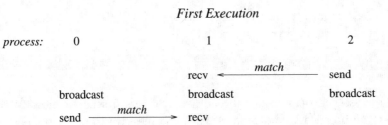

Second Execution

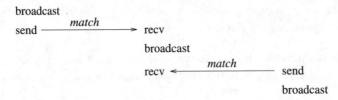

Figure 4.14
A race condition causes non-deterministic matching of sends and receives. One cannot rely on synchronization from a broadcast to make the program deterministic.

5 Communicators

In this chapter we present the important MPI abstraction of communication domains. This feature in MPI allows one to subdivide the processes into groups as well as protect against message collision in different libraries. We also introduce the ability to cache information within these communication domains. At the end of the chapter we discuss an extension of these domains to include two disjoint groups.

5.1 Introduction

It was the intent of the creators of the MPI standard to address several issues that augment the power and usefulness of point-to-point and collective communications. These issues are mainly concerned with the the creation of portable, efficient and safe libraries and codes with MPI, and will be discussed in this chapter. This effort was driven by the need to overcome several limitations in many message passing systems. The next few sections describe these limitations.

5.1.1 Division of Processes

In some applications it is desirable to divide up the processes to allow different groups of processes to perform independent work. For example, we might want an application to utilize $\frac{2}{3}$ of its processes to predict the weather based on data already processed, while the other $\frac{1}{3}$ of the processes initially process new data. This would allow the application to regularly complete a weather forecast. However, if no new data is available for processing we might want the same application to use all of its processes to make a weather forecast.

Being able to do this efficiently and easily requires the application to be able to logically divide the processes into independent subsets. It is important that these subsets are logically the same as the initial set of processes. For example, the module to predict the weather might use process 0 as the master process to dole out work. If subsets of processes are not numbered in a consistent manner with the initial set of processes, then there may be no process 0 in one of the two subsets. This would cause the weather prediction model to fail.

Applications also need to have collective operations work on a subset of processes. If collective operations only work on the initial set of processes then it is impossible to create independent subsets that perform collective operations. Even if the application does not need independent subsets, having collective operations work on subsets is desirable. Since the time to complete most collective operations increases with the number of processes, limiting a collective operation to only the processes that need to be involved yields much better scaling behavior. For example, if a matrix computation needs to broadcast information along the diagonal of a matrix, only the processes containing diagonal elements should be involved.

5.1.2 Avoiding Message Conflicts between Modules

Library routines have historically had difficulty in isolating their own message passing calls from those in other libraries or in the user's code. For example, suppose the user's code posts a nonblocking receive with both tag and source wildcarded before it enters a library routine. The first send in the library may be received by the user's posted receive instead of the one posted by the library. This will undoubtedly cause the library to fail.

The solution to this difficulty is to allow a module to isolate its message passing calls from the other modules. Some applications may only determine at run time which modules will run so it can be impossible to statically isolate all modules in advance. This necessitates a run time callable system to perform this function.

5.1.3 Extensibility by Users

Writers of libraries often want to expand the functionality of the message passing system. For example, the library may want to create its own special and unique collective operation. Such a collective operation may be called many times if the library is called repetitively or if multiple libraries use the same collective routine. To perform the collective operation efficiently may require a moderately expensive calculation up front such as determining the best communication pattern. It is most efficient to reuse the up front calculations if the same the set of processes are involved. This is most easily done by attaching the results of the up front calculation to the set of processes involved. These types of optimization are routinely done internally in message passing systems. The desire is to allow others to perform similar optimizations in the same way.

5.1.4 Safety

There are two philosophies used to provide mechanisms for creating subgroups, isolating messages, etc. One point of view is to allow the user total control over the process. This allows maximum flexibility to the user and can, in some cases, lead to fast implementations. The other point of view is to have the message passing system control these functions. This adds a degree of safety while limiting the mechanisms to those provided by the system. MPI chose to use the latter approach. The added safety was deemed to be very important for writing portable message passing codes. Since the MPI system controls these functions, modules that are written independently can safely perform these operations without worrying about conflicts. As in other areas, MPI also decided to provide a rich set of functions so that users would have the functionality they are likely to need.

5.2   Overview

The above features and several more are provided in MPI through communicators. The concepts behind communicators encompass several central and fundamental ideas in MPI. The importance of communicators can be seen by the fact that they are present in most calls in MPI. There are several reasons that these features are encapsulated into a single MPI object. One reason is that it simplifies calls to MPI functions. Grouping logically related items into communicators substantially reduces the number of calling arguments. A second reason is it allows for easier extensibility. Both the MPI system and the user can add information onto communicators that will be passed in calls without changing the calling arguments. This is consistent with the use of opaque objects throughout MPI.

5.2.1   Groups

A **group** is an ordered set of processes; processes are implementation-dependent objects. Each process in a group is associated with an integer **rank**. Ranks are contiguous and start from zero. Groups are represented by opaque **group objects**; these cannot be directly transferred from one process to another.

There is a special predefined group: MPI_GROUP_EMPTY (MPI::GROUP_EMPTY, in C++), which is a group with no members. The predefined constant MPI_GROUP_NULL (MPI::GROUP_NULL, in C++) is the value used for invalid group handles. MPI_GROUP_EMPTY, which is a valid handle to an empty group, should not be confused with MPI_GROUP_NULL, which is an invalid handle. The former may be used as an argument to group operations; the latter, which is returned when a group is freed, in not a valid argument.

Groups are, in C, objects of type `MPI_Group` and, in C++, of type `MPI::Group`. Group operations are discussed in Section 5.3.

5.2.2   Communicator

A communicator is an opaque object with a number of attributes, together with simple rules that govern its creation, use and destruction. The communicator specifies a **communication domain** which can be used for point-to-point communications. An **intracommunicator** is used for communicating within a single group of processes; we call such communication *intragroup communication*. An intracommunicator has one fixed attribute: its process group. It has one optional, predefined attribute: a topology describing the logical layout of the processes in the group. Process topologies are the subject of Chapter 6. Intracommunicators are also used for collective operations within a group of processes.

An **intercommunicator** is used for point-to-point communication between two disjoint groups of processes. We call such communication *inter-group communication*. The fixed attributes of an intercommunicator are the two groups. No topology is associated with an intercommunicator. Intercommunicators may also be used for collective communications between two groups of processes.

In addition to fixed attributes a communicator may also have user-defined attributes which are associated with the communicator using MPI's caching mechanism, as described in Section 5.6.

The table below summarizes the differences between intracommunicators and intercommunicators.

Functionality	Intracommunicator	Intercommunicator
# of groups	1	2
Communication Safety	Yes	Yes
Collective Operations	Yes	Yes (MPI-2)
Topologies	Yes	No
Caching	Yes	Yes

Communicators are, in C, objects of type `MPI_Comm`. In C++, `MPI::Comm` is the base class for communicator objects. This is an abstract base class; and one cannot instantiate objects of type `MPI::Comm`. Derived classes are provided for the different types of communicators. `MPI::Intercomm` and `MPI::Intracomm` are derived from `MPI::Comm`, and are used for intercommunicators and intracommunicators, respectively. In addition, `MPI::Cartcomm` and `MPI::Graphcomm` are derived from `MPI::Intracomm`, and are used for intracommunicators with a Cartesian or general graph topology, respectively. Topologies are discussed in Chapter 6.

Intracommunicator operations are described in Section 5.4, and intercommunicator operations are discussed in Section 5.7.

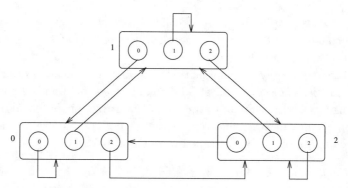

Figure 5.1
Distributed data structure for intra-communication domain.

5.2.3 Communication Domains

Any point-to-point or collective communication occurs in MPI within a **communication domain**. Such a communication domain is represented by a set of communicators with consistent values, one at each of the participating processes; each communicator is the local representation of the global communication domain. If this domain is for intragroup communication then all the communicators are intracommunicators, and all have the same group attribute. Each communicator identifies all the other corresponding communicators.

One can think of a communicator as an array of links to other communicators. An intragroup communication domain is specified by a set of communicators such that

- their links form a complete graph: each communicator is linked to all communicators in the set, including itself; and
- links have consistent indices: at each communicator, the i-th link points to the communicator for process i.

This distributed data structure is illustrated in Figure 5.1, for the case of a three member group.

We discuss inter-group communication domains in Section 5.7.

In point-to-point communication, matching send and receive calls should have communicator arguments that represent the same communication domains. The rank of the processes is interpreted relative to the group, or groups, associated with the communicator. Thus, in an intragroup communication domain, process ranks are relative to the group associated with the communicator.

Similarly, a collective communication call involves all processes in the group of an intragroup communication domain, and all processes should use a communicator argument that represents this domain.

We shall sometimes say, for simplicity, that two communicators are the same, if they represent the same communication domain. One should not be misled by this abuse of language: Each communicator is really a distinct object, local to a process. Furthermore, communicators that represent the same communication domain may have different attribute values attached to them at different processes.

Advice to implementors.   An often-used design is that each communicator is associated with an id that is process-unique, and which is identical at all communicators that define one intragroup communication domain. This id is referred as the communication *context*. Thus, each message is tagged with the context of the send communicator argument, and that context identifies the matching communicator at the receiving process.

In more detail: a group can be represented by an array group such that group[i] is the address of the process with rank i in group. An intracommunicator can be represented by a structure with components group, myrank and context.

When a process posts a send with arguments dest, tag and comm, then the address of the destination is computed as comm.group[dest]. The message sent carries a header with the tuple (comm.myrank, tag, comm.context).

If a process posts a receive with argument source, tag and comm, then headers of incoming messages are matched to the tuple (source, tag, comm.context) (first two may be dontcare).

Another design is to use ids that are process-unique, but not necessarily identical at all processes. In such case, the context component of the communicator structure is an array, where comm.context[i] is the id chosen by the process with rank i for that communication domain. A message is sent with header comm.myrank, tag, comm.context[dest]; a receive call causes incoming messages to be matched against the tuple (source, tag, comm.context[myrank]).

The latter design uses more storage for the communicator object, but simplifies the creation of new communicators, since ids can be selected locally (they still need to be broadcast to all other group members).

It is important to remember that MPI does not require a unique context to be associated with each communicator. "Context" is a possible implementation structure, not an MPI object.

With both designs we assumed a "flat" representation for groups, where each process holds a complete list of group members. This requires, at each process, storage of size proportional to the size of the group. While this presents no problem with groups of practical size (100's or 1000's of processes) it is not a scalable design. Other representations will be needed for MPI computations that span the Internet. The group information may be distributed and managed hierarchically, as are Internet addresses, at the expense of additional communication. □

MPI is designed to ensure that communicator constructors always generate consistent communicators that are a valid representation of the newly created communication domain. This is done by requiring that a new intracommunicator be constructed out of an existing parent communicator, and that this be a collective operation over all processes in the group associated with the parent communicator. The group associated with a new intracommunicator must be a subgroup of that associated with the parent intracommunicator. Thus, all the intracommunicator constructor routines described in Section 5.4.2 have an existing communicator as an input argument, and the newly created intracommunicator as an output argument. This leads to a chicken-and-egg situation since we must have an existing communicator to create a new communicator. This problem is solved by the provision of a predefined intracommunicator, MPI_COMM_WORLD (MPI::COMM_WORLD, in C++), which is available for use once the routine MPI_INIT has been called. MPI_COMM_WORLD, which has as its group attribute all processes with which the local process can communicate, can be used as the parent communicator in constructing new communicators. A second predefined intracommunicator, MPI_COMM_SELF (MPI::COMM_SELF, in C++), is also available for use after calling MPI_INIT and has as its associated group just the process itself. MPI_COMM_SELF is provided as a convenience since it could easily be created out of MPI_COMM_WORLD.

5.2.4   Compatibility with Previous Practice

The practice with older message passing libraries is to use is a unique, predefined communication universe that includes all processes available when the parallel program is initiated; the processes are assigned consecutive ranks. Participants in a point-to-point communication are identified by their rank; a collective communication (such as broadcast) always involves all processes. As such, most of these message passing libraries have no equivalent argument to the communicator. It is implicitly all the processes as ranked by the system.

This practice can be followed in MPI by using the predefined communicator MPI_COMM_WORLD wherever a communicator argument is required. Users that are content with this style can ignore most of the information in this chapter. However, everyone should seriously consider understanding the potential risks in using MPI_COMM_WORLD to avoid unexpected behavior of their programs, and the performance advantages of restricting collective communications to user-defined subgroups.

5.3   Group Management

This section describes the manipulation of process groups in MPI. These operations are local and execution of these operations does not require interprocess communication. MPI allows manipulation of groups outside of communicators but groups can only be used for message passing inside of a communicator.

5.3.1   Group Accessors

MPI_GROUP_SIZE(group, size)

IN	group	group (handle)
OUT	size	number of processes in group (integer)

```
int MPI_Group_size(MPI_Group group, int *size)
```

```
MPI_GROUP_SIZE(GROUP, SIZE, IERROR)
    INTEGER GROUP, SIZE, IERROR
```

```
int MPI::Group::Get_size() const
```

MPI_GROUP_SIZE returns the number of processes in the group. Thus, if group = MPI_GROUP_EMPTY then the call will return size = 0. (On the other hand, a call with group = MPI_GROUP_NULL is erroneous.)

MPI_GROUP_SIZE and other functions with a group argument may return the error code MPI_ERR_GROUP (MPI::ERR_GROUP, in C++) to indicate an invalid group argument.

MPI_GROUP_RANK(group, rank)

IN	group	group (handle)
OUT	rank	rank of the calling process in group (integer)

```
int MPI_Group_rank(MPI_Group group, int *rank)
```

```
MPI_GROUP_RANK(GROUP, RANK, IERROR)
    INTEGER GROUP, RANK, IERROR
```

```
int MPI::Group::Get_rank() const
```

MPI_GROUP_RANK returns the rank of the calling process in group. If the process is not a member of group then MPI_UNDEFINED is returned.

MPI_GROUP_TRANSLATE_RANKS(group1, n, ranks1, group2, ranks2)

IN	group1	group1 (handle)
IN	n	number of ranks in ranks1 and ranks2 arrays (integer)
IN	ranks1	array of zero or more valid ranks in group1 (array of integers)
IN	group2	group2 (handle)
OUT	ranks2	array of corresponding ranks in group2 (array of integers)

```
int MPI_Group_translate_ranks(MPI_Group group1, int n, int *ranks1,
    MPI_Group group2, int *ranks2)
```

```
MPI_GROUP_TRANSLATE_RANKS(GROUP1, N, RANKS1, GROUP2, RANKS2, IERROR)
    INTEGER GROUP1, N, RANKS1(*), GROUP2, RANKS2(*), IERROR
```

```
static void MPI::Group::Translate_ranks(const MPI::Group& group1,
    int n, const int ranks1[], const MPI::Group& group2,
    int ranks2[])
```

MPI_GROUP_TRANSLATE_RANKS maps the ranks of a set of processes in group1 to their ranks in group2. Upon return, the array ranks2 contains the ranks in group2 for the processes in group1 with ranks listed in ranks1. If a process in group1 found in ranks1 does not belong to group2 then MPI_UNDEFINED is returned in ranks2.

This function is important for determining the relative numbering of the same processes in two different groups. For instance, if one knows the ranks of certain processes in the group of MPI_COMM_WORLD, one might want to know their ranks in a subset of that group.

Example 5.1   Let group1 be a handle to the group {a,b,c,d,e,f} and let group2 be a handle to the group {d,e,a,c}. Let ranks1 = (0,5,0,2). Then, a call to MPI_GROUP_TRANSLATE_RANKS will return the ranks of the processes {a,f,a,c} in group2, namely ranks2 = (2,⊥,2,3). (⊥ denotes the value MPI_UNDEFINED.)

MPI_GROUP_COMPARE(group1, group2, result)

IN	group1	first group (handle)
IN	group2	second group (handle)
OUT	result	result (integer)

```
int MPI_Group_compare(MPI_Group group1, MPI_Group group2,
    int *result)
```

```
MPI_GROUP_COMPARE(GROUP1, GROUP2, RESULT, IERROR)
    INTEGER GROUP1, GROUP2, RESULT, IERROR
```

```
static int MPI::Group::Compare(const MPI::Group& group1,
    const MPI::Group& group2)
```

MPI_GROUP_COMPARE returns the relationship between two groups. MPI_IDENT results if the group members and group order is exactly the same in both groups. This happens, for instance, if group1 and group2 are handles to the same object. MPI_SIMILAR results if the group members are the same but the order is different. MPI_UNEQUAL results otherwise. (The C++ syntax for these constants is MPI::IDENT, MPI::SIMILAR, and MPI::UNEQUAL, respectively.)

5.3.2 Group Constructors

Group constructors are used to construct new groups from existing groups, using various set operations. These are local operations, and distinct groups may be defined on different processes; a process may also define a group that does not include itself. Consistent definitions are required when groups are used as arguments in communicator-building functions. MPI does not provide a mechanism to build a group from scratch, but only from other, previously defined groups. The base group, upon which all other groups are defined, is the group associated with the initial communicator MPI_COMM_WORLD (accessible through the function MPI_COMM_GROUP).

Local group creation functions are useful since some applications have the needed information distributed on all nodes. Thus, new groups can be created locally without communication. This can significantly reduce the necessary communication in creating a new communicator to use this group.

In Section 5.4.2, communicator creation functions are described which also create new groups. These are more general group creation functions where the information does not have to be local to each node. They are part of communicator creation since they will normally require communication for group creation. Since communicator creation may also require communication, it is logical to group these two functions together for this case.

Rationale.   In what follows, there is no group duplication function analogous to MPI_COMM_DUP, defined later in this chapter. There is no need for a group duplicator. A group, once created, can have several references to it by making copies of the handle. However, care should be taken when "aliasing" groups in this way since a call to free a group using MPI_GROUP_FREE may leave dangling references. □

Advice to implementors.   Each group constructor behaves as if it returned a new group object. When this new group is a copy of an existing group, then one can avoid creating such new objects, using a reference-count mechanism. □

MPI_COMM_GROUP(comm, group)

IN	comm	communicator (handle)
OUT	group	group corresponding to comm (handle)

```
int MPI_Comm_group(MPI_Comm comm, MPI_Group *group)
```

```
MPI_COMM_GROUP(COMM, GROUP, IERROR)
    INTEGER COMM, GROUP, IERROR
```

```
MPI::Group MPI::Comm::Get_group() const
```

If comm is an intracommunicator, then MPI_COMM_GROUP returns in group a handle to the group of comm. The behavior of MPI_COMM_GROUP for intercommunicator arguments is described in Section 5.7.

The following three functions do standard set type operations. The only difference is that ordering is important so that ranks are consistently defined.

MPI_GROUP_UNION(group1, group2, newgroup)

IN	group1	first group (handle)
IN	group2	second group (handle)
OUT	newgroup	union group (handle)

```
int MPI_Group_union(MPI_Group group1, MPI_Group group2,
    MPI_Group *newgroup)

MPI_GROUP_UNION(GROUP1, GROUP2, NEWGROUP, IERROR)
    INTEGER GROUP1, GROUP2, NEWGROUP, IERROR

static MPI::Group MPI::Group::Union(const MPI::Group& group1,
    const MPI::Group& group2)
```

MPI_GROUP_INTERSECTION(group1, group2, newgroup)

IN	group1	first group (handle)
IN	group2	second group (handle)
OUT	newgroup	intersection group (handle)

```
int MPI_Group_intersection(MPI_Group group1, MPI_Group group2,
    MPI_Group *newgroup)

MPI_GROUP_INTERSECTION(GROUP1, GROUP2, NEWGROUP, IERROR)
    INTEGER GROUP1, GROUP2, NEWGROUP, IERROR

static MPI::Group MPI::Group::Intersect(const MPI::Group& group1,
    const MPI::Group& group2)
```

MPI_GROUP_DIFFERENCE(group1, group2, newgroup)

IN	group1	first group (handle)
IN	group2	second group (handle)
OUT	newgroup	difference group (handle)

```
int MPI_Group_difference(MPI_Group group1, MPI_Group group2,
    MPI_Group *newgroup)

MPI_GROUP_DIFFERENCE(GROUP1, GROUP2, NEWGROUP, IERROR)
    INTEGER GROUP1, GROUP2, NEWGROUP, IERROR

static MPI::Group MPI::Group::Difference(const MPI::Group& group1,
    const MPI::Group& group2)
```

The operations are defined as follows:

union All elements of the first group (group1), followed by all elements of second group (group2) not in first.

intersection All elements of the first group that are also in the second group, ordered as in first group.

difference All elements of the first group that are not in the second group, ordered as in the first group.

Note that for these operations the order of processes in the output group is determined primarily by order in the first group (if possible) and then, if necessary, by order in the second group. Neither union nor intersection are commutative, but both are associative.

The new group can be empty, that is, equal to MPI_GROUP_EMPTY.

Example 5.2 Let group1 = $\{a, b, c, d\}$ and group2 = $\{d, a, e\}$. Then

$$\text{group1} \bigcup \text{group2} = \{a, b, c, d, e\} \text{ (union)};$$

$$\text{group1} \bigcap \text{group2} = \{a, d\} \text{ (intersection)};$$

and

$$\text{group1} \setminus \text{group2} = \{b, c\} \text{ (difference)}.$$

MPI_GROUP_INCL(group, n, ranks, newgroup)

IN	group	group (handle)
IN	n	number of elements in array ranks (and size of newgroup) (integer)
IN	ranks	ranks of processes in group to appear in newgroup (array of integers)
OUT	newgroup	new group derived from above, in the order defined by ranks (handle)

```
int MPI_Group_incl(MPI_Group group, int n, int *ranks,
    MPI_Group *newgroup)
```

```
MPI_GROUP_INCL(GROUP, N, RANKS, NEWGROUP, IERROR)
    INTEGER GROUP, N, RANKS(*), NEWGROUP, IERROR
```

```
MPI::Group MPI::Group::Incl(int n, const int ranks[]) const
```

The function MPI_GROUP_INCL creates a group newgroup that consists of the n processes in group with ranks rank[0],..., rank[n-1]; the process with rank i in newgroup is the process with rank ranks[i] in group. Each of the n elements of ranks must be a valid rank in group and all elements must be distinct, or else the call is erroneous. If n = 0, then newgroup is MPI_GROUP_EMPTY. This function can, for instance, be used to reorder the elements of a group.

Example 5.3   Let group be a handle to the group {a,b,c,d,e,f} and let ranks = (3,1,2). Then, a handle to the group {d,b,c} is returned in newgroup.

Assume that newgroup was created by a call to MPI_GROUP_INCL(group, n, ranks, newgroup). Then, a subsequent call to MPI_GROUP_TRANSLATE_RANKS(group, n, ranks, newgroup, newranks) will return $\text{newranks}[i] = i$, $i = 0, \ldots, n-1$ (in C) or $\text{newranks}(i+1) = i$, $i = 0, \ldots, n-1$ (in Fortran).

MPI_GROUP_EXCL(group, n, ranks, newgroup)

IN	group	group (handle)
IN	n	number of elements in array ranks (integer)
IN	ranks	array of integer ranks in group not to appear in newgroup (array of integers)
OUT	newgroup	new group derived from above, preserving the order defined by group (handle)

```
int MPI_Group_excl(MPI_Group group, int n, int *ranks,
    MPI_Group *newgroup)
```

```
MPI_GROUP_EXCL(GROUP, N, RANKS, NEWGROUP, IERROR)
    INTEGER GROUP, N, RANKS(*), NEWGROUP, IERROR
```

```
MPI::Group MPI::Group::Excl(int n, const int ranks[]) const
```

The function MPI_GROUP_EXCL creates a group of processes newgroup that is obtained by deleting from group those processes with ranks ranks[0],..., ranks[n-1] in C or ranks[1],..., ranks[n] in Fortran. The ordering of processes in newgroup is identical to the ordering in group. Each of the n elements of ranks must be a valid rank in group and all elements must be distinct; otherwise, the call is erroneous. If $n = 0$, then newgroup is identical to group.

Example 5.4   Let group be a handle to the group {a,b,c,d,e,f} and let ranks = (3,1,2). Then, a handle to the group {a,e,f} is returned in newgroup.

Suppose one calls MPI_GROUP_INCL(group, n, ranks, newgroupi) and MPI_GROUP_EXCL(group, n, ranks, newgroupe).   The call MPI_GROUP_-UNION(newgroupi, newgroupe, newgroup) would return in newgroup a group with the same members as group but possibly in a different order. The call MPI_GROUP_-INTERSECTION(groupi, groupe, newgroup) would return MPI_GROUP_EMPTY.

MPI_GROUP_RANGE_INCL(group, n, ranges, newgroup)

IN	group	group (handle)
IN	n	number of triplets in array ranges (integer)
IN	ranges	a one-dimensional array of integer triplets, of the form (first rank, last rank, stride) indicating ranks in group of processes to be included in newgroup (array of integers)
OUT	newgroup	new group derived from above, in the order defined by ranges (handle)

```
int MPI_Group_range_incl(MPI_Group group, int n, int ranges[][3],
    MPI_Group *newgroup)
```

```
MPI_GROUP_RANGE_INCL(GROUP, N, RANGES, NEWGROUP, IERROR)
    INTEGER GROUP, N, RANGES(3,*), NEWGROUP, IERROR
```

```
MPI::Group MPI::Group::Range_incl(int n, const int ranges[][3]) const
```

Each triplet in ranges specifies a sequence of ranks for processes to be included in the newly created group. The newly created group contains the processes specified by the first triplet, followed by the processes specified by the second triplet, etc.

Example 5.5   Let group be a handle to the group {a,b,c,d,e,f,g,h,i,j} and let ranges = ((6,7,1),(1,6,2),(0,9,4)). The first triplet (6,7,1)} specifies the processes {g,h}, with ranks (6,7); the second triplet (1,6,2) specifies the processes {b,d,f}, with ranks (1,3,5); and the third triplet (0,9,4) specifies the processes {a,e,i}, with ranks (0,4,8). The call creates the new group {g,h,b,d,f,a,e,i}.

Generally, if ranges consist of the triplets

$(first_1, last_1, stride_1), \ldots, (first_n, last_n, stride_n)$

then newgroup consists of the sequence of processes in group with ranks

$$first_1, first_1 + stride_1, \ldots, first_1 + \left\lfloor \frac{last_1 - first_1}{stride_1} \right\rfloor \cdot stride_1, \ldots$$

$$first_n, first_n + stride_n, \ldots, first_n + \left\lfloor \frac{last_n - first_n}{stride_n} \right\rfloor \cdot stride_n.$$

Each computed rank must be a valid rank in group and all computed ranks must be distinct, or else the call is erroneous. Note that a call may have $first_i > last_i$, and $stride_i$ may be negative, but cannot be zero.

The functionality of this routine is specified to be equivalent to expanding the array of ranges to an array of the included ranks and passing the resulting array of ranks and other arguments to MPI_GROUP_INCL. A call to MPI_GROUP_INCL is equivalent to a call to MPI_GROUP_RANGE_INCL with each rank i in ranks replaced by the triplet (i,i,1) in the argument ranges.

MPI_GROUP_RANGE_EXCL(group, n, ranges, newgroup)

IN	group	group (handle)
IN	n	number of triplets in array ranges (integer)
IN	ranges	an array of integer triplets of the form (first rank, last rank, stride), indicating the ranks in group of processes to be excluded from the output group newgroup. (array of integers)
OUT	newgroup	new group derived from above, preserving the order in group (handle)

```
int MPI_Group_range_excl(MPI_Group group, int n, int ranges[][3],
    MPI_Group *newgroup)
```

```
MPI_GROUP_RANGE_EXCL(GROUP, N, RANGES, NEWGROUP, IERROR)
    INTEGER GROUP, N, RANGES(3,*), NEWGROUP, IERROR
```

```
MPI::Group MPI::Group::Range_excl(int n, const int ranges[][3]) const
```

Each triplet in ranges specifies a sequence of ranks for processes to be excluded from the newly created group. The newly created group contains the remaining processes, ordered as in group.

Example 5.6   Let, as in Example 5.5, group be a handle to the group {a,b,c,d,e,-f,g,h,i,j} and let ranges = ((6,7,1),(1,6,2),(0,9,4)). The call creates the new group {c,j}, consisting of all processes in the old group omitted by the list of triplets.

Each computed rank must be a valid rank in group and all computed ranks must be distinct, or else the call is erroneous.

The functionality of this routine is specified to be equivalent to expanding the array of ranges to an array of the excluded ranks and passing the resulting array of ranks and other arguments to MPI_GROUP_EXCL. A call to MPI_GROUP_EXCL is equivalent to a call to MPI_GROUP_RANGE_EXCL with each rank i in ranks replaced by the triplet (i,i,1) in the argument ranges.

Advice to users.   The range operations do not explicitly enumerate ranks, and therefore are more scalable if implemented efficiently. Hence, it is recommend that MPI programmers use them whenever possible, as high-quality implementations may take advantage of this fact. □

Advice to implementors.   The range operations should be implemented, if possible, without enumerating the group members, in order to obtain better scalability (time and space). □

5.3.3   Group Destructors

MPI_GROUP_FREE(group)

   INOUT group   group (handle)

```
int MPI_Group_free(MPI_Group *group)
```

```
MPI_GROUP_FREE(GROUP, IERROR)
    INTEGER GROUP, IERROR
```

```
void MPI::Group::Free()
```

This operation marks a group object for deallocation. The handle group is set to MPI_GROUP_NULL by the call. Any ongoing operation using this group will complete normally.

Advice to implementors.   One can keep a reference count that is incremented for each call to MPI_COMM_CREATE and MPI_COMM_DUP, and decremented for each call to MPI_GROUP_FREE or MPI_COMM_FREE; the group object is ultimately deallocated when the reference count drops to zero. ☐

5.4 Communicator Management

This section describes the manipulation of communicators in MPI. Operations that access communicators are local and their execution does not require interprocess communication. Operations that create communicators are collective and may require interprocess communication. We describe the behavior of these functions, assuming that their comm argument is an intracommunicator; we describe later in Section 5.7 their semantics for intercommunicator arguments.

5.4.1 Communicator Accessors

The following are all local operations.

MPI_COMM_SIZE(comm, size)

IN	comm	communicator (handle)
OUT	size	number of processes in the group of comm (integer)

```
int MPI_Comm_size(MPI_Comm comm, int *size)
```

```
MPI_COMM_SIZE(COMM, SIZE, IERROR)
    INTEGER COMM, SIZE, IERROR
```

```
int MPI::Comm::Get_size() const
```

If comm is an intracommunicator, then MPI_COMM_SIZE returns the size of the group associated with comm.

This function indicates the number of processes involved in an intracommunicator. For MPI_COMM_WORLD, it indicates the total number of processes available at initialization time.

Rationale.   This function is equivalent to accessing the communicator's group with MPI_COMM_GROUP (see above), computing the size using MPI_GROUP_SIZE, and then freeing the group temporary via MPI_GROUP_FREE. However, this function is so commonly used, that this shortcut was introduced. ☐

MPI_COMM_RANK(comm, rank)

| IN | comm | communicator (handle) |
| OUT | rank | rank of the calling process in group of comm (integer) |

```
int MPI_Comm_rank(MPI_Comm comm, int *rank)
```

```
MPI_COMM_RANK(COMM, RANK, IERROR)
    INTEGER COMM, RANK, IERROR
```

```
int MPI::Comm::Get_rank() const
```

If comm is an intracommunicator, the MPI_COMM_RANK indicates the rank of the process that calls it, in the range from $0 \ldots \text{size}-1$, where size is the return value of MPI_COMM_SIZE. This rank is relative to the group associated with the intracommunicator comm. Thus, MPI_COMM_RANK(MPI_COMM_WORLD, rank) returns in rank the "absolute" rank of the calling process in the global communication group of MPI_COMM_WORLD; MPI_COMM_RANK(MPI_COMM_SELF, rank) returns rank = 0.

Rationale. This function is equivalent to accessing the communicator's group with MPI_COMM_GROUP (see above), computing the rank using MPI_GROUP_RANK, and then freeing the group temporary via MPI_GROUP_FREE. However, this function is so commonly used, that this shortcut was introduced. □

Advice to users. Many programs will be written with the manager-worker model, where one process (such as the rank-zero process) will play a supervisory role, and the other processes will serve as compute nodes. In this framework, the two preceding calls are useful for determining the roles of the various processes of a communicator. □

MPI_COMM_COMPARE(comm1, comm2, result)

IN	comm1	first communicator (handle)
IN	comm2	second communicator (handle)
OUT	result	result (integer)

```
int MPI_Comm_compare(MPI_Comm comm1,MPI_Comm comm2, int *result)
```

```
MPI_COMM_COMPARE(COMM1, COMM2, RESULT, IERROR)
    INTEGER COMM1, COMM2, RESULT, IERROR
```

```
static int MPI::Comm::Compare(const MPI::Comm& comm1,
    const MPI::Comm& comm2)
```

MPI_COMM_COMPARE is used to find the relationship between two intra-communicators. MPI_IDENT (MPI::IDENT, in C++) results if and only if comm1 and comm2 are handles for the same object (representing the same communication domain). MPI_CONGRUENT (MPI::CONGRUENT, in C++) results if the underlying groups are identical in constituents and rank order (the communicators represent two distinct communication domains with the same group attribute). MPI_SIMILAR (MPI::SIMILAR, in C++) results if the group members of both communicators are the same but the rank order differs. MPI_UNEQUAL (MPI::UNEQUAL, in C++) results otherwise. The groups associated with two *different* communicators could be gotten via MPI_COMM_GROUP and then used in a call to MPI_GROUP_COMPARE. If MPI_COMM_COMPARE gives MPI_CONGRUENT then MPI_GROUP_COMPARE will give MPI_IDENT. If MPI_COMM_COMPARE gives MPI_SIMILAR then MPI_GROUP_COMPARE will give MPI_SIMILAR.

5.4.2 Communicator Constructors

The following are collective functions that are invoked by all processes in the group associated with comm.

MPI_COMM_DUP(comm, newcomm)

IN	comm	communicator (handle)
OUT	newcomm	copy of comm (handle)

```
int MPI_Comm_dup(MPI_Comm comm, MPI_Comm *newcomm)
```

```
MPI_COMM_DUP(COMM, NEWCOMM, IERROR)
    INTEGER COMM, NEWCOMM, IERROR
```

```
MPI::Intracomm MPI::Intracomm::Dup() const
```

```
MPI::Intercomm MPI::Intercomm::Dup() const
```

```
MPI::Cartcomm MPI::Cartcomm::Dup() const
```

```
MPI::Graphcomm MPI::Graphcomm::Dup() const
```

MPI_COMM_DUP creates a new intracommunicator, newcomm, with the same fixed attributes (group, or groups, and topology) as the input intracommunicator, comm. The newly created communicators at the processes in the group of comm define a new, distinct communication domain, with the same group as the old communicators.

The association of user-defined (or cached) attributes with newcomm is controlled by the copy callback function specified when the attribute was attached to comm. For each key value, the respective copy callback function determines the attribute value associated with this key in the new communicator. User-defined attributes are discussed in Section 5.6.

The function MPI_COMM_DUP is not defined in C++ as a member function of MPI::Comm, as it is not virtual, but returns a parameter by value. On the other hand, MPI::Comm is an abstract base class that is not instantiable, hence cannot be returned by value. Instead, MPI_COMM_DUP is defined on the derived classes that can be instantiated.

The common practice in C++, when abstract base classes are used, is to use virtual functions that return objects by reference. This is supported, in C++, by a new function Clone().

```
MPI::Comm& MPI::Comm::Clone() const = 0

MPI::Intracomm& MPI::Intracomm::Clone() const

MPI::Intercomm& MPI::Intercomm::Clone() const

MPI::Cartcomm& MPI::Cartcomm::Clone() const

MPI::Graphcomm& MPI::Graphcomm::Clone() const
```

MPI::Comm::Clone() is a pure virtual function. For the derived communicator classes, Clone() behaves like Dup() except that it returns a new object by reference.

Advice to users.   MPI_COMM_DUP can be used to provide a parallel library call with a duplicate communication space that has the same properties as the original communicator. This includes any user-defined attributes (see below), and topologies (see Chapter 6). This call is valid even if there are pending point-to-point communications involving the communicator comm. A typical call might involve a MPI_COMM_DUP at the beginning of the parallel call, and an MPI_COMM_FREE of that duplicated communicator at the end of the call – see Example 5.11. Other models of communicator management are also possible. □

Advice to implementors.   Assume that communicators are implemented as described on page 260. If a unique context is used per communication domain, then the generation of a new communicator requires a collective call where processes agree on a new context value. E.g., this could be $1 + \max\{$already_used_contexts$\}$, computed using an MPI_ALLREDUCE call (assuming there is no need to garbage collect contexts). If a different context is used by each process, then a collective call is needed where each process exchange with all other processes the value of the context it selected, using an MPI_ALLGATHER call.

It is theoretically possible to agree on a group-wide unique context with no communication: e.g., one could use as context a unique encoding of the group, followed by a sequence number for intracommunicators with this group. Since all processes in the group execute the same sequence of calls to MPI_COMM_DUP with this group argument, all processes will locally compute the same id. This design may not be practical because it generates large context ids. Implementations may strike various compromises between communication overhead for communicator creation and context size.

Important: If new communicators are created without synchronizing the processes involved then the communication system should be able to cope with messages arriving for a communicator that has not yet been created at the receiving process.

When a communicator is duplicated, one need not actually copy the group information, but only add a new reference and increment the reference count.

Within their class declarations, prototypes for Clone() and Dup() would look like the following:

```
namespace MPI {
  class Comm {
    virtual Comm& Clone() const = 0;
  };
  class Intracomm : public Comm {
    Intracomm Dup() const { ... };
    virtual Intracomm& Clone() const { ... };
  };
  class Intercomm : public Comm {
    Intercomm Dup() const { ... };
    virtual Intercomm& Clone() const { ... };
  };
```

```
// Cartcomm and Graphcomm are similarly defined
```

```
};
```

⬚

MPI_COMM_CREATE(comm, group, newcomm)

IN	comm	communicator (handle)
IN	group	Group, which is a subset of the group of comm (handle)
OUT	newcomm	new communicator (handle)

```
int MPI_Comm_create(MPI_Comm comm, MPI_Group group,
    MPI_Comm *newcomm)
```

```
MPI_COMM_CREATE(COMM, GROUP, NEWCOMM, IERROR)
    INTEGER COMM, GROUP, NEWCOMM, IERROR
```

```
MPI::Intercomm MPI::Intercomm::Create(const MPI::Group& group) const
```

```
MPI::Intracomm MPI::Intracomm::Create(const MPI::Group& group) const
```

If comm is an intracommunicator then this function creates a new intracommunicator newcomm with communication group defined by group. No attributes propagate from comm to newcomm. The function returns MPI_COMM_NULL (MPI::COMM_NULL, in C++, see II-8.1.7) to processes that are not in group. The communicators returned at the processes in group define a new intragroup communication domain.

The call is erroneous if not all group arguments have the same value on different processes, or if group is not a subset of the group associated with comm (but it does not have to be a proper subset). Note that the call is to be executed by all processes in comm, even if they do not belong to the new group.

Rationale. The requirement that the entire group of comm participate in the call stems from the following considerations:

• It allows the implementation to layer MPI_COMM_CREATE on top of regular collective communications.

• It provides additional safety, in particular in the case where partially overlapping groups are used to create new communicators.

- It permits implementations sometimes to avoid communication related to the creation of communicators.

        ⬚

Advice to users.   MPI_COMM_CREATE provides a means to subset a group of processes for the purpose of separate MIMD computation, with a separate communication space. newcomm, which emerges from MPI_COMM_CREATE can be used in subsequent calls to MPI_COMM_CREATE (or other communicator constructors) further to subdivide a computation into parallel sub-computations. A more general service is provided by MPI_COMM_SPLIT, below. ⬚

MPI_COMM_SPLIT(comm, color, key, newcomm)

IN	comm	communicator (handle)
IN	color	control of subset assignment (integer)
IN	key	control of rank assignment (integer)
OUT	newcomm	new communicator (handle)

```
int MPI_Comm_split(MPI_Comm comm, int color, int key,
    MPI_Comm *newcomm)
```

```
MPI_COMM_SPLIT(COMM, COLOR, KEY, NEWCOMM, IERROR)
    INTEGER COMM, COLOR, KEY, NEWCOMM, IERROR
```

```
MPI::Intercomm MPI::Intercomm::Split(int color, int key) const
```

```
MPI::Intracomm MPI::Intracomm::Split(int color, int key) const
```

If comm is an intracommunicator then this function partitions the group associated with comm into disjoint subgroups, one for each value of color. Each subgroup contains all processes of the same color. Within each subgroup, the processes are ranked in the order defined by the value of the argument key, with ties broken according to their rank in the old group. A new communication domain is created for each subgroup and a handle to the representative communicator is returned in newcomm. A process may supply the color value MPI_UNDEFINED to not be a member of any new group, in which case newcomm returns MPI_COMM_NULL. This is a collective call, but each process is permitted to provide different values for color and key. The value of color must be nonnegative.

Example 5.7   Assume that a collective call to MPI_COMM_SPLIT is executed in a 10 element group, with the arguments listed in the table below.

rank	0	1	2	3	4	5	6	7	8	9
process	a	b	c	d	e	f	g	h	i	j
color	0	$\perp$	3	0	3	0	0	5	3	$\perp$
key	3	1	2	5	1	1	1	2	1	0

The call generates three new communication domains: the first with group {f,g,a,d}, the second with group {e,i,c}, and the third with singleton group {h}. The processes b and j do not participate in any of the newly created communication domains, and are returned a null communicator handle.

A call to MPI_COMM_CREATE(comm, group, newcomm) is equivalent to a call to MPI_COMM_SPLIT(comm, color, key, newcomm), where all members of group provide color = 0 and key = rank in group, and all processes that are not members of group provide color = MPI_UNDEFINED. The function MPI_COMM_SPLIT allows more general partitioning of a group into one or more subgroups with optional reordering.

Advice to users.   This is an extremely powerful mechanism for dividing a single communicating group of processes into k subgroups, with k chosen implicitly by the user (by the number of colors asserted over all the processes). Each resulting communication domain will be unique and their associated groups are non-overlapping. Such a division could be useful for defining a hierarchy of computations, such as for multigrid, or linear algebra.

Multiple calls to MPI_COMM_SPLIT can be used to overcome the requirement that any call have no overlap of the resulting communicators (each process is of only one color per call). In this way, multiple overlapping communication structures can be created.

Note that, for a fixed color, the keys need not be unique. It is MPI_COMM_SPLIT's responsibility to sort processes in ascending order according to this key, and to break ties according to old rank. If all the keys are specified with the same value, then all the processes in a given color will have the same relative rank order as they did in their parent group. □

5.4.3 Communicator Destructor

MPI_COMM_FREE(comm)
    INOUT comm   communicator to be destroyed (handle)

```
int MPI_Comm_free(MPI_Comm *comm)
```

```
MPI_COMM_FREE(COMM, IERROR)
    INTEGER COMM, IERROR
```

```
void MPI::Comm::Free()
```

This collective operation marks the communication object for deallocation. The handle is set to MPI_COMM_NULL. Any pending operations that use this communicator will complete normally; the object is actually deallocated only if there are no other active references to it. The delete callback functions for all cached attributes (see Section 5.6) are called in arbitrary order. It is erroneous to attempt to free MPI_COMM_NULL.

Advice to implementors.   Though collective, it is anticipated that this operation will normally be implemented with no communication, though the debugging version of an MPI library might choose to synchronize. □

Advice to users.   Aliasing of communicators (e.g., comma = commb) is possible, but is not generally advised. After calling MPI_COMM_FREE any aliased communicator handle will be left in an undefined state. □

5.5   Safe Parallel Libraries

This section illustrates the design of parallel libraries, and the use of communicators to ensure the safety of internal library communications.

Assume that a new parallel library function is needed that is similar to the MPI broadcast function, except that it is not required that all processes provide the rank of the root process. Instead of the root argument of MPI_BCAST, the function takes a Boolean flag input that is true if the calling process is the root, false, otherwise. To simplify the example we make another assumption: namely that the datatype of the send buffer is identical to the datatype of the receive buffer, so that only one datatype argument is needed. A possible code for such a modified broadcast function is shown below.

Example 5.8   Code for modified broadcast function mcast(). The algorithm uses a broadcast tree that is built dynamically. The root divides the sequence of processes that follows the root into two segments. It sends a message to the first process in the second segment, which becomes the root for this segment. The process is repeated, recursively, within each subsegment.

In this example, we use blocking communication. Also, we select the two segments to be of equal size; performance can be improved by using a biased tree, and by using nonblocking communication.

```
void mcast(void *buff, // address of output buffer at root; address
                       // of input buffer at other processes.
           int count,  // number of items to broadcast
           const MPI::Datatype& type, // type of items to broadcast
           int isroot, // 1 if calling process is root, 0 otherwise
           MPI::Comm& comm) // communicator for broadcast
{
  const int size = comm.Get_size(); // Group size
  const int rank = comm.Get_rank(); // Rank in group

  int numleaves, // number of leaves in broadcast tree
    child, // rank of current child in broadcast tree
    childleaves; // number of leaves in child's broadcast tree
  MPI::Status status;

  if (isroot)
    numleaves = size - 1;
  else {
    // receive from parent leaf count and message
    comm.Recv(&numleaves, 1, MPI::INT, MPI::ANY_SOURCE, 0, status);
    comm.Recv(buff, count, type, MPI::ANY_SOURCE, 0, status);
  }
  while (numleaves > 0) {
    // pick child in middle of current leaf processes
    child = (rank + (numleaves + 1) / 2) % size;
    childleaves = numleaves/2;

    // send to child leaf count and message
    comm.Send(&childleaves, 1, MPI::INT, child, 0);
    comm.Send(buff, count, type, child, 0);

    numleaves -= (childleaves + 1); // remaining number of leaves
  }
}
```

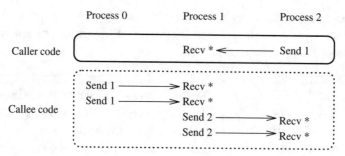

Figure 5.2
Correct invocation of mcast

Consider a collective invocation to the broadcast function just defined, in the context of the program segment shown in the example below, for a group of three processes.

Example 5.9   Before the collective invocation to mcast(), process 2 sends a message to process 1; process 1 posts a receive with a dontcare source. mcast is invoked, with process 0 as the root.

```
...
const int myrank = comm.Get_rank();
if (myrank == 2)
  comm.Send(&i, 1, MPI::INT, 1, 0);
else if (myrank == 1)
  comm.Recv(&i, 1, MPI::INT, MPI::ANY_SOURCE, 0, status);

mcast(&i, 1, MPI::INT, (myrank == 0), comm);
...
```

A (correct) execution of this code is illustrated in Figure 5.2, with arrows used to indicate communications.

Since the invocation of mcast at the three processes is not simultaneous, it may actually happen that mcast is invoked at process 0 before process 1 executed the receive in the caller code. This receive, rather than being matched by the caller code send at process 2, might be matched by the first send of process 0 within mcast. The erroneous execution illustrated in Figure 5.3 results.

How can such erroneous execution be prevented? One option is to enforce synchronization at the entry to mcast, and, for symmetric reasons, at the exit from

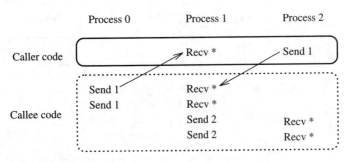

Figure 5.3
Erroneous invocation of mcast

mcast. E.g., the first and last executable statements within the code of mcast would be a call to MPI_Barrier(comm). This, however, introduces two superfluous synchronizations that will slow down execution. Furthermore, this synchronization works only if the caller code obeys the convention that messages sent before a collective invocation should also be received at their destination before the matching invocation. Consider an invocation to mcast() in a context that does not obey this restriction, as shown in the example below.

Example 5.10   Before the collective invocation to mcast(), process 2 sends a message to process 1; process 1 posts a matching receive with a dontcare source after the invocation to mcast.

```
...
const int myrank = comm.Get_rank();
if (myrank == 2)
  comm.Send(&i, 1, MPI::INT, 1, 0);

mcast(&i, 1, MPI::INT, (myrank == 0), comm);

if (myrank == 1)
  comm.Recv(&i, 1, MPI::INT, MPI::ANY_SOURCE, 0, status);
```

The desired execution of the code in this example is illustrated in Figure 5.4.

However, a more likely matching of sends with receives will lead to the erroneous execution is illustrated in Figure 5.5. Erroneous results may also occur if a process that is not in the group of comm and does not participate in the collective invocation of mcast sends a message to processes one or two in the group of comm.

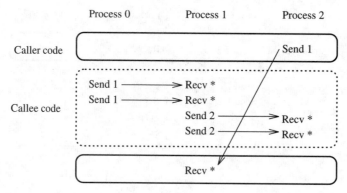

Figure 5.4
Correct invocation of mcast

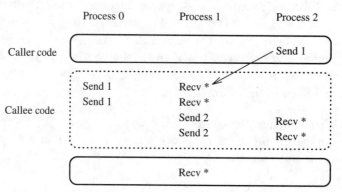

Figure 5.5
Erroneous invocation of mcast

A more robust solution to this problem is to use a distinct communication domain for communication within the library, which is not used by the caller code. This will ensure that messages sent by the library are not received outside the library, and vice-versa. The modified code of the function mcast is shown below.

Example 5.11   Code for modified broadcast function mcast() that uses a private communicator. The code is identical to the one in Example 5.8, with the following exceptions: Upon entry, a duplicate pcomm of the input communicator comm is created. This private communicator is used for communication within the library code. It is freed before exit.

```
void mcast(void *buff, int count, MPI_Datatype type,
           int isroot, MPI_Comm comm)
{
  int size, rank, numleaves, child, childleaves;
  MPI_Status status;
  MPI_Comm pcomm; /* private communicator, for internal
                     communication */

  MPI_Comm_dup(comm, &pcomm);

  MPI_Comm_size(pcomm, &size);
  MPI_Comm_rank(pcomm, &rank);

  if (isroot) {
    numleaves = size-1;
  }
  else {
    /* receive from parent leaf count and message */
    MPI_Recv(&numleaves, 1, MPI_INT, MPI_ANY_SOURCE, 0, pcomm,
             &status);
    MPI_Recv(buff, count, type, MPI_ANY_SOURCE, 0, pcomm, &status);
  }
  while (numleaves > 0) {
    /* pick child in middle of current leaf processes */
    child = (rank + (numleaves+1)/2)%size;
    childleaves = numleaves/2;
    /* send to child leaf count and message */
    MPI_Send(&childleaves, 1, MPI_INT, child, 0, pcomm);
    MPI_Send(buff, count, type, child, 0, pcomm);
    /* compute remaining number of leaves */
    numleaves -= (childleaves+1);
  }

  MPI_Comm_free(&pcomm);
}
```

Here we show the same example in C++. In this example we use Clone() rather than Dup() since the comm argument is of type MPI::Comm, an abstract base class, rather than any of the derived communicator classes. Note that pcomm must be deleted.

```cpp
void mcast(void *buff, int count, const MPI::Datatype& type,
           int isroot, MPI::Comm& comm)
{
  int numleaves, child, childleaves;
  MPI::Status status;

  MPI::Comm& pcomm = comm.Clone(); // Clone a private communicator

  const int size = pcomm.Get_size();
  const int rank = pcomm.Get_rank();

  if (isroot)
    numleaves = size - 1;
  else {
    // receive from parent leaf count and message
    pcomm.Recv(&numleaves, 1, MPI::INT, MPI::ANY_SOURCE, 0, status);
    pcomm.Recv(buff, count, type, MPI::ANY_SOURCE, 0, status);
  }
  while (numleaves > 0) {
    // pick child in middle of current leaf processes
    child = (rank + (numleaves + 1) / 2) % size;
    childleaves = numleaves / 2;

    // send to child leaf count and message
    pcomm.Send(&childleaves, 1, MPI::INT, child, 0);
    pcomm.Send(buff, count, type, child, 0);

    // compute remaining number of leaves
    numleaves -= (childleaves + 1);
  }

  pcomm.Free();
  delete &pcomm;                        // Clone() requires deletion
}
```

This code suffers the penalty of one communicator allocation and deallocation at each invocation. We show in the next section, in Example 5.12, how to avoid this overhead, by using a preallocated communicator.

5.6   Caching

5.6.1   Introduction

As the previous examples showed, a communicator provides a "scope" for collective invocations. The communicator, which is passed as parameter to the call, specifies the group of processes that participate in the call and provide a private communication domain for communications within the body of subroutine being called. In addition, it may carry information about the logical topology of the executing processes. It is often useful to attach additional persistent values to this scope; e.g., initialization parameters for a library, or additional communicators to provide a separate, private communication domain.

MPI provides a caching facility that allows an application to attach arbitrary pieces of information, called **attributes**, to both intra- and intercommunicators. More precisely, the caching facility allows a portable library to do the following:

- pass information between calls by associating it with an MPI intra- or inter-communicator,
- quickly retrieve that information, and
- be guaranteed that out-of-date information is never retrieved, even if the communicator is freed and its handle subsequently reused by MPI.

Attribute caching is part of MPI-1. MPI-2 introduced a slightly different syntax for attribute caching functions and deprecated the MPI-1 syntax for attribute caching (see Section 1.9.1 for the status of deprecated functions). We present here the MPI-2 syntax, and present in Section 5.6.3 the deprecated functions (which continue to be part of the MPI standard). The new functions should be preferably used, if available.

Each attribute is associated with a **key**.   To provide safety, MPI internally generates key values. MPI functions are provided which allow the user to allocate and deallocate key values (MPI_COMM_CREATE_KEYVAL and MPI_COMM_FREE_-KEYVAL). Once a key is allocated by a process, it can be used to attach one attribute to any communicator defined at that process. Thus, the allocation of a key can be thought of as creating an empty box at each current or future communicator object at that process; this box has a lock that matches the allocated key. (The

box is "virtual": one need not allocate any actual space before an attempt is made
to store something in the box.)

Once the key is allocated, the user can set or access attributes associated with
this key. The MPI call MPI_COMM_SET_ATTR can be used to set an attribute.
This call stores an attribute, or replaces an attribute in one box: the box attached
with the specified communicator with a lock that matches the specified key.

The call MPI_COMM_GET_ATTR can be used to access the attribute value associated with a given key and communicator. I.e., it allows one to access the content
of the box attached with the specified communicator, that has a lock that matches
the specified key. This call is valid even if the box is empty, e.g., if the attribute
was never set. In such case, a special "empty" value is returned.

Finally, the call MPI_COMM_DELETE_ATTR allows one to delete an attribute.
I.e., it allows one to empty the box attached with the specified communicator with
a lock that matches the specified key.

To be general, the attribute mechanism must be able to store arbitrary user
information. On the other hand, attributes must be of a fixed, predefined type—the
type specified by the MPI functions that access or update attributes. Attributes
are defined in C and C++ to be of type void *. Generally, such an attribute
will be a pointer to a user-defined data structure or a handle to an MPI opaque
object. In Fortran, attributes are of type INTEGER(KIND=MPI_ADDRESS_KIND), i.e.,
are address-sized integers. These can hold addresses, or can be converted, without
loss of information to INTEGERs that can be handles to opaque MPI objects.

An attribute, from the MPI viewpoint, is a pointer or an integer. An attribute,
from the application viewpoint, may contain arbitrary information that is attached
to the "MPI attribute". User-defined attributes are "copied" when a new communicator is created by a call to MPI_COMM_DUP; they are "deleted" when a
communicator is deallocated by a call to MPI_COMM_FREE. Because of the arbitrary nature of the information that is copied or deleted, the user has to specify
the semantics of attribute copying or deletion. The user does so by providing copy
and delete callback functions when the attribute key is allocated (by a call to MPI_-
COMM_CREATE_KEYVAL). Predefined, default copy and delete callback functions
are available.

All attribute manipulation functions are local and require no communication.
Two communicator objects at two different processes that represent the same communication domain may have a different set of attribute keys and different attribute
values associated with them.

MPI reserves a set of predefined key values in order to associate with MPI_COMM-
_WORLD information about the execution environment, at MPI initialization time.

These attribute keys are discussed in Chapter 7. These keys cannot be deallocated and the associated attributes cannot be updated by the user. Otherwise, they behave like user-defined attributes.

The error code MPI_ERR_KEYVAL (MPI::ERR_KEYVAL, in C++) is returned by attribute manipulation functions if they are passed an invalid key value.

Advice to users. The communicator MPI_COMM_SELF can be used to store process-local attributes, via this attribute caching mechanism. □

Rationale. A much smaller interface, consisting of just a callback facility, would allow the entire caching facility to be implemented by portable code. However, such a minimal interface does not provide good protection when different libraries try to attach attributes to the same communicator. Some convention will be needed to avoid different libraries from using the same key values. With the current design, the initialization code for each library can allocate a separate key value for that library; the code written for one library is independent of the code used by another library. Furthermore the more complete interface defined here allows high-quality implementations of MPI to implement fast attribute access algorithms (e.g., using an incrementable dictionary data structure).

Attribute keys are allocated process-wide, rather then specifically for one communicator. This often simplifies usage, since a particular type of attribute may be associated with many communicators; and simplifies implementation.

The use of callback functions for attribute copying and deletion allows one to define different behaviors for these operations. For example, copying may involve the allocation of a new data structure, if the attribute is modifiable; or, it may involve only the increment of a reference count if the attribute is not modifiable. With the current design, the implementation of attribute copying and deletion is defined when the attribute key is allocated, and need not be visible to all program modules that use this key. □

Advice to implementors. In C and C++, attributes are scalar values, equal in size to, or larger than a pointer. Fortran attributes are of type INTEGER(KIND=MPI_-ADDRESS_KIND). Attributes can always hold an MPI handle. Also, C and C++ attributes can be converted to Fortran attributes without loss of precision, and vice-versa. The issue of attribute use across languages is discussed in Section II-2.2.7.

Caching and callback functions are only called synchronously, in response to explicit application requests. This synchronous calling rule is a general property of MPI. □

5.6.2   Caching Functions

MPI provides the following services related to caching. They are all process local.

MPI_COMM_CREATE_KEYVAL(comm_copy_attr_fn,   comm_delete_attr_fn,   comm_-
keyval, extra_state)

IN	comm_copy_attr_fn	copy callback function for comm_keyval (function)
IN	comm_delete_attr_fn	delete callback function for comm_keyval (function)
OUT	comm_keyval	key value for future access (integer)
IN	extra_state	extra state for callback functions

```
int MPI_Comm_create_keyval(MPI_Comm_copy_attr_function *comm_copy_-
    attr_fn, MPI_Comm_delete_attr_function *comm_delete_attr_fn,
    int *comm_keyval, void *extra_state)
```

```
MPI_COMM_CREATE_KEYVAL(COMM_COPY_ATTR_FN, COMM_DELETE_ATTR_FN,
    COMM_KEYVAL, EXTRA_STATE, IERROR)
    EXTERNAL COMM_COPY_ATTR_FN, COMM_DELETE_ATTR_FN
    INTEGER COMM_KEYVAL, IERROR
    INTEGER(KIND=MPI_ADDRESS_KIND) EXTRA_STATE
```

```
static int MPI::Comm::Create_keyval(MPI::Comm::Copy_attr_function*
    comm_copy_attr_fn,
    MPI::Comm::Delete_attr_function* comm_delete_attr_fn,
    void* extra_state)
```

MPI_COMM_CREATE_KEYVAL allocates a new attribute key value. Key values are
unique in a process.   Once allocated, the key value can be used to associate
attributes and access them on any locally defined communicator. The special key
value MPI_KEYVAL_INVALID (MPI::KEYVAL_INVALID, in C++) is never returned by
MPI_COMM_CREATE_KEYVAL. Therefore, it can be used for static initialization of
key variables, to indicate an "unallocated" key.

The comm_copy_attr_fn function is invoked when a communicator is duplicated
by MPI_COMM_DUP. comm_copy_attr_fn should be in C of type MPI_Comm_copy_-
attr_function, which is defined as

```
typedef int MPI_Comm_copy_attr_function(MPI_Comm oldcomm,
    int comm_keyval, void *extra_state, void *attribute_val_in,
    void *attribute_val_out, int *flag);
```

A Fortran declaration for such a function is as follows:

```
SUBROUTINE COMM_COPY_ATTR_FN(OLDCOMM, COMM_KEYVAL, EXTRA_STATE,
    ATTRIBUTE_VAL_IN, ATTRIBUTE_VAL_OUT, FLAG, IERROR)
    INTEGER OLDCOMM, COMM_KEYVAL, IERROR
    INTEGER(KIND=MPI_ADDRESS_KIND) EXTRA_STATE, ATTRIBUTE_VAL_IN,
        ATTRIBUTE_VAL_OUT
    LOGICAL FLAG
```

The C++ definition is

```
typedef int MPI::Comm::Copy_attr_function(const MPI::Comm& oldcomm,
    int comm_keyval, void* extra_state, void* attribute_val_in,
    void* attribute_val_out, bool& flag);
```

Whenever a communicator is replicated using the function MPI_COMM_DUP, all callback copy functions for attributes that are currently set are invoked (in arbitrary order). Each call to the copy callback is passed as input parameters the old communicator oldcomm, the key value keyval, the additional state extra_state that was provided to MPI_COMM_CREATE_KEYVAL when the key value was created, and the current attribute value attribute_val_in. If it returns flag = false, then the attribute is deleted in the duplicated communicator. Otherwise, when flag = true, the new attribute value is set to the value returned in attribute_val_out. The function returns MPI_SUCCESS on success and an error code on failure (in which case MPI_COMM_DUP is erroneous).

comm_copy_attr_fn may be specified as MPI_COMM_NULL_COPY_FN or MPI_COMM_DUP_FN from either C or Fortran and MPI::COMM_NULL_FN or MPI::COMM_DUP_FN, respectively from C++. MPI_COMM_NULL_COPY_FN is a function that does nothing other than returning flag = false and MPI_SUCCESS. MPI_COMM_DUP_FN is a simple-minded copy function that sets flag = true, returns the value of attribute_val_in in attribute_val_out, and returns MPI_SUCCESS. That is, the attribute value is copied, with no side-effects.

The extra_state argument should not be modified by the copy or delete callback functions (this is obvious from the C and C++ binding, but not obvious from the Fortran binding).

Rationale.   The use of the extra_state argument allows one to specialize the behavior of a generic copy callback function to a particular attribute. E.g., one might have a generic copy function that allocates m bytes of storage, copies m bytes from address attribute_val_in into the newly allocated space, and returns the address of the allocated space in attribute_val_out; the value of m, i.e., the size of the data structure for a specific attribute, can be specified via extra_state. ☐

Advice to users.   Even though both formal arguments attribute_val_in and attribute_val_out are of type void * in C and C++, their usage differs. The C (C++) copy function is passed by MPI in attribute_val_in the *value* of the attribute, and in attribute_val_out the *address* of the attribute, so as to allow the function to return the (new) attribute value. The use of type void * for both is to avoid messy type casts.

A valid copy function is one that completely duplicates the information by making a full duplicate copy of the data structures implied by an attribute; another might just make another reference to that data structure, while using a reference-count mechanism. Other types of attributes might not copy at all (they might be specific to oldcomm only). ☐

Advice to implementors.   A C (respectively, Fortran or C++) interface should be assumed for copy and delete functions associated with key values created in C (respectively, Fortran, or C++). ☐

Analogous to comm_copy_attr_fn is a callback deletion function, defined as follows. The comm_delete_attr_fn function is invoked when a communicator is deleted by MPI_COMM_FREE or by a call to MPI_COMM_DELETE_ATTR or MPI_COMM_SET_ATTR. comm_delete_attr_fn should be in C of type MPI_Comm_delete_attr_function, which is defined as follows:

```
typedef int MPI_Comm_delete_attr_function(MPI_Comm comm, int
    comm_keyval, void *attribute_val, void *extra_state);
```

A Fortran declaration for such a function is as follows:

```
SUBROUTINE COMM_DELETE_ATTR_FN(COMM, COMM_KEYVAL, ATTRIBUTE_VAL,
    EXTRA_STATE, IERROR)
    INTEGER COMM, COMM_KEYVAL, IERROR
    INTEGER(KIND=MPI_ADDRESS_KIND) ATTRIBUTE_VAL, EXTRA_STATE
```

The C++ declaration is:

```
typedef int MPI::Comm::Delete_attr_function(MPI::Comm& comm,
    int comm_keyval, void* attribute_val, void* extra_state);
```

Whenever a communicator is deleted using the function MPI_COMM_FREE, all callback delete functions for attributes that are currently set are invoked (in arbitrary order). In addition the callback delete function for the deleted attribute is invoked by MPI_COMM_DELETE_ATTR and MPI_COMM_SET_ATTR. The function is passed as input parameters the communicator comm, the key value keyval, the current attribute value attribute_val, and the additional state extra_state that was passed to MPI_COMM_KEYVAL_CREATE when the key value was allocated. The function returns MPI_SUCCESS on success and an error code on failure (in which case MPI_COMM_FREE is erroneous).

delete_fn may be specified as MPI_COMM_NULL_DELETE_FN from either C or Fortran and MPI::COMM_NULL_DELETE from C++. MPI_COMM_NULL_DELETE_FN is a function that does nothing, other than returning MPI_SUCCESS.

Advice to users. The delete callback function may be invoked by MPI asynchronously, after the call to MPI_COMM_FREE returned, when MPI actually deletes the communicator object. □

MPI_COMM_FREE_KEYVAL(comm_keyval)

   INOUT   comm_keyval   key value (integer)

```
int MPI_Comm_free_keyval(int *comm_keyval)
```

```
MPI_COMM_FREE_KEYVAL(COMM_KEYVAL, IERROR)
    INTEGER COMM_KEYVAL, IERROR
```

```
static void MPI::Comm::Free_keyval(int& comm_keyval)
```

MPI_COMM_FREE_KEYVAL deallocates an attribute key value. This function sets the value of keyval to MPI_KEYVAL_INVALID. Note that it is not erroneous to free an attribute key that is in use (i.e., has attached values for some communicators); the key value is not actually deallocated until after no attribute values are locally attached to this key. All such attribute values need to be explicitly deallocated by the program, either via calls to MPI_COMM_DELETE_ATTR that free one attribute instance, or by calls to MPI_COMM_FREE that free all attribute instances associated with the freed communicator.

MPI_COMM_SET_ATTR(comm, comm_keyval, attribute_val)

   INOUT   comm   communicator from which attribute will be attache (handle)

   IN   comm_keyval   key value (integer)

IN   attribute_val   attribute value

---

int MPI_Comm_set_attr(MPI_Comm comm, int comm_keyval, void
    *attribute_val)

MPI_COMM_SET_ATTR(COMM, COMM_KEYVAL, ATTRIBUTE_VAL, IERROR)
    INTEGER COMM, COMM_KEYVAL, IERROR
    INTEGER(KIND=MPI_ADDRESS_KIND) ATTRIBUTE_VAL

void MPI::Comm::Set_attr(int comm_keyval, const void* attribute_val)
    const

MPI_COMM_SET_ATTR associates the value attribute_val with the key keyval on
communicator comm. If a value is already associated with this key on the communicator, then the outcome is as if MPI_COMM_DELETE_ATTR was first called
to delete the previous value (and the delete callback function was executed), and
a new value was next stored. The call is erroneous if there is no key with value
keyval; in particular MPI_KEYVAL_INVALID is an erroneous value for keyval.

MPI_COMM_GET_ATTR(comm, comm_keyval, attribute_val, flag)

IN	comm	communicator to which the attribute is attached (handle)
IN	comm_keyval	key value (integer)
OUT	attribute_val	attribute value, unless flag = false
OUT	flag	false if no attribute is associated with the key (logical)

---

int MPI_Comm_get_attr(MPI_Comm comm, int comm_keyval, void
    *attribute_val, int *flag)

MPI_COMM_GET_ATTR(COMM, COMM_KEYVAL, ATTRIBUTE_VAL, FLAG, IERROR)
    INTEGER COMM, COMM_KEYVAL, IERROR
    INTEGER(KIND=MPI_ADDRESS_KIND) ATTRIBUTE_VAL
    LOGICAL FLAG

bool MPI::Comm::Get_attr(int comm_keyval, void* attribute_val) const

MPI_COMM_GET_ATTR retrieves an attribute value by key. The call is erroneous
if there is no key with value keyval. In particular MPI_KEYVAL_INVALID is an erroneous value for keyval. On the other hand, the call is correct if the key value exists,

but no attribute is attached on comm for that key; in such a case, the call returns flag = false. If an attribute is attached on comm to keyval, then the call returns flag = true, and returns the attribute value in attribute_val.

Advice to users. In C and C++, the call to MPI_Comm_set_attr passes in attribute_val the *value* of the attribute; the call to MPI_Comm_get_attr passes in attribute_val the *address* of the the location where the attribute value is to be returned. Thus, if the attribute value itself is a pointer of type void*, then the actual attribute_val parameter to MPI_Comm_set_attr will be of type void* and the actual attribute_val parameter to MPI_Comm_attr will be of type void**. ☐

Rationale. The use of a formal parameter attribute_val of type void* (rather than void**) in MPI_Comm_get_attr avoids the messy type casting that would be needed if the attribute is declared with a type other than void*. ☐

MPI_COMM_DELETE_ATTR(comm, comm_keyval)

INOUT	comm	communicator from which the attribute is deleted (handle)
IN	comm_keyval	key value (integer)

```
int MPI_Comm_delete_attr(MPI_Comm comm, int comm_keyval)
```

```
MPI_COMM_DELETE_ATTR(COMM, COMM_KEYVAL, IERROR)
    INTEGER COMM, COMM_KEYVAL, IERROR
```

```
void MPI::Comm::Delete_attr(int comm_keyval)
```

MPI_COMM_DELETE_ATTR deletes the attribute attached to key keyval on comm. This function invokes the attribute delete function delete_fn specified when the keyval was created. The call will fail if there is no key with value keyval or if the delete_fn function returns an error code other than MPI_SUCCESS. On the other hand, the call is correct even if no attribute is currently attached to keyval on comm.

Example 5.12 We come back to the code in Example 5.11. Rather than duplicating the communicator comm at each invocation, we desire to do it once, and store the duplicate communicator. It would be inconvenient to require initialization code that duplicates all communicators to be used later with mcast. Fortunately, this is not needed. Instead, we shall use an initialization code that allocates an attribute key for the exclusive use of mcast(). This key can then be used to store, with each communicator comm, a private copy of comm which is used by mcast. This copy is created once at the first invocation of mcast with argument comm.

```
static int *extra_state;    /* not used */
static int mcast_key = MPI_KEYVAL_INVALID;
/* attribute key for mcast */
int mcast_delete_fn(MPI_Comm comm, int keyval, void *attr_val,
                    void *extra_state)
    /* delete function to be used for mcast_key attribute.
        The callback function frees the private communicator attached
        to this key  */
{
  return MPI_Comm_free((MPI_Comm *)&attr_val);
}


void mcast_init(void)
    /* initialization function for mcast.  It should be invoked once
        by each process before it invokes mcast */
{
  MPI_Comm_create_keyval(MPI_COMM_NULL_COPY_FN, mcast_delete_fn,
                    &mcast_key, extra_state);
}


void mcast(void *buff, int count, MPI_Datatype type,
          int isroot, MPI_Comm comm)
{
  int size, rank, numleaves, child, childleaves, flag;
  MPI_Comm pcomm;
  void *attr_val;
  MPI_Status status;

  MPI_Comm_get_attr(comm, mcast_key, &attr_val, &flag);
  if (flag) {          /* private communicator cached */
    pcomm = (MPI_Comm)attr_val;
  }
  else {                   /* first invocation; no cached communicator */
                           /* create private communicator */
    MPI_Comm_dup(comm, &pcomm);
```

```
                            /* and cache it */
        MPI_Comm_set_attr(comm, mcast_key, &pcomm);
}

/* continue now as before */
MPI_Comm_size(pcomm, &size);
MPI_Comm_rank(pcomm, &rank);

if (isroot) {
  numleaves = size-1;
}
else {
  /* receive from parent leaf count and message */
  MPI_Recv(&numleaves, 1, MPI_INT, MPI_ANY_SOURCE, 0, pcomm,
           &status);
  MPI_Recv(buff, count, type, MPI_ANY_SOURCE, 0, pcomm, &status);
}
while (numleaves > 0) {
  /* pick child in middle of current leaf processes */
  child = (rank + (numleaves+1)/2) % size;
  childleaves = numleaves/2;
  /* send to child leaf count and message */
  MPI_Send(&childleaves, 1, MPI_INT, child, 0, pcomm);
  MPI_Send(buff, count, type, child, 0, pcomm);
  /* compute remaining number of leaves */
  numleaves -= (childleaves+1);
}
}
```

The code above dedicates a statically allocated private communicator for the use of mcast. This segregates communication within the library from communication outside the library. However, this approach does not provide separation of communications belonging to distinct invocations of the same library function, since they all use the same communication domain. Consider two successive collective invocations of mcast by four processes, where process 0 is the broadcast root in the first one, and process 3 is the root in the second one. The intended execution and communication flow for these two invocations is illustrated in Figure 5.6.

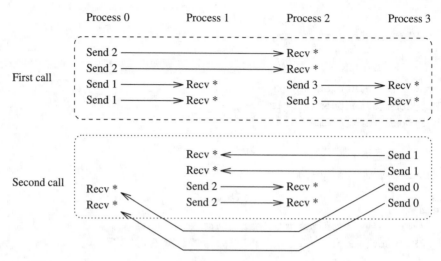

Figure 5.6
Correct execution of two successive invocations of mcast

However, there is a race between messages sent by the first invocation of mcast, from process 0 to process 1, and messages sent by the second invocation of mcast, from process 3 to process 1. The erroneous execution illustrated in Figure 5.7 may occur, where messages sent by second invocation overtake messages from the first invocation. This phenomenon is known as *backmasking*.

How can we avoid backmasking? One option is to revert to the approach in Example 5.11, where a separate communication domain is generated for each invocation. Another option is to add a barrier synchronization, either at the entry or at the exit from the library call. Yet another option is to rewrite the library code, so as to prevent the nondeterministic race. The race occurs because receives with dontcares are used. It is often possible to avoid the use of such constructs. Unfortunately, avoiding dontcares leads to a less efficient implementation of mcast. A possible alternative is to use increasing tag numbers to disambiguate successive invocations of mcast. An "invocation count" can be cached with each communicator, as an additional library attribute. The resulting code is shown below.

Example 5.13   Code in previous example is modified, to prevent backmasking: successive invocations of mcast with the same communicator use distinct tags.

```
static int *extra_state;        /* not used */
static int mcast_key = MPI_KEYVAL_INVALID;
```

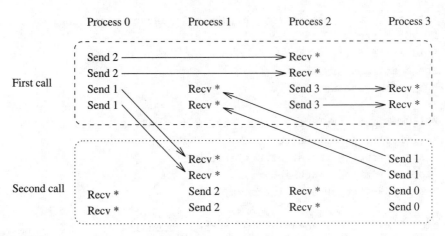

Figure 5.7
Erroneous execution of two successive invocations of mcast

```
typedef  struct {              /* mcast attribute structure */
  MPI_Comm pcomm;              /* private communicator */
  int invcount;               /* invocation count */
} Mcast_attr;

int mcast_delete_fn(MPI_Comm comm, int keyval, void *attr_val,
                    void *extra_state)
{
  MPI_Comm_free(&((Mcast_attr *)attr_val)->pcomm);
  free(attr_val);
  return(MPI_SUCCESS);
}

void mcast_init(void)    /* initialization function for mcast. */
{
  MPI_Comm_create_keyval( MPI_COMM_NULL_COPY_FN, mcast_delete_fn,
                &mcast_key, extra_state);
}

void mcast(void *buff, int count, MPI_Datatype type,
           int isroot, MPI_Comm comm)
{
```

```
int size, rank, numleaves, child, childleaves, flag, tag;
MPI_Comm pcomm;
void *attr_val;
Mcast_attr *attr_struct;
MPI_Status status;

MPI_Comm_get_attr(comm, mcast_key, &attr_val, &flag);
if (flag) { /* attribute  cached */
  attr_struct = (Mcast_attr *)attr_val;
  pcomm = attr_struct->pcomm;
  tag = ++attr_struct->invcount;
}
else { /* first invocation; no cached communicator
          create private communicator */
  MPI_Comm_dup(comm, &pcomm);
  /* create attribute structure */
  attr_struct = (Mcast_attr *)malloc(sizeof(Mcast_attr));
  attr_struct->pcomm = pcomm;
  attr_struct->invcount = 0;
  MPI_Comm_set_attr(comm, mcast_key, attr_struct);
}

/* broadcast code, using tag */
MPI_Comm_size(pcomm, &size);
MPI_Comm_rank(pcomm, &rank);

if (isroot) {
  numleaves = size-1;
 }
else {
  /* receive from parent leaf count and message */
  MPI_Recv(&numleaves, 1, MPI_INT, MPI_ANY_SOURCE, tag, pcomm,
           &status);
  MPI_Recv(buff, count, type, MPI_ANY_SOURCE, tag, pcomm, &status);
}
while (numleaves > 0) {
  /* pick child in middle of current leaf processes */
  child = (rank + (numleaves+1)/2) % size;
```

```
    childleaves = numleaves/2;
    /* send to child leaf count and message */
    MPI_Send(&childleaves, 1, MPI_INT, child, 0, pcomm);
    MPI_Send(buff, count, type, child, 0, pcomm);
    /* compute remaining number of leaves */
    numleaves -= (childleaves+1);
  }
}
```

5.6.3   Deprecated Functions

MPI-2 introduced new attribute caching functions for two reasons.

• MPI-1 Fortran attributes were of type INTEGER. The Fortran binding for the new functions specifies attributes of type INTEGER(KIND=MPI_ADDRESS_KIND). This facilitates language interoperability by ensuring that attributes can be converted from Fortran to C or C++ with no loss of information (see II-2.2.7).

• In MPI-1 attributes were cached only with communicators. MPI-2 supports attribute caching for objects other than communicators. New attribute caching operations were needed for the other objects. The new attribute caching functions for communicators are methods of the object comm in C++, and carry "COMM" in their name in C and Fortran. This is consistent with the design chosen for attribute caching on other objects.

The old attribute caching functions, while deprecated, are still part of the MPI standard.

The deprecated MPI-1 attribute caching functions are listed below. The language-neutral definitions and the C bindings are the same (expect for the different function names). The Fortran bindings of the deprecated Fortran functions differ in that all INTEGER arguments have default kind – while the new functions have attribute value arguments of type INTEGER(KIND=MPI_INTEGER_KIND).

We list the deprecated functions, with their C and Fortran binding, and specify the replacing function for each one.

MPI_KEYVAL_CREATE(copy_fn, delete_fn, keyval, extra_state)

```
int MPI_Keyval_create(MPI_Copy_function *copy_fn, MPI_Delete_function
    *delete_fn, int *keyval, void* extra_state)
```

```
MPI_KEYVAL_CREATE(COPY_FN, DELETE_FN, KEYVAL, EXTRA_STATE, IERROR)
    EXTERNAL COPY_FN, DELETE_FN
```

```
      INTEGER KEYVAL, EXTRA_STATE, IERROR
```

is replaced by

MPI_COMM_CREATE_KEYVAL(comm_copy_attr_fn, comm_delete_attr_fn, comm_keyval, extra_state)

copy_fn is defined in C as

```
typedef int MPI_Copy_function(MPI_Comm oldcomm, int keyval, void
    *extra_state, void *attribute_val_in, void *attribute_val_out, int
    *flag);
```

(same as MPI_Comm_copy_attr_function). The Fortran declaration for copy_fn is

```
SUBROUTINE COPY_FUNCTION(OLDCOMM, KEYVAL, EXTRA_STATE,
    ATTRIBUTE_VAL_IN, ATTRIBUTE_VAL_OUT, FLAG, IERR)
    INTEGER OLDCOMM, KEYVAL, EXTRA_STATE, ATTRIBUTE_VAL_IN,
    ATTRIBUTE_VAL_OUT, IERR
    LOGICAL FLAG
```

copy_fn can be specified as MPI_NULL_COPY_FN or MPI_DUP_FN (MPI::NULL_COPY_FN or MPI::DUP_FN in C++), which are the same as MPI_COMM_NULL_COPY_FN or MPI_COMM_DUP_FN, respectively, except for the different signature of the Fortran functions.

The C definition for delete_fn is

```
typedef int MPI_Delete_function(MPI_Comm comm, int keyval, void
    *attribute_val, void *extra_state);
```

(same as the C definition for MPI_Comm_delete_attr_function). The Fortran declaration for delete_fn is

```
SUBROUTINE DELETE_FUNCTION(COMM, KEYVAL, ATTRIBUTE_VAL, EXTRA_STATE,
    IERR)
    INTEGER COMM, KEYVAL, ATTRIBUTE_VAL, EXTRA_STATE, IERR
```

delete_fn can be specified as MPI_NULL_DELETE_FN (MPI::NULL_DELETE_FN, in C++), which is the same as MPI_COMM_NULL_DELETE_FN, expect for the different signature of the Fortran function.

MPI_KEYVAL_FREE(keyval)

```
int MPI_Keyval_free(int *keyval)
```

```
MPI_KEYVAL_FREE(KEYVAL, IERROR)
    INTEGER KEYVAL, IERROR
```

is replaced by
MPI_COMM_FREE_KEYVAL(comm_keyval)

MPI_ATTR_PUT(comm, keyval, attribute_val)
int MPI_Attr_put(MPI_Comm comm, int keyval, void* attribute_val)

MPI_ATTR_PUT(COMM, KEYVAL, ATTRIBUTE_VAL, IERROR)
    INTEGER COMM, KEYVAL, ATTRIBUTE_VAL, IERROR

is replaced by
MPI_COMM_SET_ATTR(comm, comm_keyval, attribute_val)

MPI_ATTR_GET(comm, keyval, attribute_val, flag)
int MPI_Attr_get(MPI_Comm comm, int keyval, void *attribute_val,
    int *flag)

MPI_ATTR_GET(COMM, KEYVAL, ATTRIBUTE_VAL, FLAG, IERROR)INTEGER
COMM, KEYVAL, ATTRIBUTE_VAL, IERROR LOGICAL FLAG
is replaced by
MPI_COMM_GET_ATTR(comm, comm_keyval, attribute_val, flag)

MPI_ATTR_DELETE(comm, keyval)
int MPI_Attr_delete(MPI_Comm comm, int keyval)

MPI_ATTR_DELETE(COMM, KEYVAL, IERROR)
    INTEGER COMM, KEYVAL, IERROR

is replaced by
MPI_COMM_DELETE_ATTR(comm, comm_keyval)
If MPI_ATTR_GET is called, in Fortran, then the the attribute value may be truncated, when converted from an address-sized integer to a default integer (truncation returns the least significant part of the value, with the sign extended). Similarly, if a copy or delete callback function that was associated with an attribute key by a Fortran call to MPI_KEYVAL_CREATE is invoked, then the attribute value may be truncated before it is passed to the callback function through the attribute_val_in argument. Conversely, attribute values passed to Fortran calls to MPI_ATTR_PUT, or returned through the attribute_val_out by old style attribute copy callback functions are converted to address-size integers.

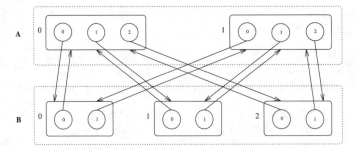

Figure 5.8
Distributed data structure for inter-communication domain.

5.7   Intercommunication

5.7.1   Introduction

This section introduces the concept of inter-communication and describes the portions of MPI that support it.

All point-to-point communication described thus far has involved communication between processes that are members of the same group. In modular and multidisciplinary applications, different process groups execute distinct modules and processes within different modules communicate with one another in a pipeline or a more general module graph. In these applications, the most natural way for a process to specify a peer process is by the rank of the peer process within the peer group. In applications that contain internal user-level servers, each server may be a process group that provides services to one or more clients, and each client may be a process group that uses the services of one or more servers. It is again most natural to specify the peer process by rank within the peer group in these applications.

An inter-group communication domain is specified by a set of intercommunicators with the pair of disjoint groups (A,B) as their attribute, such that

- their links form a bipartite graph: each communicator at a process in group A is linked to all communicators at processes in group B, and vice-versa; and
- links have consistent indices: at each communicator at a process in group A, the i-th link points to the communicator for process i in group B; and vice-versa.

This distributed data structure is illustrated in Figure 5.8, for the case of a pair of groups (A,B), with two (upper box) and three (lower box) processes, respectively.

The communicator structure distinguishes between a *local* group, namely the group containing the process where the structure reside, and a *remote* group, namely the other group. The structure is symmetric: for processes in group A, then A is the local group and B is the remote group, whereas for processes in group B, then B is the local group and A is the remote group.

An inter-group communication will involve a process in one group executing a send call and another process, in the other group, executing a matching receive call. As in intragroup communication, the matching process (destination of send or source of receive) is specified using a (communicator, rank) pair. Unlike intra-group communication, the rank is relative to the second, remote group. Thus, in the communication domain illustrated in Figure 5.8, process 1 in group A sends a message to process 2 in group B with a call MPI_SEND(..., 2, tag, comm); process 2 in group B receives this message with a call MPI_RECV(..., 1, tag, comm). Conversely, process 2 in group B sends a message to process 1 in group A with a call to MPI_SEND(..., 1, tag, comm), and the message is received by a call to MPI_RECV(..., 2, tag, comm); a remote process is identified in the same way for the purposes of sending or receiving. All point-to-point communication functions can be used with intercommunicators for inter-group communication.

Here is a summary of the properties of inter-group communication and intercommunicators:

- The syntax of point-to-point communication is the same for both inter- and intra-communication. The same communicator can be used both for send and for receive operations.
- A target process is addressed by its rank in the remote group, both for sends and for receives.
- Communications using an intercommunicator are guaranteed not to conflict with any communications that use a different communicator.
- A communicator will provide either intra- or inter-communication, never both.

Rationale. The correspondence between inter- and intracommunicators can be best understood by thinking of an intragroup communication domain as a special case of an inter-group communication domain, where both communication groups happen to be identical. This interpretation can be used to derive a consistent semantics for communicator inquiry functions and for point-to-point communication, or an identical implementation for both types of objects. Note, however, that the two groups of an intercommunicator are currently required to be disjoint, for reasons explained later in this section. ☐

Advice to implementors.   An intercommunicator can be implemented with a data structure very similar to that used for an intracommunicator. The intercommunicator can be represented by a structure with components group, myrank, local_context and remote_context. The group array represents the remote group, whereas myrank is the rank of the process in the local group.

When a process posts a send with arguments dest, tag and comm, then the address of the destination is computed as comm.group[dest]. The message sent carries a header with the tuple (comm.myrank, tag, comm.remote_context).

If a process posts a receive with argument source, tag and comm, then headers of incoming messages are matched to the tuple (source, tag, comm.local_context) (first two may be dontcares).

This design provides a safe inter-group communication domain provided that

- the local_context is process unique and is identical at all processes in the same group; and

- the local_context of one group equals to the remote_context of the other group.

Note that this data structure can be used to represent intracommunicators merely be setting local_context = remote_context. It is then identical to the first representation discussed on page 260.

Another design is to use ids which are process-unique, but not necessarily identical at all processes. In such case, the remote_context component of the communicator structure is an array, where comm.remote_context[i] is the context chosen by process i in remote group to identify that communication domain; local_context is the context chosen by the local process to identify that communication domain. A message is sent with header comm.myrank, tag, comm.remote_context[dest]; a receive call causes incoming messages to be matched against the tuple (source, tag, comm.local_context).

Comparing with the second implementation outlined on page 260, we see again that the same data structure can be used to represent an intragroup communication domain, with no changes. When used for an intracommunicator, then the identity comm.local_context = comm.remote_context[myrank] holds. □

Intercommunicators can be used as arguments to all the communicator accessor, constructor and destructor functions of Section 5.4.1, Section 5.4.2 and Section 5.4.3. The following additional accessor and constructor functions are defined in this section.

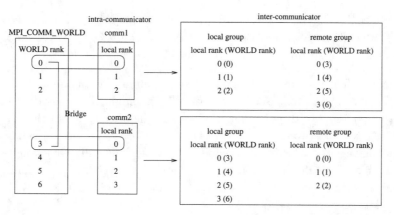

Figure 5.9
Example of two intracommunicators merging to become one intercommunicator.

The routine MPI_COMM_TEST_INTER may be used to determine if a communicator is an inter- or intracommunicator.

It is often convenient to generate an inter-group communication domain by joining together two intragroup communication domains, i.e., building the pair of communicating groups from the individual groups. This requires that there exists one process in each group that can communicate with each other through a communication domain that serves as a bridge between the two groups. For example, suppose that comm1 has 3 processes and comm2 has 4 processes (see Figure 5.9). In terms of the MPI_COMM_WORLD, the processes in comm1 are 0, 1 and 2 and in comm2 are 3, 4, 5 and 6. Let local process 0 in each intracommunicator form the bridge. They can communicate via MPI_COMM_WORLD where process 0 in comm1 has rank 0 and process 0 in comm2 has rank 3. Once the intercommunicator is formed, the original group for each intracommunicator is the local group in the intercommunicator and the group from the other intracommunicator becomes the remote group. For communication with this intercommunicator, the rank in the remote group is used. For example, if a process in comm1 wants to send to process 2 of comm2 (MPI_COMM_WORLD rank 5) then it uses 2 as the rank in the send.

Intercommunicators are created in this fashion by the call MPI_INTERCOMM_CREATE. The two joined groups are required to be disjoint. The converse function of building an intracommunicator from an intercommunicator is provided by the call MPI_INTERCOMM_MERGE. This call generates a communication domain with

a group which is the union of the two groups of the inter-group communication domain. Both calls are blocking. Both will generally require collective communication
within each of the involved groups, as well as communication across the groups.

Rationale. The two groups of an inter-group communication domain are required
to be disjoint in order to support the defined intercommunicator creation function.
If the groups were not disjoint then a process in the intersection of the two groups
would have to make two calls to MPI_INTERCOMM_CREATE, one on behalf of each
group it belongs to. This is not feasible with a blocking call. One would need to
use a nonblocking call, implemented using nonblocking collective communication,
in order to relax the disjointness condition. Another reason is that it is the intent
of the intercommunicators to

provide a communicator for communication between disjoint groups. This is reflected in the definition of MPI_INTERCOMM_MERGE, which allows the user to
control the ranking of the processes in the created intracommunicator; this ranking
makes little sense if the groups are not disjoint. In addition, the natural extension of collective operations to intercommunicators makes the most sense when the
groups are disjoint. □

5.7.2 Intercommunicator Accessors

MPI_COMM_TEST_INTER(comm, flag)

IN	comm	communicator (handle)
OUT	flag	true if comm is intercommunicator (logical)

```
int MPI_Comm_test_inter(MPI_Comm comm, int *flag)
```

```
MPI_COMM_TEST_INTER(COMM, FLAG, IERROR)
    INTEGER COMM, IERROR
    LOGICAL FLAG
```

```
bool MPI::Comm::Is_inter() const
```

MPI_COMM_TEST_INTER is a local routine that allows the calling process to
determine if a communicator is an intercommunicator or an intracommunicator. It
returns true if it is an intercommunicator, otherwise false.

When an intercommunicator is used as an input argument to the communicator
accessors described in Section 5.4.1, the following table describes the behavior.

MPI_COMM_* Function Behavior (in Inter-Communication Mode)	
MPI_COMM_SIZE	returns the size of the local group.
MPI_COMM_GROUP	returns the local group.
MPI_COMM_RANK	returns the rank in the local group

Furthermore, the operation MPI_COMM_COMPARE is valid for intercommunicators. Both communicators must be either intra- or intercommunicators, or else MPI_UNEQUAL results. Both corresponding local and remote groups must compare correctly to get the results MPI_CONGRUENT and MPI_SIMILAR. In particular, it is possible for MPI_SIMILAR to result because either the local or remote groups were similar but not identical.

The following accessors provide consistent access to the remote group of an intercommunicator; they are all local operations.

MPI_COMM_REMOTE_SIZE(comm, size)

IN	comm	intercommunicator (handle)
OUT	size	number of processes in the remote group of comm (integer)

```
int MPI_Comm_remote_size(MPI_Comm comm, int *size)
```

```
MPI_COMM_REMOTE_SIZE(COMM, SIZE, IERROR)
    INTEGER COMM, SIZE, IERROR
```

```
int MPI::Intercomm::Get_remote_size() const
```

MPI_COMM_REMOTE_SIZE returns the size of the remote group in the intercommunicator. Note that the size of the local group is given by MPI_COMM_SIZE.

MPI_COMM_REMOTE_GROUP(comm, group)

IN	comm	intercommunicator (handle)
OUT	group	remote group corresponding to comm (handle)

```
int MPI_Comm_remote_group(MPI_Comm comm, MPI_Group *group)
```

```
MPI_COMM_REMOTE_GROUP(COMM, GROUP, IERROR)
    INTEGER COMM, GROUP, IERROR
```

```
MPI::Group MPI::Intercomm::Get_remote_group() const
```

MPI_COMM_REMOTE_GROUP returns the remote group in the intercommunicator. Note that the local group is give by MPI_COMM_GROUP.

Advice to implementors.   It is necessary to expand the representation outlined on page 306, in order to support intercommunicator accessors that return information on the local group: namely, the data structure has to carry information on the local group, in addition to the remote group. This information is also needed in order to support conveniently the call MPI_INTERCOMM_MERGE. □

5.7.3   Intercommunicator Constructors and Destructors

The constructor functions defined in Section 5.4.2 will return a new intercommunicator if they are passed an old intercommunicator as input. The functions are extended to intercommunicators in the following manner.

The call MPI_COMM_DUP(comm, newcomm returns in newcomm a handle to an intercommunicator with the same groups as comm; also, the user-defined attributes associated with comm are replicated.

If MPI_COMM_CREATE(comm, group, newcomm) is invoked with an intercommunicator argument in comm, then all processes in group A of comm should invoke MPI_COMM_CREATE with the same group argument A1, which is a subgroup of A, and all processes in group B of comm should invoke MPI_COMM_CREATE with the same group argument B1, which is a subgroup of B. The call will create a new intercommunicator with groups A1 and B1. This is illustrated in Figure 5.10. The call will return a handle to this intercommunicator at those processes that are members of either of these two subgroups, and will return MPI_COMM_NULL at the other processes. MPI_COMM_NULL is returned at all processes if one or both of the two groups A1 or B1 is empty.

Rationale.   In the case when exactly on of the two subgroups is empty, a null communicator handle is returned at processes of the other subgroup. Instead one could return at these processes a handle to an intercommunicator with a an empty remote group. But such an intercommunicator has little use – the current choice was deemed to be more useful. □

If MPI_COMM_SPLIT(comm, color, key, newcomm) is invoked with an intercommunicator argument in comm, then a new intercommunicator is created for each value of color (distinct from MPI_UNDEFINED). The two groups of this intercommunicator consist of all processes of group A of that color, and of all processes of group

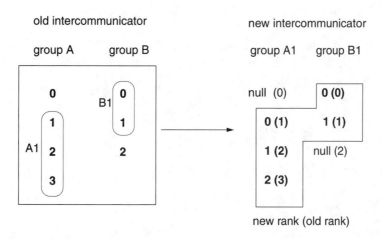

Figure 5.10
Intercommunicator create using MPI_COMM_CREATE extended to intercommunicators.

B or that color. The key argument describes the relative rank of processes in each of these two groups. This is illustrated in Figure 5.11. For those colors that are specified only on one side of the intercommunicator, MPI_COMM_NULL is returned. MPI_COMM_NULL is also returned to those processes that specify MPI_UNDEFINED as the color.

Two new functions are specific to intercommunicators.

MPI_INTERCOMM_CREATE(local_comm, local_leader, bridge_comm, remote_leader, tag, newintercomm)

IN	local_comm	local intracommunicator (handle)
IN	local_leader	rank of local group leader in local_comm (integer)
IN	bridge_comm	"bridge" communicator (handle)
IN	remote_leader	rank of remote group leader in bridge_comm (integer)
IN	tag	"safe" tag (integer)
OUT	newintercomm	new intercommunicator (handle)

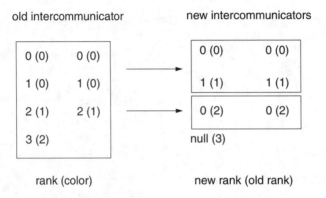

Figure 5.11
Intercommunicator construction achieved by splitting an existing intercommunicator with
MPI_COMM_SPLIT extended to intercommunicators.

```
int MPI_Intercomm_create(MPI_Comm local_comm, int local_leader,
    MPI_Comm bridge_comm, int remote_leader, int tag,
    MPI_Comm *newintercomm)
```

```
MPI_INTERCOMM_CREATE(LOCAL_COMM, LOCAL_LEADER, PEER_COMM,
    REMOTE_LEADER, TAG, NEWINTERCOMM, IERROR)
    INTEGER LOCAL_COMM, LOCAL_LEADER, PEER_COMM, REMOTE_LEADER, TAG,
    NEWINTERCOMM, IERROR
```

```
MPI::Intercomm MPI::Intracomm::Create_intercomm(int local_leader,
    const MPI::Comm& peer_comm, int remote_leader, int tag) const
```

MPI_INTERCOMM_CREATE creates an intercommunicator. The call is collective
over the union of the two groups. Processes should provide matching local_comm
and identical local_leader arguments within each of the two groups. The two leaders
specify matching bridge_comm arguments, and each provide in remote_leader the
rank of the other leader within the domain of bridge_comm. Both provide identical

tag values. These last three arguments are significant only at the leaders. Wildcards are not permitted for remote_leader, local_leader, nor tag.

This call uses point-to-point communication with communicator bridge_comm, and with tag tag between the leaders. Thus, care must be taken that there be no pending communication on bridge_comm that could interfere with this communication.

MPI_INTERCOMM_MERGE(intercomm, high, newintracomm)

IN	intercomm	InterCommunicator (handle)
IN	high	see below (logical)
OUT	newintracomm	new intracommunicator (handle)

```
int MPI_Intercomm_merge(MPI_Comm intercomm, int high,
    MPI_Comm *newintracomm)
```

```
MPI_INTERCOMM_MERGE(INTERCOMM, HIGH, NEWINTRACOMM, IERROR)
    INTEGER INTERCOMM, NEWINTRACOMM, IERROR
    LOGICAL HIGH
```

```
MPI::Intracomm MPI::Intercomm::Merge(bool high) const
```

MPI_INTERCOMM_MERGE creates an intracommunicator from the union of the two groups that are associated with intercomm. All processes should provide the same high value within each of the two groups. If processes in one group provided the value high = false and processes in the other group provided the value high = true then the union orders the "low" group before the "high" group. If all processes provided the same high argument then the order of the union is arbitrary. This call is blocking and collective within the union of the two groups. The error handler on the new intercommunicator in each process is inherited from the communicator that contributes the local group. Note that this can result in different processes in the same communicator having different error handlers.

Advice to implementors. In order to implement MPI_INTERCOMM_MERGE, MPI_COMM_FREE and MPI_COMM_DUP, it is necessary to support collective communication within the two groups as well as communication between the two groups. One possible mechanism is to create a data structure that will allow one to run code similar to that used for MPI_INTERCOMM_CREATE: A private communication domain for each group, a leader for each group, and a private bridge communication domain for the two leaders. ☐

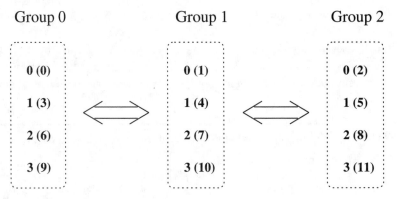

Figure 5.12
Three-group pipeline. The figure shows the local rank and (within brackets) the global rank of each process.

An intercommunicator is deallocated by a call to MPI_COMM_FREE. The call also frees user-defined attributes, using the associated callback functions.

5.7.4 Examples

Example 5.14   The following example illustrates how the first node in the left side of an intercommunicator could be joined with all members on the right side of an intercommunicator to form a new intercommunicator.

```
MPI_Comm  inter_comm, new_inter_comm;
MPI_Group local_group, group;
int       rank = 0; /* rank on left side to include in
                       new inter-comm */

/* Construct the original intercommunicator: "inter_comm" */
...

/* Construct the group of processes to be in new
   intercommunicator */
if (/* I'm on the left side of the intercommunicator */) {
  MPI_Comm_group ( inter_comm, &local_group );
  MPI_Group_incl ( local_group, 1, &rank, &group );
  MPI_Group_free ( &local_group );
}
```

```
else
  MPI_Comm_group ( inter_comm, &group );

MPI_Comm_create ( inter_comm, group, &new_inter_comm );
MPI_Group_free( &group );
```

Example 5.15   (Parallel client-server model). The following client code illustrates how clients on the left side of an intercommunicator could be assigned to a single server from a pool of servers on the right side of an intercommunicator.

```
/* Client code */
MPI_Comm  multiple_server_comm;
MPI_Comm  single_server_comm;
int       color, rank, num_servers;

/* Create intercommunicator with clients and servers:
   multiple_server_comm */
...

/* Find out the number of servers available */
MPI_Comm_remote_size ( multiple_server_comm, &num_servers );

/* Determine my color */
MPI_Comm_rank ( multiple_server_comm, &rank );
color = rank % num_servers;

/* Split the intercommunicator */
MPI_Comm_split ( multiple_server_comm, color, rank,
                 &single_server_comm );
```

The following is the corresponding server code:

```
/* Server code */
MPI_Comm  multiple_client_comm;
MPI_Comm  single_server_comm;
int       rank;

/* Create intercommunicator with clients and servers:
   multiple_client_comm */
```

```
      ...

            /* Split the intercommunicator for a single server per group
                of clients */
            MPI_Comm_rank ( multiple_client_comm, &rank );
            MPI_Comm_split ( multiple_client_comm, rank, 0,
                                &single_server_comm );
```

Example 5.16   In this example, processes are divided in three groups. Groups 0
and 1 communicate. Groups 1 and 2 communicate. Therefore, group 0 requires one
intercommunicator, group 1 requires two intercommunicators, and group 2 requires
1 intercommunicator. See Figure 5.12.

```
#include <mpi.h>

int main(int argc, char **argv)
{
   MPI_Comm    myComm; /* intracommunicator of local sub-group */
   MPI_Comm    myFirstComm; /* intercommunicator */
   MPI_Comm    mySecondComm; /* second intercommunicator
                                (group 1 only) */
   int membershipKey, rank;

   MPI_Init(&argc, &argv);
   MPI_Comm_rank(MPI_COMM_WORLD, &rank);

   /* Generate membershipKey in the range [0, 1, 2] */
   membershipKey = rank % 3;

   /* Build intra-communicator for local sub-group */
   MPI_Comm_split(MPI_COMM_WORLD, membershipKey, rank, &myComm);

   /* Build inter-communicators.  Tags are hard-coded. */
   if (membershipKey == 0) {
     /* Group 0 communicates with group 1. */
     MPI_Intercomm_create(myComm, 0, MPI_COMM_WORLD, 1, 01,
                            &myFirstComm);
   }
   else if (membershipKey == 1) {
```

```
        /* Group 1 communicates with groups 0 and 2. */
        MPI_Intercomm_create(myComm, 0, MPI_COMM_WORLD, 0, 01,
                             &myFirstComm);
        MPI_Intercomm_create(myComm, 0, MPI_COMM_WORLD, 2, 12,
                             &mySecondComm);
    }
    else if (membershipKey == 2) {
      /* Group 2 communicates with group 1. */
      MPI_Intercomm_create(myComm, 0, MPI_COMM_WORLD, 1, 12,
                           &myFirstComm);
    }

    /* Do work .. (not shown) */

    /* free communicators appropriately */
    MPI_Comm_free(&myComm);
    MPI_Comm_free(&myFirstComm);
    if(membershipKey == 1)
      MPI_Comm_free(&mySecondComm);
    MPI_Finalize();
    return 0;
}
```

6 Process Topologies

In this chapter we present the MPI mechanisms for defining logical topologies. We discuss the two topologies that MPI supports: grids and graphs. These allow for a standard mechanism for implementing common algorithmic concepts such as 2D grids in linear algebra. We also give the functions that translate between these topologies and the MPI message passing routines.

6.1 Introduction

This chapter discusses the MPI topology mechanism. A topology is an extra, optional attribute that one can give to an intracommunicator; topologies cannot be added to intercommunicators. A topology can provide a convenient naming mechanism for the processes of a group (within a communicator), and additionally, may assist the runtime system in mapping the processes onto hardware.

As stated in Chapter 5, a process group in MPI is a collection of n processes. Each process in the group is assigned a rank between 0 and n-1. In many parallel applications a linear ranking of processes does not adequately reflect the logical communication pattern of the processes (which is usually determined by the underlying problem geometry and the algorithm used). Often the processes are arranged in topological patterns such as two- or three-dimensional grids. More generally, the logical process arrangement is described by a graph. In this chapter we will refer to this logical process arrangement as the "virtual topology."

A clear distinction must be made between the virtual process topology and the topology of the underlying, physical hardware. The virtual topology can be exploited by the system in the assignment of processes to physical processors, if this helps to improve the communication performance on a given machine. How this mapping is done, however, is outside the scope of MPI. The description of the virtual topology, on the other hand, depends only on the application, and is machine-independent. The functions in this chapter deal only with machine-independent mapping.

Rationale. Though physical mapping is not discussed, the existence of the virtual topology information may be used as advice by the runtime system. There are well-known techniques for mapping grid/torus structures to hardware topologies such as hypercubes or grids. For more complicated graph structures good heuristics often yield nearly optimal results [26]. On the other hand, if there is no way for the user to specify the logical process arrangement as a "virtual topology," a random mapping is most likely to result. On some machines, this will lead to unnecessary contention in the interconnection network. Some details about predicted and measured performance improvements that result from good process-to-processor mapping on modern wormhole-routing architectures can be found in [9, 8].

Besides possible performance benefits, the virtual topology can function as a convenient process-naming structure with tremendous benefits for program readability and notational power in message-passing programming. ☐

6.2 Virtual Topologies

The communication pattern of a set of processes can be represented by a graph. The nodes stand for the processes, and the edges connect processes that communicate with each other. Since communication is most often symmetric, communication graphs are assumed to be symmetric: if an edge uv connects node u to node v, then an edge vu connects node v to node u.

MPI provides message-passing between any pair of processes in a group. There is no requirement for opening a channel explicitly. Therefore, a "missing link" in the user-defined process graph does not prevent the corresponding processes from exchanging messages. It means, rather, that this connection is neglected in the virtual topology. This strategy implies that the topology gives no convenient way of naming this pathway of communication. Another possible consequence is that an automatic mapping tool (if one exists for the runtime environment) will not take into account this edge when mapping, and communication on the "missing" link might be less efficient.

Rationale.   As previously stated, the message passing in a program can be represented as a directed graph where the vertices are processes and the edges are messages. On many systems, optimizing communication speeds requires a minimization of the contention for physical wires by messages occurring simultaneously. Performing this optimization requires knowledge of when messages occur and their resource requirements. Not only is this information difficult to represent, it may not be available at topology creation time in complex programs. A simpler alternative is to provide information about the "spatial" distribution of communication and ignore the "temporal" distribution. Though the former method can lead to greater optimizations and faster programs, the later method is used in MPI to allow a simpler interface that is well understood at the current time. As a result, the programmer tells the MPI system the typical connections, e.g., topology, of their program. This can lead to compromises when a specific topology may over- or

0 (0,0)	1 (0,1)	2 (0,2)	3 (0,3)
4 (1,0)	5 (1,1)	6 (1,2)	7 (1,3)
8 (2,0)	9 (2,1)	10 (2,2)	11 (2,3)

Figure 6.1
Relationship between ranks and Cartesian coordinates for a 3x4 2D topology. The upper number in each box is the rank of the process and the lower value is the (row, column) coordinates.

under-specify the connectivity that is used at any time in the program. Overall, however, the chosen topology mechanism was seen as a useful compromise between functionality and ease of usage. Experience with similar techniques in PARMACS [3, 7] show that this information is usually sufficient for a good mapping. □

Specifying the virtual topology in terms of a graph is sufficient for all applications. However, in many applications the graph structure is regular, and the detailed set-up of the graph would be inconvenient for the user and might be less efficient at run time. A large fraction of all parallel applications use process topologies like rings, two- or higher-dimensional grids, or tori. These structures are completely defined by the number of dimensions and the numbers of processes in each coordinate direction. Also, the mapping of grids and tori is generally an easier problem than general graphs. Thus, it is desirable to address these cases explicitly.

Process coordinates in a Cartesian structure begin their numbering at 0. Row-major numbering is always used for the processes in a Cartesian structure. This means that, for example, the relation between group rank and coordinates for twelve processes in a 3×4 grid is as shown in Figure 6.1.

6.3   Overlapping Topologies

In some applications, it is desirable to use different Cartesian topologies at different stages in the computation. For example, in a QR factorization, the ith transformation is determined by the data below the diagonal in the ith column of the matrix.

0 / (0,0)	1 / (0,1)	2 / (0,2)	3 / (0,3)
6 / (1,2)	7 / (1,3)	4 / (1,0)	5 / (1,1)
4 / (1,0)	5 / (1,1)	6 / (1,2)	7 / (1,3)
10 / (2,2)	11 / (2,3)	8 / (2,0)	9 / (2,1)
8 / (2,0)	9 / (2,1)	10 / (2,2)	11 / (2,3)
2 / (0,2)	3 / (0,3)	0 / (0,0)	1 / (0,1)

Figure 6.2
The relationship between two overlaid topologies on a 3×4 torus. The upper values in each process is the rank / (row,col) in the original 2D topology and the lower values are the same for the shifted 2D topology. Note that rows and columns of processes remain intact.

It is often easiest to think of the upper right hand corner of the 2D topology as starting on the process with the ith diagonal element of the matrix for the ith stage of the computation. Since the original matrix was laid out in the original 2D topology, it is necessary to maintain a relationship between it and the shifted 2D topology in the ith stage. For example, the processes forming a row or column in the original 2D topology must also form a row or column in the shifted 2D topology in the ith stage. As stated in Section 6.2 and shown in Figure 6.1, there is a clear correspondence between the rank of a process and its coordinates in a Cartesian topology. This relationship can be used to create multiple Cartesian topologies with the desired relationship. Figure 6.2 shows the relationship of two 2D Cartesian topologies where the second one is shifted by two rows and two columns.

6.4   Embedding in MPI

The support for virtual topologies as defined in this chapter is consistent with other parts of MPI, and, whenever possible, makes use of functions that are defined elsewhere. Topology information is associated with communicators. It can be implemented using the caching mechanism described in Chapter 5.

Rationale.   As with collective communications, the virtual topology features can be layered on top of point-to-point and communicator functionality. By doing this, a layered implementation is possible, though not required. A consequence of this design is that topology information is not given directly to point-to-point nor collective routines. Instead, the topology interface provides functions to translate between the virtual topology and the ranks used in MPI communication routines. ☐

6.5 Cartesian Topology Functions

This section describes the MPI functions for creating Cartesian topologies.

6.5.1 Cartesian Constructor Function

MPI_CART_CREATE can be used to describe Cartesian structures of arbitrary dimension. For each coordinate direction one specifies whether the process structure is periodic or not. For a 1D topology, it is linear if it is not periodic and a ring if it is periodic. For a 2D topology, it is a rectangle, cylinder, or torus as it goes from non-periodic to periodic in one dimension to fully periodic. Note that an n-dimensional hypercube is an n-dimensional torus with 2 processes per coordinate direction. Thus, special support for hypercube structures is not necessary.

MPI_CART_CREATE(comm_old, ndims, dims, periods, reorder, comm_cart)

IN	comm_old	input communicator (handle)
IN	ndims	number of dimensions of Cartesian grid (integer)
IN	dims	integer array of size ndims specifying the number of processes in each dimension (array of integers)
IN	periods	logical array of size ndims specifying whether the grid is periodic (true) or not (false) in each dimension (array of logicals)
IN	reorder	ranks may be reordered (true) or not (false) (logical)
OUT	comm_cart	communicator with new Cartesian topology (handle)

```
int MPI_Cart_create(MPI_Comm comm_old, int ndims, int *dims,
    int *periods, int reorder, MPI_Comm *comm_cart)
```

```
MPI_CART_CREATE(COMM_OLD, NDIMS, DIMS, PERIODS, REORDER, COMM_CART,
    IERROR)
    INTEGER COMM_OLD, NDIMS, DIMS(*), COMM_CART, IERROR
    LOGICAL PERIODS(*), REORDER
```

```
MPI::Cartcomm MPI::Intracomm::Create_cart(int ndims,
    const int dims[], const bool periods[], bool reorder) const
```

MPI_CART_CREATE returns a handle to a new communicator to which the Cartesian topology information is attached. In analogy to the function MPI_COMM_-CREATE, no cached information propagates to the new communicator. Also, this function is collective. As with other collective calls, the program must be written to work correctly, whether the call synchronizes or not.

If reorder = false then the rank of each process in the new group is identical to its rank in the old group. Otherwise, the function may reorder the processes (possibly so as to choose a good embedding of the virtual topology onto the physical machine). If the total size of the Cartesian grid is smaller than the size of the group of comm_old, then some processes are returned MPI_COMM_NULL, in analogy to MPI_COMM_SPLIT. The call is erroneous if it specifies a grid that is larger than the group size.

Advice to implementors.   MPI_CART_CREATE can be implemented by creating a new communicator, and caching with the new communicator a description of the Cartesian grid, e.g.,

1. `ndims` (number of dimensions),

2. `dims` (numbers of processes per coordinate direction),

3. `periods` (periodicity information),

4. `own_position` (own position in grid)

⬜

6.5.2   Cartesian Convenience Function: MPI_DIMS_CREATE

For Cartesian topologies, the function MPI_DIMS_CREATE helps the user select a balanced distribution of processes per coordinate direction, depending on the number of processes in the group to be balanced and optional constraints that can be specified by the user. One possible use of this function is to partition all the processes (the size of MPI_COMM_WORLD's group) into an n-dimensional topology.

MPI_DIMS_CREATE(nnodes, ndims, dims)

IN	nnodes	number of nodes in a grid (integer)
IN	ndims	number of Cartesian dimensions (integer)
INOUT	dims	integer array of size `ndims` specifying the number of nodes in each dimension (array of integers)

```
int MPI_Dims_create(int nnodes, int ndims, int *dims)
```

```
MPI_DIMS_CREATE(NNODES, NDIMS, DIMS, IERROR)
    INTEGER NNODES, NDIMS, DIMS(*), IERROR
```

```
void MPI::Compute_dims(int nnodes, int ndims, int dims[])
```

The entries in the array dims are set to describe a Cartesian grid with ndims dimensions and a total of nnodes nodes. The dimensions are set to be as close to each other as possible, using an appropriate divisibility algorithm. The caller may further constrain the operation of this routine by specifying elements of array dims. If dims[i] is set to a positive number, the routine will not modify the number of nodes in dimension i; only those entries where dims[i] = 0 are modified by the call.

Negative input values of dims[i] are erroneous. An error will occur if nnodes is not a multiple of $\prod_{i, dims[i] \neq 0} dims[i]$.

For dims[i] set by the call, dims[i] will be ordered in monotonically decreasing order. Array dims is suitable for use as input to routine MPI_CART_CREATE. MPI_DIMS_CREATE is local. Several sample calls are shown in Example 6.1.

Example 6.1

dims before call	function call	dims on return
(0,0)	MPI_DIMS_CREATE(6, 2, dims)	(3,2)
(0,0)	MPI_DIMS_CREATE(7, 2, dims)	(7,1)
(0,3,0)	MPI_DIMS_CREATE(6, 3, dims)	(2,3,1)
(0,3,0)	MPI_DIMS_CREATE(7, 3, dims)	erroneous call

6.5.3 Cartesian Inquiry Functions

Once a Cartesian topology is set up, it may be necessary to inquire about the topology. These functions are given below and are all local calls.

MPI_CARTDIM_GET(comm, ndims)

IN	comm	communicator with Cartesian structure (handle)
OUT	ndims	number of dimensions of the Cartesian structure (integer)

```
int MPI_Cartdim_get(MPI_Comm comm, int *ndims)
```

```
MPI_CARTDIM_GET(COMM, NDIMS, IERROR)
    INTEGER COMM, NDIMS, IERROR
```

```
int MPI::Cartcomm::Get_dim() const
```

MPI_CARTDIM_GET returns the number of dimensions of the Cartesian structure associated with comm. This can be used to provide the other Cartesian inquiry functions with the correct size of arrays. The communicator with the topology in Figure 6.1 would return ndims = 2.

This function and other functions that access topology information may return the error code MPI_ERR_TOPOLOGY (MPI::ERR_TOPOLOGY, in C++) if the communicator argument is not associated with a topology, or has a wrong topology.

MPI_CART_GET(comm, maxdims, dims, periods, coords)

IN	comm	communicator with Cartesian structure (handle)
IN	maxdims	length of vectors dims, periods, and coords in the calling program (integer)
OUT	dims	number of processes for each Cartesian dimension (array of integers)
OUT	periods	periodicity (true/false) for each Cartesian dimension (array of logicals)
OUT	coords	coordinates of calling process in Cartesian structure (array of integers)

```
int MPI_Cart_get(MPI_Comm comm, int maxdims, int *dims, int *periods,
    int *coords)
```

```
MPI_CART_GET(COMM, MAXDIMS, DIMS, PERIODS, COORDS, IERROR)
    INTEGER COMM, MAXDIMS, DIMS(*), COORDS(*), IERROR
    LOGICAL PERIODS(*)
```

```
void MPI::Cartcomm::Get_topo(int maxdims, int dims[],
    bool periods[], int coords[]) const
```

MPI_CART_GET returns information on the Cartesian topology associated with comm. maxdims must be at least ndims as returned by MPI_CARTDIM_GET. For the example in Figure 6.1, dims = $(3, 4)$. The coords are as given for the rank of the calling process as shown, e.g., process 6 returns coords = $(1, 2)$.

6.5.4   Cartesian Translator Functions

The functions in this section translate to/from the rank and the Cartesian topology coordinates. These calls are local.

MPI_CART_RANK(comm, coords, rank)

IN	comm	communicator with Cartesian structure (handle)
IN	coords	specifies the Cartesian coordinates of a process (array of integers)
OUT	rank	rank of specified process (integer)

```
int MPI_Cart_rank(MPI_Comm comm, int *coords, int *rank)
```

```
MPI_CART_RANK(COMM, COORDS, RANK, IERROR)
    INTEGER COMM, COORDS(*), RANK, IERROR
```

```
int MPI::Cartcomm::Get_cart_rank(const int coords[]) const
```

For a process group with Cartesian structure, the function MPI_CART_RANK translates the logical process coordinates to process ranks as they are used by the point-to-point routines. coords is an array of size ndims as returned by MPI_CART-DIM_GET. For the example in Figure 6.1, coords $= (1, 2)$ would return rank $= 6$.

For dimension i with periods(i) = true, if the coordinate, coords(i), is out of range, that is, coords(i) < 0 or coords(i) $\geq$ dims(i), it is shifted back to the interval $0 \leq$ coords(i) $<$ dims(i) automatically. If the topology in Figure 6.1 is periodic in both dimensions (torus), then coords $= (4, 6)$ would also return rank $= 6$. Out-of-range coordinates are erroneous for non-periodic dimensions.

MPI_CART_COORDS(comm, rank, maxdims, coords)

IN	comm	communicator with Cartesian structure (handle)
IN	rank	rank of a process within group of comm (integer)
IN	maxdims	length of vector coord in the calling program (integer)
OUT	coords	integer array containing the Cartesian coordinates of specified process (array of integers)

```
int MPI_Cart_coords(MPI_Comm comm, int rank, int maxdims,
    int *coords)
```

```
MPI_CART_COORDS(COMM, RANK, MAXDIMS, COORDS, IERROR)
```

```
INTEGER COMM, RANK, MAXDIMS, COORDS(*), IERROR
```

```
void MPI::Cartcomm::Get_coords(int rank, int maxdims, int coords[])
    const
```

MPI_CART_COORDS is the rank-to-coordinates translator. It is the inverse mapping of MPI_CART_RANK. maxdims is at least as big as ndims as returned by MPI_CARTDIM_GET. For the example in Figure 6.1, rank = 6 would return coords = $(1, 2)$.

6.5.5   Cartesian Shift Function

If the process topology is a Cartesian structure, a MPI_SENDRECV operation is likely to be used along a coordinate direction to perform a shift of data. As input, MPI_SENDRECV takes the rank of a source process for the receive, and the rank of a destination process for the send. A Cartesian shift operation is specified by the coordinate of the shift and by the size of the shift step (positive or negative). The function MPI_CART_SHIFT accepts such a specification and returns the information needed to call MPI_SENDRECV. The function MPI_CART_SHIFT is local.

MPI_CART_SHIFT(comm, direction, disp, rank_source, rank_dest)

IN	comm	communicator with Cartesian structure (handle)
IN	direction	coordinate dimension of shift (integer)
IN	disp	displacement (> 0: upwards shift, < 0: downwards shift) (integer)
OUT	rank_source	rank of source process (integer)
OUT	rank_dest	rank of destination process (integer)

```
int MPI_Cart_shift(MPI_Comm comm, int direction, int disp,
    int *rank_source, int *rank_dest)
```

```
MPI_CART_SHIFT(COMM, DIRECTION, DISP, RANK_SOURCE, RANK_DEST, IERROR)
    INTEGER COMM, DIRECTION, DISP, RANK_SOURCE, RANK_DEST, IERROR
```

```
void MPI::Cartcomm::Shift(int direction, int disp, int& rank_source,
    int& rank_dest) const
```

The direction argument indicates the dimension of the shift, i.e., the coordinate whose value is modified by the shift. The coordinates are numbered from 0 to ndims-1, where ndims is the number of dimensions.

Depending on the periodicity of the Cartesian group in the specified coordinate direction, MPI_CART_SHIFT provides the identifiers for a circular or an end-off shift. In the case of an end-off shift, the value MPI_PROC_NULL may be returned in rank_source and/or rank_dest, indicating that the source and/or the destination for the shift is out of range. This is a valid input to the sendrecv functions.

Neither MPI_CART_SHIFT nor MPI_SENDRECV are collective functions. It is not required that all processes in the grid call MPI_CART_SHIFT with the same direction and disp arguments, but only that sends match receives in the subsequent calls to MPI_SENDRECV. Example 6.2 shows such use of MPI_CART_SHIFT, where each column of a 2D grid is shifted by a different amount. Figures 6.3 and 6.4 show the result on 12 processors.

Example 6.2   The communicator, comm, has a 3×4 periodic, Cartesian topology associated with it. A two-dimensional array of REALs is stored one element per process, in variable a. One wishes to skew this array, by shifting column i (vertically, i.e., along the column) by i steps.

```
INTEGER comm_2d, rank, coords(2), ierr, source, dest
INTEGER status(MPI_STATUS_SIZE), dims(2)
LOGICAL reorder, periods(2)
REAL a, b

CALL MPI_COMM_SIZE(MPI_COMM_WORLD, isize, ierr)
IF (isize.LT.12) CALL MPI_ABORT(MPI_COMM_WORLD, MPI_ERR_OTHER, ierr)
CALL MPI_COMM_RANK(MPI_COMM_WORLD, rank, ierr)

! initialize arrays
a = rank
b = -1

! create topology
! values to run on 12 processes
dims(1) = 3
dims(2) = 4
! change to .FALSE. for non-periodic
periods(1) = .TRUE.
periods(2) = .TRUE.
reorder = .FALSE.
CALL MPI_CART_CREATE(MPI_COMM_WORLD, 2, dims, periods, reorder, &
```

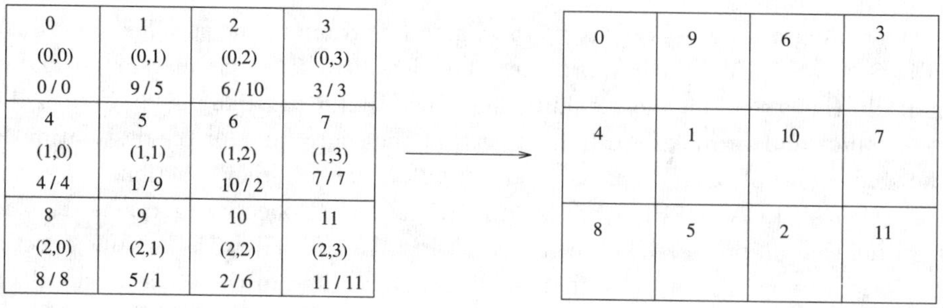

0 (0,0) 0 / 0	1 (0,1) 9 / 5	2 (0,2) 6 / 10	3 (0,3) 3 / 3
4 (1,0) 4 / 4	5 (1,1) 1 / 9	6 (1,2) 10 / 2	7 (1,3) 7 / 7
8 (2,0) 8 / 8	9 (2,1) 5 / 1	10 (2,2) 2 / 6	11 (2,3) 11 / 11

0	9	6	3
4	1	10	7
8	5	2	11

Figure 6.3

Outcome of Example 6.2 when the 2D topology is periodic (a torus) on 12 processes. In the boxes on the left, the upper number in each box represents the process rank, the middle values are the (row, column) coordinate, and the lower values are the source/dest for the sendrecv operation. The value in the boxes on the right are the results in b after the sendrecv has completed.

```
                      comm_2d, ierr)
! first 12 processes of MPI_COMM_WORLD are in group of comm_2d,
! with same rank as in MPI_COMM_WORLD

! find Cartesian coordinates
CALL MPI_CART_COORDS(comm_2d, rank, 2, coords, ierr)
! compute shift source and destination
CALL MPI_CART_SHIFT(comm_2d, 0, coords(2), source, dest, ierr)

! skew a into b
CALL MPI_SENDRECV(a, 1, MPI_REAL, dest, 13, b, 1, MPI_REAL, &
                  source, 13, comm_2d, status, ierr)
```

Rationale. The effect of returning MPI_PROC_NULL when the source of an end-off shift is out of range is that, in the subsequent shift, the destination buffer stays unchanged. This is different from the behavior of a Fortran 90 EOSHIFT intrinsic function, where the user can provide a fill value for the target of a shift, if the source is out of range, with a default which is zero or blank. To achieve the behavior of the Fortran function, one would need to have a receive from MPI_PROC_NULL put a fixed fill value in the receive buffer. A default fill cannot be easily provided since a different fill value is required for each **datatype** argument used in the sendreceive

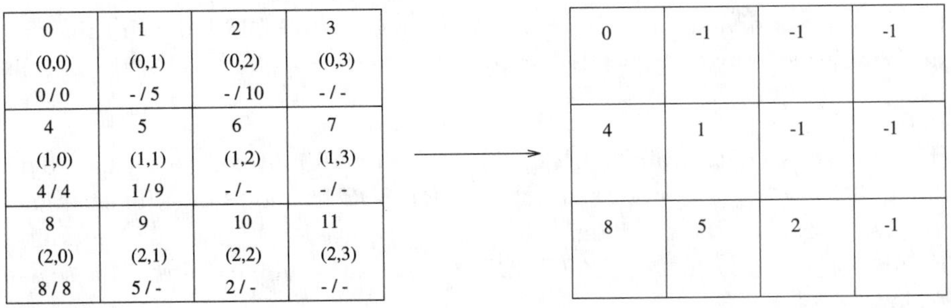

0	1	2	3
(0,0)	(0,1)	(0,2)	(0,3)
0 / 0	- / 5	- / 10	- / -
4	5	6	7
(1,0)	(1,1)	(1,2)	(1,3)
4 / 4	1 / 9	- / -	- / -
8	9	10	11
(2,0)	(2,1)	(2,2)	(2,3)
8 / 8	5 / -	2 / -	- / -

0	-1	-1	-1
4	1	-1	-1
8	5	2	-1

Figure 6.4
Similar to Figure 6.3 except the 2D Cartesian topology is not periodic (a rectangle). This results when the values of **periods(1)** and **periods(2)** are made .FALSE. A "-" in a source or dest value indicates MPI_CART_SHIFT returns MPI_PROC_NULL.

call. Since the user can mimic the EOSHIFT behavior with little additional code, it was felt preferable to choose the simpler interface. ▯

Advice to users. In Fortran, the dimension indicated by DIRECTION = i has DIMS(i+1) processes, where DIMS is the array that was used to create the grid. In C, the dimension indicated by direction = i is the dimension specified by dims[i]. ▯

6.5.6 Cartesian Partition Function

MPI_CART_SUB(comm, remain_dims, newcomm)

IN	comm	communicator with Cartesian structure (handle)
IN	remain_dims	the ith entry of remain_dims specifies whether the ith dimension is kept in the subgrid (**true**) or is dropped (**false**) (array of logicals)
OUT	newcomm	communicator containing the subgrid that includes the calling process (handle)

```
int MPI_Cart_sub(MPI_Comm comm, int *remain_dims, MPI_Comm *newcomm)
```

```
MPI_CART_SUB(COMM, REMAIN_DIMS, NEWCOMM, IERROR)
    INTEGER COMM, NEWCOMM, IERROR
    LOGICAL REMAIN_DIMS(*)
```

```
MPI::Cartcomm MPI::Cartcomm::Sub(const bool remain_dims[]) const
```

If a Cartesian topology has been created with MPI_CART_CREATE, the function MPI_CART_SUB can be used to partition the communicator group into subgroups that form lower-dimensional Cartesian subgrids, and to build for each subgroup a communicator with the associated subgrid Cartesian topology. This call is collective.

Advice to users. The same functionality as MPI_CART_SUB can be achieved with MPI_COMM_SPLIT. However, since MPI_CART_SUB has additional information, it can greatly reduce the communication and work needed by logically working on the topology. As such, MPI_CART_SUB can be easily implemented in a scalable fashion. ☐

Advice to implementors. The function MPI_CART_SUB(comm, remain_dims, comm_new) can be implemented by a call to MPI_COMM_SPLIT(comm, color, key, comm_new), using a single number encoding of the lost dimensions as color and a single number encoding of the preserved dimensions as key. In addition, the new topology information has to be added. ☐

Example 6.3 Assume that MPI_CART_CREATE(..., comm) has defined a $(2 \times 3 \times 4)$ grid. Let remain_dims = (true, false, true). Then a call to,

        MPI_CART_SUB(comm, remain_dims, comm_new),

will create three communicators each with eight processes in a 2×4 Cartesian topology. If remain_dims = (false, false, true) then the call to MPI_CART_SUB(comm, remain_dims, comm_new) will create six non-overlapping communicators, each with four processes, in a one-dimensional Cartesian topology.

6.5.7 Cartesian Low-Level Functions

Typically, the functions already presented are used to create and use Cartesian topologies. However, some applications may want more control over the process. MPI_CART_MAP returns the Cartesian map recommended by the MPI system, in order to map well the virtual communication graph of the application on the physical machine topology. This call is collective.

MPI_CART_MAP(comm, ndims, dims, periods, newrank)

IN	comm	input communicator (handle)
IN	ndims	number of dimensions of Cartesian structure (integer)
IN	dims	array of size ndims specifying the number of processes in each coordinate direction (array of integers)

| IN | periods | array of size ndims specifying the periodicity specification in each coordinate direction (array of logicals) |
| OUT | newrank | reordered rank of the calling process; MPI_UNDEFINED if calling process does not belong to grid (integer) |

```
int MPI_Cart_map(MPI_Comm comm, int ndims, int *dims, int *periods,
    int *newrank)
```

```
MPI_CART_MAP(COMM, NDIMS, DIMS, PERIODS, NEWRANK, IERROR)
    INTEGER COMM, NDIMS, DIMS(*), NEWRANK, IERROR
    LOGICAL PERIODS(*)
```

```
int MPI::Cartcomm::Map(int ndims, const int dims[],
    const bool periods[]) const
```

MPI_CART_MAP computes an "optimal" placement for the calling process on the physical machine.

Advice to implementors.   The function MPI_CART_CREATE(comm, ndims, dims, periods, reorder, comm_cart), with `reorder = true` can be implemented by calling MPI_CART_MAP(comm,   ndims,   dims,   periods,   newrank),   then   calling MPI_COMM_SPLIT(comm, color, key, comm_cart), with `color = 0` if `newrank` ≠ MPI_UNDEFINED, `color = MPI_UNDEFINED` otherwise, and `key = newrank`. □

6.6   Graph Topology Functions

This section describes the MPI functions for creating graph topologies.

6.6.1   Graph Constructor Function

MPI_GRAPH_CREATE(comm_old, nnodes, index, edges, reorder, comm_graph)

IN	comm_old	input communicator (handle)
IN	nnodes	number of nodes in graph (integer)
IN	index	describes node degrees (see below) (array of integers)
IN	edges	describes graph edges (see below) (array of integers)
IN	reorder	ranking may be reordered (true) or not (false) (logical)
OUT	comm_graph	communicator with graph topology added (handle)

```
int MPI_Graph_create(MPI_Comm comm_old, int nnodes, int *index,
    int *edges, int reorder, MPI_Comm *comm_graph)
```

```
MPI_GRAPH_CREATE(COMM_OLD, NNODES, INDEX, EDGES, REORDER, COMM_GRAPH,
    IERROR)
    INTEGER COMM_OLD, NNODES, INDEX(*), EDGES(*), COMM_GRAPH, IERROR
    LOGICAL REORDER
```

```
MPI::Graphcomm MPI::Intracomm::Create_graph(int nnodes,
    const int index[], const int edges[], bool reorder) const
```

MPI_GRAPH_CREATE returns a new communicator to which the graph topology information is attached. If reorder = false then the rank of each process in the new group is identical to its rank in the old group. Otherwise, the function may reorder the processes. If the size, nnodes, of the graph is smaller than the size of the group of comm_old, then some processes are returned MPI_COMM_NULL, in analogy to MPI_COMM_SPLIT. The call is erroneous if it specifies a graph that is larger than the group size of the input communicator. In analogy to the function MPI_COMM_CREATE, no cached information propagates to the new communicator. Also, this function is collective. As with other collective calls, the program must be written to work correctly, whether the call synchronizes or not.

The three parameters nnodes, index and edges define the graph structure. nnodes is the number of nodes of the graph. The nodes are numbered from 0 to nnodes-1. The ith entry of array index stores the total number of neighbors of the first i graph nodes. The lists of neighbors of nodes 0, 1, ..., nnodes-1 are stored in consecutive locations in array edges. The array edges is a flattened representation of the edge lists. The total number of entries in index is nnodes and the total number of entries in edges is equal to the number of graph edges.

The definitions of the arguments nnodes, index, and edges are illustrated in Example 6.4.

Example 6.4   Assume there are four processes 0, 1, 2, 3 with the following adjacency matrix:

process	neighbors
0	1, 3
1	0
2	3
3	0, 2

Then, the input arguments are:

    nnodes =   4
    index =   (2, 3, 4, 6)
    edges =   (1, 3, 0, 3, 0, 2)

Thus, in C, index[0] is the degree of node zero, and index[i] - index[i-1] is the degree of node i, i=1, ..., nnodes-1; the list of neighbors of node zero is stored in edges[j], for $0 \leq j \leq$ index$[0] - 1$ and the list of neighbors of node i, i > 0, is stored in edges[j], index$[i-1] \leq j \leq$ index$[i] - 1$.

In Fortran, index(1) is the degree of node zero, and index(i+1) - index(i) is the degree of node i, i=1, ..., nnodes-1; the list of neighbors of node zero is stored in edges(j), for $1 \leq j \leq$ index(1) and the list of neighbors of node i, i > 0, is stored in edges(j), index$(i) + 1 \leq j \leq$ index$(i + 1)$.

Rationale.   Since bidirectional communication is assumed, the edges array is symmetric. To allow input checking and to make the graph construction easier for the user, the full graph is given and not just half of the symmetric graph. ▯

Advice to implementors.   A graph topology can be implemented by caching with the communicator the two arrays

1. index,

2. edges

The number of nodes is equal to the number of processes in the group. An additional zero entry at the start of array index simplifies access to the topology information. ▯

6.6.2   Graph Inquiry Functions

Once a graph topology is set up, it may be necessary to inquire about the topology. These functions are given below and are all local calls.

MPI_GRAPHDIMS_GET(comm, nnodes, nedges)

IN	comm	communicator for group with graph structure (handle)
OUT	nnodes	number of nodes in graph (integer)
OUT	nedges	number of edges in graph (integer)

```
int MPI_Graphdims_get(MPI_Comm comm, int *nnodes, int *nedges)
```

```
MPI_GRAPHDIMS_GET(COMM, NNODES, NEDGES, IERROR)
    INTEGER COMM, NNODES, NEDGES, IERROR
```

```
void MPI::Graphcomm::Get_dims(int nnodes[], int nedges[]) const
```

MPI_GRAPHDIMS_GET returns the number of nodes and the number of edges in the graph. The number of nodes is identical to the size of the group associated with comm. nnodes and nedges can be used to supply arrays of correct size for index and edges, respectively, in MPI_GRAPH_GET. MPI_GRAPHDIMS_GET would return nnodes = 4 and nedges = 6 for Example 6.4.

MPI_GRAPH_GET(comm, maxindex, maxedges, index, edges)

IN	comm	communicator with graph structure (handle)
IN	maxindex	length of vector index in the calling program (integer)
IN	maxedges	length of vector edges in the calling program (integer)
OUT	index	contains the graph structure (array of integers)
OUT	edges	contains the graph structure (array of integers)

```
int MPI_Graph_get(MPI_Comm comm, int maxindex, int maxedges,
    int *index, int *edges)
```

```
MPI_GRAPH_GET(COMM, MAXINDEX, MAXEDGES, INDEX, EDGES, IERROR)
    INTEGER COMM, MAXINDEX, MAXEDGES, INDEX(*), EDGES(*), IERROR
```

```
void MPI::Graphcomm::Get_topo(int maxindex, int maxedges,
    int index[], int edges[]) const
```

MPI_GRAPH_GET returns index and edges as was supplied to MPI_GRAPH_CRE-ATE. maxindex and maxedges are at least as big as nnodes and nedges, respectively, as returned by MPI_GRAPHDIMS_GET above. Using the comm created in Example 6.4 would return the index and edges given in the example.

6.6.3   Graph Information Functions

The functions in this section provide information about the structure of the graph topology. All calls are local.

MPI_GRAPH_NEIGHBORS_COUNT(comm, rank, nneighbors)

IN	comm	communicator with graph topology (handle)
IN	rank	rank of process in group of comm (integer)
OUT	nneighbors	number of neighbors of specified process (integer)

```
int MPI_Graph_neighbors_count(MPI_Comm comm, int rank,
    int *nneighbors)
```

```
MPI_GRAPH_NEIGHBORS_COUNT(COMM, RANK, NNEIGHBORS, IERROR)
    INTEGER COMM, RANK, NNEIGHBORS, IERROR
```

```
int MPI::Graphcomm::Get_neighbors_count(int rank) const
```

MPI_GRAPH_NEIGHBORS_COUNT returns the number of neighbors for the process signified by rank. It can be used by MPI_GRAPH_NEIGHBORS to give an array of correct size for neighbors. Using Example 6.4 with rank = 3 would give nneighbors = 2.

MPI_GRAPH_NEIGHBORS(comm, rank, maxneighbors, neighbors)

IN	comm	communicator with graph topology (handle)
IN	rank	rank of process in group of comm (integer)
IN	maxneighbors	size of array neighbors (integer)
OUT	neighbors	ranks of processes that are neighbors to specified process (array of integers)

```
int MPI_Graph_neighbors(MPI_Comm comm, int rank, int maxneighbors,
    int *neighbors)
```

```
MPI_GRAPH_NEIGHBORS(COMM, RANK, MAXNEIGHBORS, NEIGHBORS, IERROR)
   INTEGER COMM, RANK, MAXNEIGHBORS, NEIGHBORS(*), IERROR
```

```
void MPI::Graphcomm::Get_neighbors(int rank, int maxneighbors, int
   neighbors[]) const
```

MPI_GRAPH_NEIGHBORS returns the part of the edges array associated with process rank. Using Example 6.4, rank $= 3$ would return neighbors $= 0$, 2. Another use is given in Example 6.5.

Example 6.5   Suppose comm is a communicator with a shuffle-exchange topology. The group has 2^n members. Each process is labeled by $a_1, \ldots, a_n$ with $a_i \in \{0, 1\}$, and has three neighbors: exchange$(a_1, \ldots, a_n) = a_1, \ldots, a_{n-1}, \bar{a}_n$ $(\bar{a} = 1 - a)$, unshuffle$(a_1, \ldots, a_n) = a_2, \ldots, a_n, a_1$, and shuffle$(a_1, \ldots, a_n) = a_n, a_1, \ldots, a_{n-1}$. The graph adjacency list is illustrated below for $n = 3$.

node		exchange neighbors(1)	unshuffle neighbors(2)	shuffle neighbors(3)
0	(000)	1	0	0
1	(001)	0	2	4
2	(010)	3	4	1
3	(011)	2	6	5
4	(100)	5	1	2
5	(101)	4	3	6
6	(110)	7	5	3
7	(111)	6	7	7

Suppose that the communicator comm has this topology associated with it. The following code fragment cycles through the three types of neighbors and performs an appropriate permutation for each.

```
! assume: each process has stored a real number A.
! extract neighborhood information
CALL MPI_COMM_RANK(comm, myrank, ierr)
CALL MPI_GRAPH_NEIGHBORS(comm, myrank, 3, neighbors, ierr)
!  perform exchange permutation
CALL MPI_SENDRECV_REPLACE(A, 1, MPI_REAL, neighbors(1), 0, &
                          neighbors(1), 0, comm, status, ierr)
!  perform unshuffle permutation
```

```
CALL MPI_SENDRECV_REPLACE(A, 1, MPI_REAL, neighbors(2), 0, &
                          neighbors(3), 0, comm, status, ierr)
! perform shuffle permutation
CALL MPI_SENDRECV_REPLACE(A, 1, MPI_REAL, neighbors(3), 0, &
                          neighbors(2), 0, comm, status, ierr)
```

6.6.4 Low-Level Graph Functions

The low-level function for general graph topologies as in the Cartesian topologies given in Section 6.5.7 is as follows. This call is collective.

MPI_GRAPH_MAP(comm, nnodes, index, edges, newrank)

IN	comm	input communicator (handle)
IN	nnodes	number of graph nodes (integer)
IN	index	specifies the graph structure, see MPI_GRAPH_CREATE (array of integers)
IN	edges	specifies the graph structure (array of integers)
OUT	newrank	reordered rank of the calling process; MPI_UNDEFINED if the calling process does not belong to graph (integer)

```
int MPI_Graph_map(MPI_Comm comm, int nnodes, int *index, int *edges,
    int *newrank)
```

```
MPI_GRAPH_MAP(COMM, NNODES, INDEX, EDGES, NEWRANK, IERROR)
    INTEGER COMM, NNODES, INDEX(*), EDGES(*), NEWRANK, IERROR
```

```
int MPI::Graphcomm::Map(int nnodes, const int index[],
    const int edges[]) const
```

Advice to implementors.   The function MPI_GRAPH_CREATE(comm, nnodes, index, edges, reorder, comm_graph), with reorder = true can be implemented by calling MPI_GRAPH_MAP(comm, nnodes, index, edges, newrank), then calling MPI_COMM_SPLIT(comm, color, key, comm_graph), with color = 0 if newrank ≠ MPI_UNDEFINED, color = MPI_UNDEFINED otherwise, and key = newrank. □

6.7   Topology Inquiry Functions

A routine may receive a communicator for which it is unknown what type of topology is associated with it. MPI_TOPO_TEST allows one to answer this question. This is a local call.

MPI_TOPO_TEST(comm, status)

IN	comm	communicator (handle)
OUT	status	topology type of communicator comm (state)

```
int MPI_Topo_test(MPI_Comm comm, int *status)
```

```
MPI_TOPO_TEST(COMM, STATUS, IERROR)
    INTEGER COMM, STATUS, IERROR
```

```
int MPI::Comm::Get_topology() const
```

The function MPI_TOPO_TEST returns the type of topology that is assigned to a communicator.

The output value status is one of the following:

MPI_GRAPH (MPI::GRAPH, in C++)   graph topology
MPI_CART (MPI::CART, in C++)   Cartesian topology
MPI_UNDEFINED (MPI::UNDEFINED, in C++)   no topology

6.8   An Application Example

Example 6.6   We present here two algorithms for parallel matrix product. Both codes compute a product $C = A \times B$, where A is an $n_1 \times n_2$ matrix and B is an $n_2 \times n_3$ matrix (the result matrix C has size $n_1 \times n_3$). The input matrices are initially available on process zero, and the result matrix is returned at process zero.

The first parallel algorithm maps the computation onto a $p_1 \times p_2$ 2-dimensional grid of processes. The matrices are partitioned as shown in Figure 6.5: matrix A is partitioned into p_1 horizontal slices, the matrix B is partitioned into p_2 vertical slices, and matrix C is partitioned into $p_1 \times p_2$ submatrices.

Each process (i, j) computes the product of the i-th slice of A and the j-th slice of B, resulting in submatrix (i, j) of C.

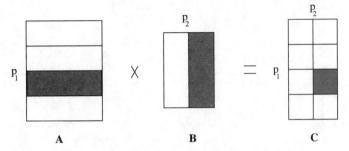

Figure 6.5
Data partition in 2D parallel matrix product algorithm.

The successive phases of the computation are illustrated in Figure 6.6:

1. Matrix A is scattered into slices on the $(x, 0)$ line;
2. Matrix B is scattered into slices on the $(0, y)$ line.
3. The slices of A are replicated in the y dimension.
4. The slices of B are replicated in the x dimension.
5. Each process computes one submatrix product.
6. Matrix C is gathered from the (x, y) plane.

```
SUBROUTINE PMATMULT(A, B, C, n, p, comm)
USE MPI
    ! subroutine arguments are meaningful only at process 0
INTEGER n(3)
    ! matrix dimensions
REAL    A(n(1),n(2)), &
        B(n(2),n(3)), &
        C(n(1),n(3))
    ! data
INTEGER p(2)
    ! dimensions of processor grid. p(1) divides n(1), p(2)
    ! divides n(3) and the product of the 2 dimensions
    ! must equal the size of the group of comm
INTEGER comm
    ! communicator for processes that participate in computation
INTEGER nn(2)
    ! dimensions of local submatrices
REAL, DIMENSION(:,:), ALLOCATABLE:: AA, BB, CC
```

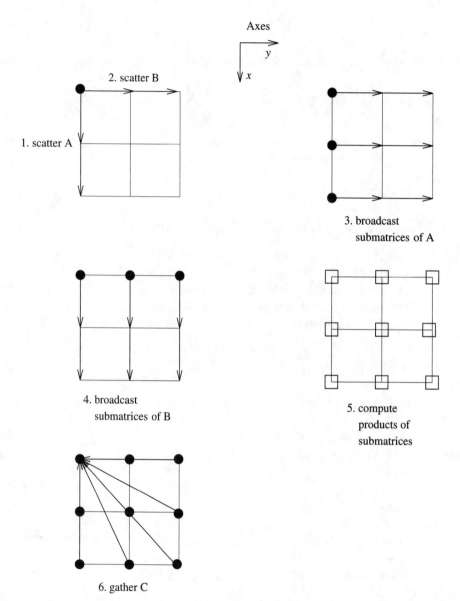

Figure 6.6
Phases in 2D parallel matrix product algorithm.

```
           ! local submatrices
INTEGER  comm_2D, comm_1D(2), pcomm
           ! communicators for 2D grid, for subspaces, and copy of comm
INTEGER coords(2)
           ! Cartesian coordinates
INTEGER rank
           ! process rank
INTEGER, DIMENSION(:), ALLOCATABLE:: dispc, countc
           ! displacement and count array for gather call.
INTEGER typea, typec, types(2), blen(2)
INTEGER(KIND=MPI_ADDRESS_KIND) disp(2), lb, sizeofreal
           ! datatypes and arrays for datatype creation
INTEGER ierr, i, j, k
LOGICAL periods(2), remains(2)

CALL MPI_COMM_DUP(comm, pcomm, ierr)

! broadcast parameters n(3) and p(2)
CALL MPI_BCAST(n, 3, MPI_INTEGER, 0, pcomm, ierr)
CALL MPI_BCAST(p, 2, MPI_INTEGER, 0, pcomm, ierr)

! create 2D grid of processes
periods = (/ .FALSE., .FALSE./)
CALL MPI_CART_CREATE(pcomm, 2, p, periods, .FALSE., comm_2D, ierr)

! find rank and Cartesian coordinates
CALL MPI_COMM_RANK(comm_2D, rank, ierr)
CALL MPI_CART_COORDS(comm_2D, rank, 2, coords, ierr)

! compute communicators for subspaces
DO i = 1, 2
   DO j = 1, 2
      remains(j) = (i.EQ.j)
   END DO
   CALL MPI_CART_SUB(comm_2D, remains, comm_1D(i), ierr)
END DO

! allocate submatrices
```

```
nn(1) = n(1)/p(1)
nn(2) = n(3)/p(2)
ALLOCATE (AA(nn(1),n(2)), BB(n(2),nn(2)), CC(nn(1),nn(2)))

IF (rank.EQ.0) THEN
   ! compute datatype for slice of A
   CALL MPI_TYPE_VECTOR(n(2), nn(1), n(1), MPI_REAL, &
                        types(1), ierr)
   ! and correct extent to size of subcolumn so that
   ! consecutive slices be "contiguous"
   CALL MPI_TYPE_GET_EXTENT(MPI_REAL, lb, sizeofreal, ierr)
   blen = (/ 1, 1 /)
   disp = (/ 0, sizeofreal*nn(1) /)
   types(2) = MPI_UB
   CALL MPI_TYPE_CREATE_STRUCT(2, blen, disp, types, typea, ierr)
   CALL MPI_TYPE_COMMIT(typea, ierr)

   ! compute datatype for submatrix of C
   CALL MPI_TYPE_VECTOR(nn(2), nn(1), n(1), MPI_REAL, &
                        types(1), ierr)
   ! and correct extent to size of subcolumn
   CALL MPI_TYPE_CREATE_STRUCT(2, blen, disp, types, typec, ierr)
   CALL MPI_TYPE_COMMIT(typec, ierr)

   ! compute number of subcolumns preceeding each successive
   ! submatrix of C.  Submatrices are ordered in row-major
   ! order, to fit the order of processes in the grid.
   ALLOCATE (dispc(p(1)*p(2)), countc(p(1)*p(2)))
   DO i = 1, p(1)
      DO j = 1, p(2)
         dispc((i-1)*p(2)+j) = ((j-1)*p(1) + (i-1))*nn(2)
         countc((i-1)*p(2)+j) = 1
      END DO
   END DO
END IF

! and now, the computation
```

```
! 1. scatter row slices of matrix A on x axis
IF (coords(2).EQ.0) THEN
   CALL MPI_SCATTER(A, 1, typea, AA, nn(1)*n(2), MPI_REAL, &
                    0, comm_1D(1), ierr)
END IF


! 2. scatter column slices of matrix B on y axis
IF (coords(1).EQ.0) THEN
   CALL MPI_SCATTER(B, n(2)*nn(2), MPI_REAL, BB, &
                    n(2)*nn(2), MPI_REAL, 0, comm_1D(2), ierr)
END IF


! 3. broadcast matrix AA in y dimension
CALL MPI_BCAST(AA, nn(1)*n(2), MPI_REAL, 0, comm_1D(2), ierr)


! 4. broadcast matrix BB in x dimension
 CALL MPI_BCAST(BB, n(2)*nn(2), MPI_REAL, 0, comm_1D(1), ierr)


! 5. compute submatrix products
DO j = 1, nn(2)
  DO i = 1, nn(1)
     CC(i,j) = 0
     DO k = 1, n(2)
        CC(i,j) = CC(i,j) + AA(i,k)*BB(k,j)
     END DO
  END DO
END DO


! 6. gather results from plane to node 0
CALL MPI_GATHERV(CC, nn(1)*nn(2), MPI_REAL, &
                 C, countc, dispc, typec, 0, comm_2D, ierr)
! clean up
DEALLOCATE(AA, BB, CC)
CALL MPI_COMM_FREE(pcomm, ierr)
CALL MPI_COMM_FREE(comm_2D, ierr)
DO i = 1, 2
   CALL MPI_COMM_FREE(comm_1D(i), ierr)
END DO
```

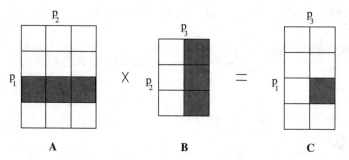

Figure 6.7
Data partition in 3D parallel matrix product algorithm.

```
IF (rank.EQ.0) THEN
   DEALLOCATE(countc, dispc)
   CALL MPI_TYPE_FREE(typea, ierr)
   CALL MPI_TYPE_FREE(typec, ierr)
   CALL MPI_TYPE_FREE(types(1), ierr)
END IF


! returns matrix C at process 0
RETURN
END
```

Example 6.7   For large matrices, performance of matrix products can be improved by using Strassen's algorithm, rather than the n^3 one. Even if one uses the simple, n^3 algorithm, the amount of communication can be decreased by using an algorithm that maps the computation on a 3-dimensional grid of processes.

The parallel computation maps the $n_1 \times n_2 \times n_3$ volume of basic products onto a three-dimensional grid of dimensions $p_1 \times p_2 \times p_3$. The matrices are partitioned as shown in Figure 6.7: matrix A is partitioned into $p_1 \times p_2$ submatrices, matrix B is partitioned into $p_2 \times p_3$ submatrices, and matrix C is partitioned into $p_1 \times p_3$ submatrices. Process (i, j, k) computes the product of submatrix (i, j) of matrix A and submatrix (j, k) of matrix B. The submatrix (i, k) of matrix C is obtained by summing the subproducts computed at processes (i, j, k), $j = 0, \ldots, p_2 - 1$.

The successive phases of the computation are illustrated in Figure 6.8.

1.   The submatrices of A are scattered in the $(x, y, 0)$ plane;
2.   The submatrices of B are scattered in the $(0, y, z)$ plane.

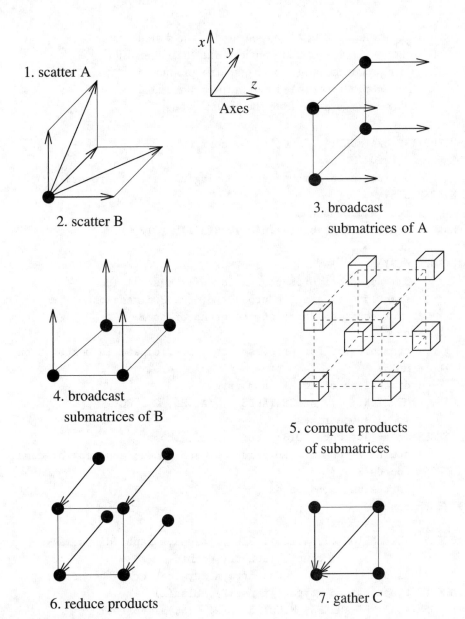

Figure 6.8
Phases in 3D parallel matrix product algorithm.

3. The submatrices of A are replicated in the z dimension.
4. The submatrices of B are replicated in the x dimension.
5. Each process computes one submatrix product.
6. The subproducts are reduced in the y dimension.
7. Matrix C is gathered from the $(x, 0, z)$ plane.

```
SUBROUTINE PMATMULT(A, B, C, n, p, comm)
USE MPI
      ! subroutine arguments are meaningful only at process 0
INTEGER n(3)
      ! matrix dimensions
REAL    A(n(1),n(2)), B(n(2),n(3)), C(n(1),n(3))
      ! data
INTEGER p(3)
      ! dimensions of processor grid. p(i) must divide
      ! exactly n(i) and the product of the 3 dimensions
      ! must equal the size of the group of comm
INTEGER comm
      ! communicator for processes that participate in computation
INTEGER nn(3)
      ! dimensions of local submatrices
REAL, DIMENSION(:,:), ALLOCATABLE :: AA, BB, CC, CC1
      ! local submatrices
INTEGER  comm_3D, comm_2D(3), comm_1D(3), pcomm
      ! communicators for 3D grid, for subspaces, and copy of comm
INTEGER coords(3)
      ! Cartesian coordinates
INTEGER rank
      ! process rank
INTEGER, DIMENSION(:), ALLOCATABLE :: dispa, dispb, dispc, &
                        counta, countb, countc
      ! displacement and count arrays for scatter/gather calls.
INTEGER typea, typeb, typec, types(2), blen(2)
INTEGER(KIND=MPI_ADDRESS_KIND) disp(2), lb, sizeofreal
      ! datatypes and arrays for datatype creation
INTEGER ierr, i, j, k
LOGICAL periods(3), remains(3)
```

```fortran
CALL MPI_COMM_DUP(comm, pcomm, ierr)

! broadcast parameters n(3) and p(3)
CALL MPI_BCAST(n, 3, MPI_INTEGER, 0, pcomm, ierr)
CALL MPI_BCAST(p, 3, MPI_INTEGER, 0, pcomm, ierr)

! create 3D grid of processes
periods = (/ .FALSE., .FALSE., .FALSE./)
CALL MPI_CART_CREATE(pcomm, 3, p, periods, .FALSE., comm_3D, ierr)

! find rank and Cartesian coordinates
CALL MPI_COMM_RANK(comm_3D, rank, ierr)
CALL MPI_CART_COORDS(comm_3D, rank, 3, coords, ierr)

! compute communicators for subspaces

! 2D subspaces
DO i = 1, 3
   DO j = 1, 3
      remains(j) = (i.NE.j)
   END DO
   CALL MPI_CART_SUB(comm_3D, remains, comm_2D(i), ierr)
END DO

! 1D subspaces
DO i = 1, 3
   DO j = 1, 3
      remains(j) = (i.EQ.j)
   END DO
   CALL MPI_CART_SUB(comm_3D, remains, comm_1D(i), ierr)
END DO

! allocate submatrices
DO i = 1, 3
   nn(i) = n(i)/p(i)
END DO
ALLOCATE (AA(nn(1),nn(2)), BB(nn(2),nn(3)), CC(nn(1),nn(3)))
```

```
IF (rank.EQ.0) THEN
   ! compute datatype for submatrix of A
   CALL MPI_TYPE_VECTOR(nn(2), nn(1), n(1), MPI_REAL, types(1), ierr)
   ! and correct extent to size of subcolumn
   CALL MPI_TYPE_GET_EXTENT(MPI_REAL, lb, sizeofreal, ierr)
   blen = (/ 1, 1 /)
   disp = (/ 0, sizeofreal*nn(1) /)
   types(2) = MPI_UB
   CALL MPI_TYPE_CREATE_STRUCT(2, blen, disp, types, typea, ierr)
   CALL MPI_TYPE_COMMIT(typea, ierr)

   ! compute number of subcolumns preceeding each
   ! submatrix of A.  Submatrices are ordered in row-major
   ! order, to fit the order of processes in the grid.
   ALLOCATE (dispa(p(1)*p(2)), counta(p(1)*p(2)))
   DO i = 1, p(1)
      DO j = 1, p(2)
         dispa((i-1)*p(2)+j) = ((j-1)*p(1) + (i-1))*nn(2)
         counta((i-1)*p(2)+j) = 1
      END DO
   END DO

   ! same for array B
   CALL MPI_TYPE_VECTOR(nn(3), nn(2), n(2), MPI_REAL, &
                        types(1), ierr)
   disp(2) = sizeofreal*nn(2)
   CALL MPI_TYPE_CREATE_STRUCT(2, blen, disp, types, typeb, ierr)
   CALL MPI_TYPE_COMMIT(typeb, ierr)
   ALLOCATE (dispb(p(2)*p(3)), countb(p(2)*p(3)))
   DO i = 1, p(2)
      DO j = 1, p(3)
         dispb((i-1)*p(3)+j) = ((j-1)*p(2) + (i-1))*nn(3)
         countb((i-1)*p(3)+j) = 1
      END DO
   END DO

   ! same for array C
   CALL MPI_TYPE_VECTOR(nn(3), nn(1), n(1), MPI_REAL, &
```

```
                          types(1), ierr)
   disp(2) = sizeofreal*nn(1)
   CALL MPI_TYPE_CREATE_STRUCT(2, blen, disp, types, typec, ierr)
   CALL MPI_TYPE_COMMIT(typec, ierr)
   ALLOCATE (dispc(p(1)*p(3)), countc(p(1)*p(3)))
   DO i = 1, p(1)
      DO j = 1, p(3)
         dispc((i-1)*p(3)+j) = ((j-1)*p(1) + (i-1))*nn(3)
         countc((i-1)*p(3)+j) = 1
      END DO
   END DO
END IF


! and now, the computation


! 1. scatter matrix A
IF (coords(3).EQ.0) THEN
   CALL MPI_SCATTERV(A, counta, dispa, typea, &
                     AA, nn(1)*nn(2), MPI_REAL, 0, Comm_2D(3), ierr)
END IF


! 2. scatter matrix B
IF (coords(1).EQ.0) THEN
   CALL MPI_SCATTERV(B, countb, dispb, typeb, &
                     BB, nn(2)*nn(3), MPI_REAL, 0, Comm_2D(1), ierr)
END IF


! 3. broadcast matrix AA in z dimension
CALL MPI_BCAST(AA, nn(1)*nn(2), MPI_REAL, 0, comm_1D(3), ierr)


! 4. broadcast matrix BB in x dimension
CALL MPI_BCAST(BB, nn(2)*nn(3), MPI_REAL, 0, comm_1D(1), ierr)


! 5. compute submatrix products
DO j = 1, nn(3)
   DO i = 1, nn(1)
      CC(i,j) = 0
      DO k = 1, nn(2)
```

```
                CC(i,j) = CC(i,j) + AA(i,k)*BB(k,j)
            END DO
        END DO
END DO


! 6. reduce subproducts in y dimension
! need additional matrix, since one cannot reduce "in place"
ALLOCATE (CC1(nn(1),nn(3)))
CALL MPI_REDUCE(CC, CC1, nn(1)*nn(3), MPI_REAL, MPI_SUM, &
                0, comm_1D(2), ierr)


! 7. gather results from plane (x,0,z) to node 0
IF (coords(2).EQ.0) THEN
    CALL MPI_GATHERV(CC1, nn(1)*nn(3), MPI_REAL, &
                     C, countc, dispc, typec, 0, comm_2D(2), ierr)
END IF


! clean up
DEALLOCATE(AA, BB, CC)
DEALLOCATE (CC1)
IF (rank.EQ.0) THEN
    DEALLOCATE (counta, countb, countc, dispa, dispb, dispc)
    CALL MPI_TYPE_FREE(typea, ierr)
    CALL MPI_TYPE_FREE(typeb, ierr)
    CALL MPI_TYPE_FREE(typec, ierr)
    CALL MPI_TYPE_FREE(types(1), ierr)
END IF
CALL MPI_COMM_FREE(pcomm, ierr)
CALL MPI_COMM_FREE(comm_3D, ierr)
DO i = 1, 3
    CALL MPI_COMM_FREE(comm_2D(i), ierr)
    CALL MPI_COMM_FREE(comm_1D(i), ierr)
END DO


! returns matrix C at process 0
RETURN
END
```

7 Environmental Management

In this chapter we present a number of topics generally involving how MPI interacts with the operating system and implementation specific information. We discuss how to start, stop, and abort an MPI program as well as how MPI interacts with other OS features including signals. Later we show how to deal with errors returned by MPI. We present the MPI mechanisms for finding out about the MPI implementation including the version and some internal values. The chapter also contains the MPI mechanisms for performing timings and inquiring about clocks.

This chapter discusses routines for getting and, where appropriate, setting various parameters that relate to the MPI implementation and the execution environment. It discusses error handling in MPI and the procedures available for controlling MPI error handling. The procedures for entering and leaving the MPI execution environment are also described here. Finally, the chapter discusses the interaction between MPI and the general execution environment.

7.1 MPI Process Startup

Each MPI implementation provides mechanisms for starting up a parallel MPI execution, and specifying the environment of the execution. Oftentimes a startup command of the form

```
mpirun <mpirun arguments> <program> <program arguments>
```

can be issued from a command shell environment. Having a standard startup mechanism extends the portability of MPI programs one step further to the command lines and scripts that manage them. For example, a validation suite script that runs hundreds of programs can be a portable script if it is written using such a standard startup mechanism.

While a standardized startup mechanism improves the usability of MPI, the range of environments is so diverse (e.g., there may not even be a command line interface) that MPI cannot mandate such a mechanism. Instead, MPI specifies an mpiexec startup command and recommends but does not require it, as advice to implementors. It is not suggested that this be the only way to start MPI programs. However, if an implementation does provide a command called mpiexec, it should be of the following form.

mpiexec -n maxproc [**-soft** soft] [**-host** host] [**-arch** arch] [**-wdir** wdir] [**-path** path] [**-file** file] ... program [program arguments]

We describe below each of the arguments.

-n Maximum number of processes started.

-soft Value specifies a set of numbers which are allowed values for the number of processes that may be started. The format of the value is a comma-separated list of Fortran-90 triplets each of which specifies a set of integers and which together specify the set formed by the union of these sets. Negative values in this set and values greater than maxproc are ignored. MPI will spawn the largest number of processes it can, consistent with some number in the set. The order in which triplets are given is not significant.

By Fortran-90 triplets, we mean:

1. a means a

2. a:b means $a, a + 1, a + 2, \ldots, b$

3. a:b:c means $a, a + c, a + 2c, \ldots, a + ck$, where for $c > 0$, k is the largest integer for which $a + ck \leq b$ and for $c < 0$, k is the largest integer for which $a + ck \geq b$. If $b > a$ then c must be positive. If $b < a$ then c must be negative.

Examples:

1. a:b gives a range between a and b

2. 0:maxproc gives full "soft" functionality

3. 1,2,4,8,16,32,64,128,256,512,1024,2048,4096 allows power-of-two number of processes.

4. 2:10000:2 allows even number of processes.

5. 2:10:2,7 allows 2, 4, 6, 7, 8, or 10 processes.

If the -soft argument is missing then exactly maxproc processes will be spawned.

-host Name of host where program will be executed.

-arch Type of host where program will be executed.

-wdir Working directory for executing processes.

-path Directory or set of directories where the implementation should look for the executable.

-file Name of a file in which additional information is specified.

program Name of file containing executable.

program arguments Arguments to be passed to program.

The format for each argument value (except **-n** and **-soft**) is implementation-dependent.

Implementations that provide the `mpiexec` command need not support all these arguments and may provide other arguments. To the least, the command

```
mpiexec -n <numprocs> <program>
```

should start `<program>` with an initial MPI_COMM_WORLD whose group contains `<numprocs>` processes.

The syntax is chosen in order that `mpiexec` be able to be viewed as a command-line version of the command MPI_COMM_SPAWN for dynamic process spawning (Chapter II-3). This syntax enables to spawn multiple processes, all running the same executable, with the same environment (working directory, host, etc.). An alternative, more complex syntax is required for spawning processes that run different programs or have different arguments. This is analogous to the command MPI_-COMM_SPAWN_MULTIPLE in Chapter II-3. For these cases there are two possible formats:

Form A:

```
mpiexec { <above arguments> } : { ... } : { ... } : ... : { ... }
```

All the arguments are optional. (Even the **-n x** argument is optional; the default is implementation-dependent. It might be 1, it might be taken from an environment variable, or it might be specified at compile time.) Each column separated segment specifies start up arguments for a group of processes.

Note that Form A, though convenient to type, prevents colons from being program arguments. Therefore an alternate, file-based form is allowed:

Form B:

```
mpiexec -configfile <filename>
```

where the lines of <`filename`> are of the form separated by the colons in Form A. Lines beginning with '**#**' are comments, and lines may be continued by terminating the partial line with '\'.

Example 7.1   Start 16 instances of `myprog` on the current or default machine:

```
mpiexec -n 16 myprog
```

Example 7.2   Start 10 processes on the machine called `ferrari`:

```
mpiexec -n 10 -host ferrari myprog
```

Example 7.3   Start three copies of the same program with different command-line arguments:

```
mpiexec myprog infile1 : myprog infile2 : myprog infile3
```

Example 7.4   Start the `ocean` program on five Suns and the `atmos` program on 10 RS/6000's:

```
mpiexec -n 5 -arch sun ocean : -n 10 -arch rs6000 atmos
```

It is assumed that the implementation in this case has a method for choosing hosts of the appropriate type. Their ranks are in the order specified.

Example 7.5   Start the `ocean` program on five Suns and the `atmos` program on 10 RS/6000's (Form B):

```
mpiexec -configfile myfile
```

where `myfile` contains

```
-n 5   -arch sun    ocean
-n 10 -arch rs6000 atmos
```

Advice to users.   Users should consult the documentation on the MPI implementation they use to find out how they can start up an MPI execution. Implementations may not support the `mpiexec` command, or may require various implementation specific options. ▯

Rationale.   Several available implementations of MPI provide an `mpirun` command to start MPI jobs. Of course, the various `mpirun` commands are not compatible. In order that the "standard" command not be confused with existing practice, which is not standard and not portable among implementations, instead of `mpirun` MPI specifies `mpiexec`. ▯

7.2   Initialization and Exit

One goal of MPI is to achieve *source code portability*. By this we mean that a program written using MPI and complying with the relevant language standards is portable as written, and must not require any source code changes when moved from one system to another. An implementation may require some setup to be performed before other MPI routines may be called, and some cleanup to be done to release resources used by MPI. To provide for this in a portable manner, MPI includes the routines listed in this section.

MPI_INIT()

```
int MPI_Init(int *argc, char ***argv)
```

```
MPI_INIT(IERROR)
    INTEGER IERROR
```

```
void MPI::Init(int& argc, char**& argv)
```

```
void MPI::Init()
```

This routine, or the routine MPI_INIT_THREAD, which is described in Section II-2.1.3, must be called before any other MPI routine (apart from MPI_INITIALIZED, MPI_FINALIZED and MPI_GET_VERSION) is called. MPI must be initialized at most once; subsequent calls to either routines are erroneous (see MPI_INITIALIZED).

In C, NULL is a valid argument for both argc and argv. In C++, the function is called with no arguments using the second binding. The Fortran version takes only IERROR. Calling MPI_INIT with no arguments (or with NULL arguments, in C) is portable. For compatibility with MPI-1, MPI also accepts calling, in C and C++, MPI_INIT with argc, argv arguments. It this then expected that the user will pass to MPI_INIT the argc, argv arguments of main, as shown in the following C example.

Example 7.6

```
int main(argc, argv)
int argc;
char **argv;
{
MPI_Init(&argc, &argv);
/* parse arguments */
```

```
/* main program     */

MPI_Finalize();      /* see below */
return 0;
}
```

The call to MPI_INIT may use and update the two arguments. The semantics of such usage is implementation-dependent.

Advice to users.   It is recommended to call MPI_INIT with no arguments for portability. □

Rationale.   MPI-1 allowed implementations to require that the argc, argv arguments of main be passed to MPI_INIT. Some implementations took advantage of this to pass to MPI_INIT information used to initialize the MPI environment. Implementations could also use argc, argv as output arguments, to set these two variables in environments where the process startup mechanism did not allow the user to supply arguments to main, or to add additional MPI specific information to argv. This was somewhat confusing. Also, the call to MPI_INIT may occur inside a library that does not have access to argc and argv. Alternative mechanisms (such as environment variables) are generally available to pass information to or from the MPI environment. This usage is encouraged by MPI-2. □

MPI_FINALIZE()

```
int MPI_Finalize(void)

MPI_FINALIZE(IERROR)
     INTEGER IERROR

void MPI::Finalize()
```

This routines must be called by each process before it exits. The call cleans up all MPI state. Once MPI_FINALIZE has been called, no MPI routine may be called, except for MPI_GET_VERSION, MPI_INITIALIZED, and MPI_FINALIZED. MPI_INIT cannot be called after a call to MPI_FINALIZE – one cannot restart MPI once the MPI environment has been cleaned up.

If the call returns, each process may continue local computations, or exit, without participating in further MPI communication with other processes. MPI_FINALIZE is collective over all connected processes. If no processes were spawned, accepted or connected then this means over MPI_COMM_WORLD. The general definition of connectivity is given in Section II-3.5.4.

Each process must complete any pending communication it initiated before it calls MPI_FINALIZE, unless there has been a call to MPI_ABORT. More precisely, each process must ensure that all pending nonblocking communications are (locally) complete before calling MPI_FINALIZE. Further, at the point at which the last process calls MPI_FINALIZE, all pending sends must be matched by a receive, and all pending receives must be matched by a send.

For example, the following program is correct:

```
Process 0                    Process 1
---------                    ---------
MPI_Init();                  MPI_Init();
MPI_Send(dest=1);            MPI_Recv(src=0);
MPI_Finalize();             MPI_Finalize();
```

Without the matching receive, the program is erroneous:

```
Process 0                    Process 1
-----------                  -----------
MPI_Init();                  MPI_Init();
MPI_Send (dest=1);
MPI_Finalize();             MPI_Finalize();
```

A successful return from a blocking communication operation or from MPI_WAIT or MPI_TEST tells the user that the buffer can be reused and means that the communication is completed by the user, but does not guarantee that the local process has no more work to do. A successful return from MPI_REQUEST_FREE with a request handle generated by an MPI_ISEND nullifies the handle but provides no assurance of operation completion. The MPI_ISEND is complete only when it is known by some means that a matching receive has completed. MPI_FINALIZE guarantees that all local actions required by communications the user has completed will, in fact, occur before it returns.

MPI_FINALIZE guarantees nothing about pending communications that have not been completed (completion is assured only by MPI_WAIT, MPI_TEST, or MPI_REQUEST_FREE combined with some other verification of completion).

Example 7.7   This program is correct:

```
Process 0                         Process 1
========================================================
...                               ...
MPI_Isend();                      MPI_Recv();
MPI_Request_free();               MPI_Barrier();
MPI_Barrier();                    MPI_Finalize();
MPI_Finalize();                   exit();
exit();
```

Example 7.8   This program is erroneous and its behavior is undefined:

```
rank 0                            rank 1
========================================================
...                               ...
MPI_Isend();                      MPI_Recv();
MPI_Request_free();               MPI_Finalize();
MPI_Finalize();                   exit();
exit();
```

If no MPI_BUFFER_DETACH occurs between an MPI_BSEND (or other buffered send) and MPI_FINALIZE, the MPI_FINALIZE implicitly supplies the MPI_BUFFER_-DETACH.

Example 7.9   This program is correct, and after the MPI_Finalize, it is as if the buffer had been detached.

```
process 0                         process 1
========================================================
...                               ...
buffer = malloc(1000000);         MPI_Recv();
MPI_Buffer_attach();              MPI_Finalize();
MPI_Bsend();                      exit();
MPI_Finalize();
free(buffer);
exit();
```

Example 7.10   In this example, MPI_Test_cancelled() must return a TRUE flag, independent of the relative order of execution of MPI_Cancel() in process 0 and MPI_Finalize() in process 1.

```
rank 0                          rank 1
==========================================================
MPI_Init();                     MPI_Init();
MPI_Isend();
MPI_Cancel();                   MPI_Finalize();
MPI_Wait();                     exit();
MPI_Test_cancelled();
MPI_Finalize();
exit();
```

Advice to implementors. An implementation may need to delay the return from MPI_FINALIZE until all potential future message cancellations have been processed. One possible solution is to place a barrier inside MPI_FINALIZE.

Even though a process has completed all the communication it initiated, such communication may not yet be completed from the viewpoint of the underlying MPI system. For example, a blocking send may have completed, even though the data is still buffered at the sender. The MPI implementation must ensure that a process has completed any involvement in MPI communication before MPI_FINALIZE returns. Thus, if a process exits after the call to MPI_FINALIZE, this will not cause an ongoing communication to fail. □

Although it is not required that all processes return from MPI_FINALIZE, it is required that at least process 0 in MPI_COMM_WORLD return, so that users can know that the MPI portion of the computation is over. In addition, in a POSIX environment, they may desire to supply an exit code for each process that returns from MPI_FINALIZE.

Example 7.11 The following illustrates the use of requiring that at least one process return and that it be known that process 0 is one of the processes that return. One wants code like the following to work no matter how many processes return.

```
    ...
    MPI_Comm_rank(MPI_COMM_WORLD, &myrank);
    ...
    MPI_Finalize();
    if (myrank == 0) {
        resultfile = fopen("outfile","w");
        dump_results(resultfile);
```

```
      fclose(resultfile);
   }
   exit(0);
```

There are times in which it is convenient to have actions happen when an MPI process finishes. For example, a routine may do initializations that are useful until the MPI job (or that part of the job being terminated in the case of dynamically created processes) is finished. This can be accomplished by attaching an attribute to MPI_COMM_SELF with a callback function. When MPI_FINALIZE is called, it will first execute the equivalent of an MPI_COMM_FREE on MPI_COMM_SELF. This will cause the delete callback function to be executed on all keys associated with MPI_COMM_SELF, in an arbitrary order. If no key has been attached to MPI_COMM_SELF, then no callback is invoked. The "freeing" of MPI_COMM_SELF occurs before any other parts of MPI are affected. Thus, for example, calling MPI_FINALIZED will return false in any of these callback functions. Once done with MPI_COMM_SELF, the order and rest of the actions taken by MPI_FINALIZE is not specified.

MPI_INITIALIZED(flag)

   OUT   flag   true if MPI_INIT has been called (logical)

```
int MPI_Initialized(int *flag)
```

```
MPI_INITIALIZED(FLAG, IERROR)
   LOGICAL FLAG
   INTEGER IERROR
```

```
bool MPI::Is_initialized()
```

This routine may be used to determine whether MPI_INIT has been called. It may be called before MPI_INIT is called. Whether MPI_FINALIZE has been called does not affect the behavior of MPI_INITIALIZED.

MPI_FINALIZED(flag)

   OUT   flag   true if MPI was finalized (logical)

```
int MPI_Finalized(int *flag)
```

```
MPI_FINALIZED(FLAG, IERROR)
```

```
LOGICAL FLAG
INTEGER IERROR
```

`bool MPI::Is_finalized()`

This routine returns true if MPI_FINALIZE has completed. It is legal to call MPI_FINALIZED before MPI_INIT and after MPI_FINALIZE.

Advice to users. The two query functions MPI_INITIALIZED and MPI_FINALIZED are useful for layered libraries. That is, a library may call MPI_INIT if MPI has not yet been initialized, execute in parallel if MPI has been initialized but not finalized, and return an error if MPI has been finalized. ☐

MPI_ABORT(comm, errorcode)

| IN | comm | communicator of tasks to abort (handle) |
| IN | errorcode | error code to return to invoking environment (integer) |

`int MPI_Abort(MPI_Comm comm, int errorcode)`

```
MPI_ABORT(COMM, ERRORCODE, IERROR)
    INTEGER COMM, ERRORCODE, IERROR
```

`void MPI::Comm::Abort(int errorcode)`

This routine makes a "best attempt" to abort all tasks in the group of comm. This function does not require that the invoking environment take any action with the error code. However, a Unix or POSIX environment should handle this as a `return errorcode` from the main program or an `abort(errorcode)`.

It may not be possible for an MPI implementation to abort only the processes represented by comm if this is a subset of the processes. In this case, the MPI implementation should attempt to abort all the connected processes but should not abort any unconnected processes. If no processes were spawned, accepted or connected then this has the effect of aborting all the processes associated with MPI_COMM_WORLD. The general definition of connectivity is given in Section II-3.5.4.

Advice to users. The behavior of MPI_ABORT(comm, errorcode) for comm other then MPI_COMM_WORLD is implementation-dependent. One the other hand, a call to MPI_ABORT(MPI_COMM_WORLD, errorcode) should always cause all processes in the group of MPI_COMM_WORLD to abort. ☐

7.3   Implementation Information

7.3.1   MPI Version Number

Though MPI is backward compatible, users may need to know what version of MPI they are running under. For example, later versions of MPI may offer additional features that can be used if they are available. Also, clarifications to the standard may change the behavior of some implementations and knowing this can be very useful. As a result, MPI offers both compile-time and runtime ways to determine which version of the standard is in use in the environment one is using.

The "version" will be represented by two separate integers, for the version and subversion. An example for MPI-1.2 is:
In C and C++,

```
#define MPI_VERSION    1
#define MPI_SUBVERSION 2
```

In Fortran,

```
INTEGER MPI_VERSION, MPI_SUBVERSION
PARAMETER (MPI_VERSION    = 1)
PARAMETER (MPI_SUBVERSION = 2)
```

For runtime determination,

MPI_GET_VERSION(version, subversion)

| OUT | version | version number (integer) |
| OUT | subversion | subversion number (integer) |

```
int MPI_Get_version(int *version, int *subversion)
```

```
MPI_GET_VERSION(VERSION, SUBVERSION, IERROR)
    INTEGER VERSION, SUBVERSION, IERROR
```

```
void MPI::Get_version(int& version, int& subversion)
```

MPI_GET_VERSION is one of the few functions that can be called before MPI_INIT and after MPI_FINALIZE.

This book describes MPI Version 2.0, i.e. MPI_VERSION = 2 and MPI_SUBVERSION = 0. (Note that this volume concentrates on features from MPI-1.1 and the direct extensions of these from MPI-2. The second volume contains most of the new material from MPI-2. Since MPI-2 is the official MPI standard, this book reflects that version of the standard.)

7.3.2   Environmental Inquiries

A set of attributes that describe the execution environment are attached to the communicator MPI_COMM_WORLD when MPI is initialized. The value of these attributes can be inquired by using the function MPI_COMM_GET_ATTR described in Chapter 5. It is erroneous to delete these attributes, free their keys, or change their values.

The list of predefined attribute keys include

MPI_TAG_UB (MPI::TAG_UB, in C++) Upper bound for tag value.

MPI_HOST (MPI::HOST, in C++) Host process rank, if such exists, MPI_PROC_-NULL, otherwise.

MPI_IO (MPI::IO, in C++) rank of a process that has regular I/O facilities (possibly rank of calling process). Processes in the same communicator may return different values for this parameter.

MPI_WTIME_IS_GLOBAL (MPI::WTIME_IS_GLOBAL, in C++).   Boolean variable that indicates whether clocks are synchronized.

Vendors may add implementation specific parameters (such as node number, real memory size, virtual memory size, etc.)

These predefined attributes do not change value between MPI initialization (MPI-_INIT) and MPI completion (MPI_FINALIZE).

Advice to users.   Note that in the C binding, the value returned by these attributes is a *pointer* to an int containing the requested value. ☐

The required parameter values are discussed in more detail below:

Tag Values   Tag values range from 0 to the value returned for MPI_TAG_UB, inclusive. This range is guaranteed to be unchanging during the execution of an MPI program. In addition, the tag upper bound value must be *at least* 32767. An MPI implementation is free to make the value of MPI_TAG_UB larger than this; for example, the value $2^{30} - 1$ is also a legal value for MPI_TAG_UB (on a system where this value is a legal int or INTEGER value).

The attribute MPI_TAG_UB has the same value on all processes of MPI_COMM_-WORLD.

Host Rank The value returned for MPI_HOST gets the rank of the HOST process in the group associated with communicator MPI_COMM_WORLD, if one is present. MPI_PROC_NULL is returned if there is no host. This attribute can be used on systems that have a distinguished *host* processor, in order to identify the process running on this processor. However, MPI does not specify what it means for a process to be a HOST, nor does it requires that a HOST exists.

The attribute MPI_HOST has the same value on all processes of MPI_COMM_WORLD.

I/O Rank The value returned for MPI_IO is the rank of a processor that can provide language-standard I/O facilities. For Fortran, this means that all of the Fortran I/O operations are supported (e.g., OPEN, REWIND, WRITE). For C, this means that all of the ISO C I/O operations are supported (e.g., fopen, fprintf, lseek). For C++, this means that all of the ANSI C++ input/output library functions are supported (e.g., iostream, fstream).

If every process can provide language-standard I/O, then the value MPI_ANY_SOURCE will be returned. Otherwise, if the calling process can provide language-standard I/O, then its rank will be returned. Otherwise, if some process can provide language-standard I/O then the rank of one such process will be returned. The same value need not be returned by all processes. If no process can provide language-standard I/O, then the value MPI_PROC_NULL will be returned.

Advice to users. MPI does not require that all processes provide language-standard I/O, nor does it specify how the standard input or output of a process is linked to a particular file or device. In particular, there is no requirement, in an interactive environment, that keyboard input be broadcast to all processes which support language-standard I/O. ☐

Clock Synchronization The value returned for MPI_WTIME_IS_GLOBAL is 1 if clocks at all processes in MPI_COMM_WORLD are synchronized, 0 otherwise. A collection of clocks is considered synchronized if explicit effort has been taken to synchronize them. The expectation is that the variation in time, as measured by calls to MPI_WTIME, will be less then one half the round-trip time for an MPI message of length zero. If time is measured at a process just before a send and at another process just after a matching receive, the second time should be always higher than the first one.

The attribute MPI_WTIME_IS_GLOBAL need not be present when the clocks are not synchronized (however, the attribute key MPI_WTIME_IS_GLOBAL is always valid).

This attribute may be associated with communicators other then MPI_COMM_-WORLD.

The attribute MPI_WTIME_IS_GLOBAL has the same value on all processes of MPI_-COMM_WORLD.

MPI_GET_PROCESSOR_NAME(name, resultlen)

OUT	name	A unique specifier for the actual (as opposed to virtual) node. (string)
OUT	resultlen	Length (in printable characters) of the result returned in **name** (integer)

```
int MPI_Get_processor_name(char *name, int *resultlen)
```

```
MPI_GET_PROCESSOR_NAME( NAME, RESULTLEN, IERROR)
    CHARACTER*(*) NAME
    INTEGER RESULTLEN,IERROR
```

```
void MPI::Get_processor_name(char* name, int& resultlen)
```

This routine returns the name of the processor on which it was called at the moment of the call. The name is a character string for maximum flexibility. From this value it must be possible to identify a specific piece of hardware; possible values include "processor 9 in rack 4 of mpp.cs.org" and "231" (where 231 is the actual processor number in the running homogeneous system). The argument name must represent storage that is at least MPI_MAX_PROCESSOR_NAME characters long (MPI::MAX_PROCESSOR_NAME, in C++). MPI_GET_PROCESSOR_NAME may write up to this many characters into name.

The number of characters actually written is returned in the output argument resultlen.

Rationale. This function allows MPI implementations that do process migration to return the current processor. Note that nothing in MPI *requires* or defines process migration; this definition of MPI_GET_PROCESSOR_NAME simply allows such an implementation. □

Advice to users. The user must provide at least MPI_MAX_PROCESSOR_NAME space to write the processor name — processor names can be this long. (See Section II-2.2.8 for a discussion of max name lengths.) The user should examine the output argument, resultlen, to determine the actual length of the name. □

The constant MPI_BSEND_OVERHEAD (MPI::BSEND_OVERHEAD, in C++) provides an upper bound on the fixed overhead per message buffered by a call to MPI_BSEND.

7.4 Timers and Synchronization

MPI defines a timer. A timer is specified even though it is not "message-passing," because timing parallel programs is important in "performance debugging" and because existing timers (both in POSIX 1003.1-1988 and 1003.4D 14.1 and in Fortran 90) are either inconvenient or do not provide adequate access to high-resolution timers.

MPI_WTIME()

```
double MPI_Wtime(void)
```

```
DOUBLE PRECISION MPI_WTIME()
```

```
double MPI::Wtime()
```

MPI_WTIME returns a floating-point number of seconds, representing elapsed wall-clock time since some time in the past.

The "time in the past" is guaranteed not to change during the life of the process. The user is responsible for converting large numbers of seconds to other units if they are preferred.

This function is portable (it returns seconds, not "ticks"), it allows high-resolution, and carries no unnecessary baggage. One would use it like this:

```
{
    double starttime, endtime;
    starttime = MPI_Wtime();
     ....  stuff to be timed  ...
    endtime  = MPI_Wtime();
    printf("That took %f seconds\n",endtime-starttime);
}
```

The times returned are local to the node that called them. There is no requirement that different nodes return "the same time." (But see also the discussion of MPI_WTIME_IS_GLOBAL in Section 7.3.2).

MPI_WTICK()

```
double MPI_Wtick(void)
```

```
DOUBLE PRECISION MPI_WTICK()
```

```
double MPI::Wtick()
```

MPI_WTICK returns the resolution of MPI_WTIME in seconds. That is, it returns, as a double precision value, the number of seconds between successive clock ticks. For example, if the clock is implemented by the hardware as a counter that is incremented every millisecond, the value returned by MPI_WTICK should be 10^{-3}.

7.5   Error Handling

MPI provides the user with reliable message transmission. A message sent is always received correctly, and the user does not need to check for transmission errors, time-outs, or other error conditions. In other words, MPI does not provide mechanisms for dealing with failures in the communication system. If the MPI implementation is built on an unreliable underlying mechanism, then it is the job of the implementor of the MPI subsystem to insulate the user from this unreliability, or to reflect unrecoverable errors as exceptions.

Of course, errors can occur during MPI calls for a variety of reasons. A **program error** can occur when an MPI routine is called with an incorrect argument (non-existing destination in a send operation, buffer too small in a receive operation, etc.) This type of error would occur in any implementation. In addition, a **resource error** may occur when a program exceeds the amount of available system resources (number of pending messages, system buffers, etc.). The occurrence of this type of error depends on the amount of available resources in the system and the resource allocation mechanism used; this may differ from system to system. A high-quality implementation will provide generous limits on the important resources so as to alleviate the portability problem this represents.

An MPI implementation cannot or may choose not to handle some errors that occur during MPI calls. These can include errors that generate exceptions or traps, such as floating point errors or access violations; errors that are too expensive to detect in normal execution mode; or "catastrophic" errors which may prevent MPI from returning control to the caller in a consistent state.

Another subtle issue arises because of the nature of asynchronous communications. MPI can handle only errors that can be attached to a specific MPI call. MPI calls (both blocking and nonblocking) may initiate operations that continue asynchronously after the call returned. Thus, the call may complete successfully, yet the operation may later cause an error. If there is a subsequent call that relates to the same operation (e.g., a Wait or Test call that completes a nonblocking call, or a Receive that completes a communication initiated by a blocking Send) then the error can be associated with this call. In some cases, the error may occur after all calls that relate to the operation have completed. (Consider the case of a blocking ready mode send operation, where the outgoing message is buffered, and it is subsequently found that no matching receive is posted.) Such errors will not usually be handled by MPI though they can be handled if an implementation can detect the error.

The set of errors in MPI calls that are handled by MPI is implementation-dependent. Each such error generates an MPI **exception**. A high-quality implementation will attempt to handle as many errors as possible as MPI exceptions. Errors that are not handled by MPI will be handled by the error handling mechanisms of the language run-time or the operating system. Typically, errors that are not handled by MPI will cause the parallel program to abort.

The occurrence of an MPI exception has two effects:

- An MPI **error handler** will be invoked.
- If the error handler did not cause the process to halt, then a suitable error code will be returned by the MPI call.

Some MPI calls may cause more than one MPI exception (see Section 2.9). In such a case, the MPI error handler will be invoked once for each exception, and multiple error codes will be returned.

After an error is detected, the state of MPI is undefined. That is, the state of the computation after the error-handler executed does *not* necessarily allow the user to continue to use MPI. The purpose of these error handlers is to allow a user to issue user-defined error messages and to take actions unrelated to MPI (such as flushing I/O buffers) before a program exits. An MPI implementation is free to allow MPI to continue after an error but is not required to do so.

Advice to implementors.   A high-quality implementation will, to the greatest possible extent, circumscribe the impact of an error, so that normal processing can continue after an error handler was invoked. The implementation documentation will provide information on the possible effect of each class of errors. ▯

7.5.1   Error Handlers

Error handlers are associated at each process with each communicator, file, or window object. (The last two objects are described in Section II-7.7 and Section II-4.6, respectively.) The specified error handling routine will be used for any MPI exception that occurs during a call to MPI for a call with this object as input parameter. Most MPI calls that are not related to any such object will raise the exception handler associated with the communicator MPI_COMM_WORLD. The exception is the MPI IO calls with no file argument that raise the exception handler "associated" with the null file handle MPI_FILE_NULL. The attachment of error handlers to MPI objects is purely local: for example, different processes may attach different error handlers to the same communicator.

Several predefined error handlers are available in MPI:

MPI_ERRORS_ARE_FATAL (MPI::ERRORS_ARE_FATAL, in C++) The handler, when called, causes the program to abort on all executing processes. This has the same effect as if MPI_ABORT was called by the process that invoked the handler.

MPI_ERRORS_RETURN (MPI::ERRORS_RETURN, in C++) The handler has no effect (other than returning the error code to the user).

MPI::ERRORS_THROW_EXCEPTIONS (C++ only!) The handler, when called (in C++), causes an MPI::Exception to be thrown for any MPI result code other than MPI::SUCCESS. The public interface to MPI::Exception class is defined as follows:

```
namespace MPI {
  class Exception {
  public:

    Exception(int error_code);

    int Get_error_code() const;
    int Get_error_class() const;
    const char *Get_error_string() const;
  };
};
```

The user can use these methods to find out the code and class of the error that caused the abnormal termination of the MPI call. Some MPI functions that complete multiple communications, such as MPI_WAITALL, may return an error code

of MPI_ERR_IN_STATUS and return an error code for each communication in the
status associated with this communication in the array_of_statuses argument (see
Section 2.9). In such a case, Get_error_code will return MPI::ERR_IN_STATUS and
the error fields of the status objects in array_of_statuses will be set before the exception is thrown.

Implementations may provide additional predefined error handlers and programmers can code their own error handlers.

A communicator, window, or file is associated with a default error handler, according to the following rules.

• The error handler MPI_ERRORS_ARE_FATAL is associated by default to the predefined communicators (MPI_COMM_WORLD, MPI_COMM_SELF, and MPI_COMM_-
PARENT). Other communicators inherit the error handler that is associated with
the input "parent" communicator at the local process. Most communicator creating calls have only one input communicator argument, in which case this definition
is unambiguous. There is one exception: MPI_INTERCOMM_CREATE(local_comm,
local_leader, bridge_comm, remote_leader,tag, newintercomm) – the parent communicator is the local_comm intracommunicator.
• New windows are associated by default with the error handler MPI_ERRORS_-
ARE_FATAL.
• New files inherit the error handler that is "associated" with MPI_FILE_NULL.
MPI_FILE_NULL is associated, by default, with MPI_ERRORS_RETURN.

Users may attach a new error handler to a communicator, file (including MPI_-
FILE_NULL), or window, and may query the error handler attached to such an object.
If the user does not change the default error handlers, then all communication errors
will be treated as fatal (handled by MPI_ERRORS_ARE_FATAL), while all I/O errors
will be treated as non-fatal (handled by MPI_ERRORS_RETURN).

Advice to users.   The user can specify a "global" error handler for all communicators by associating on each process this handler with the communicator
MPI_COMM_WORLD immediately after MPI was initialized on the process.

The user should test the return code of MPI calls that invoke the error handler
MPI_ERROR_RETURNS, and execute suitable recovery code when the call was un-
successful. Thus, normally, the user should test the error code returned by an
MPI I/O call, so as to recover from errors such as attempts to open a nonexistant

file, attempts to read past end-of-file, etc. On the other hand, users need not normally test the error code returned by a message passing call since they are fatal by default. ☐

Rationale.   The current design treats, by default, communication errors as fatal, and treats, by default I/O errors as non-fatal. This corresponds to current practice since we assume that communication is reliable so communication errors usually are program errors. Programs normally do not check the return codes of communication calls. On the other hand, I/O errors, such as attempting to read past end-of-file, are normally treated as non-fatal errors, and programs normally check whether such a condition occurred.

Communicators are always created from communicators, hence it is natural to have error handler inheritance. Files or windows are also created from communicators, but, since they are a different type of object, there is a good argument that they should not inherit their error handler from the "parent" communicator. There is not a strong reason why a different default scheme is used for windows and for files (why windows do not inherit from MPI_WIN_NULL). This is an oversight of the MPI Forum that might to be corrected in the future. ☐

An MPI error handler is an opaque object which is accessed by a handle. MPI calls are provided to create new error handlers, to associate error handlers with communicators, files, or windows, and to test which error handler is associated with an object.

MPI_COMM_CREATE_ERRHANDLER(function, errhandler)

IN	function	user defined error handling procedure (function)
OUT	errhandler	MPI error handler (handle)

```
int MPI_Comm_create_errhandler(MPI_Comm_errhandler_fn *function,
    MPI_Errhandler *errhandler)
```

```
MPI_COMM_CREATE_ERRHANDLER(FUNCTION, ERRHANDLER, IERROR)
    EXTERNAL FUNCTION
    INTEGER ERRHANDLER, IERROR
```

```
static MPI::Errhandler
    MPI::Comm::Create_errhandler(MPI::Comm::Errhandler_fn* function)
```

MPI_COMM_CREATE_ERRHANDLER registers the user routine function for use as an MPI exception handler to be associated with communicators. Returns in errhandler a handle to the registered exception handler.

The user routine should be, in C, a function of type MPI_Comm_errhandler_fn, which is defined as

```
typedef void MPI_Comm_errhandler_fn(MPI_Comm *, int *, ...);
```

The first argument is the communicator on which the error occurred; the second is the error code to be returned by the MPI function for the error that occurred. If the routine would have returned multiple error codes (see Section 2.9), it is the error code returned in the status for the request that caused the error handler to be invoked. The remaining arguments are "stdargs" arguments whose number and meaning is implementation-dependent. An implementation should clearly document these arguments.

In Fortran, the user routine should be of the form:

```
SUBROUTINE COMM_ERRHANDLER_FN(COMM, ERROR_CODE, ...)
    INTEGER COMM, ERROR_CODE
```

In C++, the user routine should be of the form:

```
typedef void MPI::Comm::Errhandler_fn(MPI::Comm &, int *, ...);
```

Similar functions are provided to register an error handler that can be used for windows or for files.

MPI_WIN_CREATE_ERRHANDLER(function, errhandler)

IN	function	user defined error handling procedure (function)
OUT	errhandler	MPI error handler (handle)

```
int MPI_Win_create_errhandler(MPI_Win_errhandler_fn *function,
    MPI_Errhandler *errhandler)
```

```
MPI_WIN_CREATE_ERRHANDLER(FUNCTION, ERRHANDLER, IERROR)
    EXTERNAL FUNCTION
    INTEGER ERRHANDLER, IERROR
```

```
static MPI::Errhandler
    MPI::Win::Create_errhandler(MPI::Win::Errhandler_fn* function)
```

MPI_WIN_CREATE_ERRHANDLER registers an error handler to be associated with windows. The user routine should be, in C, a function of type MPI_Win_errhandler_fn, which is defined as

```
typedef void MPI_Win_errhandler_fn(MPI_Win *, int *, ...);
```

In Fortran, the user routine should be of the form:

```
SUBROUTINE WIN_ERRHANDLER_FN(WIN, ERROR_CODE, ...)
    INTEGER WIN, ERROR_CODE
```

In C++, the user routine should be of the form:

```
typedef void MPI::Win::Errhandler_fn(MPI::Win&, int*, ...);
```

MPI_FILE_CREATE_ERRHANDLER(function, errhandler)

IN	function	user defined error handling procedure (function)
OUT	errhandler	MPI error handler (handle)

```
int MPI_File_create_errhandler(MPI_File_errhandler_fn *function,
    MPI_Errhandler *errhandler)
```

```
MPI_FILE_CREATE_ERRHANDLER(FUNCTION, ERRHANDLER, IERROR)
    EXTERNAL FUNCTION
    INTEGER ERRHANDLER, IERROR
```

```
static MPI::Errhandler
    MPI::File::Create_errhandler(MPI::File::Errhandler_fn* function)
```

The user routine should be, in C, a function of type MPI_File_errhandler_fn, which is defined as

```
typedef void MPI_File_errhandler_fn(MPI_File *, int *, ...);
```

In Fortran, the user routine should be of the form:

```
SUBROUTINE FILE_ERRHANDLER_FN(FILE, ERROR_CODE, ...)
    INTEGER FILE, ERROR_CODE
```

In C++, the user routine should be of the form:

```
typedef void MPI::File::Errhandler_fn(MPI::File&, int*, ...);
```

Advice to users. Users are discouraged from using a Fortran error handler function since these routines expects a variable number of arguments using ISO C stdargs. As a result, it will not, in general, be possible to create portable code with a Fortran error handler function.

Both error handler function arguments are input arguments. They are passed by reference, rather than by value, in C, so as to make the C interface closer to the Fortran interface. ⬚

Rationale. There is only one type of MPI error handler handle, even though there are three types of error handling functions in C and C++. The three MPI functions MPI_{COMM|WIN|FILE}_CREATE_ERRHANDLER have as input parameters error handling functions with different signatures, as they expect a communicator argument, a window argument, or a file argument, respectively. They all return a handle of type MPI_Errhanlder. The MPI implementation may record internally the type of error handling function that is associated with the error handler, and raise an error if this error handler is subsequently associated with an object of the wrong type.

An alternative design would be to have a different type of error handler (in C and C++) for each type of error handling function, thus supporting compile time checking, rather than run time checking. As calls to functions that manipulate error handlers are not frequent, the overhead of run-time type checking was not deemed to be significant and not worth the additional multiplication of types and constant for error handlers.

The variable argument list is provided because it provides an ISO-standard hook for providing additional information to the error handler; without this hook, ISO C prohibits additional arguments. ⬚

Advice to implementors. As is the case elsewhere with callback functions, the implementation must keep track of the language where the callback was defined so that, when it is invoked, the correct argument passing convention is used. ⬚

MPI_COMM_SET_ERRHANDLER(comm, errhandler)

INOUT	comm	communicator (handle)
IN	errhandler	new error handler for communicator (handle)

```
int MPI_Comm_set_errhandler(MPI_Comm comm, MPI_Errhandler errhandler)
```

```
MPI_COMM_SET_ERRHANDLER(COMM, ERRHANDLER, IERROR)
```

```
    INTEGER COMM, ERRHANDLER, IERROR
```

void MPI::Comm::Set_errhandler(const MPI::Errhandler& errhandler)

MPI_COMM_SET_ERRHANDLER associates the new error handler errhandler with communicator comm at the calling process. This replaces the error handler that was previously associated with the communicator. The error handler must be either a predefined error handler, or an error handler created by a call to MPI_COMM_-CREATE_ERRHANDLER.

Similar functions are available for windows and files.

MPI_WIN_SET_ERRHANDLER(win, errhandler)

INOUT	win	window (handle)
IN	errhandler	new error handler for window (handle)

---

int MPI_Win_set_errhandler(MPI_Win win, MPI_Errhandler errhandler)

MPI_WIN_SET_ERRHANDLER(WIN, ERRHANDLER, IERROR)
```
    INTEGER WIN, ERRHANDLER, IERROR
```

void MPI::Win::Set_errhandler(const MPI::Errhandler& errhandler)

and

MPI_FILE_SET_ERRHANDLER(file, errhandler)

INOUT	file	file (handle)
IN	errhandler	new error handler for file (handle)

---

int MPI_File_set_errhandler(MPI_File file, MPI_Errhandler errhandler)

MPI_FILE_SET_ERRHANDLER(FILE, ERRHANDLER, IERROR)
```
    INTEGER FILE, ERRHANDLER, IERROR
```

void MPI::File::Set_errhandler(const MPI::Errhandler& errhandler)

MPI_COMM_GET_ERRHANDLER(comm, errhandler)

IN	comm	communicator (handle)

OUT	errhandler	error handler currently associated with communicator (handle)

```
int MPI_Comm_get_errhandler(MPI_Comm comm, MPI_Errhandler
    *errhandler)
```

```
MPI_COMM_GET_ERRHANDLER(COMM, ERRHANDLER, IERROR)
    INTEGER COMM, ERRHANDLER, IERROR
```

```
MPI::Errhandler MPI::Comm::Get_errhandler() const
```

MPI_COMM_GET_ERRHANDLER retrieves the error handler currently associated with a communicator. This error handler can be associated only with a communicator.

Similar functions are available for windows and for files.

MPI_WIN_GET_ERRHANDLER(win, errhandler)

IN	win	window (handle)
OUT	errhandler	error handler currently associated with window (handle)

```
int MPI_Win_get_errhandler(MPI_Win win, MPI_Errhandler *errhandler)
```

```
MPI_WIN_GET_ERRHANDLER(WIN, ERRHANDLER, IERROR)
    INTEGER WIN, ERRHANDLER, IERROR
```

```
MPI::Errhandler MPI::Win::Get_errhandler() const
```

and

MPI_FILE_GET_ERRHANDLER(file, errhandler)

IN	file	file (handle)
OUT	errhandler	error handler currently associated with file (handle)

```
int MPI_File_get_errhandler(MPI_File file, MPI_Errhandler
    *errhandler)
```

```
MPI_FILE_GET_ERRHANDLER(FILE, ERRHANDLER, IERROR)
    INTEGER FILE, ERRHANDLER, IERROR
```

```
MPI::Errhandler MPI::File::Get_errhandler() const
```

MPI_ERRHANDLER_FREE(errhandler)

    INOUT   errhandler   MPI error handler (handle)

```
int MPI_Errhandler_free(MPI_Errhandler *errhandler)
```

```
MPI_ERRHANDLER_FREE(ERRHANDLER, IERROR)
    INTEGER ERRHANDLER, IERROR
```

```
void MPI::Errhandler::Free()
```

MPI_ERRHANDLER_FREE marks the error handler associated with errhandler for deallocation and sets errhandler to MPI_ERRHANDLER_NULL (MPI::ERRHANDLER_-NULL, in C++). The error handler will be deallocated after all operations associated with it have been deallocated.

7.5.2 Deprecated Functions

The three error handler functions that deal with error handling for communicators are available under different names in MPI-1.

    The function MPI_COMM_CREATE_ERRHANDLER has replaced the old function MPI_ERRHANDLER_CREATE(function, errhandler)

    The function MPI_COMM_SET_ERRHANDLER has replaced MPI_ERRHANDLER_SET(comm, errhandler)

    The function MPI_COMM_GET_ERRHANDLER has replaced MPI_ERRHANDLER_GET(comm, errhandler)

    The user routine MPI_Comm_errhandler_fn has replaced MPI_Handler_function and MPI_COMM_ERRHANDLER_FN has replaced HANDLER_FUNCTION.

    The associated user routines in C (MPI_Handler_function) and Fortran (HANDLER_FUNCTION) are also deprecated.

    In each case, the old function has the same definition and the same binding as the corresponding new function. The old functions have been deprecated. (See Section 1.9.1 for a discussion of deprecated functions.)

Rationale.   MPI-1 attached error handlers only with communicators. The file and window objects, and the attachment of error handlers to those, was introduced by MPI-2. The new function names were introduced so as to be consistent with the names of the functions used with the other objects, and so as to be consistent with the C++ binding. □

7.5.3 Error Codes

Most MPI functions return an error code indicating successful execution (MPI_SUC-CESS, MPI::SUCCESS, in C++), or provide information on the type of MPI exception that occurred. In certain circumstances, when the MPI function may complete several distinct operations and therefore may generate several independent errors, the MPI function may return multiple error codes. This may occur with some of the calls described in Section 2.9 that complete multiple nonblocking communications. As described in that section, the call returns MPI_SUCCESS, or it returns the code MPI_ERR_IN_STATUS (MPI::ERR_IN_STATUS, in C++), and a detailed error code is returned with the status of each communication.

The error codes returned by MPI are left entirely to the implementation (with the exception of MPI_SUCCESS, MPI_ERR_IN_STATUS and MPI_ERR_PENDING). This is done to allow an implementation to provide as much information as possible in the error code. Error codes can be translated into meaningful messages using the function below.

MPI_ERROR_STRING(errorcode, string, resultlen)

IN	errorcode	Error code returned by an MPI routine (integer)
OUT	string	Text that corresponds to the errorcode (string)
OUT	resultlen	Length (in printable characters) of the result returned in string (integer)

```
int MPI_Error_string(int errorcode, char *string, int *resultlen)
```

```
MPI_ERROR_STRING(ERRORCODE, STRING, RESULTLEN, IERROR)
    INTEGER ERRORCODE, RESULTLEN, IERROR
    CHARACTER*(*) STRING
```

```
void MPI::Get_error_string(int errorcode, char* name, int& resultlen)
```

MPI_ERROR_STRING returns the error string associated with an error code or class. The argument string must represent storage that is at least MPI_MAX_ERROR_-STRING characters long (MPI::MAX_ERROR_STRING, in C++).

The number of characters actually written is returned in the output argument resultlen.

Rationale. The form of this function was chosen to make the Fortran and C bindings similar. A version that returns a pointer to a string has two difficulties. First, the returned string must be statically allocated and different for each error message (allowing the pointers returned by successive calls to MPI_ERROR_STRING to point to the correct message). Second, in Fortran, a function declared as returning CHARACTER*(*) can not be referenced in, for example, a PRINT statement. □

The use of implementation-dependent error codes allows implementors to provide more information, but prevents one from writing portable error-handling code. To solve this problem, MPI provides a standard set of specified error values, called **error classes**, and a function that maps each error code into a suitable error class. The classes defined in MPI-1 are given for C and Fortran in Table 7.1 and for C++ in Table 7.2. Additional error classes are defined in Book 2.

Most of these classes are self explanatory. The use of MPI_ERR_IN_STATUS and MPI_ERR_PENDING is explained in Section 2.9.

The error codes satisfy,

$$0 = \text{MPI\_SUCCESS} < \text{MPI\_ERR}.... \leq \text{MPI\_ERR\_LASTCODE}.$$

MPI_ERROR_CLASS(errorcode, errorclass)

| IN | errorcode | Error code returned by an MPI routine (integer) |
| OUT | errorclass | Error class associated with errorcode (integer) |

```
int MPI_Error_class(int errorcode, int *errorclass)
```

```
MPI_ERROR_CLASS(ERRORCODE, ERRORCLASS, IERROR)
    INTEGER ERRORCODE, ERRORCLASS, IERROR
```

```
int MPI::Get_error_class(int errorcode)
```

The function MPI_ERROR_CLASS maps each standard error code (error class) onto itself.

MPI_ERROR_STRING can be used to compute the error string associated with an error class.

Rationale. The difference between MPI_ERR_UNKNOWN and MPI_ERR_OTHER is that MPI_ERROR_STRING can return useful information about MPI_ERR_OTHER.

Table 7.1
C and Fortran error classes

MPI_ERR_ARG	Invalid argument of some other kind
MPI_ERR_BASE	Invalid base argument
MPI_ERR_BUFFER	Invalid buffer pointer
MPI_ERR_COMM	Invalid communicator
MPI_ERR_COUNT	Invalid count argument
MPI_ERR_DIMS	Invalid dimension argument
MPI_ERR_GROUP	Invalid group
MPI_ERR_IN_STATUS	Error code is in status
MPI_ERR_INFO_KEY	Invalid info key
MPI_ERR_INFO_NOKEY	Missing info key
MPI_ERR_INFO_VALUE	Invalid info value
MPI_ERR_INTERN	Internal MPI error
MPI_ERR_KEYVAL	Invalid attribute key
MPI_ERR_LASTCODE	Last error code
MPI_ERR_NO_MEM	No memory available for allocation
MPI_ERR_OP	Invalid operation
MPI_ERR_OTHER	Known error not in this list
MPI_ERR_PENDING	Pending request
MPI_ERR_RANK	Invalid rank
MPI_ERR_REQUEST	Invalid request
MPI_ERR_ROOT	Invalid root
MPI_ERR_TAG	Invalid tag argument
MPI_ERR_TOPOLOGY	Invalid topology
MPI_ERR_TRUNCATE	Message truncated on receive
MPI_ERR_TYPE	Invalid datatype argument
MPI_ERR_UNKNOWN	Unknown error
MPI_SUCCESS	No error

Note that MPI_SUCCESS = 0 is necessary to be consistent with C practice; the separation of error classes and error codes allows us to define the error classes this way. Having a known LASTCODE is often a nice sanity check as well. ☐

Advice to implementors.   An MPI implementation may use error classes as the error codes returned by some or all MPI functions. Another choice is to use these values as "major error codes", extended with additional bits that provide "minor"

Table 7.2
C++ error classes

MPI::ERR_ARG	Invalid argument of some other kind
MPI::ERR_BASE	Invalid base argument
MPI::ERR_BUFFER	Invalid buffer pointer
MPI::ERR_COMM	Invalid communicator
MPI::ERR_COUNT	Invalid count argument
MPI::ERR_DIMS	Invalid dimension argument
MPI::ERR_GROUP	Invalid group
MPI::ERR_IN_STATUS	Error code is in status
MPI::ERR_INFO_KEY	Invalid info key
MPI::ERR_INFO_NOKEY	Missing info key
MPI::ERR_INFO_VALUE	Invalid info value
MPI::ERR_INTERN	Internal MPI error
MPI::ERR_KEYVAL	Invalid attribute key
MPI::ERR_LASTCODE	Last error code
MPI::ERR_NO_MEM	No memory available for allocation
MPI::ERR_OP	Invalid operation
MPI::ERR_OTHER	Known error not in this list
MPI::ERR_PENDING	Pending request
MPI::ERR_RANK	Invalid rank
MPI::ERR_REQUEST	Invalid request
MPI::ERR_ROOT	Invalid root
MPI::ERR_TAG	Invalid tag argument
MPI::ERR_TOPOLOGY	Invalid topology
MPI::ERR_TRUNCATE	Message truncated on receive
MPI::ERR_TYPE	Invalid datatype argument
MPI::ERR_UNKNOWN	Unknown error
MPI::SUCCESS	No error

error codes. Then, the MPI_ERROR_CLASS function merely needs to truncate the full error code.

Implementations may go beyond this document in supporting MPI calls that are defined here to be erroneous. For example, MPI specifies strict type matching rules between matching send and receive operations: it is erroneous to send a floating point variable and receive an integer. Implementations may go beyond these type matching rules and provide automatic type conversion in such situations. It will be helpful to generate warnings for such nonconforming behavior. □

7.6 Interaction with Executing Environment

There are a number of areas where an MPI implementation may interact with the operating environment and system. While MPI does not mandate that any services (such as I/O or signal handling) be provided, it does strongly suggest the behavior to be provided if those services are available. This is an important point in achieving portability across platforms that provide the same set of services.

7.6.1 Independence of Basic Runtime Routines

MPI programs require that library routines that are part of the basic language environment (such as `date` and `write` in Fortran and `printf()` and `malloc()` in ISO C) and are executed after MPI_INIT and before MPI_FINALIZE operate independently and that their *completion* is independent of the action of other processes in an MPI program.

Note that this in no way prevents the creation of library routines that provide parallel services whose operation is collective. However, the following program is expected to complete in an ISO C environment regardless of the size of MPI_COMM_-WORLD (assuming that I/O is available at the executing nodes).

```
int rank;
MPI_Init( &argc, &argv );
MPI_Comm_rank( MPI_COMM_WORLD, &rank );
if (rank == 0) printf( "Starting program\n" );
MPI_Finalize();
```

The corresponding Fortran and C++ programs are also expected to complete.

An example of what is *not* required is any particular ordering of the action of these routines when called by several tasks. For example, MPI makes neither requirements nor recommendations for the output from the following program (again assuming that I/O is available at the executing nodes).

```
MPI_Comm_rank( MPI_COMM_WORLD, &rank );
printf( "Output from task rank %d\n", rank );
```

In addition, calls that fail because of resource exhaustion or other error are not considered a violation of the requirements here (however, they are required to complete, just not to complete successfully).

7.6.2 Interaction with Signals in POSIX

MPI does not specify either the interaction of processes with signals, in a UNIX environment, or with other events that do not relate to MPI communication. That is, signals are not significant from the view point of MPI, and implementors should attempt to implement MPI so that signals are transparent: an MPI call suspended by a signal should resume and complete after the signal is handled. Generally, the state of a computation that is visible or significant from the view point of MPI should only be affected by MPI calls.

The intent of MPI to be thread and signal-safe has a number of subtle effects. For example, on Unix systems, a catchable signal such as SIGALRM (an alarm signal) must not cause an MPI routine to behave differently than it would have in the absence of the signal. Of course, if the signal handler issues MPI calls or changes the environment in which the MPI routine is operating (for example, consuming all available memory space), the MPI routine should behave as appropriate for that situation (in particular, in this case, the behavior should be the same as for a multithreaded MPI implementation).

A second effect is that a signal handler that performs MPI calls must not interfere with the operation of MPI. For example, an MPI receive of any type that occurs within a signal handler must not cause erroneous behavior by the MPI implementation. Note that an implementation is permitted to prohibit the use of MPI calls from within a signal handler and is not required to detect such use.

It is highly desirable that MPI not use SIGALRM, SIGFPE, or SIGIO. An implementation is *required* to clearly document all of the signals that the MPI implementation uses; a good place for this information on a Unix system is the 'man' page on MPI. A comparable facility can be used on non-Unix systems.

8 The MPI Profiling Interface

In this chapter we present the MPI mechanism for profiling the performance of MPI routines. We discuss how this mechanism allows for portable code to be written to perform this important function.

8.1 Requirements

To satisfy the requirements of the MPI profiling interface, an implementation of the MPI functions *must*

1. provide a mechanism through which all of the MPI defined functions may be accessed with a name shift. Thus all of the MPI functions (which normally start with the prefix "MPI_") should also be accessible with the prefix "PMPI_". In C++ the nameshift is accomplished by provision of a PMPI namespace.

2. ensure that those MPI functions which are not replaced may still be linked into an executable image without causing name clashes.

3. document the implementation of different language bindings of the MPI interface if they are layered on top of each other, so that the profiler developer knows whether the profile interface must be implemented for each binding, or whether it needs to be implemented only for the lowest level routines.

4. ensure that where the implementation of different language bindings is done through a layered approach (e.g. the Fortran binding is a set of "wrapper" functions which call the C implementation), these wrapper functions are separable from the rest of the library. This is necessary to allow a separate profiling library to be correctly implemented, since (at least with Unix linker semantics) the profiling library must contain these wrapper functions if it is to perform as expected. This requirement allows the person who builds the profiling library to extract these functions from the original MPI library and add them into the profiling library without bringing along any other unnecessary code.

5. provide a no-op routine MPI_PCONTROL in the MPI library (MPI::Pcontrol() in C++).

Details of the profiling interface specific to C++ are provided in II-8.1.10.

8.2   Discussion

The objective of the MPI profiling interface is to ensure that it is relatively easy for authors of profiling (and other similar) tools to interface their codes to MPI implementations on different machines.

Since MPI is a machine independent standard with many different implementations, it is unreasonable to expect that the authors of profiling tools for MPI will have access to the source code which implements MPI on any particular machine. It is therefore necessary to provide a mechanism by which the implementors of such tools can collect whatever performance information they wish *without* access to the underlying implementation.

The MPI Forum believed that having such an interface is important if MPI is to be attractive to end users, since the availability of many different tools will be a significant factor in attracting users to the MPI standard.

The profiling interface is just that, an interface. It says *nothing* about the way in which it is used. Therefore, there is no attempt to lay down what information is collected through the interface, or how the collected information is saved, filtered, or displayed.

While the initial impetus for the development of this interface arose from the desire to permit the implementation of profiling tools, it is clear that an interface like that specified may also prove useful for other purposes, such as "internetworking" multiple MPI implementations. Since all that is defined is an interface, there is no impediment to it being used wherever it is useful.

As the issues being addressed here are intimately tied up with the way in which executable images are built, which may differ greatly on different machines, the examples given below should be treated solely as one way of implementing the MPI profiling interface. The actual requirements made of an implementation are those detailed in Section 8.1; the whole of the rest of this chapter is only present as justification and discussion of the logic for those requirements.

The examples below show one way in which an implementation could be constructed to meet the requirements on a Unix system (there are doubtless others which would be equally valid).

8.3   Logic of the Design

Provided that an MPI implementation meets the requirements listed in Section 8.1, it is possible for the implementor of the profiling system to intercept all of the MPI calls which are made by the user program. Whatever information is required can then be collected before calling the underlying MPI implementation (through its name shifted entry points) to achieve the desired effects.

8.3.1 Miscellaneous Control of Profiling

There is a clear requirement for the user code to be able to control the profiler dynamically at run time. This is normally used for (at least) the purposes of

- Enabling and disabling profiling depending on the state of the calculation.
- Flushing trace buffers at non-critical points in the calculation
- Adding user events to a trace file.

These requirements are met by use of MPI_PCONTROL.

MPI_PCONTROL(level, ...)

    IN   level   Profiling level (integer)

```
int MPI_Pcontrol(const int level, ...)
```

```
MPI_PCONTROL(LEVEL)
    INTEGER LEVEL
```

```
void MPI::Pcontrol(const int level, ...)
```

MPI libraries themselves make no use of this routine, and simply return immediately to the user code. However the presence of calls to this routine allows a profiling package to be explicitly called by the user.

Since MPI has no control of the implementation of the profiling code, the MPI Forum was unable to specify precisely the semantics which will be provided by calls to MPI_PCONTROL. This vagueness extends to the number of arguments to the function, and their datatypes.

However to provide some level of portability of user codes to different profiling libraries, the MPI Forum requested the following meanings for certain values of level.

- `level = 0`: Profiling is disabled.
- `level = 1`: Profiling is enabled at a normal default level of detail.
- `level = 2`: Profile buffers are flushed. (This may be a no-op in some profilers).

- All other values of level have profile library defined effects and may have additional arguments.

The MPI Forum also requested that the default state after MPI_INIT has been called is for profiling to be enabled at the normal default level. (i.e., as if MPI_PCONTROL had just been called with the argument 1). This allows users to link with a profiling library and obtain profile output without having to modify their source code at all.

The provision of MPI_PCONTROL as a no-op in the standard MPI library allows users to modify their source code to obtain more detailed profiling information, but still be able to link exactly the same code against the standard MPI library.

8.4 Examples

8.4.1 Profiler Implementation

Suppose that the profiler wishes to accumulate the total amount of data sent by the MPI_Send() function, along with the total elapsed time spent in the function. This could trivially be achieved thus

```
static int totalBytes;
static double totalTime;
int MPI_Send(void * buffer, const int count, MPI_Datatype datatype,
             int dest, int tag, MPI_Comm comm)
{
  double tstart = MPI_Wtime();        /* Pass on all the arguments */
  int extent;
  int result     = PMPI_Send(buffer,count,datatype,dest,tag,comm);

  totalTime   += MPI_Wtime() - tstart;

  MPI_Type_size(datatype,&extent);  /* Compute size */
  totalBytes += count * extent;

  return result;
}
```

8.4.2 MPI **Library Implementation**

On a Unix system in which the MPI library is implemented in C, there are various possible options of which two of the most obvious are presented here. Which is better depends on whether the linker and compiler support weak symbols.

Systems with weak symbols If the compiler and linker support weak external symbols (e.g., Solaris 2.x, other system V.4 machines), then only a single library is required through the use of #pragma weak thus

```
#pragma weak MPI_Send = PMPI_Send
int PMPI_Send(/* appropriate args */)
{
    /* Useful content */
}
```

The effect of this #pragma is to define the external symbol MPI_Send as a weak definition. This means that the linker will not complain if there is another definition of the symbol (for instance in the profiling library), however if no other definition exists, then the linker will use the weak definition. This type of situation is illustrated in Fig. 8.1, in which a profiling library has been written that profiles calls to MPI_Send() but not calls to MPI_Bcast(). On systems with weak links the link step for an application would be something like

```
% cc ... -lprof -lmpi
```

References to MPI_Send() are resolved in the profiling library, where the routine then calls PMPI_Send() which is resolved in the MPI library. In this case the weak link to PMPI_Send() is ignored. However, since MPI_Bcast() is not included in the profiling library, references to it are resolved via a weak link to PMPI_Bcast() in the MPI library.

Systems without weak symbols In the absence of weak symbols, one possible solution would be to use the C macro pre-processor thus

```
#ifdef PROFILELIB
#    ifdef __STDC__
#        define FUNCTION(name) P##name
#    else
#        define FUNCTION(name) P/**/name
#    endif
```

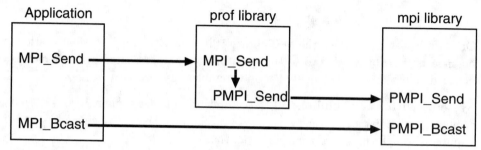

Figure 8.1
Resolution of MPI calls on systems with weak links.

```
#else
#     define FUNCTION(name) name
#endif
```

Each of the user visible functions in the library would then be declared thus

```
int FUNCTION(MPI_Send)(/* appropriate args */)
{
    /* Useful content */
}
```

The same source file can then be compiled to produce the MPI and the PMPI versions of the library, depending on the state of the PROFILELIB macro symbol.

It is required that the standard MPI library be built in such a way that the inclusion of MPI functions can be achieved one at a time. This is a somewhat unpleasant requirement, since it may mean that each external function has to be compiled from a separate file. However this is necessary so that the author of the profiling library need only define those MPI functions that are to be intercepted, references to any others being fulfilled by the normal MPI library. Therefore the link step can look something like this

```
% cc ... -lprof -lpmpi -lmpi
```

Here libprof.a contains the profiler functions which intercept some of the MPI functions. libpmpi.a contains the "name shifted" MPI functions, and libmpi.a contains the normal definitions of the MPI functions. Thus, on systems without weak links the example shown in Fig. 8.1 would be resolved as shown in Fig. 8.2

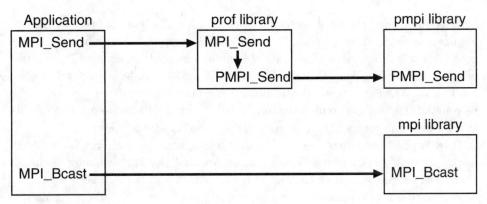

Figure 8.2
Resolution of MPI calls on systems without weak links.

8.4.3   Complications

Multiple counting   Since parts of the MPI library may themselves be implemented using more basic MPI functions (e.g. a portable implementation of the collective operations implemented using point to point communications), there is potential for profiling functions to be called from within an MPI function which was called from a profiling function. This could lead to "double counting" of the time spent in the inner routine. Since this effect could actually be useful under some circumstances (e.g. it might allow one to answer the question "How much time is spent in the point to point routines when they're called from collective functions?"), the MPI Forum decided not to enforce any restrictions on the author of the MPI library which would overcome this. Therefore the author of the profiling library should be aware of this problem, and guard against it. In a single threaded world this is easily achieved through use of a static variable in the profiling code which remembers if you are already inside a profiling routine. It becomes more complex in a multithreaded environment (as does the meaning of the times recorded!).

Linker oddities   The Unix linker traditionally operates in one pass. The effect of this is that functions from libraries are only included in the image if they are needed at the time the library is scanned. When combined with weak symbols, or multiple definitions of the same function, this can cause odd (and unexpected) effects.

Consider, for instance, an implementation of MPI in which the Fortran binding is achieved by using wrapper functions on top of the C implementation. The author of the profile library then assumes that it is reasonable to provide profile functions only for the C binding, since Fortran will eventually call these, and the cost of the wrappers is assumed to be small. However, if the wrapper functions are not in the profiling library, then none of the profiled entry points will be undefined when the profiling library is called. Therefore none of the profiling code will be included in the image. When the standard MPI library is scanned, the Fortran wrappers will be resolved, and will also pull in the base versions of the MPI functions. The overall effect is that the code will link successfully, but will not be profiled.

To overcome this we must ensure that the Fortran wrapper functions are included in the profiling version of the library. We ensure that this is possible by requiring that these be separable from the rest of the base MPI library. This allows them to be extracted out of the base library and placed into the profiling library using the Unix `ar` command.

8.5   Multiple Levels of Interception

The scheme given here does not directly support the nesting of profiling functions, since it provides only a single alternative name for each MPI function. The MPI Forum gave consideration to an implementation which would allow multiple levels of call interception; however, it was unable to construct an implementation of this which did not have the following disadvantages

- assuming a particular implementation language.
- imposing a run time cost even when no profiling was taking place.

Since one of the objectives of MPI is to permit efficient, low latency implementations, and it is not the business of a standard to require a particular implementation language, the MPI Forum decided to accept the scheme outlined above.

Note, however, that it is possible to use the scheme above to implement a multi-level system, since the function called by the user may call many different profiling functions before calling the underlying MPI function.

Unfortunately such an implementation may require more cooperation between the different profiling libraries than is required for the single level implementation detailed above.

9 Conclusions

This final chapter addresses some important topics that either do not easily fit into the other chapters, or which are best dealt with after a good overall understanding of MPI-1 has been gained. These topics are concerned more with the interpretation of the MPI-1 specification, and the rationale behind some aspects of its design, rather than with semantics and syntax. The current status of MPI implementations will also be discussed.

9.1 Design Issues

9.1.1 Why Is MPI So Big?

One aspect of concern, particularly to novices, is the large number of routines comprising the MPI specification. In all there are 128 routines in MPI-1, and 287 functions in all of MPI. There are two fundamental reasons for the size of MPI. The first reason is that MPI was designed to be rich in functionality. This is reflected in MPI's support for derived datatypes, modular communication via the communicator abstraction, caching, application topologies, and the fully-featured set of collective communication routines. The second reason for the size of MPI reflects the diversity and complexity of today's high performance computers. This is particularly true with respect to the point-to-point communication routines where the different communication modes (see Sections 2.1 and 2.13) arise mainly as a means of providing a set of the most widely-used communication protocols. For example, the synchronous communication mode corresponds closely to a protocol that minimizes the copying and buffering of data through a rendezvous mechanism. A protocol that attempts to initiate delivery of messages as soon as possible would provide buffering for messages, and this corresponds closely to the buffered communication mode (or the standard mode if this is implemented with sufficient buffering). One could decrease the number of functions by increasing the number of parameters in each call. But such approach would increase the call overhead and would make the use of the most prevalent calls more complex. The availability of a large number of calls to deal with more esoteric features of MPI allows one to provide a simpler interface to the more frequently used functions.

9.1.2 Should We Be Concerned about the Size of MPI?

There are two potential reasons why we might be concerned about the size of MPI. The first is that potential users might equate size with complexity and decide that MPI is too complicated to bother learning. The second is that vendors might decide that MPI is too difficult to implement. The design of MPI addresses the first of these concerns by adopting a layered approach. For example, novices can avoid having to worry about groups and communicators by performing all communication in the predefined communicator MPI_COMM_WORLD. To allay the concerns of potential implementors the MPI Forum at one stage considered defining a core subset of MPI known as the MPI subset that would be substantially smaller than MPI and include just the point-to-point communication routines and a few of the more commonly-used collective communication routines. However, early work by Lusk, Gropp, Skjellum, Doss, Franke and others on early implementations of MPI showed that it could be fully implemented without a prohibitively large effort [12, 18]. Thus, the rationale for the MPI subset was lost, and this idea was dropped.

9.1.3   Why Does MPI Not Guarantee Buffering?

MPI does not guarantee to buffer arbitrary messages because memory is a finite resource on all computers. Thus, all computers will fail under sufficiently adverse communication loads. Different computers at different times are capable of providing differing amounts of buffering, so if a program relies on buffering it may fail under certain conditions, but work correctly under other conditions. This is clearly undesirable.

Given that no message passing system can guarantee that messages will be buffered as required under all circumstances, it might be asked why MPI does not guarantee a minimum amount of memory available for buffering. One major problem is that it is not obvious how to specify the amount of buffer space that is available, nor is it easy to estimate how much buffer space is consumed by a particular program.

Different buffering policies make sense in different environments. Messages can be buffered at the sending node or at the receiving node, or both. In the former case,

- buffers can be dedicated to one destination in one communication domain, or
- dedicated to one destination for all communication domains, or
- shared by all outgoing communications, or
- shared by all processes running at a processor node, or
- part of the buffer pool may be dedicated and part shared.

Similar choices occur if messages are buffered at the destination. Communication buffers may be fixed in size, or they may be allocated dynamically out of the heap in competition with the application. The buffer allocation policy may depend on the size of the messages (preferably buffering short messages), and may depend on communication history (preferably buffering on busy channels).

The choice of the right policy is strongly dependent on the hardware and software environment. For instance, in a dedicated environment, a processor with a process blocked on a Send is idle and so computing resources are not wasted if this processor copies the outgoing message to a buffer. In a time shared environment, the computing resources may be used by another process. In a system where buffer space can be in paged memory, such space can be allocated from heap. If the buffer space cannot be paged or has to be in kernel space, then a separate buffer is needed. Flow control may require that some amount of buffer space be dedicated to each pair of communicating processes.

The optimal strategy strongly depends on various performance parameters of the system: the bandwidth, the communication start-up time, scheduling and context switching overheads, the amount of potential overlap between communication and computation, etc. The choice of a buffering and scheduling policy may not be entirely under the control of the MPI implementor as it is partially determined by the properties of the underlying communication layer.

Attempts by the MPI Forum to design mechanisms for querying or setting the amount of buffer space available to standard communication led to the conclusion that such mechanisms will either restrict allowed implementations unacceptably, or provide bounds that will be extremely pessimistic on most implementations in most cases. Another problem is that parameters such as buffer sizes work against portability. Rather then restricting the implementation strategies for standard communication, the choice was taken to provide additional communication modes for those users that do not want to trust the implementation to make the right choice for them.

9.2   Portable Programming with MPI

The MPI specification was designed to make it possible to write portable message passing programs while avoiding unacceptable performance degradation. Within the context of MPI, "portable" is synonymous with "safe." Unsafe programs may exhibit a different behavior on different systems because they are non-deterministic: Several outcomes are consistent with the MPI specification, and the actual outcome to occur depends on the precise timing of events. Unsafe programs may require resources that are not always guaranteed by MPI, in order to complete successfully. On systems where such resources are unavailable, the program will encounter a resource error. Such an error will manifest itself as an actual program error or will result in deadlock.

There are three main issues relating to the portability of MPI programs (and, indeed, message passing programs in general).

1.   The program should not depend on the buffering of messages by MPI or lower levels of the communication system. A valid MPI implementation may or may not buffer messages of a given size (in standard mode).

2.   The program should not depend upon whether collective communication routines, such as MPI_Bcast(), act as barrier synchronizations. In a valid MPI implementation collective communication routines may or may not have the side effect of performing a barrier synchronization.

3.   The program should ensure that messages are matched by the intended receive call. Ambiguities in the specification of communication can lead to incorrect or non-deterministic programs since race conditions may arise. MPI provides message tags and communicators to help avoid these types of problem.

If proper attention is not paid to these factors, a message passing code may fail intermittently on a given computer or may work correctly on one machine but not on another. Clearly such a program is not portable. We shall now consider each of the above factors in more detail.

9.2.1   Dependency on Buffering

A message passing program is dependent on the buffering of messages if its communication graph has a cycle. The communication graph is a directed graph in which the nodes represent MPI communication calls and the edges represent dependencies between these calls: a directed edge uv indicates that operation v might not complete before operation u has started. Calls may be dependent because they have to be executed in succession by the same process, or because they are matching Send and Receive calls. Consider the code in Example 9.1.

Example 9.1   Code for periodic shift in which the processes are arranged with a ring topology (i.e. a one-dimensional, periodic topology) and each communicates data to its clockwise neighbor. A degenerate instance of this is when a process sends a message to itself. The following code uses a blocking send in standard mode to send a message to its clockwise neighbor, and a blocking receive to receive a message from its anti-clockwise neighbor.

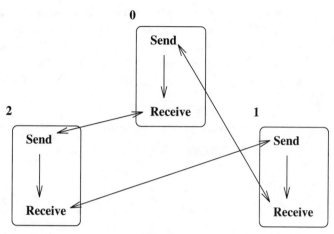

Figure 9.1
Cycle in communication graph for cyclic shift.

```
...
MPI_Comm_size(comm, &size);
MPI_Comm_rank(comm, &rank);
clock = (rank+1)%size;
anticlock = (rank+size-1)%size;

MPI_Send (buf1, count, MPI_INT, clock, tag, comm);
MPI_Recv (buf2, count, MPI_INT, anticlock, tag, comm, &status);
```

The execution of the code results in the dependency graph illustrated in Figure 9.1, for the case of a three process group.

The arrow from each Send to the following Receive executed by the same process reflects the program dependency within each process: the receive call cannot be executed until the previous send call has completed. The double arrow between each Send and the matching Receive reflects their mutual dependency: Obviously, the Receive cannot complete unless the matching Send was invoked. Conversely, since a standard mode Send is used, it may be the case that the Send blocks until a matching Receive occurs.

The dependency graph has a cycle. This code will only work if the system provides sufficient buffering, in which case the send operation will complete locally, the call to MPI_Send() will return, and the matching call to MPI_Recv() will be performed. In the absence of sufficient buffering MPI does not specify an outcome, but for most implementations deadlock will occur, i.e., the call to `MPI_Send()` will never return: each process will wait for the next process on the ring to execute a matching Receive. Thus, the behavior of this code will differ from system to system, or on the same system, when message size (`count`) is changed.

There are a number of ways in which a shift operation can be performed portably using MPI. These are

1.   reverse the order of send and receive calls on some, but not all, processes (only works if there is more than one process), or

2.   use a blocking send in buffered mode, or

3.   use a nonblocking send and/or receive, or

4.   use a call to `MPI_Sendrecv()`.

If at least one process in a shift operation calls the receive routine before the send routine, and at least one process calls the send routine before the receive routine, then at least one communication can proceed, and, eventually, the shift will complete successfully. One of the most efficient ways of doing this is to alternate the send and receive calls so that all processes with even rank send first and then receive, and all processes with odd rank receive first and then send. (Odd numbers of processors complicates this picture.) Thus, the following code is portable provided there is more than one process, i.e., `clock` and `anticlock` are different:

```
...
if (rank%2) {
   MPI_Recv (buf2, count, MPI_INT, anticlock, tag, comm, &status);
   MPI_Send (buf1, count, MPI_INT, clock, tag, comm);
   }
else {
   MPI_Send (buf1, count, MPI_INT, clock, tag, comm);
   MPI_Recv (buf2, count, MPI_INT, anticlock, tag, comm, &status);
   }
```

The resulting communication graph is illustrated in Figure 9.2. This graph is acyclic.

If there is only one process then clearly blocking send and receive routines cannot be used since the Send must be called before the Receive, and so cannot complete in the absence of buffering.

We now consider methods for performing shift operations that work even if there is only one process involved. A blocking send in buffered mode can be used to

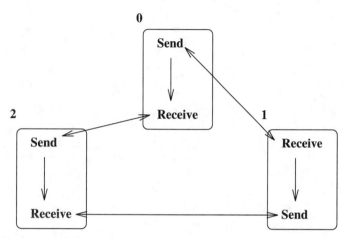

Figure 9.2
Cycle in communication graph is broken by reordering Send and Receive.

perform a shift operation. In this case the application program passes a buffer to the MPI communication system, and MPI can use this to buffer messages. If the buffer provided is large enough, then the shift will complete successfully. The following code shows how to use buffered mode to create a portable shift operation.

```
...
MPI_Buffer_attach (userbuf, count*sizeof(int));
MPI_Bsend (buf1, count, MPI_INT, clock, tag, comm);
MPI_Recv  (buf2, count, MPI_INT, anticlock, tag, comm, &status);
```

MPI guarantees that the buffer supplied by a call to MPI_Buffer_attach() will be used if it is needed to buffer the message. (In an implementation of MPI that provides sufficient buffering, the user-supplied buffer may be ignored.) Each buffered send operations can complete locally, so that a deadlock will not occur. The acyclic communication graph for this modified code is shown in Figure 9.3. Each Receive depends on the matching Send, but the Send does not depend anymore on the matching Receive.

Another approach is to use nonblocking communication. One can either use a nonblocking Send, a nonblocking Receive, or both. If a nonblocking Send is used, the call to MPI_Isend() initiates the send operation and then returns. The call to MPI_Recv() can then be made, and the communication completes successfully. After the call to MPI_Isend(), the data in buf1 must not be changed until one is

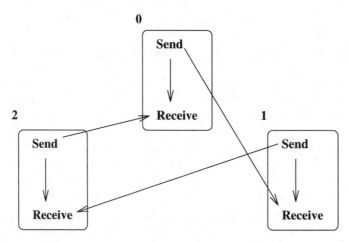

Figure 9.3
Cycle in communication graph is broken by using buffered sends.

certain that the data have been sent or copied by the system. MPI provides the routines `MPI_Wait()` and `MPI_Test()` to check on this. Thus, the following code is portable,

```
...
MPI_Isend (buf1, count, MPI_INT, clock, tag, comm, &request);
MPI_Recv (buf2, count, MPI_INT, anticlock, tag, comm, &status);
MPI_Wait (&request, &status);
```

The corresponding acyclic communication graph is shown in Figure 9.4. Each Receive operation depends on the matching Send, and each Wait depends on the matching communication; the Send does not depend on the matching Receive, as a nonblocking Send call will return even if no matching Receive is posted.

(Posted nonblocking communications do consume resources: MPI has to keep track of such posted communications. But the amount of resources consumed is proportional to the number of posted communications, not to the total size of the pending messages. Good MPI implementations will support a large number of pending nonblocking communications, so that this will not cause portability problems.)

An alternative approach is to perform a nonblocking receive first to initiate (or "post") the receive, and then to perform a blocking send in standard mode.

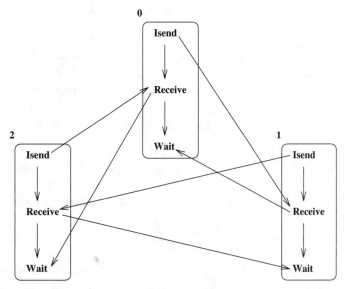

Figure 9.4
Cycle in communication graph is broken by using nonblocking sends.

```
...
MPI_Irecv (buf2, count, MPI_INT, anticlock, tag, comm, &request);
MPI_Send (buf1, count, MPI_INT, clock, tag, comm);
MPI_Wait (&request, &status);
```

The call to `MPI_Irecv()` indicates to MPI that incoming data should be stored in `buf2`; thus, no buffering is required. The call to `MPI_Wait()` is needed to block until the data have actually been received into `buf2`. This alternative code will often result in improved performance, since Sends complete faster in many implementations when the matching Receive is already posted.

Finally, a portable shift operation can be implemented using the routine MPI-_Sendrecv(), which was explicitly designed to send to one process while receiving from another in a safe and portable way. In this case only a single call is required;

```
...
MPI_Sendrecv (buf1, count, MPI_INT, clock, tag,
              buf2, count, MPI_INT, anticlock, tag, comm, &status);
```

9.2.2   Collective Communication and Synchronization

The MPI specification purposefully does not mandate whether or not collective communication operations have the side effect of synchronizing the processes over which they operate. Thus, in one valid implementation collective communication operations may synchronize processes, while in another equally valid implementation they do not. Portable MPI programs, therefore, must not rely on whether or not collective communication operations synchronize processes. Thus, the following assumptions must be avoided.

1.   We assume `MPI_Bcast()` acts as a barrier synchronization and it doesn't.

```
MPI_Irecv (buf2, count, MPI_INT, anticlock, tag, comm, &request);
MPI_Bcast (buf3, 1, MPI_CHAR, 0, comm);
MPI_Rsend (buf1, count, MPI_INT, clock, tag, comm);
```

Here if we want to perform the send in ready mode we must be certain that the receive has already been initiated at the destination. The above code is nonportable because if the broadcast does not act as a barrier synchronization we cannot be sure this is the case.

2.   We assume that `MPI_Bcast()` does not act as a barrier synchronization and it does. Examples of this case are given in Examples 4.27, 4.28, and 4.29 starting on page 250.

9.2.3   Ambiguous Communications and Portability

MPI employs the communicator abstraction to promote software modularity by allowing the construction of independent communication streams between processes, thereby ensuring that messages sent in one phase of an application are not incorrectly intercepted by another phase. Communicators are particularly important in allowing libraries that make message passing calls to be used safely within an application. The point here is that the application developer has no way of knowing if the tag, group, and rank completely disambiguate the message traffic of different libraries and the rest of the application. Communicators, in effect, provide an additional criterion for message selection, and hence permits the construction of independent tag spaces.

If communicators are not used to disambiguate message traffic there are two ways in which a call to a library routine can lead to unintended behavior. In the first case, the processes enter a library routine synchronously when a send has been

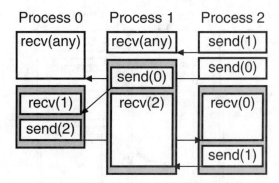

Figure 9.5
Use of communicators. Time increases down the page. Numbers in parentheses indicate the process to which data are being sent or received. The gray shaded area represents the library routine call. In this case the program behaves as intended. Note that the second message sent by process 2 is received by process 0, and that the message sent by process 0 is received by process 2.

initiated for which the matching receive is not posted until after the library call. In this case the message may be incorrectly received in the library routine. The second possibility arises when different processes enter a library routine asynchronously, as shown in the example in Figure 9.5, resulting in nondeterministic behavior. If the program behaves correctly processes 0 and 1 each receive a message from process 2, using a wildcarded selection criterion to indicate that they are prepared to receive a message from any process. The three processes then pass data around in a ring within the library routine. If separate communicators are not used for the communication inside and outside of the library routine this program may intermittently fail. Suppose we delay the sending of the second message sent by process 2, for example, by inserting some computation, as shown in Figure 9.6. In this case the wildcarded receive in process 0 is satisfied by a message sent from process 1, rather than from process 2, and deadlock results. By supplying a different communicator to the library routine we can ensure that the program is executed correctly, regardless of when the processes enter the library routine.

More examples and further discussion of this problem occur in Section 5.5.

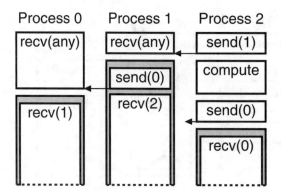

Figure 9.6
Unintended behavior of program. In this case the message from process 2 to process 0 is never received, and deadlock results.

9.3 Heterogeneous Computing with MPI

Heterogeneous computing uses different computers connected by a network to solve a problem in parallel. With heterogeneous computing a number of issues arise that are not applicable when using a homogeneous parallel computer. For example, the computers may be of differing computational power, so care must be taken to distribute the work between them to avoid load imbalance. Other problems may arise because of the different behavior of floating point arithmetic on different machines. However, the two most fundamental issues that must be faced in heterogeneous computing are,

- incompatible data representation, and
- interoperability of differing implementations of the message passing layer.

Incompatible data representations arise when computers use different binary representations for the same number. In MPI all communication routines have a datatype argument so implementations can use this information to perform the appropriate representation conversion when communicating data between computers.

Interoperability refers to the ability of different implementations of a given piece of software to work together as if they were a single homogeneous implementation. A prerequisite of interoperability for MPI would be the standardization of the MPI's internal data structures, of the communication protocols, of the initialization, termination and error handling procedures, of the implementation of collective operations, and so on. Since this has not been done, there is no support for interoperability in the MPI standard. In general, hardware-specific implementations of MPI will not be interoperable. However it is still possible for different architectures to work together if they both use the same portable MPI implementation or if different implementations agree to interoperate.

9.4 MPI **Implementations**

MPI-1 is currently available on practically any parallel platform. There are close to ten free MPI implementations, most of which are available in source form. These can be used on many systems, including DEC Alpha (Digital UNIX), Cray T3D, Fujitsu AP1000 (CellOS), HP PA-RISC (HP-UX), IBM RS/6000 (AIX), Intel X86 (Linux, NT), Sequent Symmetry (DYNIX) SGI (IRIX), and Sun SPARC (Solaris) systems, as well as TCP/IP connected clusters of such systems. Proprietary vendor implementations are available from Fujitsu, Hitachi, HP, IBM, Intel, NEC, and SGI and from several independent software vendors. Information on these implementations can be found at `http://www.osc.edu/mpi/`, or at the MPI site `http://www.mpi-forum.org`.

References

[1] V. Bala and S. Kipnis. Process groups: a mechanism for the coordination of and communication among processes in the Venus collective communication library. Technical report, IBM T. J. Watson Research Center, October 1992. Preprint.

[2] V. Bala, S. Kipnis, L. Rudolph, and Marc Snir. Designing efficient, scalable, and portable collective communication libraries. In *SIAM 1993 Conference on Parallel Processing for Scientific Computing*, pages 862–872, March 1993.

[3] Luc Bomans and Rolf Hempel. The Argonne/GMD macros in FORTRAN for portable parallel programming and their implementation on the Intel iPSC/2. *Parallel Computing*, 15:119–132, 1990.

[4] J. Bruck, R. Cypher, P. Elustond, A. Ho, C-T. Ho, V. Bala, S. Kipnis, , and M. Snir. Ccl: A portable and tunable collective communicationlibrary for scalable parallel computers. *IEEE Trans. on Parallel and Distributed Systems*, 6(2):154–164, 1995.

[5] R. Butler and E. Lusk. User's guide to the p4 programming system. Technical Report TM-ANL–92/17, Argonne National Laboratory, 1992.

[6] Ralph Butler and Ewing Lusk. Monitors, messages, and clusters: the p4 parallel programming system. *Journal of Parallel Computing*, 20(4):547–564, April 1994.

[7] Robin Calkin, Rolf Hempel, Hans-Christian Hoppe, and Peter Wypior. Portable programming with the parmacs message–passing library. *Parallel Computing*, 20(4):615–632, April 1994.

[8] S. Chittor and R. J. Enbody. Performance evaluation of mesh–connected wormhole–routed networks for interprocessor communication in multicomputers. In *Proceedings of the 1990 Supercomputing Conference*, pages 647–656, 1990.

[9] S. Chittor and R. J. Enbody. Predicting the effect of mapping on the communication performance of large multicomputers. In *Proceedings of the 1991 International Conference on Parallel Processing, vol. II (Software)*, pages II–1 – II–4, 1991.

[10] R. Cypher and E. Leu. The semantics of blocking and nonblocking send and receive primitives. In *8th International Parallel Processing Symposium*, pages 729–735, April 1994.

[11] J. J. Dongarra, R. Hempel, A. J. G. Hey, and D. W. Walker. A proposal for a user-level, message passing interface in a distributed memory environment. Technical Report TM-12231, Oak Ridge National Laboratory, February 1993.

[12] Nathan Doss, William Gropp, Ewing Lusk, and Anthony Skjellum. A model implementation of MPI. Technical report, Argonne National Laboratory, 1993.

[13] Edinburgh Parallel Computing Centre, University of Edinburgh. *CHIMP Concepts*, June 1991.

[14] Edinburgh Parallel Computing Centre, University of Edinburgh. *CHIMP Version 1.0 Interface*, May 1992.

[15] Message Passing Interface Forum. MPI: A message-passing interface standard. *International Journal of Supercomputer Applications*, 8(3/4):157–416, 1994. Special issue on MPI.

[16] Message Passing Interface Forum. MPI: A Message-Passing Interface Standard (version 1.1). Technical report, 1995. http://www.mpi-forum.org.

[17] Message Passing Interface Forum. MPI-2: Extensions to the Message-Passing Interface. Technical report, 1997. http://www.mpi-forum.org.

[18] H. Franke, H. Wu, C.E. Riviere, P.Pattnaik, and M. Snir. MPI programming environment for IBM SP1/SP2. In *15th International Conference on Distributed Computing Systems*, pages 127–135, June 1995.

[19] A. Geist, A. Beguelin, J. Dongarra, W. Jiang, R. Manchek, and V. Sunderam. *PVM: A Users' Guide and Tutorial for Networked Parallel Computing*. MIT Press, 1994. The book is available electronically, the url is ftp://www.netlib.org/pvm3/book/pvm-book.ps.

[20] G. A. Geist, M. T. Heath, B. W. Peyton, and P. H. Worley. A user's guide to PICL: a portable instrumented communication library. Technical Report TM-11616, Oak Ridge National Laboratory, October 1990.

[21] William D. Gropp and Barry Smith. Chameleon parallel programming tools users manual. Technical Report ANL-93/23, Argonne National Laboratory, March 1993.

[22] IEEE, New York. *IEEE Standard for Information Technology— POSIX Fortran 77 Language Interfaces —Part 1: System Application Program Interface (API)*, 1992.

[23] Institute of Electrical and Electronics Engineers, New York. *IEEE Standard for Binary Floating-Point Arithmetic, ANSI/IEEE Standard 754-1985*, 1985.

[24] International Organization for Standardization, Geneva. *Information processing—8-bit single-byte coded graphic character sets—Part 1: Latin alphabet No. 1*, 1987.

[25] Charles H. Koelbel, David B. Loveman, Robert S. Schreiber, Guy L. Steele Jr., and Mary E. Zosel. *The High Performance Fortran Handbook*. MIT Press, 1993.

[26] O. Krämer and H. Mühlenbein. Mapping strategies in message-based multiprocessor systems. *Parallel Computing*, 9:213–225, 1989.

[27] nCUBE Corporation. *nCUBE 2 Programmers Guide, r2.0*, December 1990.

[28] Parasoft Corporation, Pasadena, CA. *Express User's Guide*, version 3.2.5 edition, 1992.

[29] Paul Pierce. The NX/2 operating system. In *Proceedings of the Third Conference on Hypercube Concurrent Computers and Applications*, pages 384–390. ACM Press, 1988.

[30] A. Skjellum and A. Leung. Zipcode: a portable multicomputer communication library atop the reactive kernel. In D. W. Walker and Q. F. Stout, editors, *Proceedings of the Fifth Distributed Memory Concurrent Computing Conference*, pages 767–776. IEEE Press, 1990.

[31] A. Skjellum, S. Smith, C. Still, A. Leung, and M. Morari. The Zipcode message passing system. Technical report, Lawrence Livermore National Laboratory, September 1992.

[32] Inc. Sun Microsystems. Xdr: External data representation standard, June 1987. RFC1014.

[33] V.S. Sunderam, G.A. Geist, J. Dongarra, and R. Manchek. The PVM concurrent computing system: Evolution, experiences, and trends. *Parallel Computing*, 20(4):531–545, April 1994.

[34] *The Unicode Standard, Version 2.0*. Addison-Wesley, 1996. ISBN 0-201-48345-9.

[35] D. Walker. Standards for message passing in a distributed memory environment. Technical Report TM-12147, Oak Ridge National Laboratory, August 1992.

Constants Index

Function Index

Index